Peacemaker

SHORENSTEIN
APARC
STANFORD

The publication of *Peacemaker* has been made possible through the generosity of the Koret Foundation of San Francisco, California.

PEACEMAKER

TWENTY YEARS OF INTER-KOREAN RELATIONS AND THE NORTH KOREAN NUCLEAR ISSUE

A memoir by
Lim Dong-won

SHORENSTEIN
APARC
STANFORD

THE WALTER H. SHORENSTEIN
ASIA-PACIFIC RESEARCH CENTER

THE WALTER H. SHORENSTEIN ASIA-PACIFIC RESEARCH CENTER
(Shorenstein APARC) is a unique Stanford University institution focused
on the interdisciplinary study of contemporary Asia. Shorenstein APARC's
mission is to produce and publish outstanding interdisciplinary, Asia-Pacific–
focused research; educate students, scholars, and corporate and governmental
affiliates; promote constructive interaction to influence U.S. policy toward
the Asia-Pacific; and guide Asian nations on key issues of societal transition,
development, U.S.-Asia relations, and regional cooperation.

The Walter H. Shorenstein Asia-Pacific Research Center
Freeman Spogli Institute for International Studies
Stanford University
Encina Hall
Stanford, CA 94305-6055
tel. 650-723-9741
fax 650-723-6530
http://aparc.stanford.edu

Peacemaker may be ordered from:
The Brookings Institution
c/o DFS, P.O. Box 50370, Baltimore, MD, USA
tel. 1-800-537-5487 or 410-516-6956
fax 410-516-6998
http://www.brookings.edu/press

First printing, 2012.
13-digit ISBN 978-1-931368-27-8

CONTENTS

APPENDIX: ESSENTIAL DOCUMENTS

FIGURES

Map of the Korean Peninsula

FOREWORD

Four years have passed since Lim Dong-won's memoir *Peacemaker* was first published in Korean, but its appearance now in English translation is important and may be, in fact, even timelier than the original publication. In the past three years alone, North Korea conducted its second test of a nuclear device; attempted to launch two long-range rockets; sank the South Korean corvette *Cheonan* in a sneak attack resulting in the loss of forty-six sailors; killed four more South Koreans in an unprecedented artillery attack on a South Korean island; and revealed to my Stanford colleagues Siegfried S. Hecker and John W. Lewis the existence of a full-scale uranium enrichment facility that could be used to make nuclear weapons. The succession of the inexperienced Kim Jong-un in April 2012 as North Korea's supreme leader, in the wake of his father Kim Jong-il's sudden death in December 2011, has only heightened international concerns about North Korea's direction and the possibility of peace and stability on the Korean Peninsula.

Why is North Korea doing these things? In 1939, Winston Churchill said of the Soviet Union: "I cannot forecast to you the action of Russia. It is a riddle, wrapped in a mystery, inside an enigma. . . ." North Korea, though, is far more of a puzzle than was ever the former Soviet Union. Americans know more about North Korea since the United States government began sporadic talks with Pyongyang in 1992, but there is much that we still do not know and even more that we do not understand.

Peacemaker helps to fill major gaps in our understanding of North Korea and how to deal with it. It also tells the story of Lim's life and especially his passionate efforts of the past twenty years to bring about the reconciliation of the two Koreas and eventually *de facto* if not *de jure* unification of a tragically divided nation. Some Americans will know that Lim was the architect and implementer of the Sunshine policy of engaging North Korea, pursued by the late President Kim Dae-jung, who won a Nobel Prize for his efforts, and his successor, the late President Roh Moo-hyun. Far fewer will know that Lim was already playing a key role in intra-Korean reconciliation efforts as early as 1990, and that he helped to achieve the North-South Basic

Agreement and the Joint Declaration of the Denuclearization of the Korean Peninsula the following year.

I myself first met Lim when President Bill Clinton asked me in late 1998 to conduct a review of North Korea policy after Pyongyang launched its first long-range missile. For the next two years, Lim and I, along with Ryozo Kato from Japan, worked together to craft a joint position to present to the North. Lim brought to the discussion an intimate understanding of President Kim's North Korea policy and an irreplaceable grasp of North Korea informed by his unique experiences with Pyongyang's leaders.

Lim's own life in some ways mirrors the suffering of the Korean people of his generation. As a seventeen-year-old boy, he fled South during the Korean War, only to be permanently separated from the family he left behind. Desperately poor, he managed to obtain a job with a U.S. military unit, and, studying intensively after work, managed to be accepted to the Korean Military Academy two years later. He rose quickly to become a general and, in hindsight ironically, became known in South Korea for his book and lectures on *Communist Revolutionary War and Counterinsurgency*. After Lim's retirement from the military, he served as his country's ambassador to Nigeria and Australia before being named to head the foreign ministry's research and training center.

But it was Lim's encounter with Kim Dae-jung, a few years later when both were retired, that set him on the path to becoming North Korea policy architect when Kim returned to politics to be elected president in 1997. In *Peacemaker*, Lim recounts in detail his relationship with Kim Dae-jung, the fascinating and important contents of his private meetings with Kim Jong-il, and the many obstacles and frustrations he encountered in dealing with both South Koreans and Americans who opposed the Sunshine policy.

Whether one agrees fully with Lim's analysis and recommendations for dealing with North Korea, *Peacemaker* is not only a moving personal memoir, but also essential reading for everyone, especially Americans, concerned about North Korea, our South Korean ally, and the future of the Korean Peninsula.

Bill Perry
Stanford University
April 2012

PREFACE TO THE ENGLISH EDITION

Peacemaker is a memoir of my forty years of public service, published four years ago in Korean, then later in Japanese with the added subtitle, *Two Decades of Inter-Korean Relations and the North Korean Nuclear Issue.* I am very pleased with the publication of this English edition, which benefits enormously from the generosity of the Stanford Korean Studies Program (KSP) at the Walter H. Shorenstein Asia-Pacific Research Center (Shorenstein APARC). I am indebted to Professor Gi-Wook Shin, KSP and Shorenstein APARC director, who initiated the project to publish this edition. I also thank Professor Tong Kim for translating the Korean version into English, and Dr. Yoon S. Choi and George Krompacky, Shorenstein APARC publications manager, for editing the manuscript.

The twenty years following the end of the Cold War were a turbulent period of transformation for the Korean Peninsula. During this period, the North and South were exerting efforts to end hostile relations, to reconcile with each other, and to undertake the tasks of resolving the North Korean nuclear issue and improving hostile relations between the United States and the Democratic People's Republic of Korea (DPRK, or simply North Korea). This was a time during which South Korea and the United States undertook a peace process to dismantle the Cold War structure on the peninsula. However, the path to these goals was not easy. It was a long and winding road between accomplishment and frustration, progress and retreat, and stability and crisis.

This memoir is a record of the history, for two decades beginning in 1988, of the bold attempts and arduous efforts by the Korean people that aimed to end the Cold War on the peninsula and establish a new relationship of reconciliation and cooperation. This book details the two most significant events of the period—the North-South High-Level Talks (1989–92), which sought a new post–Cold War relationship, and the historic inter-Korean summit of June 2000, which set the tone for reconciliation and cooperation. *Peacemaker* also discusses the Kim Dae-jung and Clinton summit in Washington (June 1998) as well as the peace process for the peninsula, known as the Perry Process.

Regarding the North Korean nuclear issue, my memoir focuses on the origin of the suspicion of North Korea's nuclear program that emerged in 1991; the Geneva Agreed Framework of 1994, which was implemented for eight years until it collapsed; and the Six-Party Talks and the disabling of the plutonium facilities, which continued until 2008. *Peacemaker* deals with President George W. Bush's hostile policy toward North Korea and provides an insider's description of Bush's meeting with Kim Dae-jung in Seoul (February 2002).

This book speaks of the facts based on my experience as a key player in the formulation and implementation of North Korea policy for the South Korean government, in which I served in various capacities including national security advisor, unification minister, director of the National Intelligence Service, presidential special envoy, and several other positions. The views expressed in the book are solely mine and based on my experience as a negotiator, a policy formulator, and a policy practitioner.

Through this English edition, I hope the readers gain a better understanding and give support for the ardent desire of the Korean people for peace and unification. Our final goal is clearly to end the national division and achieve unification. Korea is a country that had existed for more than a thousand years as a single unified state. As long as the division continues, it is inevitable for the two sides to compete in a zero-sum game for their claims of legitimacy to the sovereignty of the whole nation. The division causes confrontation, tension, an arms race, and risk of war. Under the division, the nation wastes resources that should be used instead for improving the lives of its people. The division of the Korean Peninsula affects the peace and stability of the entire Northeast Asia region.

In the historic first inter-Korean summit of June 2000, the two leaders agreed to pursue a gradual and peaceful unification. They agreed that "unification is a goal and a process at the same time" and that we should work together to prevent the perpetuation of the division. Before achieving the ultimate state of *de jure* unification, the two sides would first establish *de facto* unification through exchange and cooperation in peaceful coexistence. In this unification process, we would build an inter-Korean economic community, realize arms control, and, with support from the great powers, replace the Armistice Agreement with a unification-oriented peace regime.

I believe this peace unification model would meet the interests of those countries who have a stake in the security and stability of the Korean

Peninsula. In my view, this ideal and realistic model can win the support and cooperation of neighboring countries, including the United States and China.

A peace regime in Korea is directly related to the dismantlement of the Cold War structure in Northeast Asia. It has been twenty years since China and Russia normalized their relations with the Republic of Korea and since the two Koreas were admitted to the United Nations. However, the United States and Japan have not normalized their relations with North Korea, which pursues a reckless nuclear program.

In 2005, the September 19 Joint Statement of the Six-Party Talks, in which the United States, China, Russia, Japan, and the two Koreas participated, reaffirmed that the resolution of the nuclear issue and the normalization of the relations of the United States and Japan with North Korea should be promoted in parallel in a phased and reciprocal manner. Through the joint statement, the participants also agreed to seek a cooperative security arrangement for Northeast Asia and to hold peace talks among the parties concerned to build a peace regime on the Korean Peninsula. The joint statement set the right direction for the dismantlement of the Cold War structure in the region. The resolution of the North Korean nuclear issue and the elimination of hostility between the United States and North Korea would provide new momentum for the peace process on the peninsula and in the region.

Unfortunately, during the four years following the publication of my memoir in 2008, the peace process came to a standstill. Inter-Korean relations were strained, and no progress was made on the nuclear issue or in U.S.-DPRK relations. On the other hand, North Korea has strengthened its strategic cooperative relationship with China.

The Lee Myung-bak administration chose to pursue a policy opposite to those of the previous administrations. Preoccupied by the "wishful thinking" that North Korea would soon collapse and the South would be able to achieve unification by absorption, it rejected all the inter-Korean agreements for reconciliation and cooperation. It discarded the policy of gradual and peaceful unification. Instead of the engagement policy of reconciliation and cooperation, the Lee administration carried out a policy of confrontation through pressure and sanctions in a futile attempt to force North Korean surrender. It adhered to its pronounced principle of refusing to improve inter-Korean relations without the resolution of the nuclear issue. When North Korea leader Kim Jong-il's health problems became known in August 2008, the Lee administration toughened its hardliner policy with a higher expectation of sudden upheaval in the North and unification by absorption. North Korea reacted strongly to such a Southern policy, and both sides clashed over every issue with conflict, contradictions, and confrontation. As a result, tension reached the level of military clashes. All dialogue, exchange, trade, economic cooperation, and even humanitarian assistance were halted, except for the minimum operation of the Kaesong Industrial Complex.

After the failure of its "Southern Policy" for improving relations with South Korea, the United States, and Japan, which had been pursued for the past two decades, North Korea shifted to a "Northern Policy" to reinforce its relations with China and Russia. North Korea's economic cooperation with China has been going well, as it serves China's practical interest in developing the economy of its three northeastern provinces, securing a new source of underground resources, and obtaining access to seaports towards the East Sea. In return, North Korea's economic situation started improving from China's supply of strategic goods and a sharp increase in trade between the two allies. With China's "strategic engagement" since the fall of 2009, North Korea has become closer to China in terms of economic relations as well as foreign affairs and security.

As for the nuclear issue, North Korea recklessly conducted a missile (satellite rocket) launch and a second underground nuclear test at the beginning of the Obama administration, resulting in the deterioration of relations with the United States and inviting UN sanctions. It has been three years since the Obama administration started waiting for North Korea's change under the so-called "strategic patience" policy and the Six-Party Talks were suspended.

At the January 2011 summit in Washington, the United States and China emphasized the importance of an improvement in North-South relations and agreed that a sincere and constructive inter-Korean dialogue is an essential step. Agreeing on the crucial importance of denuclearization of the Korean Peninsula in order to preserve peace and stability in Northeast Asia, China and the United States reiterated the need for concrete and effective steps to achieve the goal of denuclearization and full implementation of the other commitments made in the September 19, 2005 Joint Statement of the Six-Party Talks. However, the efforts of the concerned parties to restart the process of the Six-Party Talks have not made any progress so far.

North Korea's leader Kim Jong-il died in December 2011, and the planned power succession by the young Kim Jong-un, the third son of Kim Jong-il, was carried out in an atmosphere of stability. The North Korean constitution declares that "Kim Il-sung is the founding father of the Democratic People's Republic of Korea." It appears that the ruling elites of the North are committed to maintaining the succession system and the North Korean people, who have had no exposure to democracy or civil society, are not rejecting the dynastic regime.

It seems that North Korea will be run by a small inner circle, and Kim Jong-un will play the role of the main protagonist as that circle moves gradually to solidify its monolithic leadership, which has been rooted in the North for more than half a century. Any possible power struggle that might emerge down the road would not target the supreme leader but it would more likely reflect an internal disagreement over the basic policy line and specific policy issues. Kim Jong-un is facing a daunting task to build a "prosperous economy" following his grandfather Kim Il-sung's "strong political state" of *juche* ideology, and his father Kim Jong-il's "strong military state" of the military-first policy.

Kim Jong-il's military-first policy, which was adopted for a crisis situation, will gradually diminish. Instead, North Korea will focus on economic vitalization to improve the people's livelihoods. They will strengthen their cooperation with China, while seeking an improved relationship with the United States, which they regard as very important.

The past foretells the future. The past two decades of our experience taught us that we could not change North Korea or achieve its denuclearization through containment, coercion, or sanctions. We learned the lesson that pressure measures only produced adverse effects. Instead, we need to convince the North Koreans that they can live safely and thrive without nuclear weapons. When the people's lives have improved and when the information and culture of the outside world are accessible, the people's perception will change, bringing change to their society.

The changes of leadership in South Korea and the United States next year may provide a good opportunity to undertake a new version of a comprehensive engagement policy that would contribute to bringing about the right environment and conditions for change in the North. Such a policy could succeed in inducing reform and opening in North Korea. Without efforts to make peace, it would be difficult to keep peace. The peace process for the Korean Peninsula must resume.

Lim Dong-won
February 2012

TRANSLATOR'S NOTE

It was an honor and a great pleasure to translate Minister Lim Dong-won's *Peacemaker* for publication in English. My fundamental goal was to accurately and correctly convey the author's meaning in English. I tried not to omit words or repetitive phrases, or to rewrite any parts of the book, as long as I could extract meaning from them. I used English terms and phrases as they had been used by the South Korean government.

However, due to differences in linguistic, cultural, and institutional practices between Korea—North and South—and the United States, some subtleties and nuances may have been lost in translation. It is common that translators find no exact equivalents for certain words or expressions that derive from a country's unique history and cultural background.

As a translator for several decades, I tried to provide an understandable version of this important book. I could not have done it without thorough reviews of the initial translation drafts and valuable advice from Minister Lim. I also appreciate the efforts of copyeditors at Stanford.

As a former State Department interpreter who participated in many negotiations with North Korea, I support the authenticity of the author's descriptions of what transpired between Washington and Pyongyang, and Washington and Seoul. In particular, Kim Jong-il's conversations with the author appear very real to me in terms of his speaking style and personality, which I observed when I interpreted for Secretary of State Madeline Albright during her meeting with the North Korean leader.

As a teacher for two years at the Johns Hopkins University School of Advanced International Studies and one who is still teaching at Korea University in Seoul, I have used the Korean version in my classes. It has much information about the history of inter-Korean relations and a constructive vision for the future of the Korean Peninsula; it also provides an insightful analysis of how the Kim Dae-jung administration formulated and executed its policy. As such, I recommend that this book be included in the reading list for students who study U.S. relations with the two Koreas.

Tong Kim
April 2012

PREFACE TO THE ORIGINAL
KOREAN EDITION

Almost twenty years have passed since the end of the Cold War. Those countries divided in the wake of World War II have since been united; the exception is Korea, still divided, where the legacy of the Cold War continues, much to the shame of Koreans, who had lived as one people and one unified country[1] for more than a thousand years.

Nevertheless, the Korean people have worked hard over the past two decades of the post–Cold War era to achieve peace on the Korean Peninsula. The two Koreas entered the United Nations at the same time and adopted the North-South Basic Agreement in search of a new inter-Korean relationship. We held the historic Inter-Korean Summit and produced the June 15 Joint Declaration, opening an era of reconciliation and cooperation.

We removed landmines from the Demilitarized Zone that divides our land, built the "peace corridor," and reconnected the national artery between the two sides. Now, for the first time in a half-century, people are traveling and goods are being shipped through this peace corridor between the North and the South. Frequent inter-Korean traffic has helped to reduce tensions, mitigate hostile attitudes, and has contributed to confidence building. The seventy million people of Korea have undertaken a national task—to realize a virtual state of *de facto* unification, where people can travel freely and help each other between the North and the South, in advance of achieving a *de jure* unification.

The bitter modern history shows that, as we went through national division, war, armistice, and the Cold War, the fate of our nation was de-

---

1   This cannot be overstated: while Koreans are a homogeneous people who, for five thousand years, lived under different nation-states, sometimes concurrently, those states were unified under the Koryŏ (Goryeo) dynasty more than a thousand years ago. Korea remained unified as a single country until its division in 1945.

termined by foreign forces. During the Cold War era, it was impossible to hope that the North and South would work together to resolve the issue of the divided Korean Peninsula. However, the historic Inter-Korean Summit of June 2000 gave us confidence that, if the North and South combined their strengths, we could determine the fate of our nation with the support and blessing of neighboring countries.

I believe we should further develop and deepen our exchanges and cooperation toward a national economic community. At the same time, we should pursue a denuclearized Korean Peninsula and carry out arms reduction. We should replace the Armistice Agreement with a durable peace framework toward unification.

As a soldier and a diplomat during the Cold War, my mission was to deter war; I am proud of what I was able to achieve as a peacekeeper. In the past two decades of the post–Cold War era, I worked as a policymaker, a negotiator, and a policy implementer to improve inter-Korean relations and to end the legacy of the Cold War on the Korean Peninsula.[2] Fulfilling my role as a "peacemaker" on the Peninsula was an honorable mission, and I thank the Lord for blessing me with this privilege.

A witness to history, I felt a sense of obligation to keep the records, notes, and other materials of my experience and observations during the many important events in which I played a role. The purpose of this book, an edited compilation of those materials, is to share my experiences and views with the reader. I want to share with you what went on during each of these events and what it was like to go through them.

This book is a record of the process of our efforts to overcome the many ordeals and challenges that confronted the North and South in the post–Cold War era, and our efforts to resolve hostilities and improve relations for a new inter-Korean relationship of exchange and cooperation.

It describes the process of forming President Roh Tae-woo's Northern Policy, the North-South High-level Talks that produced the North-South Basic Agreement, and the peace process that began with President Kim Dae-jung's Sunshine policy of reconciliation and cooperation, one which had the support of the Clinton administration. It discusses the process of holding the first historic Inter-Korean Summit and producing the June 15 Joint Declaration.

This book is also a record of the efforts to resolve hostile relations between Washington and Pyongyang, and of North Korea's nuclear weapons program. The issue of the Korean Peninsula has a dual nature, involving

2   The Cold War had already ended, except in Korea.

both inter-Korean relations and international relations. The United States, maintaining an alliance with South Korea, has enormous influence on the Korean Peninsula.

Also discussed are the origin of the North Korean nuclear program, the process of negotiating the Joint Declaration of the Denuclearization of the Korean Peninsula, the Clinton administration's engagement policy, the abrogation of the U.S.-DPRK Agreed Framework that had suspended North Korea's nuclear program for eight years, the Bush administration's North Korea policy under the six-year influence of the neoconservatives, as well as the development of the second nuclear crisis following the suspected highly enriched uranium program (HEUP) in the North.

I admit that there are still sensitive areas related to North Korea and the United States that I cannot reveal, even today. On the other hand, most of the information concerning these events should no longer be kept secret, and I frankly wrote about it as a witness to history and in deference to the people's right to know. For the parts of the book that were related to my role as the director of the National Intelligence Service, I make it known that those were reviewed and approved for printing by the established procedure.

I am indebted to many individuals who provided me with their valuable guidance, assistance, encouragement, and advice while I carried out my past mission. If there was any contribution that I was able to make, it was made possible only because of their contributions. I hope I may be excused for failing to mention all of the names of those who helped me, as well as for the shortcomings of this book—I have tried to do my best.

I humbly pay respect and dedicate this book to all those who have devoted their lives to the improvement of inter-Korean relations through exchange and cooperation, who have worked for peace and the unification of the Korean Peninsula, and who have maintained interest in the resolution of issues of peace and security in Northeast Asia.

Lim Dong-won
Spring 2008

1 INTER-KOREAN SUMMIT, 2000

FIRST MEETING WITH
KIM JONG-IL

New Responsibility as NIS Director

Christmas Eve, 1999—the end of a century. The city was blanketed from the previous night's snowfall. It signaled a new year, a new millennium, and a new life for me as director of the National Intelligence Service (NIS).

On the morning of December 23, I was unexpectedly summoned to the presidential residence at the Blue House. When I arrived, President Kim Dae-jung said he wanted me to be the director of the NIS. He added that I should immediately prepare to assume the position. I was completely caught off guard. I responded that I was not the right person for the job, and said, "I have no interest in politics and, therefore, do not have a good knowledge of politics. How could I possibly be qualified for such an important position? I am not the man for the job."

"You are the right man *because* you are not interested in politics."

From the beginning of his administration, President Kim Dae-jung had expressed his intent to transform the NIS into an intelligence organization that did not interfere with politics.

The next morning, on December 24, President Kim presented me a letter of appointment at the Blue House. "The National Intelligence Service," he said, "should not interfere with political activities, but should only carry out its legitimate mission as defined by law." Asking me to do my best on the job, he added, "The new year will be an important year for relations between the North and South. We must improve our relations through an active promotion of dialogue."

* * * * * * * * *

On February 3, 2000, the Thursday afternoon before the beginning of the long Lunar New Year break, I gave the president my fifth weekly report since taking the NIS job. President Kim had never skipped the regular one-on-one meetings with the NIS directors. Every Thursday he received an intelligence report on all of the major developments.

After I had completed my briefing, the president informed me of surprising news:

> North Korea has sent us a message regarding their intent to promote an inter-Korean summit. Yesterday, Minister of Culture and Tourism Park Ji-won met with Hyundai Chairman Lee Ik-chi and a man by the name of Yoshida, through whom Minister Park received the message. But I am not sure of the credibility of this proposal or the possibility of carrying out an inter-Korean summit.

He instructed me to review the proposal and return to him with an assessment.

I was shocked. Although it had been less than a month since taking the job as chief of intelligence, I should not have been so completely kept in the dark regarding such important information on North-South relations. President Kim had proposed an inter-Korean summit in his inauguration speech, and he had repeatedly asked North Korea to respond to his proposal.

In the meantime, the government had asked civilian channels, particularly Hyundai, to assess North Korea's position on exchanging special envoys and holding an inter-Korean summit. At the same time, NIS maintained its own channel with the North to learn of their intentions. Why did the North Koreans convey their decision to Minister Park Ji-won through Hyundai Chair, Lee Ik-chi? What conditions were they imposing? Why hadn't NIS known about this development? A series of questions went through my head.

On the last day of the holiday break, I met with Minister Park Ji-won. But he was unable to provide me with any more information than the president had. I followed up with a dinner invitation to the chairman of Hyundai Security, Lee Ik-chi. I asked Lee detailed questions about the information in order to gain an overall understanding of the situation. Lee shared that he had received a top-secret request from Minister Park Ji-won to help arrange an inter-Korean summit to take place during the month of May or June. Lee had begun to actively work on the request through Yoshida Takeshi.

According to Chairman Lee Ik-chi, Yoshida was a reliable man who had brokered successful business deals between Hyundai and North Korea since the late 1980s. Lee gave me a copy of a December 1995 article published by the monthly Japanese magazine *Bungeishunjū*. It read,

Yoshida Takeshi was born in 1948. He is a pro-North Korean Japanese. His father was born in North Korea but became a Japanese citizen who fostered a good relationship with Kim Il-sung. In 1963, the elder Yoshida set up a trading business with North Korea called the "New Japan Industry." He had his oldest son work in Tokyo and his younger son, Takeshi, worked in Pyongyang.

The father had publicly declared that he had "dedicated Takeshi to Kim Il-sung." In 1986, he died of an illness in Pyongyang, and Takeshi inherited his father's company, which continued to trade with North Korea, serving as a bridge between the North and South.

He is known to have worked behind the scenes for the Shin Kanemaru delegation visit to the North in 1990; he did likewise during Japan's provision of 150,000 tons of rice to the North in 1995; the recent Japan-North Korea talks; Hyundai Chairman Chung Ju-young's visits to the North in 1989 and 1998; and for the Mount Kumgang tourism industry as well.

During a naval clash on the West Sea in June 1999, North Korea promptly sent a message to Hyundai through Yoshida Takeshi that they wanted to continue tourism at Mount Kumgang. Having worked with Yoshida for more than 10 years, Hyundai had a high degree of trust in him.

Working for Honorary Chairman Chung Ju-young and Chairman Chung Mong-heon, Lee Ik-chi was responsible for Hyundai's business dealings with the North. Lee was frank with me about the reason Hyundai was actively helping to promote an inter-Korean summit. Hyundai had several business plans in addition to the Kumgang tourism project, which included constructing an industrial complex on the west coast, relinking and doubling the Seoul-Shinuiju railroad between the North and the South, installing communications systems, and investing in the North's energy industry. Lee said that an early summit was required to effectively carry out these projects.

Judging from what Lee Ik-chi shared, it was clear that he had asked Yoshida to help arrange an inter-Korean summit at the request of Minister Park Ji-won; Yoshida, in turn, had visited Pyongyang in January 2000 and conveyed the message to two close assistants of Chairman Kim Jong-il of the National Defense Commission.

The North Korean leadership was responding positively to the South's proposal to hold a summit in May or June. The North now wanted to confirm the South's proposal in a secret meeting to be held in a country other than China. In addition, Yoshida was instructed by the North to visit Seoul, where he met with Hyundai Chairman Lee Ik-chi and Minister Park Ji-won on February 2 at the Lotte Hotel. During this meeting, Yoshida conveyed the North's positive response to Park Ji-won, confirming that the intent of the proposal was indeed sincere. I also learned that Yoshida had reported to Pyongyang about our meeting and was awaiting further instruction from the North. On February 12, I made a full report to the president on my findings.

* * * * * * * * *

Two weeks later on February 27, President Kim summoned me to the Blue House residence again. "The North side sent a new message through Yoshida again," he told me. "They want to have a secret meeting with Minister Park Ji-won in Singapore soon. I am going to appoint Minister Park Ji-won as a special envoy. I want the NIS to support Minister Park and provide two experts to aid in the negotiation process with the North, and provide all other necessary support. And you should assist me."

Upon my return to NIS, I made it a priority to assign two top North Korean specialists, Kim Bo-hyun and Seo Hoon, to Minister Park.

A few days before the scheduled secret contact between Park Ji-won and his North Korean counterpart, Song Ho-kyong, the North side warned: "No involvement by the National Intelligence Service will be tolerated on this matter." And a commentary in the *Rodong Sinmun* stated:

> For genuine dialogue, all interference by the gang of the National Intelligence Service must first be excluded. . . . We know from the past processes of North-South dialogue that the National Security Planning Agency [a precursor to the NIS] interfered in the talks to manipulate them, leading to a failure to produce results. . . . If the NIS were to be involved again, it would make a mockery of the North-South dialogue and be an intolerable insult to us as counterparts. We will not sit idly by and watch.

This position was echoed approximately ten days later in a statement by the Secretariat of the Committee for the Peaceful Unification of the Fatherland, who said: "If the National Intelligence Service shamelessly rears its head in the North-South talks, we will regard it as a machination to disrupt the talks and will take appropriate measures against it."

It was clear that the North believed the NIS would impede the talks and they wanted to obviate this. But this type of threat did not faze us.

Secret Envoy Meeting

On the morning of March 9, a secret meeting between Park Ji-won and Song Ho-kyong was held in Singapore. From our side, Kim Bo-hyun and Seo Hoon also attended the meeting. The North Koreans did not say much other than that they wanted to confirm the exact intent of the South's highest leadership.

In response, Minister Park confirmed the South's proposal that the first North-South summit be held sometime in May or June, to discuss important national issues such as the improvement of inter-Korean relations and the settlement of peace on the Korean Peninsula. Park told his counterpart, Song Ho-kyong, that President Kim Dae-jung could come to Pyongyang first. Park also said that pending a successful summit, the South would be willing to provide humanitarian support. In addition, North-South economic cooperation would be enhanced. Song only said that he would report it to the highest authority. The meeting ended with no further discussion, except for an agreement to meet again the following week.

* * * * * * * * *

During this time, President Kim Dae-jung was visiting the Free University of Berlin, where he announced the "Berlin Declaration," stating, "The government of the Republic of Korea is ready to help North Korea tide over its economic difficulties." In addition, in a speech entitled "The Lessons of the German Unification and the Korean Peninsula," President Kim said:

> Presently, private-sector economic cooperation is underway. However, to realize meaningful economic collaboration, the social infrastructure, including highways, railroads, harbors, power generation, and communications facilities, must be expanded. And the overall agricultural structure must be reformed. The time is ripe for government-to-government cooperation. The government of the Republic of Korea is ready to respond positively to any North Korean request in this regard.
>
> The Republic of Korea is making three central promises to Pyongyang—to guarantee their national security, assist in their economic recovery efforts, and actively support them in the international arena. In return, the Republic of Korea wants three guarantees from Pyongyang: first, the North must abandon any armed provocations against the South once and for all; second, it must comply with its previous promises not to develop nuclear weapons; and third, it must give up ambitions to develop long-range missiles.
>
> North Korea should also respond positively to reconciliation and cooperation for the purpose of ending the Cold War and achieving peace. In addition, North Korea should exert efforts to resolve the issue of separated families. And above all, we urge the North Korean side to come forward to accept government-to-government talks for the implementation of the North-South Basic Agreement.

The projects President Kim openly mentioned were the same projects that the North Korean authorities were promoting through Hyundai. At this point, the North was suffering from a severe shortage of energy, and, through the United States, they were requesting the provision of one million kilowatts of electricity from our government.

While aboard the plane en route to Europe, President Kim had written the Berlin speech himself, sending it to Seoul in advance so that our allies, including the United States, would have it one day before he delivered it. A copy was also provided to North Korea through Panmunjom in order to ensure that they understood the speech was not propaganda, but a serious proposal.

* * * * * * * * *

One week after the preliminary meeting in Singapore, the first envoys' meeting took place in Shanghai. At the second envoys' meeting, held in Beijing on March 23, the North took issue against using the expression, "the summit meeting between President Kim Dae-jung and Chairman Kim Jong-il." The North argued that since the head of state representing North Korea was Kim Young-nam, president of the Presidium of the Supreme People's Assembly, the meeting should be labeled "the Kim Dae-jung–Kim Young-nam Summit." At the same time, the North insisted that "in consideration of the South's wishes," they would accept President Kim's request for a meeting with Chairman Kim Jong-il on the sidelines during the summit.

At dawn that morning, I received a call from Minister Park from Beijing. After he debriefed me on the talks, I surmised that the North Koreans were wielding their negotiation tactics in order to gain more concessions from us, since we were facing the upcoming general elections for the National Assembly that spring. The North clearly appeared interested in a summit. Nevertheless, I could not accept their appeal.

With President Kim's instructions, I sent the following message to our team: "Just tell them you will see them again after the general elections. And come back home." President Kim was firm in his stance that it would be impossible to agree upon such a sensitive issue before the elections. As such, he was unwilling to make any concrete promises regarding economic aid before a summit meeting.

At the envoys' meeting, the North even asked for a certain amount of cash support. But Special Envoy Park firmly rejected the request, saying, "After we hold a summit, we can provide humanitarian assistance or economic cooperation, but cash support is impossible." In the end, the second envoys' meeting adjourned after the first day, and Special Envoy Park and his delegates returned to Seoul that afternoon.

* * * * * * * * * *

About ten days after the second envoys' meeting, the North sent us a follow-up proposal through Hyundai that both sides meet for working-level contacts in Beijing, stating: "Since compromise is possible, we request that the South send a draft of the agreement to the North." On April 4, working-level representatives from both sides met in Beijing and they were able to agree on a joint press statement regarding the summit, which was based on the South's draft statement.

On the morning of April 7, after receiving a report on the result of the third working-level meeting, President Kim instructed Special Envoy Park Ji-won to go to Beijing the next morning to reach a final agreement. The president said,

> A rich older brother should not visit his poor younger brother's home empty-handed. As we are about to succeed in holding a historic summit, isn't it right that we consider providing food aid for the North Koreans who are under difficult circumstances? Special Envoy Park, you tell them we will offer $100 million as a gift for the summit. That's the bottom line for your negotiation.

In fact, until this point, we had been embroiled in an internal debate over whether we should give $100 million worth of rice and fertilizer as a summit gift, or cash as the North had requested. As found in a special prosecutor's investigation three years later, the idea of providing $100 million was never realized.

* * * * * * * * * *

Only very few people had known about the secret inter-Korean special envoy meeting: Prime Minister Park Tae-joon and four or five officials of the U.S. government, including the U.S. president and the secretary of state, who were informed of the development through U.S. Ambassador to Korea Stephen Bosworth.

At the third special envoys' meeting that took place Saturday evening, April 8, both sides signed a joint statement of agreement. It had taken one month since initial contact in Singapore to agree to hold a summit. The following earth-shaking news was simultaneously announced in Seoul and Pyongyang on the morning of Monday, April 10:

> At the invitation of Chairman Kim Jong-il of the National Defense Commission, President Kim Dae-jung will visit Pyongyang from June 12 to June 14 this year. During the visit, there will be a historic meeting between President Kim Dae-jung and Chairman Kim Jong-il for a North-South summit.

There had been one particular matter of concern during the month-long process of negotiation with the North: the April 13 general elections to be held in the South. We were concerned because it was difficult to predict what impact or repercussions the announcement about the North-South summit would have on the elections.

I reported to the president NIS views that were based on internal analysis regarding this matter. We predicted the opposition party would criticize and oppose it as the government's political strategy to gain victory in the general elections. And we anticipated there would be rumors circulating about suspicious secret deals and an obsession to win a Nobel Peace Prize. In any case, it would negatively affect the general elections for the governing party. Our recommendation was to hold off on announcing the agreement about the summit until after the elections.

As it later turned out, the governing party had failed to gain the majority party status as a result of the general elections, which were held without the involvement of the National Intelligence Agency for the first time in Korea. The governing party suffered a devastating defeat in the Gyeongsang provinces, and the results from the metropolitan areas were unsatisfactory. The opposition Grand National Party (GNP) grabbed 133 seats, the ruling Democratic Party 114, the United Liberal Democrats (ULD) 17 seats, and other minor parties and independents won 8 seats.

Whisper of American Support

After the agreement to hold the summit was reached, we were very busy for the two months until the summit was actually held. By the order of the president, I assumed the important responsibility of overseeing the process of preparing for the summit.

President Kim wanted to put me, as director of the NIS, in charge of dealing with essential issues and strategies related to negotiations with the North. Accordingly, I set up a summit support team at NIS to recommend a summit strategy and provide necessary documents, while supporting the summit preparation and planning group.

Preparations proceeded smoothly. Preparation talks between the South the North were held five times at Panmunjom. Through these talks, both sides were able to agree on the technical details and agenda for the summit. It was also agreed that our side's presidential delegation would include 130 people to accompany the president and fifty press reporters to cover the event. Direct telephone lines would be installed between Seoul and Pyongyang and a satellite network would be set up for the first time in the history of the Korean division for a live television broadcast.

One of the difficult issues to negotiate was related to determining the number of press reporters to cover the summit in Pyongyang. We had proposed eighty reporters, but the North, raising complaints about the so-called anti-North machination by the *Chosun Ilbo*, the monthly *Chosun*, and the Korean Broadcasting System (KBS), stubbornly insisted that the number be limited to thirty or forty at the most.

It was not an easy task to select members of the presidential delegation. Twenty-four special delegates included representatives from a broad range of organizations, including political parties, social organizations, representatives from economic organizations, business entities carrying out business deals with the North, press organizations, and academia. However, the Grand National Party refused to join the presidential delegation.

＊　＊　＊　＊　＊　＊　＊　＊　＊

The official response from the United States was, "We welcome and support the North-South summit." However, some Americans continued raising questions, concerns, and doubts. They were worried the North and South might agree on the withdrawal of U.S. troops without the knowledge of the United States. They also raised concerns about the possibility that the summit might reach a radical agreement on a peace treaty, or cause a negative impact on U.S.-DPRK talks. In the midst of this speculative atmosphere, U.S. Secretary of Defense William Cohen issued a statement that "U.S. troops will remain in Korea."

President Kim received a courtesy call from Ambassador Wendy Sherman when she came to Seoul with her delegation as the U.S.–North Korea Policy Coordinator; the president kindly explained to her his position on the summit. My role was to host a dinner for her and her delegation and to further expound on the details of President Kim's thoughts. I told them that we would address the issues of North Korea's nuclear and missile programs during the upcoming summit. I made clear that we would tell the North that we would only be able to proceed to improve our relations with the North and engage in economic cooperation when these issues were resolved through agreement between the United States and North Korea.

I also told Wendy Sherman and her party that we would persuade the North that the continued U.S. military presence in Korea was the balancer of peace and stability in the region of Northeast Asia—even beyond the point of Korean unification—and that it served the interests of the Korean people. To make them feel comfortable, I reemphasized that it was President Kim's firm conviction that "the United States is the most important friendly country to the Republic of Korea and we should develop relations with the North based on the robust ROK-U.S. alliance."

In addition, I also briefed them in detail on our objectives for the summit, negotiating strategy, and anticipated results. In response, Ambassador Sherman thanked me, saying that after listening to the president and to my explanation, "all concerns were completely resolved." In particular, she praised me as the "architect of the Perry Process," and said she "appreciated our close coordination regarding the summit." She said, "Now we have found a path to end the Cold War on the Korean Peninsula."

Then she whispered in my ear, "I am well aware that you candidly informed the United States of everything through Ambassador Bosworth. President Clinton and Secretary Albright both trust you and they are grateful to you. I am also pleased that our close and cooperative relations are better now than ever before."

Hyundai's Seven Projects

On the evening of May 4, I was surprised again after I received a call from Minister Park Ji-won. That evening Minister Park had met with the Hyundai people. They informed Minister Park that the North side had issued an agreement with Hyundai to give them the exclusive business rights for "seven business projects." In addition, Hyundai would soon apply for approval by the Ministry of Unification. What surprised me was that Hyundai had made a secret deal to pay $400 million dollars for the exclusive business rights. Minister Park said, "I have just reported to the president on this matter and he 'could not understand what in the world was going on.' The president instructed me to find out the details and report them to him. So I need your help, Director Lim."

I had no idea what was going on either. I immediately instructed Kim Bo-hyun to find out the facts and review them to come up with a countermeasure. On May 6, Park Ji-won, Senior Economic Secretary Lee Ki-ho, and I received a fact-finding report from Kim Bo-hyun on Hyundai's agreement on economic cooperation with the North. The agreement was as follows:

- The North side grants exclusive business rights to Hyundai for thirty years on all social overhead capital (SOC) projects and basic industrial facilities.
- Hyundai will undertake the seven projects as early as possible, including linking and doubling of the rail tracks between Seoul and Shinuiju, construction of an industrial park on the west coast, modernization of communication systems, and building power generation facilities.

- Hyundai will form a business consortium to include domestic business entities and related organizations to promote the projects.
- The North side guarantees Hyundai free provision of land and all other benefits applicable to Special Economic Zones.

Hyundai agreed to pay the North $400 million in a secret deal. Kim Bo-hyun also reported that Hyundai was going to apply for business approval by the unification ministry as soon as possible and move on to raise the required funds. Hyundai was expecting the government to willingly provide support since it was assisting the promotion of a summit with the North.

After receiving the report, all three of us felt negatively about the Hyundai business projects. We understood that it was not atypical for big businesses to make secret deals. But the idea that a business would be the sole organization to implement such large SOC projects seemed unrealistic. We also concluded that there would be a procedural problem for the government to approve such a business deal before holding the summit. The three of us agreed that Senior Economic Secretary Lee Ki-ho should contact Hyundai to verify the findings, develop countermeasures, and report them to the president.

* * * * * * * * *

A few days later, Senior Secretary Lee reported the results of his discussion with Hyundai to the president. Minister Park and I were present during Lee's report to the president, who was very disturbed by the deal between the North and Hyundai. Although the president recognized Hyundai's contribution in getting the North to hold a summit—as well as Hyundai's cooperation in building a North-South economic community—it was hard for the government to accept Hyundai's unilateral actions. The president asked,

> Is Hyundai not taking advantage of the summit, forcing us to retroactively support them after they have already made the agreement? Don't they know that the government's actions might be misconstrued as trying to buy a summit? If Hyundai wanted to promote business the right way, they should have worked for international cooperation with their business competitors. Can they really achieve cooperation this way? Isn't Hyundai's behavior disrespectful to the president and the nation? We could have promoted these projects in a transparent manner after the summit with the blessing of the people and the world. Why would they want to push for agreement before the summit, under pressures of the North?

President Kim also did not hide his displeasure with the North on this matter. He said the North Korean attitude was unforgivable. Given the special nature of North-South relations, these large-scale projects would be impossible to carry out without governmental cooperation. The president could not believe Hyundai did not know this. He disliked Hyundai's ways of doing business. To conclude the matter, he instructed Senior Secretary Lee: "Make sure you persuade Hyundai to correct their behavior!"

* * * * * * * * *

The Ministry of Unification had declined Hyundai's application for business approval on the grounds of a lack of supporting documents for the application. However, it was not easy to ignore the problem Hyundai had already created. Although Hyundai had promoted the project without government approval, the North had already agreed upon it. We concluded that the government should intervene and cancel the deal. This was the backdrop for the alleged "incident of sending money to the North," which would be investigated by the special prosecutor appointed by President Roh Moo-hyun three years later.

During that time, the press had been actively reporting on the troubling management problems within the Hyundai Group. In an effort to overcome the International Monetary Fund (IMF) restrictions imposed on Korea, the government had increased pressure on big corporations for structural reform and rational management. Honorary Chairman Chung Ju-young was sick in bed from old age, while his three sons competed fiercely for succession to the chairman's throne. It was like a war of the princes. At the same time, due to Hyundai Construction's financial demise, a government-led group of creditors was demanding that Honorary Chairman Chung, and his protégé managers such as Chairman Lee Ik-chi, step down from their management positions in order to create true business reform. This was directly linked to the issue of restoring the overall market credibility of the Hyundai Group.

Some believed that due to these unfavorable circumstances, Lee Ik-chi and Chung Mong-heon were taking unreasonable steps to find a breakthrough to the crisis. It was also clear that North Korea wanted to link the business deal with Hyundai to the holding of a summit, to ensure they could cash in on the promised "rebates" from Hyundai.

Contentious Advance Meeting in Pyongyang

Until the middle of May, the NIS had provided the president with all types of information necessary for the summit. We prepared personal information on Chairman Kim Jong-il by writing reports and summarizing more than ten books that were published about him in the South. However, President Kim was dissatisfied with the information about Kim Jong-il, as most of it was negative.

President Kim expressed his concerns, saying, "If all this information is true, how am I to sit face-to-face with such a person ?" He wanted more objective, accurate, and concrete information.

He also wanted to know details about the North's intent for the summit. When it became apparent it would be impossible to gather such information through the vice ministerial level contacts at Panmunjom, President Kim decided to dispatch a special envoy to Pyongyang. He instructed this be carried out without fail. He said to me,

> Director Lim, I think you have to go to Pyongyang as a presidential special envoy, to meet Chairman Kim Jong-il. You have three missions: first, find out what kind of person Chairman Kim Jong-il really is. Second, fully explain in advance the issues to be discussed at the summit, and find out what the North's position is. Third, obtain the North's agreement on a draft joint declaration to be released after the summit."

On the dawn of Saturday, May 27, the previous night's rain had begun to taper off, but dark clouds remained. I left for Pyongyang along with four assistants from my staff. At six o'clock that morning, we crossed the Military Demarcation Line (MDL) through Panmunjom and reached the Tongilgak (Unification Pavilion) on the North side of the Joint Security Area (JSA). On the way to Panmunjom, a U.S. Army major who had been assigned to the United Nations Command escorted us from the vicinity of the Imjin River. As the envoy on a peacemaking mission, crossing the fifty-year-old division between our two nations was the opening of a new millennium of reconciliation and cooperation.

The last time I had visited the Tongilgak had been eight years prior when I had been frequenting the North as a representative of the North-South High-Level Talks. Those memories flickered through my mind.

At the Tongilgak, a familiar face—Lim Dong-ok, the first deputy director of the Workers Party's Department of the United Front—was there to meet us. Four others accompanied him.

As our delegation was transported by car to a helipad four kilometers north of Kaesong, we passed a milestone that read "168 kilometers to Pyongyang." After a fifty-minute helicopter flight, we arrived at the Baekhwawon—the best guesthouse for foreign dignitaries visiting North Korea—at 7:40 a.m.

I sat down with Lim Dong-ok, who was practically in charge of North-South relations. I explained the purpose of my visit. I told him that I wanted to meet with Chairman Kim Jong-il to present to him a personal letter from President Kim Dae-jung, and to explain the latter's intentions. I also said I wanted to discuss the main aspects of the summit agenda and obtain Chairman Kim's agreement on a joint declaration. After I finished, Lim Dong-ok briefed me on the major items on the itinerary for President Kim's visit. The North's itinerary raised an issue about which I had been concerned.

He said, "A visit in which you pay tribute to the late President Kim Il-sung, who lies in state at the Geumsusan Memorial Palace, must be included. This is the practice and 'protocol politics' for state visitors to our Republic."

I reluctantly, but firmly, expressed my disapproval, saying, "As you know, this issue was never raised at the working-level contacts. This will likely create problems in public opinion. I cannot agree to this."

Lim Dong-ok did not back down:

> Aside from practice and protocols, isn't this a matter of courtesy? It will pose many difficulties if you are unable to accommodate this civility during such a historic visit. President Kim visited President Ho Chi-minh's mausoleum when he went to Hanoi. How is it that you cannot perform this important act between us, the same nation?"

I explained my reasons. I said this was a sensitive issue in North-South relations. But he remained adamant and showed no sign of concession. He went on:

> We are well aware that the South Korean press insists on "the impossibility of a visit to the Geumsusan Memorial Palace." But, you should also understand there is harsh resistance from our hardliners due to such opposition. You should cease your unconditional opposition. This is an issue you, Director Lim, should report to President Kim, and for which you should get his approval when you return to Seoul.

As had been the case in previous inter-Korean talks, once the atmosphere turned sour, Lim Dong-ok's attitude became harder and more uncompromising.

I rejected Lim Dong-ok's request for President Kim's visit to Kim Il-sung's mausoleum that day. Upset by my firm rejection, Lim Dong-ok notified me that it would now be impossible for me to see Chairman Kim Jong-il. He went so far as to unilaterally cancel my appointment with Secretary Kim Yong-soon. Then, he read to me a prepared statement:

> It is the North's position that in the event that the president does not visit the Geumsusan Palace, it will be impossible for him to meet with Chairman Kim Jong-il; it will still be possible to hold a summit meeting with Kim Young-nam, president of the Presidium of the Supreme People's Assembly.

I called President Kim, using the Inmarsat satellite phone that I had brought with me, and reported what had transpired in Pyongyang. After that, I decided to return to Seoul. My call to the president was not reporting a positive result. Nevertheless, it was the first historic satellite call connecting the North and South. The audibility was as good as the local calls made in Seoul.

That evening I boarded a helicopter, which flew through the night rain, low above the Pyongyang-Kaesong highway of the "dark republic." There were no lights lit under the path of our flight. We all were worried about the safety of flying through a dark stormy night.

Approximately seventy minutes later, there was a blinking light pointing to the landing site. We landed near Kaesong around nine thirty at night. Only then, were we able to let out a sigh of relief. Thirty minutes later, I crossed the Military Demarcation Line back to the bright land of freedom. Although the mission had not been successful, I felt great joy in returning to the South. I realized I had managed to skip supper during the tense hours with the North Koreans and was now hungry.

Although it was late, President Kim was still waiting for me at the Blue House. After listening to my report, he appeared disappointed, yet maintained his presidential dignity. He comforted me by saying, "We'll think of some good measures tomorrow afternoon." When I got up to leave, it was ten minutes before midnight.

First Encounter with Kim Jong-il

A week later on Saturday, June 3, I crossed the border through Panmunjom again at six o'clock in the morning, and boarded a helicopter. This time the helicopter landed at the entrance of Cholima Street in Pyongyang City. We drove through very quiet streets and arrived at the Moranbong Guest House. It was about eight o'clock in the morning. I could see a clear sky, through which a grand view of Nungla Island on the Daedong River appeared. The clean and pleasant morning air I was breathing seemed auspicious.

Prior to this trip, President Kim had made an agonizing decision:

> Holding the summit is more important than the issue of visiting the Geumsusan Memorial Palace. Improving North-South relations is more important than protocol. If we fail to hold a summit now, it would bring despair to our nation's seventy million people, and we would become the laughing stock of the world. We must hold a summit and announce a joint declaration. Tell them I can visit the palace after I do these things.

I interpreted the president's intentions as him wanting to have a summit with Chairman Kim Jong-il first—but he was not really willing to visit

Geumsusan Palace. If this was correct, my mission was clear. Based on the angst in President Kim's proposal, my mission was to remind Chairman Kim Jong-il of the importance of the planned summit and to persuade him to give up his interest in having President Kim visit his deceased father's palace. I knew it would not be an easy task. But, I had to try my best. I went to Pyongyang remembering the saying that "a general will win a battle of war without fail if he fights it with the conviction of victory."

* * * * * * * * *

At the Moranbong guesthouse, I sat across from Kim Yong-soon, the party secretary in charge of South Korean affairs, and the director of the Department of the United Front. Also present at the meeting was Deputy Director Lim Dong-ok. I first conveyed to them the decision President Kim had made after agonizing deliberation. I proceeded to express my own views as the special envoy:

> It is not acceptable to the South Korean people that their president pay tribute to the body of the late President Kim Il-sung. His leadership would be undermined, and it would also trigger tremendous turmoil even if we were to hold a historic North-South summit. Suppose Chairman Kim Jong-il came to Seoul—would he be able to visit the National Cemetery and pay tribute to the fallen soldiers of South Korea? What's more, the opposition party is in control of the National Assembly and it surely would oppose inter-Korean economic cooperation and humanitarian assistance to the North. If this happens, a summit agreement would lose its significance. I ask for a wise decision on the North's part.

My words undoubtedly sounded negative to Kim Yong-soon and Lim Dong-ok. Nevertheless, they listened carefully and took notes because I told them my view was based on the premise of President Kim's decision. They promised they would provide an accurate report to the highest authority. Few people from the North would know more about South Korea than these two individuals. My first meeting with Kim Yong-soon thus ended relatively successfully.

* * * * * * * * *

That evening I was escorted to Sunan Airport, where I boarded an airplane for a thirty-five-minute flight to a military air base near Shinuiju. There I got in a Mercedes-Benz sedan driven by an Army captain. We drove about thirty minutes on an unpaved road. As we approached our destination, we passed through a one-kilometer-long stretch of road. A row of thick-leaved trees lined both sides of the road and blocked the sky. Before finally arriving at Chairman Kim Jong-il's Special House, we were stopped at three separate

Acting as presidential special envoy, the author meets Kim Jong-il (*right*) for the first time in Shinuiju in June 2000. Courtesy Lim Dong-won.

checkpoints, where we were thoroughly screened by Korean People's Army (KPA) majors. It was approximately seven o'clock in the evening. The big interior walls and the spacious floors in the house were faced with cream-colored marble. The hall was bright but for some reason looked chilly.

"I am pleased to meet you. Thank you for your trouble in coming here." Chairman Kim Jong-il extended his hand to me. He looked impressive. He had a big, stout body, and he was wearing his customary brown jacket and his shoes with lifts. He had a raised hairstyle that also helped him appear taller.

The first order of business was to take pictures with him. Then, he showed us into a room, where we sat facing each other across a big long table. Sitting to my right and left were Kim Bo-hyun and Seo Hoon, and on either side of Chairman Kim Jong-il were Kim Yong-soon and Lim Dong-ok.

Chairman Kim said, "I am staying here on my way home from China, after a visit from May 29 to May 31. I am really sorry to have asked you to come this far. How is the president doing?"

After this greeting, Chairman Kim Jong-il asked me to speak first.

I explained to him my mission: to present the president's letter to Chairman Kim and find out more about his intentions; to exchange views about how to establish a successful summit; to secure his agreement on a joint declaration based on the draft statement we sent to the North; and to coordinate other issues of interest, including the president's itinerary.

I also explained the substance of the president's letter in detail:

> The president told me to convey his appreciation to Chairman Kim Jong-il for the invitation to Pyongyang you have extended to him. The president sent me as his special envoy to ensure that the upcoming summit produces good results. The president is asking that you trust me, acting on his behalf, to discuss all issues with you.

In his letter to Chairman Kim Jong-il, President Kim proposed four issues for the agenda of the summit. They included improvement of North-South relations and unification; reduction of tension to establish peace; exchanges and cooperation for coexistence and co-prosperity; reunions of separated families; and other issues of mutual interest. President Kim also proposed in his letter that the summit announce "a joint declaration" that should include basic principles and practical measures to begin a new North-South relationship. This kind of agreement would provide a source of self-respect, joy, and hope for the Korean nation.

* * * * * * * * *

Of the president's four agenda items, I first took up the issue of unification to explain the South's fundamental views based on our "National Community Unification Formula." I said we understood that unification would not be realized immediately, but gradually and peacefully. I said that since unification was a goal and a process at the same time, we should first realize a "state of *de facto* unification," in which people could travel freely between the North and South through reconciliation and cooperation. Only after this phase would "*de jure* unification" be possible. I continued,

> To this end, we should institutionalize a "Confederation of the North and South" by joining the strengths of the North and South to form and develop a national economic community. We should also remove the legacies of the Cold War through arms control to attain peace and continue to resolve other important pending issues. These are the president's thoughts. This also means that we should implement the 1991 North-South Basic Agreement.

I was encouraged by Chairman Kim Jong-il's consistently well-composed posture and his attentiveness during my explanation. He continued to show interest in the discussion of unification at dinner that evening. He also asked some specific questions.

* * * * * * * * *

The next topic was the issue of reducing tensions and establishing peace. I emphasized that, in order to alleviate the South's anxieties about the North's threats and its policy of unification by communization, as well as the North's concerns about unification by absorption and invasion by the South, it was important to build political and military confidence between both parties. We should take measures to prevent accidental armed confrontations, make peaceful use of the Demilitarized Zone, promote military cooperation, and resolve the issues of denuclearization of the Korean Peninsula and weapons of mass destruction. I said,

> The president believes that the North should make efforts to improve relations with the United States and Japan. We are willing to earnestly help you if you make such efforts. And the president has asked that the North consider the issue of the presence of U.S. troops in the South from a broad and positive perspective. The president holds a view that the U.S. military presence is necessary now and even after unification, as it contributes to the balance that will be essential in achieving peace and stability in the Northeast Asia region.

* * * * * * * * *

Regarding the issue of exchanges and cooperation, I explained our position as detailed in President Kim's "Berlin Declaration": that we are willing to cooperate with the North Korean authorities and to work with them to carry out projects that the North wishes to promote. In addition, to guarantee the active promotion of economic cooperation, I emphasized the need to reach a North-South agreement regarding practical issues such as an investment guarantee, avoidance of double taxation, and account clearance. I also added that we should promote exchange and cooperation in social, cultural, academic, and other areas.

On the issue of separated families, I told Chairman Kim Jong-il that President Kim regarded this issue as the most urgent humanitarian issue to resolve. I shared that we should first ascertain whether family members were alive or not, promote exchanges of letters, and allow reunions by free will. I proposed that the two sides agree to begin an exchange of family meetings on the anniversary of Liberation Day that year.

* * * * * * * * *

It took more than an hour to finish my explanation. Throughout my presentation, Chairman Kim Jong-il listened attentively, keeping his fingers crossed on the table, without showing any sign of fatigue on his face. He occasionally took notes and sometimes he nodded, showing his interest and favorable attitude. After I finished, I gave him the papers that contained the topics I had covered. I asked him to take time to review and consider our positions. Later at the actual summit, Chairman Kim Jong-il said those papers were very helpful to him.

"Director Lim, I was able to fully understand President Kim's intentions, thanks to your explanation. Thank you."

After expressing his respectful appreciation, Chairman Kim Jong-il began talking in a lively manner, as though he was talking to somebody with whom he regularly spoke.

> I know well that President Kim is an elder politician, who suffered hardship, kidnapping, a death sentence, and all kinds of humiliation while he was an opposition figure. He championed the struggle for democratization and finally became president. I know he is doing very well as the incumbent president. I must first tell you that I personally respect him. I understand he is a humble person by nature.
>
> When he comes to Pyongyang, I will treat him as a respected elder leader. We will elevate the dignity of his visit and we will make sure there will be no inconveniences during his stay. I am going to be frank with you since you have come all the way here. I know your job is to catch Communists. We will host the best, grandest reception ever for President Kim—better than those we provided for China's General Secretary Jiang Zemin or any other heads of state who have visited Pyongyang. You don't have to worry about that. We will do our best to make sure that the visit will be an enjoyable one.

Chairman Kim Jong-il was serious and decisive—contrary to the negative portrayal of his personality throughout the Western world as mischievously secretive, eccentric, and violent.

> Above all, I would like to listen to President Kim at length and have candid, informal discussions. Well, as far as intellectual dialogues, he can have those when he talks to President Kim Young-nam [of the Presidium]. During this first meeting, we should not try to agree upon many things, but agree on the things that we can implement. Is there not a saying that you won't be full after the first spoonful of food? Were there not three good documents between the North and the South? [He was referring to the July 4 Joint Statement, the North-South Basic Agreement, and the Joint Declaration of Denuclearization.]

But, none of them has been implemented properly. Since the fundamental nature of our relations has not changed, what would be the purpose of continuing to make similar agreements? It is more important to implement the agreements we have already produced.

If we agree on a simple, declaratory statement of hope, I think that should be sufficient. And this is not the kind of a thing that you would write in advance. It would be fine to write it after the holding of the summit. After that, we should gradually carry out our agreements, one by one. The Chinese leadership is surprised at the news of the upcoming summit. They asked us, "How did you suddenly make such a decision?" Let's not surprise our neighbors too much, but let's move forward calmly with one thing at a time.

Chairman Kim said, "We are particularly concerned about President Kim's personal safety," and he complained that the South side had revealed the details of the president's plan of movement, including his departure time from Seoul:

We must be thoroughly ready to protect the safety of President Kim. We are in a situation in which we don't know what the obstructive external forces might do. Internally, we don't know what trouble some impure elements might cause. Therefore, I think it would be prudent to have a plan to move up or put off the president's arrival by one day without notice, so that we can confuse the obstructive forces."

I responded, however, that changing the arrival date was difficult to accept, saying, "I fully appreciate and agree with Chairman Kim's concerns about the safety issue. But changing the date is difficult. What's worse, moving up by one day is impossible."

However, immediately preceding the president's scheduled visit, the arrival date was delayed by one day at the North's request. The North asked for the delay for "the inevitable reasons of technical preparations" and we accepted their request. We took it as a signal that Chairman Kim Jong-il would come out to the airport to welcome President Kim. In fact, North Korea was most concerned about Chairman Kim Jong-il's safety. The security of Chairman Kim's itinerary was always tightly protected; the sudden change in schedule of the president's arrival was not an isolated case for North Korea. We decided to respect the North side's caution.

Regarding North Korea's relations with the United States, Chairman Kim Jong-il expressed his frank views:

The Korean Peninsula is an area where the interests of its neighboring countries clash in acute conflict. The neighbors prefer the continued division of the peninsula. Therefore, it is important that we, as the same nation, independently work together to resolve issues ourselves without the interference of external forces. Of course, whether from a historical or geopolitical perspective, it is important to maintain relations with the United States. President Kim argues that U.S. troops should remain in Korea for peace and stability in Northeast Asia even after unification. As a matter of fact, I don't think that is a bad idea, provided that the status and the role of U.S. troops be changed.

It is desirable that U.S. troops stay as a peacekeeping force in Korea, instead of a hostile force against the Republic [in reference to the Democratic People's Republic of Korea]. We already sent Secretary Kim Yong-soon to the United States in 1992 to officially convey this to the U.S. government. The point is if we become too anti-American, it could hurt the interest of our nation. I think it is an important task to end this historically hostile relationship and achieve normalization of relations with the United States. If relations are normalized, we can resolve all security concerns of the United States. Therefore, we propose an early peace treaty to replace the Armistice Agreement.

I was quite relieved by Chairman Kim's frank and candid attitude. I took this opportunity to bring up the sensitive issue of a visit to the Geumsusan Memorial Palace to find out his thoughts on the subject. I said,

Concerning the North's request that President Kim pay a visit to the Geumsusan Memorial Palace, he said he could do so after holding a successful summit and releasing a joint declaration. However, as I have told Secretary Kim Yong-soon, it is my position as the special envoy that this matter be handled with caution and, considering the sentiments of the South Korean people, that this visit be cancelled altogether.

Nevertheless, Chairman Kim was firm as far as this issue was concerned:

I would think that the president should visit the Geumsusan Memorial Palace before we hold a summit meeting. Why do you only think of the sentiments of the South Korean people? Do you think that the sentiments of the North Korean people are not important? Is it not natural, according to our traditional customs, for the South to demonstrate its courtesy by paying tributes in consideration of the people and me, the principal mourner of the bereaved family? It is not that I don't understand that both the North and South still have bad feelings towards one another. Rather than saying it cannot be done, let's think of a positive solution. One idea would be for you to announce a visit to the Geumsusan Palace before the president comes here and persuade the opposition party and the people. We could consider delaying the visit until this is possible.

The author (*second from left*) and Chairman Kim view a documentary on Kim's May 2000 visit to China. Courtesy Lim Dong-won.

Kim Jong-il's Good Sense of Humor

After leading the conversation on various pending issues, Chairman Kim Jong-il said he had prepared a dinner for the president's special envoy. He suggested that we continue our discussion during dinner. He also suggested that before dinner, we watch a documentary film that covered his recent visit to China.

We moved to a large room, where I sat beside Chairman Kim on a long sofa. Before the film started, he said to me,

> In the North, the supply of electricity can be a problem. Very often, the current becomes unstable. This happens while watching movies, too. If this happens during the film, please understand. This film shows my activities during the meetings with the highest-ranking leaders of China and the banquets I attended. The film has just arrived from Pyongyang, where they edited it.

It was almost nine o'clock at night when we moved to the dining room after watching the film. Chairman Kim kindly showed me to my seat at a large round table more than three meters in diameter. He did this to show his respect for the older man that I was. When he sat down, he raised his glass and requested a welcome toast to the president's special envoy. French red wine was served in Riedel crystal. It was a lavish dinner. Chairman Kim said he only drank wine: "In the past I used to drink a lot of whisky and cognac. But now I comply with the doctor's advice and drink red wine for good health."

The dinner lasted more than three hours, during which we talked about several subjects. Again, it was Chairman Kim Jong-il who led the conversation, but this time with a more frank attitude. At one point, we exchanged our views on democracy.

Kim Jong-il began by saying "I don't really understand what the South refers to as democracy. It allows partisan fights, similar to the days of the Yi dynasty, and the opposition Grand National Party only criticizes the government and opposes it for opposition's sake. Is that what democracy is about?"

I replied by saying that a characteristic of democracy was to seek harmony in diversity. I added that the opposition party's role was to point out the mistakes of the government. This prevented the government from making such mistakes. I agreed that sometimes they went too far. But I thought it was better to have an opposition party for the development of the country. He switched subjects:

> I think it would be good if President Kim comes here with former presidents. The whole world will be surprised. Come to think of it, President Chun Doo-hwan and President Roh Tae-woo would probably come, but I don't think President Kim Young-sam would come. When President Kim Il-sung passed away in 1994, President Kim took threatening hostile measures against us, including issuing an emergency alert to the military while we were in mourning. We can never forget this. And at that time the South was caught in a big controversy over the question of whether to send a condolence delegation. In fact, it would have been more difficult for us if the South had actually sent mourners.

A special broadcast from Pyongyang at noon on July 9, 1994, had reported that President Kim Il-sung died of myocardial infarction at two o'clock in the morning on July 8. Upon receipt of this urgent news, President Kim Young-sam issued an emergency alert order to all the armed forces. However, the United States Forces Korea (USFK) did not respond, considering it to be inappropriate. Before the funeral took place on July 17, an opposition member of the National Assembly raised a question of "condolence diplomacy" for the sake of North-South dialogue and confidence building. The opposition member recalled an exchange of condolence delegations between China and Taiwan for the funerals of Chiang Kai-shek and Mao Zedong. But the governing party criticized the suggestion, asking, "How could anyone talk about sending a condolence delegation for a war criminal?" Thus the governing party provoked anti-North Korean sentiments in the South at that time. On the other hand, President William Clinton issued a condolence statement, and the U.S. head of delegation for negotiation, Robert Gallucci, who was at Geneva, went to the North Korean mission to express his condolences on the death of President Kim Il-sung.

Chairman Kim and I continued our conversation. He said,

> I think it would be best for President Kim to come here by air. We are going to hold a big welcome reception at the airport. We are also considering having military honor guards from all three branches of service. What if I myself go out to the airport to welcome him, and then we ride in the same car to go directly to the Geumsusan Memorial Palace? I am the senior member of the bereaved family. Don't you think he would come with me? [This was a genuine request that he was making with respect.]
>
> If President Kim reluctantly conforms to this formality, would the people in the South not understand it? Another alternative would be that instead of me going out to the airport, I go to the Geumsusan Palace to wait for the president and welcome him there. Or, we can consider another method: on the second day of his visit, before the beginning of the summit meeting, I escort him there. Instead of insisting that the visit is possible only after the summit meeting, let's think about which of these three ideas would be the best.

I replied,

> I would like to ask you to reconsider this issue, because I believe it would be more beneficial to both the North and the South if President Kim is free to exercise his leadership to improve North-South relations. The people still have bad feelings from the fratricidal war, and the conservative opposition party is in control of the National Assembly. What's more, we cannot ignore the cold reality of the influence of the conservative press. As I have repeatedly said, I oppose a visit to the Geumsusan Memorial Palace because it would certainly diminish the significance of the summit and cause negative repercussions afterwards. It is the president's thought that this summit should soon be followed by a second summit in Seoul, where Chairman Kim would come. However, a visit to the Geumsusan Palace would cause trouble for such an idea. Please understand my sincere views regarding this matter. I again ask for your prudent consideration.

Kim Jong-il answered,

> I have looked at the recent opinion poll in the South that was conducted by the *Dong-A Ilbo*: 60 percent [actually it was 80 percent] of the people welcome my visit to Seoul, and 30 percent think I am a dictator. I can

fully understand that. Anyway, it is premature to discuss my visit to Seoul at this point. It might be possible that President Kim Young-nam of the Presidium could visit Seoul first. Then he would visit the tomb of President Park Chung-hee. Of course, I will visit President Park's tomb myself if I come to Seoul. Although it was bad that President Park severely suppressed politics with the Yushin system, he deserves high marks for his initiation of the Saemaeul [New Community] Movement and his contribution to the development of the South Korean economy. I understand that President Park in his early days mobilized soldiers for economic development; he would drink *makkolli* [Korean rice wine] with farmers in the field, and he developed the rural areas through the Saemaeul Movement. In the North, we don't make *makkolli*. Hyundai said they would bring *makkolli* here, so I am waiting. Ha, ha, ha . . .

Chairman Kim Jong-il freely led our conversation with his talent to switch from sensitive topics to light topics, and vice versa. He had the keen ability to make his listeners feel comfortable, but not to feel relaxed. We went on.

He began to speak of South Korea, saying, "I saw a documentary film of Gorbachev's visit to South Korea. Jeju Island looked exotic and beautiful. I felt like going there to see it. I think it would be a great idea if we alternately held summit meetings between Mount Baekdu and Mount Halla."

I said,

Jeju Island was developed with special care as an international tourist attraction. Many foreign dignitaries have visited the island, and several summit meetings between heads of states have been held there. I think we could consider beginning the second summit in Seoul first and continuing it on Jeju Island. I surely hope you visit the South.

Chairman Kim said, "I hear that in the South, 'palace cuisine' is famous, but I have not had a chance to try it." I replied, "I will recommend to President Kim during his visit here that the South serve palace cuisine for the return dinner."

In fact, at the return dinner hosted by President Kim, palace cuisine was served. Twelve expert palace cuisine chefs were selected, and they brought enough ingredients by two refrigerated trucks to prepare an impressive eight-course dinner of palace cuisine for the function.

The conversation continued. Kim Jong-il said,

In the past, the National Security Planning agency interfered in North-South talks and disrupted them. Therefore, in the beginning, we did not want the NIS to get involved in this summit. But trusting President Kim, and after learning that Director Lim greatly contributed to the conclusion of the North-South Basic Agreement, I decided to let it go and see what happens.

I told him, "Thank you for saying that. By the way, I hope that you have made a positive decision regarding the issue of separated families. It would become a memorable gift for President Kim to take home from his trip to Pyongyang." He replied,

> At no time have I ever opposed the issues of separated families. I am more than willing to allow meetings between them. You may tell President Kim of my proposal that we first hold an exchange of meetings between Seoul and Pyongyang on a trial basis for a year. After that, we can even come up with even better ways. Also, I want to make sure that the first lady sees many things during this summit. We are considering the Pyongyang Birth Hospital, a daycare center, a school, the Embroidery Institute, and other places for her visit. We are also considering her meetings with female leaders. Not too long ago, I saw a South Korean movie called *Festival*. That movie successfully portrayed our virtues as the "country of courtesy in the East," and reflected our national emotion. Both the North and the South should well-preserve our national tradition.

At this point, I stressed the need for an exchange of special envoys, and proposed that Secretary Kim Yong-soon visit Seoul as my counterpart. Chairman Kim accepted it on the spot. This was another result of my visit as special envoy. On that year's Chuseok (a traditional Thanksgiving holiday celebrating the fall harvest), Secretary Kim Yong-soon did come to Seoul.

Chairman Kim Jong-il seemed to strongly recognize the need to improve inter-Korean relations and open the door to the Western world to improve North Korea's underdeveloped economy. Nevertheless, he did not want to hide his reservations. As long as the United States maintained a hostile policy, opening would lead to disarmament and collapse of the system. It was apparent that to avoid that kind of a crisis, he wanted to get President Kim Dae-jung's help in improving relations with the United States. He seemed to have been influenced by President Kim's close relationship with President Clinton, the Korea Peninsula Peace Process (the Perry Process) that was led by the South, and President Kim's advocacy for the West to normalize relations with the North and to provide humanitarian aid.

* * * * * * * * *

The dinner with Chairman Kim ended at midnight. I flew back to Pyongyang that night. It was two o'clock in the morning when I arrived at my quarters. At eight o'clock that morning, I called President Kim over the satellite phone, and briefly reported to him on the results of my talks with Chairman Kim the night before.

That morning I walked to the Eulmildae, and in the afternoon, I visited the Tomb of Dangun–the legendary founder of Korea 5,000 years ago. Later I went to the Moran Theater to see the performance of the Pyongyang Symphony Orchestra. I particularly liked their performances of "A Good Harvest on the Chungsan Field," "My Sweet Hometown," and *The Barber of Seville*, among others. I also learned that the same orchestra would play for President Kim and his delegation when they came.

While attending the performance, a thought occurred to me. An exchange of orchestra performances between the North and the South would be a good start to cultural exchange. I promised then and there that I would promote the Pyongyang Symphony Orchestra's visit to Seoul. In fact, the same orchestra was able to come to Seoul on August 15 (Liberation Day) that year.

When it became dark, our party traveled by helicopter back to Kaesong again and returned to Seoul through Panmunjom. I reported to President Kim on my first impressions of Chairman Kim Jong-il:

> He is the type of person who enjoys listening to his counterpart. He is well-informed. He is clever, and quick to judgment. He is pleasant and has a good sense of humor. If persuaded, he agrees immediately and makes a decision. His way of thinking is open and pragmatic. Although his use of language is not logical, he never loses the point of the subject matter being discussed. I got the impression that he is a good counterpart to talk to. In particular, I felt that he respects elder people.

President Kim said he was relieved after hearing my report. He was pleased with the result of my visit.

I provided the president, his chief bodyguard, and his chief protocol secretary with a forty-minute tape covering Chinese party's General Secretary Jiang Zemin's visit to Pyongyang in March 1990. The tape contained the scenes of the arrival reception at the airport and other welcome events. The Presidential Protective Force and the protocol team prepared their plans after watching this video. This later turned out to have been a great help, as the scenes contained in the video were actually repeated during the president's visit.

Prior to the summit in Pyongyang, a Pyongyang Student Arts Performing Troupe and the Pyongyang Acrobatic Group performed in Seoul. A festive atmosphere was developing.

Kim Jong-il was born in 1942. After graduating from Kim Il-sung University and majoring in political economics (1960-64), he began his career as a guidance member of the Organizational Guidance Department of the Workers Party. In 1967, he became a division chief at the Department of Propaganda and Agitation, and continued to be promoted to director of the department. In 1974, he was already designated as heir apparent at the age of 32. In 1980, he became a standing member of the Politburo, a party secretary, and a member of the Party Central Committee of Military Affairs. He was promoted to first vice chairman of the National Defense Commission (May 1990), the Supreme Commander of the Korean People's Armed Forces (December 1991), Marshal of the Republic (April 1992), Chairman of the National Defense Commission (April 1993), and after the death of President Kim Il-sung (July 1994), became the general secretary of the party (October 1997). He was confronted by devastating natural disasters in the wake of President Kim Il-sung's death, and he experienced an "arduous march." In September 1998, he amended the Constitution and finally became the leader of North Korea with the slogans of "military-first politics" and "a strong and prosperous great nation."

CHAPTER 2

HISTORIC INTER-KOREAN SUMMIT

A Half-Century Meeting

On the morning of June 13, 2000, the Republic of Korea's Air Force One (the presidential aircraft) took off from Seoul Airport and flew one hour through clear skies; there was not even a trace of clouds over the West Sea, and we arrived at Pyongyang's Sunan Airport by ten thirty in the morning. A row of honor guards and a military band stood in formation alongside a wide red carpet on the airport apron. In addition, a crowd of women wearing colorful traditional Korean clothes waved flowers in honor of the president's arrival.

When the aircraft stopped before the row of honor guards, Chairman Kim Jong-il, dressed in his brown jacket, appeared on the scene, accompanied by his attendants. At that moment, I was reminded of Chairman Kim's earlier words that he would hold "the finest welcome ceremony."

I could not hold back my tears as I watched the historic scene of President Kim Dae-jung and Chairman Kim Jong-il cheerfully shaking hands. In particular, I was touched and excited to watch President Kim and Chairman Kim standing side by side, inspecting the honor guards and reviewing their parade. Who would have imagined that the commander-in-chief of the Armed Forces of the Republic of Korea would ever be appraising the enemy honor guard while the two sides were still technically at war?

Following the review of the honor guard, each member of the North's welcome committee was introduced to President Kim, one by one. Notable among them were Kim Young-nam, President of the Presidium of the Supreme People's Assembly; Jo Myung-rok, in military uniform, First Vice Chairman of the National Defense Commission; Choi Tae-bok, Speaker of

Chairman Kim Jong-il (*foreground, left*) and President Kim Dae-jung (*foreground, right*) meeting for their historic summit on June 13, 2000. Courtesy Lim Dong-won.

the Supreme People's Assembly; Kim Yong-soon, Party Secretary for South Korean Affairs; and Kang Sok-ju, First Vice Minister of Foreign Affairs. In turn, the official members of our delegation were introduced to Chairman Kim Jong-il.

Upon conclusion of the arrival ceremony, the two heads of state boarded the same car and started their motorcade through the streets of Pyongyang. It was a grand spectacle to see close to 500,000 people crowding the sidewalks, enthusiastically waving flowers, and repeatedly chanting "Hurrah! Hurrah! Hurrah!" After passing the welcoming crowds, our motorcade stopped in front of the Baekhwawon guesthouse, where we would check in for lodging. It was approximately 11:45 a.m. and the temperature in Pyongyang was 28 or 29 degrees Celsius.

The Baekhwawon was built in 1982 as the finest guesthouse to accommodate foreign dignitaries at the head of state level. Chinese Party General Secretary Jiang Zemin, former U.S. president Jimmy Carter, and the members of the South Korean delegation to the North-South High-level Talks had previously stayed at the same guesthouse. It was my sixth stay there.

* * * * * * * * *

As the president walked into the Baekhwawon guesthouse, we were escorted to a large reception room decorated with wall paintings of the four seasons. There, Chairman Kim Jong-il greeted us again in a loud, husky voice, "Welcome to Pyongyang. Our people are very glad to see you." At the request of Secretary Kim Yong-soon, I introduced the official members of our delegation to Chairman Kim one by one.

The two summit leaders talked to each other in the room for about thirty minutes and their conversation was covered by live television. This was the first time that Chairman Kim Jong-il's voice was broadcast around the world. His speech was uninhibited, dignified, and lively. In particular, Chairman Kim proudly spoke of the people who had come out to welcome President Kim.

> The people were informed of the route and the streets President Kim would pass through two days in advance. Many people came out to show their pride as the people of the "country of courtesy in the East." They were moved by the president's bold visit to Pyongyang, and they bravely ventured into the streets.

He then explained the name of Baekhwawon, naturally evoking the memory of the late President Kim Il-sung.

> The literal meaning of Baekhwawon is "a place where one hundred kinds of flowers bloom." It was named by my father. If he were here alive, he would be meeting you, Mr. President, instead of me. . . . In fact, it was his long cherished desire to hold a North-South summit meeting.

Chairman Kim's impressive greeting continued:

> Mr. President, you bravely overcame dread and fear and came to Pyongyang. On the front line, our soldiers are confronting each other with guns. One pull of the trigger, and bullets go off. In spite of this, you were able to witness an honor guard parade in your honor. This is not an ordinary contradiction, is it? Now the world is watching us. Several questions pique their interest, including why President Kim has come and why Chairman Kim accepted his visit. In two nights and three days we should answer those questions.

Indeed, this was true. In a way, President Kim had embarked on a dangerous adventure. It was adventurous visiting the heart of this hostile country to resolve the "contradiction" that our nation had suffered for a half century. Contradiction! The contradiction was that a nation that had existed as one state and shared a history of more than one thousand years had been divided against its will by external forces for half a century. Whereas the countries that had driven our nation into division and to the Cold War had reconciled and ended their Cold War, we were still maintaining the Cold War status of confrontation and distrust. The purpose of President Kim's Pyongyang visit was to resolve this very contradiction.

President Kim Dae-jung (*foreground, center*) discusses with Kim Jong-il (*left*) South Korean press coverage of their first meeting on the previous day. The papers were shipped overnight from Seoul. Courtesy Lim Dong-won.

* * * * * * * * * *

While watching the two leaders meet, I was still uneasy and concerned about the difficult issues that had yet to be resolved. One of them was the question of President Kim's visit to the Geumsusan Memorial Palace. All along our way to the guesthouse, I had been gravely worried that they would take President Kim to the Geumsusan Palace to have him pay tribute to the body of the late President Kim Il-sung.

Thank God that did not happen. However, this issue remained. Resolving this was my first mission to undertake in Pyongyang. Early the next morning, I was sitting down with Lim Dong-ok to discuss this issue at the request of the North. Lim Dong-ok wanted to discuss a suggestion that President Kim visit the Geumsusan Palace before the scheduled summit meeting at three o'clock in the afternoon. I reiterated the reasons against such a visit and asked him to report this to Chairman Kim. But he said it was difficult to do so, considering his moral obligation as a subordinate. I said: "Deputy Director Lim, if this compromises your position, then please convey my direct message to Chairman Kim."

Then I read to Lim Dong-ok a message that I had prepared in Seoul in the event of this situation and had him write it down:

I understand the North's stance and feelings regarding this matter. This is the time to free ourselves from the past and move forward to promote reconciliation and cooperation for the future of the North and South. We are holding this summit to create the right atmosphere for that goal. At the same time, we should also recognize the hard reality that still obstructs our path.

As you know, the budget for inter-Korean cooperation is subject to approval by the National Assembly, which is currently controlled by the opposition party. It is not easy to get cooperation from the press. We also need public support, but more than seventy percent of the people are against the president's visit to the Geumsusan Palace.

It is in your best interest to help President Kim Dae-jung strengthen his political position so that he may improve North-South relations and fulfill the economic cooperation that the North side needs. A visit to the Geumsusan Palace would damage President Kim's leadership. It would diminish the significance of this summit, and it would make it difficult to carry out our agreement.

We should find a solution to this issue that would help the interests of both sides. We could provide an appropriate expression of condolence to Chairman Kim Jong-il, the chief mourner of the bereaved family. I recommend that your insistence upon a visit to the Geumsusan Palace come to an end.

That day, a visit to the Geumsusan Memorial Palace did not take place despite the North's insistence that it be done before the start of the summit meeting. At a banquet that evening in a place called Magnolia Hall, Chairman Kim told me that the president did not have to go to the Geumsusan Palace, even after the summit. With that, the issue was resolved.

Another difficult issue was the task of writing a "North-South Joint Declaration" and getting the North's agreement. In a sense, this issue was the most important aspect of the summit, but the North side, from Chairman Kim Jong-il down, did not seem to care much about it, saying that it could be dealt with after the summit meeting. I was very concerned about whether we would even agree to issue such a statement. If we did, what would be the substance and the form of the declaration look like? In the end, I decided that there was no other way than to resolve this issue at the summit meeting.

Some press reports commented that the meeting of the two leaders itself was very significant. But President Kim's thoughts were different. He wanted to secure a concrete agreement at the summit regarding the realization of meetings between separated families and reconciliation and cooperation. I had attempted to decline the invitation to accompany the president to the summit for fear of disclosing my position as the NIS director, who was required to carry out his activities in secret. Yet, President Kim decided to have me accompany him because he wanted me to closely assist him on the scene; he wanted me to be responsible for reaching an agreement and putting it in the form of a joint declaration, while resolving the issue of a visit to the Geumsusan Palace.

* * * * * * * * *

The first event of the day was President Kim's courtesy visit to the nominal head of state for North Korea, Kim Young-nam, at the Parliament Building. The latter was the president of the Presidium of the Supreme People's Assembly. Afterwards, President Kim, escorted by his host, watched a welcome performance at the Mansudae Arts Theater. In the evening there was a state dinner hosted by President Kim Young-nam at the People's Palace of Culture.

On the morning of the second day, June 14, President Kim had a substantive meeting with President Kim Young-nam prior to the summit meeting with Chairman Kim Jong-il. After the meeting with Kim Young-nam, the president visited the Mangyungdae Boys and Girls Palace, where he watched the children's extracurricular activities and their artistic performances. From there we went to the famous Okryugwan restaurant to have Pyongyang-style cold noodles.

Kim Young-nam was born in Pyongyang in 1928. While attending Kim Il-sung University, he went to Moscow University to study diplomacy. In 1956, he started working at the Party's Department of International Relations. He was promoted to Director of International Relations for the party (1972) and to Party Secretary for International Relations (1975). For fifteen years beginning in 1983, he concurrently served as a Vice Cabinet Premier and as the Minister of Foreign Affairs for the DPRK. In 1998, Kim Yong-nam was elected as president of the Presidium of the Supreme People's Assembly, representing the DPRK as its nominal head of state. His area of expertise was foreign relations.

Eight representatives from the North attended the meeting with President Kim Young-nam. On our side, the official delegates attended. The meeting lasted about an hour. President Kim Young-nam started off with a statement: "During this summit meeting, we should build a foundation for unification that transcends the division." He explained the North's basic position as described in the so-called Three Principles of Unification. By emphasizing the "Principle of Independence," he indirectly criticized the South side's coordination with the United States and Japan. He also stressed the "Principle of National Unity," insisting that the South repeal its National Security Law that "obstructs exchanges and cooperation," and he called for a guarantee of "patriotic unification activities."

Then came President Kim Dae-jung's turn to speak. He spoke with confidence: "We made good agreements in the past, including the July 4 Joint Statement, the North-South Basic Agreement, and the Joint Declaration of Denuclearization. But they were not implemented. We all should carry out these agreements."

The president's emphasis was on implementation. Regarding the trilateral coordination between South Korea, the United States, and Japan that President Kim Young-nam had criticized, President Kim commented:

> Trilateral coordination, as it is called, does not contradict the principle of independence and national unity at all. With our leadership, we want to help North Korea improve its relations with the United States and Japan. This will contribute to peace on the Korean Peninsula. Even if external forces were to interfere, the North and South must be united in our actions. I brought four agendas: Let us avoid war and live in peace at all costs. Let us resolve the issues by ourselves, through reconciliation, exchanges and cooperation, and by building mutual confidence. Let us carry out holding meetings of separated families. Let us open a joint North-South economic committee to connect the rail tracks between Seoul and Shinuiju and move forward to resolve economic and other issues one by one. These are the things I want to discuss.

The ROK Flag and the DPRK Flag

The historic summit meeting between President Kim Dae-jung and Chairman Kim Jong-il took place on one day between three o'clock and seven o'clock at the Baekhwawon conference room. Chairman Kim showed up in his gray "people's suit." From our side, three delegates in addition to the president attended the meeting: myself as the presidential special envoy, Senior Secretary for National Security Hwang Won-tak, and Senior Economic Secretary Lee Ki-ho. From the North, only Secretary for South Korean Affairs Kim Yong-soon joined the meeting, despite an agreement that three staffers from each side would accompany their leaders.

An exchange of greetings was followed by their conversation. Back in Seoul, 1,200 reporters, including 500 journalists from 170 different foreign news organizations, were competing for coverage at the press center set up for them at the Lotte Hotel. The conversation was as follows.

[KIM JONG-IL] I watched Seoul television for quite a long time last night. The people in the South all seemed to be in a welcoming mood. Separated family members and defectors from the North were all shedding tears. They seem hopeful they will be able to go to their hometowns.

[KIM DAE-JUNG] I heard that more than a thousand reporters gave a standing ovation as they watched Chairman Kim shake my hand and welcome me at the airport.

[KIM JONG-IL] When I welcomed you? Isn't that merely a basic courtesy to show in honor of Mr. President's visit? That's hardly exceptional. People in the West often said I was living a hidden life, and now people say I am appearing for the first time. I have visited China, Indonesia, and made many confidential trips to foreign countries. They say that your visit has released me from seclusion. I suppose I deserve such comments since I went to those countries without their knowledge.

[KIM DAE-JUNG] Pyongyang's food tastes very good.

[KIM JONG-IL] When I went to China this past time, they served Korean kimchi. I know kimchi has been widely introduced in China, Japan, and Europe. It is a great accomplishment that South Koreans exported kimchi to the entire world. North Korean kimchi has a lot of juice, whereas South Korean kimchi is salty and spicy. Maybe that's why South Koreans are spicy.

After the press team retreated, Chairman Kim brought up an offensive topic.

If President Kim's visit had been handled solely by the National Intelligence Service, we would not have agreed to this summit. Our impression of the Central Intelligence Agency and the National Security Planning Agency, which preceded the NIS, was very negative. Fortunately, the Asia Pacific Peace Commission and Hyundai had been working well together on civilian economic projects. That gave us the opportunity to consider the holding of a summit. What's more, when I had heard Minister Park Ji-won was actively involved, I thought Mr. President was using a different channel. Later, we learned that the NIS was involved and Director Lim Dong-won was maneuvering things from behind the scenes. Nevertheless, I decided to go ahead with the summit, since the regimes have changed and there are different people now.

President Kim tactfully responded, "The government has changed, and the NIS has changed a lot as well."

Chairman Kim Jong-il now opened an offensive:

There is one thing that made me feel bad while watching Seoul television last night. They were talking about prosecuting students who violated the National Security Law by raising the DPRK flag on a college campus. Isn't this an attempt to spoil the summit? How can they do this? I really felt bad. Yesterday at the airport, I saw the South side flying their ROK national flag on the plane, and all the members of your delegation were wearing ROK national flag pins. But I was not even concerned. Later I had much to think about. I thought that since you had already had a welcome dinner with President Kim Young-nam, I could say goodbye and you could return. But, my assistants said I should not do so. So I came to this meeting.

It was an intentional offensive on his part. At this moment, I was reminded of incidents that had often happened during our earlier negotiations with the North Koreans. Before moving to serious discussions, the North would bring up an unexpected issue to attack and embarrass their counterpart in order to capture the lead in the talks and secure favorable grounds for negotiation. This has been the typical North Korean style of negotiation. Fortunately, however, President Kim responded to this first challenge in a calm and controlled fashion.

[KIM DAE-JUNG:] This is the first time I am hearing about it. When I go back, I will find out more. In the South, there are different groups of people with different thoughts. Chairman Kim should not be too concerned about it.

[KIM JONG-IL] Well, I recognize that the political climate is different from ours. Maybe at the airport yesterday, we should have let the South Korean national flag fly on the ground and let them sing the South Korean national anthem. If we had done so, I would be able to say more about this issue . . . to put this to rest, the South should not punish the students involved in the incident—at least not during the period of this summit. I would ask Mr. President to take special care of this matter. Why in the world don't you abolish the National Security Law? On our side, we are also trying to amend the old party covenant and charters through a party convention, which the South often takes issue with. It is not a big deal [to do so]. . . . We should make new replacements, one by one, as we move forward.

I later learned after my return to Seoul that students at more than seven universities had raised ROK national flags and DPRK flags with "Korean Peninsula flags" in the middle of their campuses, including Seoul National University and Korea University. It was intended to be a gesture of support for the North-South summit. The prosecution authority was known to have decided to search for, arrest, and prosecute the students.

Kim Dae-jung's Four Agendas

"I am sorry to bring up such an issue first. Please, Mr. President, you speak first."

Until this invitation, President Kim had calmly maintained an attentive listening manner for almost half an hour. After thanking him again for the invitation to visit Pyongyang and for the warm hospitality he received, President Kim started by saying, "You've completed your filial duty of a three-year mourning period. I am touched by your compliance with the tradition of the 'country of courtesy in the East.'"

By expressing his respect for Chairman Kim's filial piety, President Kim succeeded in fulfilling a mourner's role without paying tribute to the deceased President Kim Il-sung. Then he followed by suggesting an open discussion on possible agreements on a range of issues. The president, in line with his prepared notes, prudently began to outline the details of our position on the four issues—unification, reduction of tension and peace, promotion of exchange and cooperation, and separated families. His initial discussion took exactly thirty minutes.

President Kim first underlined his views on the issue of reconciliation and unification.

> The international Cold War is over. As the world is transitioning from an industrial community to an informational community, an era of unlimited competition is open to us. We, too, must end the Cold War and reconcile for the survival and prosperity of our nation. We cannot defer this matter any further. We are a nation that has a strong foundation in education, information technology, and cultural creation. Our nation is primed to achieve the highest level of development and prosperity. It is important that we now reconcile and cooperate to move forward towards mutual development and prosperity. I suggest that Chairman Kim and I become role models in this effort.

Then the president explained in detail our side's position on the issue of unification, to refresh the chairman's mind. "We should gradually promote unification. The North and the South should cooperate to manage the process of unification. To this end, I propose to institutionalize a 'Confederation of States.' This concept was also reflected in the North-South Basic Agreement."

The second topic President Kim addressed was the issue of tension reduction and peace. The president's points were, in summary:

> The North and the South have been mutually concerned about their security: the North about unification by absorption or invasion from the South, and the South about communization or invasion from the

North. In reality, these are impossible perspectives. War would only drive the nation into common destruction. Our position is firm. I promise that under no conditions will the South seek invasion of the North or unification by absorption. I can assure you that the North need not be concerned about that. As stipulated in the North-South Basic Agreement, let us create a joint military committee to discuss the issue of preventing accidental armed clashes and to address the issue of arms reduction.

However, in order to resolve North-South issues, we also need the cooperation of neighboring countries. When I went to the United States in June 1998, I proposed the lifting of economic sanctions on the North. In my talks with Japanese prime minister Mori, I urged him to normalize Japan's relations with the North and we seriously discussed how to approach this issue. We will actively support the North so that you can soon develop good relationships with the United States, Japan, and European countries.

Therefore, I ask that the North comply with the Agreed Framework signed in Geneva to resolve the nuclear issue and make progress in missile talks with the United States. We should move forward in this way . . . towards the settlement of peace on the Korean Peninsula. And let us work together to create and manage a six-nation Northeast Asia security cooperation organization – with the participation of the United States, Japan, China, and Russia for peace and security on the Korean Peninsula and in Northeast Asia.

The third topic on the agenda was the issue of inter-Korean exchange and cooperation, in which the North recently showed increasing interest. President Kim continued:

Economic cooperation is important to resolving North-South issues in an appropriate fashion. Earlier, our government held the principle of separation of politics and economy. However, considering the special nature of North-South relations, we are willing to work with the authorities of the North side to vitalize cooperation in the fields of railways, communications, harbor facilities, electric power, and agriculture. Let us connect the railways that have been cut off, and build an industrial park on the west coast. And let us further develop tourism to extend it from Mount Kumgang to Mountain Baekdu and Pyongyang City. We will eagerly support the North in joining international financial institutions for your financial benefit. Therefore, we should expeditiously negotiate for successful agreements on the requirements of economic cooperation, including an investment guarantee.

President Kim also proposed that the North should participate in the 2002 World Cup:

Let us revive the Seoul-Pyongyang Soccer Match on a regular basis and hold it alternatively between Seoul and Pyongyang like in the old days. We should also enter the Sydney Olympics opening ceremony as a unified team. In addition to sports, we should bolster exchange and cooperation in all other areas, including social, cultural, academic, health, and environmental areas.

President Kim's fourth topic concerned the issue of separated families. He presented a concrete proposal that included the task of finding out the status of life or death among separated families, their addresses, and exchanges of letters and reunion by free will. He insisted that an exchange of visits by separated families begin in conjunction with Liberation Day that year. Then he continued:

> It has already been twenty-eight years since the announcement of the July 4 Joint Statement, which underlined the principles of independence, peace, and national unity. It has been eight years since the adoption of the North-South Basic Agreement, which presented a perfect method for developing North-South relations. What is left for us now—for Chairman Kim and me—is to implement them according to the principles and already agreed upon method. Let us give hope and confidence to our nation through our cooperation and actual implementation. Let us hold inter-Korean ministerial meetings, joint economic committee meetings, and joint military committee meetings. And let us cooperate to realize meetings of separated families, and also implement exchange and cooperation in a variety of other areas.
>
> Now I officially invite Chairman Kim to visit Seoul. Public opinion surveys indicate eighty-one percent of the people believe that you should come to Seoul. I would like to ask you to visit Seoul sooner or later. I have two years and eight months left of my presidency. For thirty or forty years, I suffered a great deal: I was imprisoned numerous times, and I escaped death five times—but I always did my best for national reconciliation and unification. I hope that Chairman Kim and I work together to carry out my will during the two years and eight months remaining in my tenure. And, I want to firmly make sure that the next administration cannot change this path. That is my wish.

President Kim revealed his meticulous care by giving Chairman Kim a written copy of the talking points to which he had just referred.

* * * * * * * * *

Chairman Kim Jong-il, who had listened quietly for thirty minutes, started to speak again:

It was very helpful when I received a personal letter from you last time, and I was briefed thoroughly by Special Envoy Lim Dong-won. By listening to your explanation today, Mr. President, I can understand more fully now what your design is. Once again, I would like to thank you for your excellent explanation.

In contrast to President Kim's logical and orderly style of presenting, Chairman Kim was free-flowing and led the conversation in a disorderly fashion, while making all the points he wished to make. He said that he "agreed with the president that none of the good North-South agreements of the past had been implemented." Then he talked about the aborted summit meeting of July 1994, and he switched subjects to the events that led to the death of President Kim Il-sung.

> President Kim Il-sung was planning to propose to President Kim Young-sam practical projects for North-South economic cooperation. First, he was going to promote the modernization of the Seoul-Shinuiju railroad. The night before he passed away, President Kim Il-sung summoned economic advisors to the Myohyang-san villa to listen to their views on how to deal with the issues of economic cooperation with the South, while reviewing relevant documents at the same time. Then he called me when I was in Pyongyang to tell me, "Now I have finished my preparations." One hour afterwards, he unexpectedly died. He had suffered some heart ailments four or five years before his passing. Since then, he had been using a pacemaker provided by the Soviet Union's Kremlin Hospital.
>
> Last year we sent doctors to the United States and they brought a U.S.-made pacemaker of this size [he indicated the size with a pen]. That one functioned very well. But it was half the size of the Soviet product at that time, when the Soviets' medical science was primitive compared to the United States. They say the installation of a pacemaker brings the risk of a sudden death because it tends to clog the blood. I hear that aspirin is used to help prevent it in the West. China also learned this from the United States after its opening, and now the Chinese too use aspirin. . . .
>
> At that time, the Soviet medical team did not recommend the use of aspirin. It was a mistake that we just depended on our conventional wisdom that it was best to eat fish. I recognize that the South has many doctors who were trained in the United States, and therefore, the South is more advanced than us in the health and medical field. As the president mentioned, I fully agree that we should look out to a broader world.

To my surprise, Chairman Kim Jong-il acknowledged the negative consequences of a closed society.

Confederation versus Federation

Regarding the issue of an agreed-upon declaration, Chairman Kim Jong-il offered that a summit agreement should only be of "a declaratory nature, and the rest of the work should be left to ministerial-level meetings." His intention was for President Kim and him to mainly agree upon a broad, declaratory statement of hope and encouragement, and that the details be worked out at the ministerial level in compliance with the will of their superiors. He explained:

> By this, I mean that the president and I just mention general issues such as the principle of self-resolution or the method of unification. Other specific issues, including North-South exchange and cooperation, and separated families, should be delegated to ministers. The important thing is to supervise and control the implementation of agreements.

President Kim's vision was different. He replied,

> The principles of unification and the method for developing North-South relations were already agreed upon in the July 4 Joint Statement and the North-South Basic Agreement. Therefore, based on these principles and methods, we should agree on the specific details of the pending issues for implementation. Only then will we be able to give hope to the nation and build mutual confidence through our summit—a meeting that was not easy to hold. We should be in alignment on meetings of separated families, how to cooperate on economic and social issues, cultural exchange, as well as Chairman Kim's visit to Seoul, and document all of these agreements.

> [KIM JONG-IL] The South does not trust us, and they call us the "main enemy" or "puppets." Under these circumstances, even if I were to concede on a few big issues to save President Kim face, would the opposition party be placated? The South still calls us "puppets," even as they speak about coexistence. We no longer call the South a "puppet clique." Perceptions are a problem. We have to educate people to have the right understanding. We should teach them to recognize that the North and the South are brothers. The South treated us as a Soviet satellite, calling us "North Korean puppets." After the Soviet Union collapsed, didn't they say the collapse of North Korea would soon follow? In fact, unlike South Korea, we pushed for the withdrawal of Soviet troops very early after liberation. There are no foreign troops in the North. We have maintained our independence to this day.

> [KIM DAE-JUNG] The opposition party is not a real problem. The important thing is that we show the nation and the world that we have really produced good results this time, and convince them that we are a nation that can resolve North-South issues by ourselves and continue

doing so in the future. Moreover, we don't use the word "puppets" in the South either.

At this point, Secretary Kim Yong-soon, who was unhappily looking at his document, intervened: "On May 24, 1999, did Defense Minister Cho Seong-tae not say that North Korea is the 'main enemy' and call us 'puppets'? Even these days, is he not openly saying so?"

Chairman Kim excitedly resumed speaking.

> Neighboring countries will still continue to perpetuate the division of our nation to "divide and rule Korea." Nevertheless, Mr. President travels to different countries seeking balance and cooperation between them. This should come to a stop. Instead, we should try to independently find solutions amongst ourselves, people of the same nation.

It was like déjà vu of the debate the president had had with President Kim Young-nam of the Presidium. President Kim began persuading Chairman Kim with unswerving determination.

> We maintain an alliance with the United States and we have good relations with Japan. We have good relations with China and Russia, two countries I know North Korea also closely cooperates with. It would be helpful for the peace and unification of the Korean Peninsula when the North and the South both have good relations with these four countries. Therefore, the North should improve relations with the United States and Japan soon.
>
> As long as the North maintains a hostile relationship with the United States, it is difficult to expect peace on the Korean Peninsula. In order to expedite the normalization of relations with the United States, Chairman Kim should strictly comply with the Agreed Framework to resolve the nuclear issue and produce good results in the missile talks. I will actively support the North in your efforts to develop good relations with the United States, Japan, and European countries. The cooperation of these countries is a prerequisite to achieving peace on the Korean Peninsula. I, too, believe that independence is important in dealing with our national issues. But we should not pursue independence for exclusion. We must seek open independence.
>
> [KIM JONG-IL] What the president is saying is not wrong. But, as far as unification is concerned, the North and the South, we of the same nation, should combine our own strengths to achieve it. What I mean is that it should be resolved between the direct parties concerned.

Through this discussion, the two summit leaders came to share the same view that with the cooperation of neighboring countries, the North and South should lead the efforts for peace on the Korean Peninsula. The summit leaders' discussion then continued to the topic of unification.

[KIM JONG-IL] This time we should first declare our commitment to national independence. Second, we should move towards unification through the creation of a federation [*yonbang*]. At this stage, let us agree upon a low-level federation. And for a third item, would it be all right if we agreed to start dialogue between the authorities of the North and South immediately in order to resolve the political, economic and social issues?

[KIM DAE-JUNG] I cannot accept your proposed unification formula of a dual-system federation. The confederation of states [*yonhap*] that I uphold is a formula that would allow a cooperative form of two systems and two governments. In any case, let us agree to discuss the unification issue further in the future. At this time, it would be the best if we agreed upon what the North and the South should do before we get to that stage, and then what we should do in the present.

[KIM JONG-IL] The confederation system that the president describes is the same as the low-level federation that I am proposing.

Chairman Kim explained that the concept of the "low-level federation" that he was proposing and the concept of a "confederation of states" were the same. Yet, he insisted on the use of the word *yonbang*. At this point, I interjected and asked if I could speak:

The concepts of "federation" and "confederation" are different. Under your proposed "federation," a federal government would serve as the central government that exercises the rights over military and diplomatic affairs, while the local governments are only responsible for internal affairs. In contrast, the form of confederation that we envision refers to a cooperative system of two sovereign states that maintain their respective rights over military and diplomatic affairs. It would be similar in function to the Confederation of Independent States (CIS) that was created after the disintegration of the Soviet Union.

The type of "confederation" upon which we insist is not a form of unification, but an institutional device for the two governments to mutually cooperate towards peace and unification at a stage preceding unification. I would like you to understand the conceptual difference with your "federation" system, which indicates a governmental form of a unified country. How can two different systems suddenly be unified in a federation? A federation would also require a unified military and diplomacy. Would this be be possible in reality? Yemen is a good example. North Yemen and South Yemen quickly unified in the form of a federation, but they failed to unify their militaries. They eventually completed their unification through war.

We must not repeat the Yemen experience. We should first begin with a "Confederation of the North and the South" to cooperate on arms reduction and the elimination of security threats before we unify our militaries. After this point, we will be able to achieve unification. The North and South should unite their strengths to move gradually forward, step by step towards unification. In this context, President Kim believes that it is more important to discuss and agree on what we should immediately do to pave the way towards that end, rather than debate future issues such as the form of unification.

When I finished, Chairman Kim Jong-il wished to add his thoughts:

I understand the president has said that unification would take ten to twenty years. But I think unification would take forty to fifty years. And, I didn't mean that unification should be achieved immediately through *yonbang* [federation]. That was what we used to say during the Cold War era. The concept of the "low-level federation" to which I referred is that the governments of the North and the South reserve their respective rights over military and diplomatic affairs, similiar to what the South prefers to call *yonhap* [confederation], while we gradually move towards unification.

A salient characteristic of North Korea's unification formula—the "Federal Republic of Koryo"—was to call a meeting of national leaders. The intent was to immediately establish a unified federal government to promote inter-Korean exchange and cooperation. Now Chairman Kim was stating that such an approach was "an unrealistic product of the Cold War." In fact, after it failed in 1990 to enter the United Nations with the South as a single country based on the concept of "federation," North Korea signed the North-South Basic Agreement, which prefaced a gradual approach to unification. Since that time, the North has called for a "loose federation."

President Kim prudently resumed his discussion:

A formula for unification, given its nature, is not something we can agree on at this meeting. But we can agree to continue our discussion in the future of the "confederation" that the South maintains, and the "low-level federation" that the North maintains.

Chairman Kim quickly responded:

Well, then let us agree to do the following: since the South side's "confederation" and the North side's "low-level federation" are the same thing, let us agree to state, "the North and the South will cooperate in the direction of a 'low-level federation.'"

Although Chairman Kim Jong-il recognized the rationality, practicality, and feasibility behind the confederation, he was not ready to concede on using the language of "low-level federation."

President Kim tried to bring the discussion to a conclusion:

The North has proposed a "low-level federation" and the South has proposed a "confederation." As you have stated, there are many common elements between the two concepts. Therefore, I suggest that we agree to continue this discussion in the future.

Chairman Kim agreed. "Okay. Well then, let us close the discussion of the subject here."

I noticed that Chairman Kim Jong-il's adamant persistence did not frustrate President Kim. The significance of the two leaders' discussion here was reinforced by the fact that they had agreed upon the paradoxical nature of unification as both a goal and a process. They also agreed unification should take a "gradual and step by step approach." The two summit leaders thus came to hold the shared view that both sides should cooperate closely in the process of unification to peacefully manage the state of division and promote the vitalization of exchange and cooperation.

The two leaders also shared the view that war would only lead to common destruction. They firmly pledged not to invade the other. They agreed to free both sides from their mutual fears: to free the North from of "unification by absorption" and "invasion from the South"; and to free the South from fears of "unification by Communization" and "invasion of the North." To this end, they agreed on the importance of building mutual trust. To take concrete measures of implementing the agreement of non-aggression based on the North-South Basic Agreement, they also agreed to hold inter-Korean defense ministerial meetings. These meetings would work on confidence-building measures to avoid accidental armed collisions. In fact, three months later that year, the first defense ministerial meeting was held on Jeju Island.

Hotline

The next topic for the summit discussion was the issue of North-South economic cooperation. President Kim went first.

According to Hyundai's assessment it would be advantageous to build an industrial complex in an area near Haeju, closer to the South, instead of Shinuiju, which is adjacent to China. I would like Chairman Kim to make a prompt decision on this matter. In addition, the linking of the Seoul-Shinuiju railway and its expansion to double tracks would be beneficial to both sides. It would produce a great deal of profit for the North and reduce logistical costs for the South. It would of course be symbolic to reconnect the national artery that has been disconnected for so long. If we go a step further and connect it to Europe, the Korean Peninsula can become a logistics hub.

After listening to President Kim, Chairman Kim expressed his full support for North-South economic cooperation. He supported the construction of an industrial park and the project of reconnecting the railroad, but in compliance with the North's agreement with Hyundai. As I mentioned in the previous chapter, Hyundai had signed an agreement to promote "seven economic cooperation projects" in early May that year.

At this point, I intervened again to explain the position of our government.

> Our government is willing to encourage Hyundai to pursue these projects. However, a private business company cannot carry out such large-scale infrastructure projects alone. These projects will be impossible without the government's involvement and support. Therefore, we must include an agreement on economic cooperation in a joint declaration at this time.

More than two hours had already passed since we began the meeting. Chairman Kim proposed a break. But President Kim wanted successful closure on the points he had discussed with Chairman Kim thus far:

> Before we take a break, I think we should document everything we have agreed upon to this point. What do you think of asking Director Lim Dong-won and Secretary Kim Yong-soon to work together on a draft joint statement of agreement? I also request that the issue of separated families also be incorporated into the draft declaration. We must reach agreement on this issue.

Chairman Kim Jong-il gladly agreed with President Kim's conditional acceptance:

> As I told Special Envoy Lim Dong-won last time, I can't think of any reason for not holding something for separated families. We can carry out an exchange of meetings for separated families on Liberation Day this year as a trial. One hundred family members from one side can meet their relatives from the other side in Seoul, and another set can meet in Pyongyang. This way we can learn from these experiences and gradually expand such meetings. By the way, I have one issue I have to raise at this point. Why do the South's National Intelligence Service and Ministry of Unification persist in accepting defectors from the North, and then defend those criminals who have run away from here, using them for propaganda and to slander the North? Uh. . . .

North Korea was very unhappy with the issue regarding defectors from the North, and they were extremely sensitive about it. In consideration of President Kim's position, I spoke on his behalf:

No governmental institution of ours ever encourages defectors from the North. However, is it not right to accept those who want to come to Seoul since they are members of the same nation? As the Director of the NIS, I can confidently say there has been no instance in which defectors were used for propaganda purposes. As agreed upon in the North-South Basic Agreement, we should not slander or defame each other. In my view, it would be a significant accomplishment if the two summit leaders would take this opportunity to agree not to slander or defame each other.

Chairman Kim gave his unreserved concurrence on my proposal, saying, "That's great. Let us agree on this occasion not to slander or defame one another. Also, let us suspend military broadcasts directed at each other."

But it occurred to me that due to our different systems, the North and South might have different interpretations of "slander and defame." I added a premise:

On our side, we can suspend all government and military broadcasts toward the North. However, what is reported in the civilian press should not be regarded as slander or defamation. The civilian press in the South is outside of the government's control. Therefore, it should be excluded from discussion at this meeting.

Secretary Kim Yong-soon intervened again, adding, "Even so, they should not use terms such as 'the main enemy.'"

Chairman Kim then made an interesting comment.

It's natural for the military to use terms such as the "main enemy" or the "enemies." The troops facing them in the frontline are their enemies. They are not friendly troops, are they? It is natural for our training to cultivate hostility. Comrade Kim's point is that it is contradictory to talk about reconciliation and cooperation if the South is publicly using the term the "main enemy" in government publications. Is it not problematic for reporters to emphasize the term to instill a sense of hostility in the South? If we want reconciliation and cooperation, the authorities should first stop using the term.

After this battle of nerves, President Kim presented a neat summary of the points of agreement.

First, we resolve national issues independently.

Second, in light of the sufficient overlap between the "low-level federation" proposed by the North and the "confederation" proposed by the South, the authorities of both sides agree to continue discussion.

Third, we resolve the issue of separated families.

Fourth, we build mutual confidence by vitalizing exchange and cooperation in all arenas, including economic, social, and cultural areas.

Fifth, we hold meetings between the authorities of both sides to agree on concrete solutions and measures of implementation.

President Kim also proposed to include in a joint statement of agreement "Chairman Kim Jong-il's visit to Seoul" and the holding of a "second summit meeting." To push for this agreement, the president used traditional culture to his advantage:

The whole world knows Chairman Kim Jong-il as the leader of the "country of courtesy in the East" who greatly respects his elders. . . . One difference between Chairman Kim and myself is age. I am a little older than him. . . . Since the older party first came to Pyongyang, would it not be right for Chairman Kim to come to Seoul next time? You must come to Seoul. When you come to Seoul, we, too, will greatly welcome you and host you with our best.

President Kim's invitation was extended in a persuasive and earnest manner. Consequently, Chairman Kim's attitude was appreciative but his answer was still negative. I felt the need to intervene again to save face for both leaders.

Chairman Kim, how would you like to agree to the following statement? "President Kim Dae-jung cordially invited Chairman Kim Jong-il to visit Seoul, and Chairman Kim Jong-il has agreed to visit Seoul at a convenient time in the future." Of course, it would be better if we can fix the date of the visit now. But, since we cannot agree on the date at this time, can we discuss it later?

Chairman Kim repeated "a convenient time?...a convenient time?" as if he was talking to himself. "I would do that at a convenient time. . . ." Finally, he showed a positive response. Later in the Joint Declaration, "a convenient time" was changed to "an appropriate time."

Instead of immediately agreeing upon his visit to Seoul, Chairman Kim said: "If any problems arise during the implementation process, Mr. President, please send Director Lim Dong-won to Pyongyang as often as necessary." President Kim replied,

I also hope that Chairman Kim will not be concerned about speculative press reports or disorderly or rough comments from political circles every so often. In addition to these issues, if something important develops, let us summit leaders directly communicate with one another. What do you think of the idea of installing an emergency hotline between us?

[KIM JONG-IL] That's a good idea. Let's do it.

As result, a hotline was set up. It served as an important communication line for the resolution of North-South issues until the end of President Kim's administration. Personally, I thought the opening of this hotline was one of the best results of the summit meeting.

Then we took a break. It was about half past five in the evening. On display outside the conference room were morning newspapers for the leaders to look at. The newspapers, shipped from Seoul, carried reports on the summit. The front pages were fully covered with pictures of the two leaders greeting one another at the Pyongyang Airport welcome ceremony. After a thirty-minute break, we went back into the room.

Jeolla Province Chairman and Gyeongsang Province President

The second session of talks began with Chairman Kim asking President Kim a few questions:

> What is the opposition party's position on the method of unification? Why does the opposition party keep criticizing and causing friction on every aspect related to improving North-South relations? And why did they not send a single member of their party to Pyongyang this time?

This time, President Kim answered the questions himself.

> Our unification formula was adopted by agreement between the governing and opposition parties in 1989 when the present opposition party was in power. Therefore, the opposition party does not fundamentally oppose it. But the Grand National Party claims that we should not, by seeking improved North-South relations, undermine the sovereignty and security of the Republic of Korea. Of course, that is an unfounded fear. And, regarding the provision of assistance to the North, they demand a policy of "strict reciprocity." But they have no support from the people on that. As a matter of fact, there were quite a few opposition members who wanted to come this time as individual members. For example, National Assembly member Park Geun-hye, daughter of former President Park Chung-hee, had announced that she would join our delegation, but to our dismay, the Grand National Party disallowed her travel.

Chairman Kim asked a future-oriented question:

> Even if we produce solid agreements and make progress in the improvement of our relations, if the Grand National Party were to regain the reins of government, wouldn't we revert to the beginning? Mr. President, what do you think is going to happen to the South's policy on the North if the Grand National Party comes into power next time?

> [KIM DAE-JUNG] The Grand National Party is currently the opposition party, so its behavior is politically motivated. But, if they assume power, I don't think their policy line would be much different. A con-

federation is something they also advocated, and they would not object to peaceful coexistence. Of course, there might be some adjustments in the implementation of specific details.

Chairman Kim revealed an interesting piece of information:

I am going to officially share with you classified background information regarding our views on the presence of U.S. troops. . . . In early 1992, we sent Secretary Kim Yong-soon to the United States as a special envoy. Through him, we told the United States that we would not fight with South Korea. Then we asked that the U.S. troops remain in South Korea to help prevent fighting between the North and the South. We explained the numerous historical instances of foreign invasions because of the geopolitical interests of our big neighboring powers. We told them that in view of the power dynamics of Northeast Asia, the U.S. military presence would contribute to the maintenance of peace on the Korean Peninsula. I know President Kim has said that the U.S. troops should stay beyond unification. I, too, share your view. The continued presence of U.S. troops in South Korea may be a big burden to your government. But isn't this something you have to overcome?

Chairman Kim's point was that North Korea had conveyed a message to the United States that Pyongyang wanted to improve DPRK-U.S. relations. The North explained the North-South Basic Agreement of December 1991 to Washington, which included a non-aggression pact. During that time, North Korea had also expressed its desire that "the status and role of the U.S. troops in Korea be changed from a hostile military to a peacekeeping force."

President Kim asked why North Korea had, then, continued demanding troop withdrawal through the media. Chairman Kim answered, "Please, understand that our call for troop withdrawal was necessary to placate the people at home."

Chairman Kim did not hide his ardent desire for an improved relationship with the United States. It appeared clear that he would be ready to give up North Korea's nuclear and missile programs upon resolution of the issue of normalization. And this was exactly what President Kim was hoping for. Their conversation went on.

[KIM DAE-JUNG] I was really surprised when I first heard about your views regarding the U.S. troops in Korea from Special Envoy Lim Dong-won after his meeting with you. . . . I did not know you had such a superb perspective of this national issue. Yes, you're right. It would create much hardship for our nation if the neighboring powers strive for hegemony. However, with U.S. troops in Korea to help maintain a balance of power, the stability of our nation would be promoted.

[KIM JONG-IL] Mr. President, although of different origin, you and I share the same family name. Perhaps that's the reason why we share the same thoughts.

At this joke, the attendants at the meeting all burst into laughter, momentarily releasing themselves from the tension. Then the president asked about where Chairman Kim's family originated from. The Chairman said it was Jeonju, which meant Chairman Kim's family belonged to "the Kims of Jeonju." The president said,

Jeonju? Then you are a true man of Jeolla Province! I belong to the Kims of Gimhae. That means originally, my family came from Gyeongsang Province.

Everyone burst into laughter once again.

Even in the midst of this pleasant atmosphere, Chairman Kim reemphasized, "We should not depend on foreign forces for the Korean issue, but must resolve it by ourselves." In response, the president expressed his "fundamental agreement on such a view." President Kim wanted to stress the need for a commitment to make a joint decision:

This summit meeting is not being held at some other country's wishes but by our own will. Isn't that a surprise to the world? As you said, we should unite our strengths to take the initiative on the issue of the Korean Peninsula. Yet, it is my view that we need support and cooperation from neighboring countries. I repeat, we should not confine ourselves to "exclusive independence" but embrace "open independence." Whatever decision we make this time will determine the fate of our nation. If we make a mistake, it could bring disasters like war. If we do well, we could pave the path to peace and unification. Nobody lives forever. Nobody stays in the same position forever. Let us work together for the nation while we are responsible for it.

As we were approaching the end of the summit meeting, the two sides faced one another in argument over two other issues: deciding on the time of adopting a joint declaration and determining who should sign it. Chairman Kim went first to propose his suggestion, saying, "I think we have sufficiently discussed and coordinated the issues. I would like to suggest that each side bring its draft declaration tomorrow morning and agree on a final declaration to announce at noon." But President Kim insisted that "a final statement should be adopted this evening so that it would be published in the morning papers, although the official date of announcement could be fixed for tomorrow, June 15."

[KIM DAE-JUNG] If we announce it tomorrow at noon, it would be published in the newspapers the day after tomorrow. That would be too late. We must agree on a final version tonight so that people can read it tomorrow.

[KIM JONG-IL] Well, then let's agree that the document should be signed by Secretary Kim Yong-soon of the Central Committee of the Korean Workers' Party and Director Lim Dong-won of the National Intelligence Service of the Republic of Korea by "order of the superiors."

[KIM DAE-JUNG] Chairman Kim and I must sign it. There is no other way. Otherwise, wouldn't it be like a good picture of a dragon missing its eyes?

[KIM JONG-IL] Well, I don't mean to lower the level of agreement. . . . What I mean is, it's better for me not to sign it, since in the North, we have President Kim Young-nam of the Presidium of the Supreme People's Assembly who represents the country. In this situation, it would be all right if President Kim Young-nam signed the document and I guaranteed the substance of the agreement.

President Kim was adamantly against this suggestion. We had agreed on the time to announce the declaration, but the issue of the signature was getting more difficult. Secretary Kim Yong-soon stepped in, "How about if you two leaders put only your names without titles?" The president rejected that also, saying "if we do not sign the declaration, it may cause various misunderstandings." The leaders' discussion continued:

[KIM JONG-IL] We have a precedent. The July 4th Joint Statement was signed by Lee Hu-rak and Kim Young-ju also "by the order of the superiors." Let's settle this issue by the signatures of Lim Dong-won for President Kim Dae-jung, and Kim Yong-soon for Chairman Kim Jong-il of the National Defense Commission.

[KIM DAE-JUNG] Isn't it the case that Mr. Lee Hu-rak had come at that time, but this time, I, the president, have come to have a summit meeting? Don't you think you should give me a better solution?

The president was quite disappointed. I intervened again.

Mr. Chairman, both sides recognize that the North-South relationship is a special interim relationship stemming from the process of unification. Therefore, it does not require the signature of the Chairman of the Presidium of the Supreme People's Assembly. The joint declaration this time must have the signatures of the two leaders who have met and agreed on the declaration. For your title, either the Chairman of the National Defense Commission or the General Secretary of the Korean Workers' Party will be fine. But, your name "Kim Jong-il" must be included in the declaration.

Don't you think we should start with a clause in the opening of the declaration, stating something to the effect of: "President Kim Dae-jung of the Republic of Korea and Chairman Kim Jong-il of the National Defense Commission of the Democratic People's Republic of Korea met when in Pyongyang, had a summit meeting, and agreed to the following . . . "? And at the bottom of the declaration, we should rightly put "President Kim Dae-jung of the Republic of Korea" and "Chairman Kim Jong-il, of the National Defense Commission, the Democratic People's Republic of Korea" for your signatures? This declaration will be a monumental document providing a turning point in the history of our nation. Wouldn't it be right for the two leaders who made this agreement possible to sign it themselves? What a historic and proud achievement this is! Wouldn't your signatures guarantee the implementation of the agreement?

[KIM JONG-IL] I see President Kim is very persistent—maybe because he is a native of Jeolla Province.

Chairman Kim cracked a joke again during this tense moment. The president did not yield: "Isn't it true that Chairman Kim is also from the Kims of Jeonju, in Jeolla Province?" This provoked another burst of laughter in the room. Chairman Kim was a good match for President Kim's assertiveness.

[KIM JONG-IL] You seem to want the title of the "general of triumphal return."

[KIM DAE-JUNG] What's wrong with you helping me to become the "general of triumphal return"? You should help me since I came all the way here.

With a smile after this exchange, Chairman Kim expressed his willingness to sign the statement by asking me, "When should we sign it?" I replied, "As soon as this meeting is over, we will present our draft statement and discuss it with Secretary Kim Yong-soon. After we finish coordinating, we will immediately prepare it for signatures." Secretary Kim Yong-soon then supported me by saying, "Now that both of you have agreed, we will do it as soon as possible."

Division Chief Kim Chun-sik, the note-taker for our side, prepared our copy. It was satisfactory to me, and very similar to my own draft. Typing and preparing the document took less than twenty minutes. Handing the draft version of our side to Secretary Kim, I proposed that the document be titled "North-South Joint Declaration." Secretary Kim, who was working on their version with Lim Dong-ok, did not object.

Celebration at Last

A dinner was hosted by President Kim at Magnolia Hall that evening. At Chairman Kim Jong-il's suggestion, the two leaders would arrive to dinner in the same car. The two met again at the lobby of Baekhwawon at 7:40 p.m. When Chairman Kim saw me, he said in a loud voice, "It was 99 percent well done. I am referring to the joint declaration." He was referring to our draft version. I was relieved by the thought that it would be possible to adopt the joint declaration that night.

Since the summit meeting had gone on beyond schedule, President Kim's return dinner did not begin until one hour later at eight o'clock in Magnolia Hall. More than 150 ranking people from the North, including Chairman Kim Jong-il, attended the dinner event. Approximately fifty people from the South, including the official and unofficial members of the presidential delegation, attended as well. It was a celebratory atmosphere dedicated to the successful historic summit. The ambiance in the room was filled with visceral and emotional excitement. It felt like a drama continuing to unfold.

President Kim made his dinner remarks first:

> Chairman Kim Jong-il and I have successfully concluded the summit. For the first time, the Korean people can see a bright future—a dawn of hope for reconciliation, cooperation and unification is breaking.
>
> It is now time for the Korean people to stop shedding the tears that have flowed for the past hundred years. It is time for us to heal the wounds we have inflicted upon one another. We must proceed on the path toward reconciliation, cooperation, peace, and unification.

At this short opening, the audience felt an air of solemnity in the room. President Kim continued:

> All of us must work to dismantle the wall of mutual distrust that was built over the half-century of the division of our country, chase away the fear of war from our land, and join in our wisdom and strength to herald an age of exchange and cooperation.
>
> From now on, June must be recorded in history not as a month of tragedy but a month of hope for the future of our people. Thus, June will be the proudest of months for our descendants who will live on this land forever.

Next, President Kim Young-nam of the Presidium of the Supreme People's Assembly delivered the North's return remarks, on behalf of Chairman Kim Jong-il of the National Defense Commission.

> Through this summit meeting we have confirmed the North and South's inalienable brotherhood. One of the greatest outcomes of this summit meeting is that we now have confidence in our nation's ability to work and walk together towards a common goal. Rather than think about unification as a matter for the future, we should unite in wisdom to handle it as it unfolds in the present.

At dinner, royal palace cuisine was served according to Chairman Kim's wishes. It was a full-course dinner, which started with an assorted vegetable salad mixed with cucumber, stewed fish, and shrimp; this was followed by pumpkin soup and citron-flavored roasted silver cod, and by a tri-seafood stew prepared with abalone, red clam, sea cucumber, chestnuts, gingkoes, and pine nuts. The main course was served with *sinseollo* (different kinds of food kept warm on a small burner), barbequed ribs, roasted fresh ginseng, *bibimbab* (mixed vegetables with rice), and pomegranate soup. The desert included tangerines, watermelon, musk melon, *shikhye* (a cold, sweetly brewed rice drink), and traditional Korean cookies. The drinks on the table were a number of South Korean alcoholic drinks—"Majuang Maedok," "Moonbaeju," and "Jinro Soju"—and a variety of soft drinks.

* * * * * * * * *

At dinner that evening, Chairman Kim appeared pleasant, talking garrulously in a cheerful voice and creating an atmosphere of celebration. President Kim also looked happy but did not speak much. I thought this was because he wanted to give Chairman Kim more time to speak. Everyone—not just the people at the head table—was engaged and seemed enchanted by the congenial mood of the evening.

During the height of this excitement, Secretary Kim Yong-soon escorted me out of the banquet hall. He showed me the final draft for the joint declaration, and wanted to discuss it with me. The final draft was the same as ours, except that the North had inserted their favorite phrase: "by the joint strengths of our nation." In their draft I also noticed an inclusion of "exchange visits of separated families." But there was also an additional phrase they had added: resolution of the "question of former long-term prisoners who had refused to renounce Communism." In my judgment, the draft was acceptable. However, it was still subject to the president's approval.

Chairman Kim Jong-il first reviewed the draft copy of the joint declaration that he received from Secretary Kim Yong-soon, and then passed it to me. I explained to President Kim the differences from our draft before obtaining his approval. President Kim then expressed to Chairman Kim his acceptance of the draft declaration. In this moment, the joint declaration was officially adopted.

Looking fully satisfied, President Kim went up to the platform with Chairman Kim, and declared: "Ladies and gentlemen, please congratulate us on this accomplishment. The two of us have just agreed fully upon on the North-South Joint Declaration!"

The president grabbed Chairman Kim's hand and raised it high. A thunderous standing ovation lasted until the atmosphere reached its climax. This scene was repeated one more time because the camera crews were not available the first time.

June 15 Joint Declaration, 2000

In accordance with the noble will of the entire people who yearn for the peaceful reunification of the nation, President Kim Dae-jung of the Republic of Korea and National Defense Commission Chairman Kim Jong-il of the Democratic People's Republic of Korea held a historic meeting and summit talks in Pyongyang from June 13 to June 15, 2000.

The leaders of the South and the North, recognizing that the first meeting and the summit talks since the division of the country were of great significance in promoting mutual understanding, developing South-North relations and realizing peaceful reunification, declared as follows:

1. The South and the North have agreed to resolve the question of reunification through their own initiative and through the joint efforts of the Korean people, who are the masters of the country.

2. Acknowledging that there are common elements for achieving reunification in the South's proposal for a confederation as well as the North's proposal for a federation of lower stage as the formula, the South and the North agreed to promote reunification in that direction.

3. The South and the North have agreed to promptly resolve humanitarian issues such as exchange visits by separated family members and relatives on the occasion of the August 15 National Liberation Day and the question of former long-term prisoners who had refused to renounce Communism.

4. The South and the North have agreed to consolidate mutual trust by promoting balanced development of the national economy through economic cooperation, and by stimulating cooperation and exchanges in civic, cultural, sports, public health, environmental and all other fields.

5. The South and the North have agreed to hold a dialogue between relevant authorities in the near future to expeditiously implement the above agreement.

President Kim Dae-jung cordially invited National Defense Commission Chairman Kim Jong-il to visit Seoul, and Chairman Kim Jong-il decided to visit Seoul at an appropriate time.

June 15, 2000

Kim Dae-jung	Kim Jong-il
President	Chairman
Republic of Korea	National Defense Commission
	Democratic People's Republic of Korea

Kim Dae-jung (*left*) and Kim Jong-il respond to applause following the June 14, 2000, announcement of the North-South Joint Declaration. Courtesy Lim Dong-won.

Upon returning to the table, Chairman Kim whispered into my ear in a low voice, "I received a report on your recommendation this morning. I told President Kim in the car on our way here that he doesn't have to go to the Geumsusan Palace. Director Lim, you won!"

When I heard this, I did not know how to express the great joy and sense of accomplishment I felt. I simply said, "Thank you, Chairman. Everything will go well."

The footage of this important scene was televised by the South Korean media several times. Later, this scene became the pretext for the opposition party and the conservative press to criticize me. They claimed: "Instead of catching spies, the NIS director is whispering secretly with the head of North Korean spies." With a big smile, Chairman Kim filled my glass to the brim with wine. As we raised our glasses and emptied them, loud applause was heard from the floor.

Moments later, Chairman Kim proposed that everybody at the head table raise their glasses. The festive mood at the head table caused a chain reaction and the people at other tables joined in raising their glasses as well. President Kim Young-nam of the Presidium proposed a toast to President Kim and Chairman Kim Jong-il. He also proposed a separate toast to me. Chairman Kim Jong-il then called his KPA generals and had each of them offer greetings and pour drinks for President Kim. Six generals, including

At the banquet on June 14, 2000: "President Kim does not have to go to Geumsusan Palace. Director Lim, you won!" (*left to right*) Kim Jong-il, the author, Kim Dae-jung. Courtesy Lim Dong-won.

Vice Marshal Jo Myong-rok and General Park Jae-kyong, lined up in a row to pour wine for President Kim. In return, the president poured wine into their glasses one by one.

The dinner ended with an unscheduled finale performance: a recitation of a poem. Poet Koh Eun was attending the dinner as a special member of the South Korean delegation. That morning he wrote a poem, "Standing in front of the Daedong River." After he was introduced, he read his poem in a powerful voice, displaying strong emotion and vibrant body gestures. His poem ended with the line, "We are going back carrying a flower in our hand." The audience seemed solemnly touched.

*   *   *   *   *   *   *   *   *

The dinner lasted past half past ten that night, upon which we all returned to the Baekhwawon Guesthouse. Finally, at approximately 11:40 p.m., a signing ceremony took place to adopt the North-South Joint Declaration. As agreed upon between protocol secretaries, Secretary Kim Yong-soon sat next to Chairman Kim Jong-il and I sat next to President Kim Dae-jung as the two leaders signed the historic document. After signing, the two leaders along with their staff raised their glasses of champagne. This was a historic moment.

Returning Home with a Flower in Hand

The next day, June 15, Chairman Kim Jong-il hosted a luncheon reception at Baekhwawon's Banquette Hall, which lasted three hours, from noon to three o'clock in the afternoon. It was a dual-purpose event: to celebrate the adoption of the North-South Joint Declaration and to bid farewell to President Kim and his party.

The luncheon was attended by fifty people from each side. On our side, all official and special delegates, as well as strategic members, came to the event. When I entered the room, Secretary Kim Ha-joong approached me closely and said, "First Vice Chairman Jo Myong-rok of the National Defense Commission will make luncheon remarks on behalf of Chairman Kim Jong-il. The president wants you to make return remarks." I could not help but be befuddled because I had not prepared any remarks. I was given a copy of the remarks that were prepared for the president. After I looked at it, I knew I should not use it as it was.

Before I had even finished looking at the draft of the president's remarks a second time, Vice Chairman Jo Myong-rok had already finished his remarks. Though his remarks were brief, they were significant in that he, in the capacity of a KPA vice marshal and on behalf of the Korean People's Armed Forces, expressed the North Korean military's full support and guaranteed the implementation of the June 15 Joint Declaration. It was a "pledge of the military." Conversely, I had a hard time simultaneously revising and reading the prepared speech. Still, I began with an emotional opening:

> The scene of the two summit leaders shaking hands and smiling widely as they met for the first time reached all corners of the world. What person watching this scene was not moved? Both Pyongyang and Seoul wept tears of joy.

Then I expressed our thanks for the enthusiastic welcome at the airport and the North's warm hospitality, ending with an emphasis on Chairman Kim's visit in return.

> We look forward to Chairman Kim Jong-il's visit to Seoul at an appropriate time and hope to return the hospitality we have received.

At the luncheon, Chairman Kim led the conversation again, soliciting comments from some of our people who had visited a chicken factory that morning. Like before, Chairman Kim was not shy to express his views:

> I thank the South for sending us fertilizer. The people are very grateful. The 100,000 tons of fertilizer increased grain production by 300,000 tons. It tripled production. Last night I was deeply moved by the president's remarks that we should work together to change the month of

June from a "tragic month of remembering the war" to a "month of hope and promise for reconciliation and cooperation."

This morning I told the members of the National Defense Commission to cease what they were doing to prepare for the anniversary of the June 25 war, which is coming up in ten days. What's more, this will be the fiftieth anniversary. They complained that the South had not changed their position on the occasion. Understandably, their attitude is a product of fifty years of mutual hostility. I think it is important to put an end to the hostile feelings of these people.

While listening to the two leaders' candid conversation, it occurred to me that Chairman Kim had only been eight years old during the war, and his thoughts ought to have been different from the revolutionary or war generation.

At the table, Chairman Kim announced, "As of noon today, I, as the Supreme Commander of the Korean People's Armed Forces, have ordered the military to suspend all slanderous and defamatory broadcasts in the frontline area directed to the South." In response, the South also took the same measure the next day, ending the critical broadcasts. This was the first concrete action that was taken as a result of the summit. However, even after the broadcasts of criticism stopped, propaganda on each side continued for four years until the loudspeaker systems were removed from the frontline area.

That day's luncheon was more like an atmosphere of colleagues dining together or a farewell party, rather than an official or diplomatic function. People moved freely from one table to another, offering drinks to one another, sometimes singing together, all in a festive mood. Chairman Kim was the leading contributor to this jovial mood. Same as the night before, Chairman Kim called members of the National Defense Commission and executive cadres of the Workers Party to the head table and told them to offer drinks to President Kim. Among those who stood in line waiting for their turn to offer drinks to the president were Yon Hyong-muk, Vice Chairman of the National Defense Commission, who was the cabinet premier during the North South High-Level Talks; Vice Marshal Jo Myong-rok; Secretary Kim Kuk-tae, who was responsible for party cadres; Secretary Kim Yong-soon, head of South Korean affairs; Chang Sung-taek, the Party's Director for Organization; and First Vice Minister of Foreign Affairs Kang Sok-ju.

Special members of our delegation offered an exchange of drinks and a conversation with Chairman Kim before getting up to sing together in chorus. Minister Park Ji-won used this opportunity to ask Chairman Kim to approve a visit by a group of presidents of South Korean press organizations to Pyongyang. The chairman gladly accepted, saying, "It would be even better if politicians also accompanied the press people."

* * * * * * * * * *

The impression Chairman Kim had made disproved all of the preconceived notions of him held by President Kim and the official and unofficial members of his delegation, and demonstrated the inaccuracy of the West's information about him.

Our previous image of Kim Jong-il was simply that he was a strange dictator. We believed he had succeeded to power despite his incompetency and had been failing to feed the people, while consistently practicing a tyranny of fear. He had been known to be a depressed, eccentric man with a speech impediment. He was also known to be impulsive and unpredictable, making it difficult to anticipate what trouble he might cause next. He was known to be obstinate, militant, and cruel, and to lead an extravagant lifestyle that involved drinking parties and performances of "pleasure teams."

But the Kim Jong-il we actually saw was a different person. He was well-informed, intelligent, smart, and quick-witted; he had a vast accumulation of knowledge from his long, more than thirty-years of experience in important party positions. He was pleasant and had a good sense of humor. He showed charisma and leadership. At times, he led conversations in a rough voice in disregard of other people. When the situation permitted, he was very frank and candid. He also seemed to try to conform to proper courtesy.

Our overall assessment of Chairman Kim Jong-il was that he was emotional and intuitive, rather than rational or logical. It is said that the left side of the human brain controls reason, rationality, and logic, whereas the right brain manages the areas of emotion, intuition, and artistic creativity. In this context, President Kim Dae-jung seemed to use more of the left side of his brain, and Chairman Kim Jong-il the right side.

After the luncheon, we all began our trip to the airport to return to Seoul. From our motorcade, we saw the people of Pyongyang lined up again on both sides of the streets to Sunan Airport, where President Kim along with Chairman Kim reviewed the KPA honor guard. After that, the two summit leaders hugged each other three times in farewell. On the day of our arrival, the president and Chairman Kim had merely shook hands, but on the day of departure, they were now hugging each other. This was a sign of the close relationship that had developed through their interactions during President Kim's stay in Pyongyang. While observing the transformation in their relationship, I genuinely prayed that the North and South would also become so close.

During his fifty-four-hour stay in Pyongyang, the president spent a total of eleven hours conducting open discussions with Chairman Kim Jong-il: they held two meetings involving substantive talks, a dinner, and a luncheon, and shared four rides in the same car. Remarkably, in the first summit since the history of the division, the two leaders were able to open their hearts to one another. I hoped that such trust and care between the two leaders would lead to the building of inter-Korean trust and confidence.

According to arms control theory, war breaks out when there is misunderstanding, misjudgment, and miscalculation based on wrong information or distrust between highest leaders in power. Conversely, if leaders sit down together to share accurate information, the right understanding and judgment, and trust each other, war can be avoided.

＊　＊　＊　＊　＊　＊　＊　＊　＊

The June 15 Joint Declaration provided a turning point from distrust and confrontation to reconciliation and cooperation between the North and the South. The Declaration was an agreement to pursue a peaceful, gradual process to unification rather than absorption or unification by force. Recognizing unification as a matter of process and a goal, the North and South agreed to reconcile and coexist, and to peacefully and gradually promote unification. This allowed us to reach a state of *de facto* unification in which people could freely travel between the two sides and help each other on the path to an eventual *de jure* unification.

Since liberation, we went through a bitter history that began with the national division, which then led to war, armistice, and the Cold War. External forces determined the fate of our nation, and it was difficult to autonomously seek solutions to our national issues. Nevertheless, this North-South summit indeed produced an inspiring achievement for the nation by charting a new course for resolving national issues without depending on the intervention of external forces.

Public support in the South for the North-South summit was very strong. According to the polls conducted by seven major news organizations, 93 to 98 percent said they were either "satisfied with the summit" or "support the North-South Joint Declaration." Approval of Chairman Kim Jong-il's visit to Seoul was about 70 percent. The conservative media that was previously suspicious of the summit had clearly changed their attitudes now. The whole international community, which of course included the United States, Japan, China, Russia, and Europe, highly commended the result of the North-South summit in one voice. On October 31 that year, the United Nations General Assembly unanimously adopted a resolution to welcome and support the North-South summit and the June 15 Joint Declaration. It was around this time that the foreign press started reporting on the possibility that President Kim Dae-jung might be awarded the Nobel Peace Prize.

II THE SEARCH FOR NEW INTER-KOREAN RELATIONS, 1989-1993

CHAPTER 3

FROM PEACEKEEPER TO PEACEMAKER

A Soldier's Path to Peacekeeping

My father raised me according to the following teaching: "Be joyful always, pray at all times, be thankful in all circumstances" (Paul's First Letter to the Thessalonians, 5:16–18). This was the code of conduct for my family. Throughout my life, these family principles helped me to revere the Lord and always have a positive, optimistic view of life.

I was born on July 25, 1933, in a small town near the Yalu River in Wiwon, North Pyeongan Province, as the first son to my father, Lim Eui-young, and my mother, Kim Myung-soon. My parents had two sons and six daughters. My father, a Protestant elder, owned and ran a pharmacy. He tried hard to follow the life of Jesus Christ by serving the sick, the poor, and the hungry. My father's piety and Christian faith greatly influenced my life.

When I was in elementary school in 1940, Japan's colonial rule had deprived Koreans of their language and alphabet, history, culture, and even their family names. My generation grew up indoctrinated by a Japanese education that attempted to mold Koreans into Japanese citizens. We were taught in Japanese and were told not to speak Korean. In my sixth year in elementary school, Korea was liberated from Japanese rule. It was only then that I started learning the Korean alphabet (*hangul*) for the first time. The following year, I entered the newly-established middle school in my hometown.

Along with liberation came the division of the Korean Peninsula between the North and South. Soviet troops moved in to occupy the North, and when they began to strictly enforce Communist rule, my family packed twice in preparation to escape from the North. However, in the last moments before each attempt, we unpacked at my father's wish. Returning from an entire night of prayer at church, he told us that it was the Lord's will for us to safeguard the church and share hardships with our fellow Christians.

My father had always wanted me to go to Shinseong Middle School, a Christian mission school in Seonchon, which was known as "Korea's Jerusalem." His wishes were fulfilled at last when I was accepted to Shinseong High School. After spending winter vacation as a third-year middle school student, I skipped one year and entered high school in the new semester. Consequently, because I had gone to Seonchon and finished three full years of high school, I was later able to come to the South. Without my high school education, I would not have been admitted into the Republic of Korea Military Academy. I think this was a blessing. It was guidance from the Lord who must have answered the prayers of my father, whose faith was demonstrated by his decision to protect the church by forsaking opportunities to come down to the South. Since then, I have always expressed thanks to my father and the Lord.

The North and the South set up their respective governments, hardening the territorial division. Then came the fratricidal war. The North Korean aggressors, aiming for Communist unification, advanced to the Nakdong River. Later they were repelled by UN forces that were led by the U.S. Armed Forces. At one point, the Communist invaders were pushed up to the Yalu River. It seemed that unification was in sight. Then Chinese troops intervened and the UN forces retreated south of the 38th parallel. The battle then reached a stalemate.

When the UN forces were retreating from Pyongyang, I joined a group of refugees fleeing to the South. I was 17 years old. Passing through Seoul, I boarded a southbound freight train, which led me to the 40th National Guard Training Center, located in Jain near Daegu, North Gyeongsang Province. There I suffered through a cold winter in an unheated orchard warehouse with straw mats on the floor. I saw many people die from disease and hunger.

After the National Guard was dissolved, I stayed in Yeongcheon for a while, struggling for survival just like the other refugees, until I found a job with a U.S. Army unit. I was extricated from the valley of death. It was a blessing that I happened to meet a U.S. Army sergeant on the street by chance one day. He took me to his unit, where I was given a job cleaning machine guns in its armory. Thanks to my first encounter with the American soldier, I was able to work two years at the U.S. Army's 772nd Military Police Battalion. During my employment, the unit moved to Busan and my job was changed to warehouse keeper. Whenever I had time for myself, I studied hard to prepare for the college entrance exam.

* * * * * * * * *

I passed the entrance examination for the Korean Military Academy in the winter of 1952. To my surprise, honor, and gratitude, I was accepted as a cadet in the academy's 13th class. Meanwhile, the war fiercely waged on. After completing a four-year course in June 1957, I was commissioned as an army second lieutenant with a bachelor of science degree. How joyful and proud I was to start a new life as an army officer of the Republic of Korea!

When I finished my duty as a rifle platoon leader in the eastern sector of the front line, I was given an opportunity to study at a civilian university in an army program designed to train officers to become faculty members for the Korean Military Academy. I enrolled in Seoul National University's Department of Philosophy, where I encountered an entirely different world. While attending university, I witnessed the April 1960 Student Revolution, through which I came to firmly believe in freedom and democracy. After completing my bachelor's program, I matriculated to a graduate program in the School of Public Administration at Seoul National University in order to broaden the scope of my academic foundation.

The Cold War between the free world and the Communist camp was developing more intensely on both ideological and military levels. On the Korean Peninsula, the armistice had ceased gunfire, which was followed by an intensification of the Cold War that put the North and South at the forefront of confrontation between the West and the Communist camp.

A year after the Student Revolution, in 1961, the May 16 military coup took place in South Korea. During this time, North Korea declared a Vietnamese-type revolutionary war against the South. The North proceeded to carry out the so-called "four-point military line," which included the fortification of the entire North, and the strengthening of "three revolutionary forces." Under these circumstances, I was selected to attend the U.S. Army Special Warfare School at Fort Bragg in North Carolina. Prior to my departure for the U.S. Army School in 1964, I was given four months of a captain's salary in advance. I exchanged the entire amount of my $27 monthly pay into dollars, so all I had in my pocket to take with me on my journey to the United States was $100.

I enrolled in the counterinsurgency course at the U.S. Army School. It covered topics such as preventing or countering "national liberation wars" by Communists. I learned a lot from this course, and from that time on I began developing an interest in applying such theories to the unique situation on the Korean Peninsula.

While in the United States, I had an opportunity to visit several cities on observation tours, including Washington, D.C. and New York. Having grown up in the rubble of the war, I was amazed at America's brilliant development. At that time, South Korea's per capita income was only $100, while the United States was the world's richest country with a per capita income of $3,700.

* * * * * * * * *

Upon my return to Korea, I was assigned as a faculty member in the Korean Military Academy and taught *Criticism of Communism* and *Strategy Against the North*. While teaching at the Academy, I wrote a book entitled *Communist Revolutionary War and Counterinsurgency*. In the book, I proposed countermeasures against predictable North Korean strategies toward the South. Three months after the book's publication, commandos from the 124th North Korean Army Unit carried out an attempted attack on the presidential residence in Seoul. In November of that year, 120 North Korean commandos infiltrated into the Taebaek Mountains. These two incidents increased the demand for my book, which was soon adopted as a textbook by the Korean Military Academy, the National Police, and the Central Intelligence School. The media also showed a great interest in my book. As an army major, I was very busy giving lectures, writing articles for contribution to the press, and responding to interview requests.

Soon after my return from the United States in April 1965, I married Yang Chang-kyoon, a graduate from Ehwa University's Department of Pharmacy. She was a working pharmacist. While I was writing the book, we were still in the honeymoon stages of our marriage, but my wife assisted me a great deal. She proofread the draft manuscript for my book and also borrowed money from one of her friends to pay for its publication. Due to the sudden increase in demand for the book, 30,000 copies were sold in two years.

An Architect for Self-Reliant Defense

In the wake of the North's attempted attack on the Blue House in 1968, the government took measures to strengthen its defense posture under the banner of the "establishment of a firm self-reliant defense system." In the spring of 1970, I was selected to go to Israel as a member of the Israeli Defense System Research Group. Our task was to invent a "self-reliant defense system."

I enrolled at the Israeli Armed Forces Command and General Staff College and studied Israeli's sources of strength, travelling across the country. Later I presented a report on my observation tour of Israel, using slides of the pictures I took, to military generals and government leaders, including President Park Chung-hee. This report drew a sensational response and the military began to learn from the Israeli model.

After completing my duties as a special forces airborne battalion commander and a division staff officer, I was assigned to the Joint Chiefs of Staff where I worked on the task of developing a national security policy for self-reliant defense. This period coincided with the aftermath of the "Nixon Doctrine," which led to a peace agreement with North Vietnam, followed by the withdrawal of U.S. troops from Vietnam. On the Korean Peninsula, the North Korean military capability suddenly surged, shifting the balance of power in favor of the North. In spite of this, the United States withdrew one army division of the U.S. Forces in Korea. South Korea's sense of crisis was also aggravated by a lack of hope for U.S. military aid. Fortunately, President Park concentrated on a policy to develop heavy and chemical industries by designating six major strategic industrial sectors. This policy gave us hope for potentially building a defense industry.

＊　＊　＊　＊　＊　＊　＊　＊　＊　＊

After Lt. General Lee Byong-hyung, a superb military strategist, was assigned as the director of the Joint Chiefs of Staff, we began to work on the development of an ambitious self-reliant defense program. I was given the important responsibility of designing the program. General Lee and I constructed South Korea's first "Grand Military Strategy," and I developed a "self-reliant force improvement program" to support the strategy. I named it the Yulgok Program in consideration of Yulgok, the famous Yi dynasty scholar who taught that "preparation prevents worries."

In addition, I recommended that the government adopt a defense tax system that would help meet the costs of self-reliant defense. We also projected the potential demand for a defense industry and recommended construction of such an industry. This was the starting point of South Korea's gradual shift from the era of dependence on foreign assistance toward an era of "self-reliant defense" in which we autonomously built and managed our military capabilities.

Upon completion of my assignment as a frontline infantry regiment commander, I was transferred to the ROK Army Headquarters to serve as coordinator for the Force Improvement Committee, which later produced the "Army Development Plan of the 1980s." This was how I returned to the work of strategic planning.

＊　＊　＊　＊　＊　＊　＊　＊　＊　＊

I was able to serve as an architect of the Republic of Korea's self-reliant defense program and peacekeeper of the Korean Peninsula during this historic turning point for the ROK Armed Forces. I still feel proud to have answered the call of duty at that time.

The military helped me grow, and I loved and dedicated myself to it. The military provided me with opportunities to study at the Korean Military Academy, Seoul National University, the U.S. Army Special Warfare School, the Israeli Armed Forces Command and General Staff College, the ROK Army College, and the U.S. Naval Postgraduate School, and to teach at the Korean Military Academy. Based on what I learned and studied, I did my best to contribute to the development of the military.

* * * * * * * * *

Following President Park Chung-hee's death, General Chun Doo-hwan came to power through a military coup on December 12, 1979 and after suppressing the uprising of the Democratic Movement in Gwangju. I opposed the military's intervention in politics. As a result, I was forced to retire from the army under pressure from General Chun's "new military group."

I did not have an interest in promotion to a higher position, but I had a strong desire to work harder and better. Now I was suddenly told to leave the army, and I was going to greatly miss serving the military. On the other hand, I took great pride that I had done my best to partake in the historical mission to develop the military—especially serving as a pioneer in the area of strategic planning for self-reliant defense. I felt rather fortunate that I could leave the service with a sense of accomplishment as a peacekeeper.

On the last day of October 1980, I retired from the army as a major general, ending my twenty-seven-year military career. At the same time, I was appointed as a foreign service officer. I was feeling bad for having to retire against my will, not knowing it was the Lord's blessing that would turn bad fortune into good.

In the Currents of Change

In early 1981, I arrived in Nigeria to serve as the Korean ambassador. I had no experience in diplomacy and did not think my foreign language skills were good. With the assistance of members of the embassy, I did my best to perform my role as ambassador, learning about my duties step by step. During my tenure at the embassy, I focused on President Chun Doo-hwan's state visit to Nigeria, while helping private Korean companies to find business opportunities in Africa.

For four years, I survived terrible living conditions by taking malaria prevention medicine, fighting tropical heat, enduring a poor supply of electricity and water, and living in an unsafe city with no cultural facilities whatsoever. The embassy staff members were staying at a hotel without their families, whom they had left in Korea. It was my wife's job to prepare food for them as well.

With a special permit from the president, I constructed an embassy and apartment building for the embassy staff. Their families later came to Nigeria to join them. We were granted a special seven-day annual leave for diplomats serving in tough areas, which I used to travel to various countries in Europe. I still have good memories of those trips.

My second assignment after four years in Nigeria was to serve as the Korean ambassador to Australia. My wife was delighted. She said, "It was like moving to heaven from hell." Australia and South Korea had a close relationship. Australia participated in the Korean War, and South Korea was Australia's fourth-largest export market.

In Australia, I focused on economic cooperation and trade promotion, visiting various parts of the country to help the local business people. Another area of my efforts was to help create more opportunities for Koreans to immigrate into Australia. As the June 1987 democratization struggle became fiercer in Korea, my job as ambassador was difficult, as I was subject to hearing the protests of the Australian parliament and other Australian friends of Korea against the dictatorial military regime in Seoul.

* * * * * * * * *

After serving abroad for seven years, I finally returned to Seoul when the new government of President Roh Tae-woo came to power. In March 1988 the new administration appointed me as the chancellor of the Institute of Foreign Affairs and National Security. In the new position, despite some difficulties, I pushed for the construction of a new building for the institute in Seoul's Yangjae-dong neighborhood, where it still stands today.

Inspired by foreign models, I undertook the reform of the institute's education system. I established a better organizational standard to train diplomats to be patriotic servants. I also encouraged studies of diplomacy and national security issues in the post-Cold War era.

During my four years at the Institute of Foreign Affairs and National Security (from March 1988 to February 1992), the forty-year-long Cold War was ending, and there was a transformation of international dynamism. In the mid-1980s, Soviet leader Mikhail Gorbachev launched a reform policy of *perestroika* and a new paradigm for national security and foreign policy.

This reform sent great waves of change across the Communist camp. A big shift was also taking place in the international order. The United States and the Soviet Union started promoting nuclear arms reduction, and Europe agreed to reduce conventional armed forces. Following the fall of the Berlin Wall came the collapse of the East European Communist system, which finally ended the Cold War. This was a groundbreaking change in the history of the modern world.

In consideration of this changing world, I encouraged my research staff to study the best diplomatic approaches for Korea. I supported Korea's diplomatic activities and promoted exchanges between think tanks with China and the Soviet Union to prepare for eventual normalization of relations with these countries. I frequently sponsored seminars to exchange views and information to create the right atmosphere for the subsequent normalization.

In those days I was absorbed in the study of Gorbachev's *perestroika* reform and the national security and foreign policy he had created based on a new way of thinking. Given my long experience in dealing with the enhancement of military capability, I was greatly interested in the European process of reducing conventional armed forces (CFE).

* * * * * * * * *

It was about this time that I advocated that we end the Cold War on the Korean Peninsula and undertake negotiations of arms reduction between the North and South. I started urging people of all walks of life to prepare for that possibility. I began writing articles for the mass media, including the *Chosun Ilbo*, discussing a prospective process of ending the Cold War and dealing with the arms reduction issue.

At the request of Senior Secretary for National Security Kim Chong-whi at the Blue House, I took a new job as the Director of Arms Control Planning. I wrote the "ROK's Arms Control Policy," which was approved by the National Security Council. Based on this policy, our side presented its basic position on arms control at the North-South High-Level Talks that were later held.

When the North-South High-Level Talks began in 1990, I was appointed to join the South Korean delegation as a member responsible for arms control and diplomatic issues. I attended more than sixty inter-Korean negotiation sessions, travelling back and forth between Pyongyang and Seoul. I am proud and honored to have served as the midwife for the birth of the North-South Basic Agreement and the Joint Declaration for the Denuclearization of the Korean Peninsula through this role. These two documents set the direction for the inter-Korean relationship in the post-Cold War era.

An Advocate for Unification

In March 1993 I left the government after forty years of service. I first joined a civilian organization as the chairman of the Central Committee of National Unification. Next, I joined the Sejong Institute as a visiting scholar. I spent one year with each of the two organizations. These two years were valuable to me as I was able to do research and put into perspective all the experience and knowledge I had accumulated from my earlier career. During this period, my three sons got married, and I was a happy father.

As the Vice Minister of Unification in the beginning of 1993, I had turned over the Ministry's duties to the incoming administration's transition team. President-elect Kim Young-sam had campaigned as the candidate of the ruling party on an ambitious pledge that he would "realize unification within the century." He asked the Ministry of Unification to construct a new unification formula for his administration. At that time, I thought that *de jure* unification would be impossible to achieve in seven years. However, I thought that if things went well, the beginning of *de facto* unification might be possible. In the stage of a *de facto* unification, people would be able to travel between the North and the South and to aid one other.

Based on a unification concept that was developed two years earlier, I presented a three-stage unification formula. In the first stage, we would promote reconciliation and cooperation, and build mutual trust between the North and South. In the second stage, we would institutionalize a confederation of the North and the South, ending the legacies of the Cold War and achieving *de facto* unification. And in the third and final stage, we would arrive at *de jure* unification to fully unify the two parts. This three-stage formula became an official government policy, called the Three Stages for the National Community Unification Formula, after it was announced in President Kim Young-sam's speech on the commemoration of Liberation Day, August 15.

In order to begin meeting the conditions for *de facto* unification, I believed we needed to develop a patient and consistent policy of proactive reconciliation and engagement, and carry out the implementation of the North-South Basic Agreement. I recommended that the South, having gone through the presidential election, take diplomatic measures to cancel the joint Team Spirit exercise and encourage direct talks between the United States and North Korea toward the resolution of North Korea's nuclear program.

At the start of the new government, I stepped down as vice unification minister but was selected as the chairman of the National Unification

Central Committee, which had been organized in 1981 as a civilian institute dedicated to cultivating national strength for the unification of the fatherland. My tenure with the unification committee was busy. I spent many days traveling, giving speeches, and making presentations at various academic conferences.

* * * * * * * * *

On March 12, 1993, North Korea suddenly announced its withdrawal from the Nuclear Non-Proliferation Treaty (NPT), and the United States, which had been trying to extend the term of the treaty, was confounded. Nuclear non-proliferation was one of the most important foreign policy issues for the newly-inaugurated Clinton administration. Many experts thought that North Korea was determined to develop nuclear weapons. Selig Harrison, a Korean Peninsula expert, invited me to Washington. He wanted to exchange views on North Korea's thorny decision to withdraw from the NPT and discuss what could be done about it.

Selig Harrison had visited Pyongyang as the Tokyo bureau chief of the *Washington Post* and he had been the first American to interview President Kim Il-sung. He had since published several essays and articles on the subject of the Korean Peninsula. He and I had frequently exchanged views for a number of years. Accepting Harrison's invitation, I went to Washington. At a discussion forum sponsored by the Carnegie Endowment for International Peace, I presented my views on the subject and had a good exchange of views with an impressive audience. The participants included former American ambassador to Korea James Lilley; Retired Lieutenant General John H. Cushman, former commander of I Corps (ROK/US) Group in Korea; General Edward C. Meyer, former U.S. Army Chief of Staff; and officials from the departments of state and defense.

The two dominant views of the American specialists were either that North Korea's announcement to withdraw from the NPT was a "reaction to U.S. pressure and sanctions" or that the North had clearly "made its decision to develop nuclear weapons." However, my view was that North Korea seemed to be using the nuclear issue as leverage to induce high-level political talks and improve its relations with the United States.

In fact, in 1992 North Korea accepted International Atomic Energy Agency (IAEA) safeguards inspections in the hopes of having direct talks with the United States. But the North was disappointed when such hope evaporated. In my opinion, the North Koreans would have even gone to the point of shock therapy to draw the attention of the new U.S. administration.

At the Carnegie conference, I argued, "As the world's only superpower, the new U.S. administration should gracefully engage North Korea to resolve the nuclear issue through negotiation and improve relations with the North, and the United States should come up with a fundamental policy to end the Cold War on the Korean Peninsula."

Even afterwards, debates over the North Korean nuclear issue continued in the United States until the initiation of high-level political talks between Washington and Pyongyang in June 1993. At the end of the difficult negotiations, the Agreed Framework was adopted in Geneva in October 1994.

* * * * * * * * *

When I resigned as chairman of the Central Committee of National Unification, I was invited as a visiting scholar to the Sejong Institute. At the institute, I had opportunities to discuss issues of national strategy and North-South relations with young researchers, and wrote two research papers.

One of my papers, entitled "South Korea's National Strategy," was published in the first edition of the institute's journal *The National Strategy*. The other piece was a long paper on the subject of "Strategy for North-South High-Level Talks," which was incorporated in a book called *North Korean Negotiating Strategy and Inter-Korean Relations*, published by the Institute of Far East Studies. Around that time, I also presented a paper on "Arms Control Within the Context of the Unification Process" at the international conference on *Restarting the Peace Process on the Korean Peninsula*, sponsored by the RAND Corporation, located near Los Angeles.

Why a Peacemaker?

Having gone through the entire process of the North-South High-Level Talks, which took place against the backdrop of the ending of the Cold War in the early 1990s, I changed my views. From a strong anti-Communist conservative, I had become a rational pragmatist, switching my role from peacekeeper to peacemaker. I voluntarily assumed the role of a peacemaker, believing that it was the Lord's new mission for me: "Blessed are the peacemakers, for they will be called children of God."

When I was serving as Presidential Secretary for Foreign Affairs and National Security in 1998, I spoke before an audience at the Veterans Association on the topic of "Our Security Posture and North Korea Policy." There were many retired generals, including ones who contributed to the founding of the ROK Armed Forces. One of them, apparently quite disappointed, got up and asked, "You were formerly critical of Communism and taught anti-Communist strategy, advocating self-reliant defense and force improvement. How could you have changed so much?"

I listed two reasons in answer to the question.

First, the world has changed. The drastic change in the strategic environment surrounding the Korean Peninsula has changed me and the new post-Cold War era is facing new demands from history. When I was lecturing on anti-Communist strategy in the 1960s, and when I was planning national security strategy in the 1970s, these were periods of confrontation between the free world and the Communist camp, in which the United States employed a containment policy to resist Soviet expansionism.

Korea too had to confront the threat of Communist aggression at the forefront of the free world. But, now the international Cold War has ended. The Communist camp has collapsed, and democracy and market economy are spreading all over the world. The Communist camp has lost its *raison d'être* in terms of ideology or political system. Other countries divided since the end of World War II have been unified. Anti-Communism is not an issue anymore. Now the question is how we should end the Cold War on the Korean Peninsula and overcome the division to achieve peaceful unification. All ideologies and policies are the products of a given era. We would be outdated if we insisted upon holding onto the ideas and thoughts of the old era and did not change with the times.

The second reason for my change in perception was related to my personal experiences. Through my observations and conversations with the North Koreans during numerous visits to Pyongyang, I came to realize that we had held an unnecessary sense of victimization and an exaggerated assessment of the North due to inaccurate information. Given the huge gap in national power between the North and South, an unfavorable development of the international environment for the North, and a bankrupt economy, North Korea is seeking survival amidst fears of absorption by the South. Yet, we have overestimated North Korea's capability. Of course, we should not underestimate the North's capability to launch a suicidal attack. Nonetheless, overestimation is a problem. We should have the right assessment of North Korea. With confidence, we should build the right environment for the North to change. We should peacefully manage the division. North Korea's change is inevitable. The whole world is now in great transformation. Of course we have to maintain "negative peace" by maintaining a robust security posture to deter war. At the same time, we should work hard to make "positive peace" by wisely inducing North Korean change to resolve the fundamental cause of security threats and to replace the Armistice Agreement with a peace regime. To this end, we should work with neighboring countries to dismantle the Cold War structure and build a peace regime toward unification. This is what we should strive for, a strategy to achieve our goal without having to fight a war.

Based on these two reasons, I explained, I wanted to change my role from keeping a negative peace to that of actively making a positive peace.

CHAPTER 4

INTER-KOREAN
HIGH-LEVEL TALKS

Prelude to the End of the Cold War

In early December 1989, the two leaders of the United States and the Soviet Union met in Malta and officially declared an end to the Cold War. The crumbling of the more than forty-year old foundation, which had rested securely upon confrontation and distrust, shook the international system to the core. For the Korean Peninsula, the end of the Cold War afforded the North and South an opportunity to forge a new relationship. After a long period of hostile confrontation, this paved the way for the High-Level Talks that took place.

Around this time, I experienced another life-changing moment: I was appointed as a member of the delegation of the North-South High-Level Talks, which were headed by prime ministers. I knew I had been appointed because of my experience and expertise, since the North-South High-Level Talks were going to focus on the issues of arms control and a peace regime. I learned that President Roh Tae-woo had known about my career and had personally appointed me to join the prime ministerial talks with the North.

On the afternoon August 20, 1990—the same day we had been appointed—seven of us met at the official residence of the prime minister to prepare for the North-South High-Level Talks. Present were the head of the delegation, Prime Minister Kang Young-hoon; Minister of Unification, Hong Seong-chol; Chairman of the Joint Chiefs of Staff, General Chung Ho-gun; Blue House Senior Secretary for National Security, Kim Chong-whi; Vice Minister of the Economic Planning Board, Lee Jin-seol; Special Assistant to the Director of the National Security Planning Agency, Lee Byong-yong; and myself as the Director of the Institute of Foreign Affairs and National

Security. With the exception of myself, everyone had been appointed because of the prestigious positions they held in their organizations. In our first meeting, we were briefed on the plan for the North-South High-Level Talks.

* * * * * * * * *

Three objectives for the talks had been defined: achieve the National Community Unification Formula; build confidence through exchange and cooperation; and develop a new relationship of coexistence and co-prosperity. The strategy for the talks was to adopt a basic agreement to improve inter-Korean relations, agree on the steps required to implement exchange and cooperation in various fields between the North and South, and agree on political and military confidence-building measures. Further, the South would seek a regular meeting of the "Council of North-South Ministers." The strategy would help institutionalize a "Confederation of the North and South." I specifically noticed the premise that the institutionalization of a "confederation" would be realized in compliance with the National Community Unification Formula. Part of the strategy was also bringing about a North-South summit meeting.

Three days later, our delegation called on President Roh Tae-woo at the Blue House and he approved our strategy to promote the North-South High-Level Talks. President Roh emphasized, "We should begin a process to end the Cold War on the Korean Peninsula by capturing the momentum of the Cold War's end. To do so, we should first end hostile relations between the North and the South and begin a new inter-Korean relationship." The president also approved the basic guidelines that through talks we should induce exchange and cooperation, reduce tension, and build a peace mechanism. He also added that talks should not be "talks for the sake of talks" but "talks for implementation."

Our goal and strategy for the talks were thus fixed. This decision was made against the backdrop of the new international environment in the wake of the Cold War's end. The decision reflected a consistent forward-looking engagement policy for the realization of the National Community Unification Formula, based on public support and the July 7 Special Declaration on North Korea policy. The Roh Tae-woo government, which was born from the June Democracy Movement of 1987, focused on democratization at home, while capturing the currents of international politics to externally promote a Northern Policy (*Nordpolitik*).

In 1988 President Roh Tae-woo announced the "Special Declaration in the Interest of National Self-Respect, Unification and Prosperity," later simply known as the July 7 Special Declaration, which presented a progressive proposal to transform the "enemy" into a "partner" for peace and unification. The declaration paved a path to engagement for promoting exchange and travels, and opening trade with the North. To support the declaration, the government actually took a series of concrete measures to make such visits and trade possible. The Roh government also announced the National Community Unification Formula, which suggested a gradual approach to unification through the formation of a national community by way of peaceful coexistence between the two different systems. The announcement certainly contributed to the creation of a favorable atmosphere for dialogue. The formula was the basis of logic for promoting the North-South High-Level Talks.

The Roh administration's future-oriented policy toward North Korea was largely formulated by a joint effort between Senior Secretary for National Security Kim Chong-whi and Director of the National Security Planning Agency Seo Dong-gwon. Kim was a rational realist with an acute sense of judgment and expertise in national security affairs, who maintained a close working relationship with the United States. Seo was a former prosecutor who also had acute judgment and a sense of historical demand for the future. Minister of Unification Lee Hong-koo, a longtime political scientist, should also be credited for his contribution to the birth of the National Community Unification Formula.

* * * * * * * * *

After the successful hosting of the 1988 Seoul Olympic Games, which enhanced the Republic of Korea's international prestige, Pyongyang accepted Seoul's proposal for a high-level North-South talk. Preparatory meetings began at Panmunjom starting from early February 1989. After eight rounds of meetings that took place over the course of a year and a half, the final agreement to hold inter-Korean high-level talks was reached. The major agreement was that the high-level meeting would be labeled as the "North-South High-Level Talks" and the first meeting would convene in Seoul on September 4, 1990. The agreed-upon agenda for the talks was "issues related to resolving the political and military confrontation and implementing exchange and cooperation in various fields between the North and the South." Each side's delegation would consist of seven members, thirty-three staffers to accompany them, and fifty press reporters—a total of ninety on each side.

The historical context during this period was a series of monumental developments throughout Eastern Europe, including democratic revolutions replacing Communist rule in Poland, Hungary, and Czechoslovakia. In addition, there was an exodus from East Germany, followed by a civil revolution, and the fall of the Berlin Wall. The two Germanys had undertaken economic and social integration. In Romania, Ceauşescu's own people executed the dictator in a blood-spattered revolution, and the Soviet Union adopted a multiparty system.

The confrontational structure between the free democratic camp and the Communists came to an end when the two presidents of the United States and the Soviet Union, George H. W. Bush and Mikhail Gorbachev, declared on December 2, 1989 in Malta that the Cold War was over. A sensitive situation developed on the Korean Peninsula as the United States revised its Northeast Asia strategy and announced a three-phase reduction plan for U.S. forces in Korea.

In order to survive these enormous changes in the international environment, North Korea had to be flexible to avoid future international isolation and economic difficulties. The North-South High-Level Talks seemed to be an exit strategy.

The Roh Tae-woo government chose not to accept the imminent collapse theory that the U.S. intelligence community and some North Korea specialists supported. Unlike Romania, North Korea would not suddenly collapse, and to suppose so was wishful thinking. The administration determined that as long as North Korea had China's support, it was unrealistic to expect its rapid disintegration. This assessment also took into account North Korea's differing stages of political, economic, and social development from those of the Eastern European countries. Instead, the government held the view that North Korea would follow the Chinese model and undertake a process of gradual transformation.

"First Time Meeting a South Korean"

Once the goal and strategy for the talks were fixed, preparation work began immediately. The delegates and their support staff met every day in the conference room of the Secretariat Bureau of North-South Affairs in Samcheong-dong. We wrote and edited statements for the talks and reviewed and discussed the final versions. We even held mock meetings. Yet, nobody was sure whether the talks would indeed be held. Many of us were pessimistic.

A week prior to the holding of the talks scheduled for September 5 that year, the delegates and staff had dinner together at a restaurant. We were concerned because the North had not sent us a list of their delegates yet. At the dinner, Minister Hong Seong-chol asked the people at the table to predict "yes" or "no" to the prospect of the North Koreans coming to Seoul.

Out of twenty people, approximately 80 percent replied "no." Their rationale was that it was unlikely for the North Korean premier to come to Seoul so soon after a contentious disagreement, which had already raised tensions, over how to jointly celebrate the August 15 holiday. On the other hand, four people, including Senior Secretary Kim Chong-whi and myself, said the North Koreans would come as agreed.

The North sent a list of delegates only four days before the scheduled date of the talks. The atmosphere of skepticism dissipated and the preparation work was reenergized. Early on the morning of September 4, our delegation departed for Panmunjom to meet the North Korean delegation. That was my first visit to Panmunjom.

Panmunjom became well known to the world because of the Korean War. It is a site that holds the history of the national division. Located sixty-two kilometers northwest of Seoul, Panmunjom was the site of 1,076 meetings before the Armistice Agreement was finally signed on July 27, 1953. After the armistice went into effect, 459 Military Armistice Commission meetings were held there. On the southern side of Panmunjom stands the octagonal Freedom House, and on the northern side lies a two-story building called Panmungak. For the inter-Korean dialogue during the 1980s, the South and the North respectively built the "House of Peace" and the Tongilgak (Unification Pavilion) on their sides of the demarcation.

Here, South Korean and American soldiers assigned to a combined unit are on guard twenty-four hours a day, standing directly across from North Korean soldiers. Yet, Panmunjom seemed peaceful that morning. The place that once held two hostile parties meeting to discuss armistice negotiations had now been transformed into a location in which the delegates of the North-South High-Level Talks, represented by prime ministers and government representatives, were meeting to negotiate. Since that morning, I have visited or passed through Panmunjom more than eighty times.

* * * * * * * * *

My task that morning was to cross the Military Demarcation Line to the North side to meet and escort the Northern delegates to the South. I was in one of nine cars carrying sky blue flags that crossed the line. After I was ushered into a large hall to meet the North Korean delegates, I introduced myself to Yon Hyong-muk, the North's head of delegation. I said respectfully, "How are you? I am pleased to meet you. I am here to escort you to the House of Peace."

After my introduction, Cabinet Premier Yon Hyong-muk immediately got up to shake my hand and welcome me.

"I am glad to see you. Thank you for coming. Please meet the delegates from our side. This is Comrade Kim Kwang-jin, Vice Minister of the People's Armed Forces."

General Kim Kwang-jin was in uniform, with four big stars on his shoulder. After meeting him, I shook hands with the rest of the members, one by one. Among them were Ahn Byung-soo, Director of the Secretariat for the Committee of the Peaceful Unification of the Fatherland (his real name was Ahn Kyong-ho; he had a soft look, like a South Korean); Paek Nam-joon, Chief Cabinet Councilor (Paek Nam-sun was his real name and he later became a foreign minster—he was a familiar face on television since he served as the head of the preparatory meetings for the High-Level Talks); Kim Jong-woo, Deputy Minister for External Economic Affairs at the State Cabinet (Kim had a young and pleasant look); and Choi Woo-jin, a Roving Ambassador from the Ministry of Foreign Affairs (he looked like a warm and interesting person). They all smiled at me as though we were old acquaintances.

In contrast, Kim Young-cheol, a young one-star major general in uniform (who had sharp eyes and a cold look), shook hands with me without saying a word. I also met Lim Chun-choo, Special Assistant to the North Korean Head of Delegation (his real name was Lim Dong-ok, and he was actually a man of influence for the North Korean delegation).

When the greetings were done, I sat down beside Premier Yon and had a light conversation with him about the weather and the distance to Seoul, while drinking ginseng tea. He said:

> Today is my first time visiting Seoul or meeting a South Korean. Mr. Lim, you are the first South Korean I have ever met. This is a special meeting. I see nothing different between North Koreans and South Koreans. We look the same and we speak the same language. I would say we probably have the same mind . . .

Somebody jumped in and spoiled the conversation.

"Is it true that South Korean elementary school students are taught that North Korean people are animals with horns on their heads?"

Nervous laughter with a hint of disapproval was heard throughout the room. Then Premier Yon quickly resumed the conversation, changing the mood,

"We should expedite unification. By the way, where is your hometown?"

That was an expected question.

"Seonchon, North Pyeongan Province. I came to the South during the war."

Premier Yon, of course, and others seemed surprised. They did not know I was a native of the North. Later I learned that they had thought I was born in Seoul. There was a mutual lack of information regarding one another.

My twenty-minute conversation with Premier Yon that day gave me reason to believe that regardless of ideological differences, North-South talks could proceed. I also had a good impression of Premier Yon, who seemed informal and warmhearted. Before we got up to leave, he said:

> Mr. Lim, like you said, through the North-South talks, we should hasten the day when people can travel between the North and the South and help each other.

I hopped in the first car and sat beside Premier Yon in the passenger seat. As we left the Tongilgak area, we received military salutes from the Korean People's Army security guards. The motorcade carrying the North Korean delegates crossed the demarcation line, turning the corner at a Quonset hut to the east. There was no road connecting the two sides of the demarcation line. We drove for about ten meters over the gravel-covered ground known as the "ten-meter heartbreak section" to get to the Southern zone.

I took this opportunity to remind Premier Yon that there was no road connecting the North and the South. As we traveled this road of national tragedy, Premier Yon said in a serious and somber voice: "We should connect the road as soon as possible. . . ." Twelve years later, the first connecting road between the North and the South was completed, and a temporary road to Mount Kumgang on the east coast opened in February 2002.

There were many foreign and domestic press photographers and reporters waiting for the arrival of the North Korean delegation in the front of the House of Peace. Premier Yon got out of the car, smiling brightly, and raised his hand high to greet the South.

Yon Hyong-muk (1931–2006), born in North Hamkyong Province, attended the Mankyungdae School for the bereaved families of revolutionaries and studied at a college of engineering in Czechoslovakia. He worked for the Korea Workers Party until he was appointed as vice cabinet premier and concurrently the chairman of the Committee of the Metal and Machinery Industry in 1985. In 1988, he was promoted to the premier of the Cabinet for the DPRK. He was known to be sixth in the order of power as a member of the Politburo. Later Yon worked as vice chairman of the National Defense Commission and the party secretary for Jagang Province.

Meeting of Prime Ministers

The first round of the North-South High-Level Talks convened with live television coverage throughout the world at ten o'clock on the morning of September 5, 1990, at the Intercontinental Hotel in Seoul. After exchanging greetings, the two senior delegates—Kang Young-hoon (South) and Yon Hyong-muk (North)—delivered their opening statements.

Our side presented a basic draft agreement that listed eight items based on the National Community Unification Formula, as well as an agenda for the talks to include measures to implement multifaceted exchange and cooperation, measures to build political and military confidence, and promotion of arms reduction.

The eight items listed included mutual recognition and respect for each other's system; non-interference in internal affairs; suspension of slander and vilification; prohibition of actions of sabotage or subversion; peaceful resolution of disputes; and replacement of the armistice with a peace regime. These issues became the basis for discussion in the talks, and in the end they were actually adopted for the final version of the North-South Basic Agreement. Our proposed agenda became a point of contention for negotiation during the first round of the talks.

On the other hand, the North presented agenda items that included "three principles of compliance" for observation during the entire process of the talks and "three urgent tasks" for immediate resolution in the first round of the talks. The three tasks were the issues of admission to the United Nations; suspension of the combined U.S.-ROK Team Spirit exercises; and release of detainees who have visited the North. With emphasis on the necessity of resolving the state of political and military confrontation, the North presented "measures to end the state of political confrontation" and "measures to resolve the state of military confrontation." Their representative stressed, "We can end the state of confrontation when we adopt a non-aggression accord between the North and the South, and conclude a peace treaty with the United States." Reflecting North Korea's security concerns, he concluded, "Such issues as economic cooperation and exchange are not essential but collateral, and they will naturally be realized once the state of political and military confrontation is resolved."

* * * * * * * * *

The second day of talks proceeded in a closed session to clarify earlier discussions. Asserting the principle of "one Korea," the North waged a critical offensive by insisting, "The South's proposal was not intended to move toward unification, but was divisive to the nation and conducive to perpetuating the status quo of division." Reiterating the so-called three urgent tasks, the North then argued, "The task that first has to be resolved between the North and the South is not the issue of exchange and cooperation as the South claims, but the resolution of the political and military issue." In response, our side maintained, "Under the premise that we should gradually move toward unification through the improvement of North-South relations and establishment of peaceful coexistence, we should first resolve relatively easy issues, such as separated family members and economic cooperation."

The two sides disagreed on two fundamental points. The first was how to define a new relationship between the North and the South. The point of contention was choosing between a "one-Korea theory" versus a "strategy of recognizing the state of division and improving relations between the two existing political entities." This contention stemmed from the two different approaches to unification.

The other point of contention was the question of what the North and the South should discuss and resolve first. It was a matter of determining priorities between the political and military issue and the exchange and cooperation issue. The debate on these issues continued for a year until the adoption of the agreement in the fifth round of the talks.

On the second day of the talks, the North side proposed a meeting between the representatives of both sides to discuss a "single-seat admission to the United Nations" to represent both the North and the South. Our side accepted the proposal. As for the issue of separated families, the two sides agreed to commission the Red Crosses of both sides to discuss it.

* * * * * * * * *

The North-South High-Level Talks provided the first opportunity in the forty years following the Korean War to allow a large delegation of ninety members, including journalists, to travel openly between Seoul and Pyongyang. The talks allowed us to collect firsthand information on the North side's social and economic conditions. That helped the South gain a better understanding of the North. In addition, both sides tried to use the talks as an opportunity to demonstrate the superiority of their systems.

From the first evening after their arrival in Seoul, we took the North Koreans to the best hotels—the Hilton, the Walkerhill Sheraton, and the Lotte—for dinners and shows. Starting from the Intercontinental Hotel, we drove them through Teheran Road where high-rise buildings line the Gangnam district. As we intended, the North Koreans took note of the modern skyline buildings, heavy automobile traffic, crowds of people walking on the street, merchandise in show windows, and night scenes all brightly lit by neon signs. The North Korean delegates kept asking about the role of so many banks and television commercials.

UN Membership: Two in One, or One in Two?

The question of United Nations entry was important. It was closely related to the unification formulas of both parties and inevitably linked to the issue of establishing a new relationship between the North and the South. It was arguable, however, whether or not this question should be resolved before the other issues.

One week before the first round of the North-South High-Level Talks, the South Korean foreign minister revealed the South Korean government's intention to apply for UN membership as a separate country that year, saying, "If North Korea refuses joint entry to the United Nations along with the Republic of Korea, we will seek separate admission."

By the end of September that year, South Korea normalized relations with the Soviet Union, and in October an agreement was reached to exchange trade offices with China. South Korea's Northern Policy had thus started yielding results and the prospect of admission to the United Nations appeared bright. For North Korea, these developments presented a diplomatic crisis it could not overlook.

In accordance with the agreement of the first round of High-Level Talks, on the morning of September 18, representatives from both sides discussed the issue of UN admission in the conference room of the Neutral Nations Supervisory Commission at Panmunjom. This meeting was followed by two more in the following months. During these meetings, I, along with my two assistants, represented the South, and Choi Woo-jin and his two assistants represented the North.

Choi Woo-jin and I had a few things in common. We both had served as ambassadors in Africa during the same period. At Pyongyang's Ministry of Foreign Affairs he, like me, had worked on arms control issues, and we were the same age. He had an unusually pleasant personality for a North Korean representative.

In the first round of the High-Level Talks, Choi Woo-jin was my counterpart from day one. We rode in the same car and exchanged candid views. At times, we argued with one another. At times, we raised our voices. Yet, we tried to build a good working relationship by treating each other as problemsolvers rather than adversaries. Our relationship contributed to solving several issues that arose at the High-Level Talks.

That day, Choi Woo-jin expressed the North's basic position regarding the issue of UN membership:

In order to prevent the perpetuation of national division, the North and South should seek admission to the United Nations as a single country once unification has been achieved. If we were to join the UN before unification, we should not seek two separate seats but a single seat.

If the North and South were to enter the United Nations as two separate countries, it would signify international legalization of the division. It would not only obscure the path to unification but also make it difficult to avoid North-South confrontations on the world stage, and therefore, from the perspective of national dignity, should not be allowed.

I rebutted, saying,

There are no grounds for the North's claim that the two separate seats in the United Nations would perpetuate and legalize the division.

I presented a few examples.

North Yemen and South Yemen, which entered the United Nations with separate seats, have already been integrated. Also, in view of the fact that West Germany and East Germany will soon be unified, your argument has no basis. In the case of Yemen and Germany, their separate admission to the United Nations has, in fact, worked positively towards the promotion of their unification. Your side's insistence on a single seat for two states in the United Nations is unrealistic. In the current state of North-South relations, not a single letter is delivered across the border, nor are there any other means of communication. Considering the reality that the two sides cannot even agree on trivial things, your side's argument that the North and South should cooperate to exercise a joint voting right is impractical.

After this refutation, I explained the South's position:

Accepting the cold reality of the division, the North and South should recognize and respect each other and coexist until unification. First, we should recognize there are two of us. We need to work through reconciliation and cooperation to become one. A simultaneous dual entry into the United Nations as separate states is a realistic way to promote the unification of the Korean Peninsula. Of course, it will be an interim measure until the day of unification. In the meantime, we should maintain a unification-oriented special relationship and we should closely cooperate in the United Nations to promote common interests and peaceful unification.

The concept of a "unification-oriented special relationship," as a definition for the North-South relationship, had never been introduced until I used it at that meeting. This concept was later adopted in the preamble of the North-South Basic Agreement.

Although we were not able to reach a negotiated solution to the issue of UN admission, these meetings were very helpful in clarifying the other side's position on the issue and other related problems. In addition, South Korea had followed a cooperative approach to UN admission, as recommended by the permanent members of the UN Security Council, including China and the Soviet Union, creating favorable conditions for the South's admission. At the same time, the North was able to block South Korea's UN entry as a separate country that year.

* * * * * * * * *

A breakthrough on this issue came from the shifting strategic environment on the Korean Peninsula. The Soviet Union and Eastern European countries were transforming into market economies and democracies; Germany had been unified, and China was accelerating reform and opening. Even worse for North Korea, the Soviet Union and China, their longtime allies, had changed their attitudes.

In September 1990, Soviet foreign minister Eduard Shevardnadze visited Pyongyang to notify North Korea of the Soviet decision to normalize relations with South Korea. The North Korean leadership was shocked by this abrupt change. A memorandum that Pyongyang sent to Moscow stated, "Normalization of relations with South Korea will recognize and extend the Korean division, and unlike in the case of other countries, it will legitimize the 'two Koreas.'" The memorandum also alleged that normalization would contribute to "the realization of South Korea's Northern Policy" designed to isolate the North, and to the "promotion of the South's policy of unification by absorption."

In addition, the memorandum alluded to North Korea's intent to develop nuclear weapons and its prior warning of an "intensified arms race on the Korean Peninsula": "In such circumstances, the DPRK-Soviet alliance would become meaningless and we would have to prepare countermeasures to produce our own weapons to replace the weapons we had depended upon for our alliance."

The North fiercely denounced the Soviet Union's change and "betrayal" when ROK-Soviet diplomatic normalization was later announced at the end of the month: "The Soviet Union sold its dignity and lost the trust of its ally for the price of $2.3 billion." The North was referring to South Korea's cash loan to the Soviet Union, negotiated during the process of normalization of relations and granted after normalization.

Even afterwards, the tide continued to turn against North Korea. The Soviet Union decided to end its barter trade with the North and demanded

The author (*seated, first from right*) and the North's Choi Woo-jin (*seated, second from left*) negotiating UN admission of the two Koreas at Panmunjom on October 5, 1990. Courtesy Lim Dong-won.

payment in hard currency beginning in 1991. China also decided to terminate barter trade with North Korea, after agreeing with South Korea to exchange trade missions. To add to the series of diplomatic crises, the North was about to face serious economic difficulties with shortages in food, energy, and foreign exchange.

Concurrent with the ominous prospect of an economic crisis for the North, in spite of their adamant objections, China decided to support South Korea's UN admission in May of 1991. On his visit to Pyongyang, Chinese Vice Premier Li Peng notified President Kim Il-sung of the Chinese Communist Party's decision not to veto South Korea's UN admission, encouraging North Korea's simultaneous UN entry with South Korea. The North accepted China's advice and made a 180-degree turn from its previous position.

Pyongyang released a foreign ministry statement on May 27, 1991:

> If we allow South Korea to enter the United Nations as a separate state, this will lead to prejudiced discussions at the United Nations regarding important issues related to the interest of the Korean nation. This may lead to grave consequences. . . . To resolve this interim difficulty which South Korean authorities have created, we have no choice at this stage but to enter the United Nations.

North Korea joined the United Nations in September 1991. With that, the North lost the grounds to insist upon its prior positions of "immediate unification by a federation with two systems" and its "one-Korea theory," which it had advocated on the premise of a single-seat membership in the UN. The North came to recognize the existence of two states; they also came to consider the South's proposal that the North and South work together to promote unification through peaceful coexistence and a gradual step by step process. Thus, the UN admissions created an opportunity to establish a new North-South relationship.

Unification Fever

On October 16, 1990, our delegation was on its way to Pyongyang to attend the second round of the North-South High-Level Talks. That morning we passed through Panmunjom to arrive at Kaesong Railroad Station, where we boarded a special train bound for Pyongyang.

Each member of our delegation was assigned to a large compartment furnished with a bed, a desk, and a spacious toilet. I pushed the window curtain to look outside and saw a view of the North Korean land that I had been unable to see for forty years. I could not help but feel deep emotion and excitement.

I saw barren mountains stripped of vegetation, interspersed with patches of arable slopes. This image was a stark contrast to the thick wooded mountains in the South. I could see some small traces of farming on the edge of the bare mountains. There were piles of straw in the rice fields and dry farming fields, but no farmers were working. The fields looked serene and quiet after the harvest season.

However, the modest rural homes from Kaesong to Pyongyang were impressive. They seemed to have been built with clay blocks and were all painted in white. More noticeable were the placards and slogans: "*Juche* for the entire society!" "Self-reliant Economy!" "All-out March to Economic Reconstruction through a Speedy Battle of Annihilation Warfare!" "Let's Live by Our Style!" and "The Party Decides, We Carry It Out." Written in big, bold type, these slogans were conspicuous throughout all the areas we passed through.

The distance from Kaesong to Pyongyang was about 150 kilometers— about the same distance from Seoul to Daejeon. Yet, it took us four hours without stopping to arrive in Pyongyang at 1:40 p.m. The train ran at an average speed of 40 kilometers an hour. I thought it was strange that there were no trains waiting on other tracks at the big stations like Hwangju and

The second round of the North-South High-Level Talks, held in Pyongyang in October 1990. Courtesy Lim Dong-won.

Sariwon that we passed. I observed the same thing on our return train ride to Kaesong later. It was clear to me that the lack of traffic and logistics was a sign of a halted economy. Nevertheless, it was hard to understand why the train speed was so slow. Perhaps, it might have been due to a safety problem from the poor maintenance of the tracks, bridges, or the locomotive and cars.

My first impression of North Korea was surprise over its economic backwardness. How had this part of Korea become such a pathetic, poor country! I could not help thinking that we had overestimated the North's capability in the past.

South Korea's per capita GNP had already passed $5,000 by then, but North Korea's was known to be about $1,000. Once I stepped foot in the North, I had a difficult time believing that figure. The North's economy was equivalent to that of South Korea in the mid-1960's. I resolved to help expedite unification so that both sides could have a better life and coexist in peace.

* * * * * * * * *

After disembarking the train, we drove through the streets of Pyongyang. We saw crowds of people in the city. Buildings in the heart of the city were balanced and of the same height. I was frequently attracted to certain large and impressive buildings that exhibited artistic grandeur.

There were gigantic symbolic structures throughout Pyongyang. These included the "Arch of Triumph," the largest arch of its kind in the world and a source of pride in the North; the enormous gold-colored Statue of Kim Il-sung, erected on Mansudae Hill; the 170-meter-high Juche Tower; and the Statue of the Flying Horse.

Unlike in the South, the state owned all the land in the North, and it was therefore free to plan and use the land according to its wishes. The state determined the site, scale, and height for the buildings it wished to construct. In this sense, it was not a surprise to see several gigantic structures throughout Pyongyang.

Perhaps because there was little traffic in the city, the streets looked very wide but nearly empty. There were several green areas that made me feel refreshed. Pyongyang truly seemed to be a city free of pollution. It had been completely reconstructed from the rubble of war. At first glance, Pyongyang appeared to be a very beautiful city. I was also surprised at the stark difference between Pyongyang and the rural areas, which we passed through on our way up.

Our delegation unpacked at Baekhwawon, where we would be staying, near the presidential palace. It was a state guesthouse built in 1983 to host visiting foreign dignitaries at the head-of-state level. It was a large three-story building, and the doors inside were three meters high. The marble floors of the guesthouse were covered with thick rugs, and small and large chandeliers hung down from the four-meter-high ceilings.

The second round of the High-Level Talks was held over two days on October 17 and 18 at the People's Palace of Culture. In his opening statement, the North's head of delegation, Yon Hyong-muk, presented a comparative analysis of both parties' positions as presented in the first round of the talks and a draft of the "declaration of nonaggression between the North and the South." The draft did not differ much in substance in that it included a list of subjects that we had been considering, including the universal principle of nonaggression, establishment of the borderline, no territorial aggression, and peaceful resolution of disputes.

According to Yon's analysis, "The different positions between the North and the South stemmed from both sides' differing unification formulas and prioritization of the issues to be resolved." He criticized the South by saying, "Unification as stipulated by the South's single-system unification formula is impossible to accomplish because under that formula, one side must eliminate the other, either peacefully or through war." He claimed, "The 'Koryo

Federation' is the only solution for unification that does not allow one side to take the other or be taken by the other. This federation would unify the nation into a single state with two systems and two local governments."

He continued, "The biggest internal impediment to unification is mutual distrust, and the key to the resolution of distrust is resolving political and military confrontation." Reemphasizing that political and military confrontation was the priority issue, he proposed the adoption of a declaration of nonaggression.

During his turn, our head of delegation, Kang Young-hoon, presented a supplementary proposal regarding issues for discussion. It contained a long list of thirty-two items, including passage, trade, economic exchange, and cooperation. In contrast to the North's "three urgent tasks," he argued in favor of resolving the South's own "three major issues": the abandonment of the North's revolutionary line, early realization of separated family members' visits to their hometowns, and vitalization of economic exchange and cooperation.

However, during the course of discussion, the North adopted a new position, saying that both political and military confrontation, and exchange and cooperation could be discussed in parallel. This resolved the question of having to prioritize issues for discussion. However, there was still the unresolved question of determining whether to put the North-South agreement in the form of a basic agreement or a nonaggression declaration.

When our delegation made a courtesy call on President Kim Il-sung, our head of delegation, Kang Young-hoon, cautiously proposed an inter-Korean summit, saying, "I hope the two leaders meet as soon as possible to have an openhearted discussion so that they may give us guidance." But President Kim's response showed that he was not ready for a summit:

> Please convey my message to President Roh Tae-woo. I am also looking forward to meeting him as soon as possible. But such a meeting must produce good results. Otherwise, it would only disappoint the people. So I hope that you effectively lead the work so that we can meet.

Our meeting with President Kim lasted only ten minutes. We moved to one side of the central hall to take pictures by the wall. I followed President Kim and Prime Minister Kang closely from behind. I saw the infamous egg-sized bump behind President Kim's right ear. He walked in a wobbly manner, as though his legs were struggling to support the weight of his upper body. I felt uneasy as I watched him walk. Prime Minister Kang, noting President Kim's health, tactfully asked, "So, what is your secret to maintaining your good health?" In a thick and strong voice, President Kim replied:

> I have an optimistic attitude towards life. I am confident that there is always a way to make the best out of a disaster. Even if the sky falls upon you, there is a way to rise up.

In those days during the wake of the collapse of Communism, North Korea was enthusiastically campaigning for unification. This was intended to serve as some type of shock treatment to prevent the influence of liberalization from Eastern Europe. The campaign seemed excessively zealous to me. From the children we met at the Youth Students Palace, to the reporters and guides from North Korean organizations, I heard the same urgently-pitched voice for unification. They all were calling for unification. Some of them cried out in tears, saying, "Unification will come soon."

Delaying Tactics

Having gone through two rounds of the High-Level Talks, both sides clarified their positions and the differences were made clear. The next task was to negotiate and reduce or resolve the differences. While our delegation was preparing for forthcoming negotiations, something odd happened.

The negotiating headquarters of our government, which until that point had been pushing the talks with a positive attitude, started raising suspicions about North Korea's intent and suddenly instructed us to delay the talks. We did not understand the rationale for the government's sudden shift in policy. Ultimately, although the representatives of both sides continued to meet, we failed to produce any results.

Three months later, I learned that Seo Dong-gwon, director of the National Security Planning Agency, had secretly visited Pyongyang in early October, and Yun Ki-bok, the Workers' Party Secretary for South Korean Affairs, had visited Seoul in early November. They met with the respective leader of each side and discussed the possibility of a summit, without much success.

From the beginning, our government had proposed an inter-Korean summit through the High-Level Talks. In subsequent secret contacts, we suggested to the North that the leaders of the two sides meet in a summit to sign a document of agreement that would be produced by the High-Level Talks, and to discuss ways to further improve North-South relations.

In response, the North insisted that "a summit should discuss national issues of high dimensions such as unification; therefore, before holding a summit, the High-Level Talks should first yield certain results." I learned that the North had turned down an early summit by saying, "a summit would disappoint the people if it does not produce good results, and no summit is better than just a photo opportunity." The more interest our side showed in a summit, the more high-handed the North became. The North simply kept asking the South to accept its unification formula of a "federation of two states with two systems."

Once it became obvious that the North would not agree to a summit, the South's negotiating headquarters decided to employ a delaying tactic as a means to pressure the North, which desired an early conclusion of negotiations. The North needed an early inter-Korean agreement of non-aggression and peace before it could start negotiations with the United States to resolve its hostile relationship with them and obtain U.S. assurance for its survival. North Korea also had a plan to pursue an early normalization of its relationship with Japan, from which the North wanted to receive reparations for Japan's colonial rule. The North needed financial assistance to rescue its struggling economy.

Since the North was in a desperate situation, the South's strategy to stick to its position while pressing the North for a summit through tactical delays seemed to make sense. However, this made no difference to the North.

Early April 1992, after the North-South Basic Agreement went into force, Yun Ki-bok came to Seoul again, carrying a message from President Kim Il-sung. The timing of Yun's visit coincided with the North's busy preparations for a grand celebration of Kim Il-sung's eightieth birthday. The message contained an unexpected proposal: "On the occasion of President Kim Il-sung's birthday on April 15, North Korea invites President Roh to Pyongyang for a summit meeting." This time, our government rejected the offer. The South did not want to be taken advantage of by the North, which was obviously trying to hold a summit as part of Kim Il-sung's birthday celebration.

* * * * * * * * *

The third round of the High-Level Talks was held from December 4, 1990, at the Shilla Hotel's Dynasty Hall in Seoul. Our side reiterated the position that "a basic agreement must first be adopted to improve relations, and then a joint military committee should be formed to discuss the issue of nonaggression."

The North came up with a new proposal that combined our proposal made at the second round of talks regarding a "joint declaration of reconciliation and cooperation between the North and the South," with their proposal of a "declaration of nonaggression." This time the North suggested that we label an integrated agreement as a "Declaration of Nonaggression, Reconciliation, and Cooperation." In fact, our side's proposal of a basic agreement and the North's revised proposal had by then become very similiar in substance. The North definitely desired an agreement, and we could have pulled off a deal if we had been willing.

Intent on a summit, however, the South implemented a delaying tactic on the issue of nonaggression, and we ended up losing an opportunity for a successful conclusion to the negotiations. This was our big mistake. In the end, we failed to hold a summit and agree on an inter-Korean basic agreement. Our mistake caused a deadlock that lasted for an entire year.

By the time we adopted the agreement, President Roh's term in office was in its final phase, and a presidential election campaign had already started warming up. The political situation simply did not allow the government to push its ambitious plans to improve relations with the North. This was unfortunate for the improvement of North-South relations and for the future of the nation.

After the third round, the High-Level Talks entered a long stalemate. It was agreed that a fourth round would convene in Pyongyang on February 25, 1991, but the North unilaterally cancelled it on the grounds of the start of the Gulf War in January 1991 and the combined U.S.-ROK Team Spirit exercise in March 1991. It took ten more months before the talks resumed. During this period, North Korea was confronted with various difficulties in political, economic, social, and diplomatic areas.

* * * * * * * * *

On the international scene, there were several significant developments that decisively impacted the strategic situation on the Korean Peninsula. The Soviet Union had normalized relations with South Korea. China had set up a trade mission in Seoul to increase trade and elevate the level of economic cooperation with the South. Both the Soviet Union and China had been firm in their positions to support the dual entry of the North and South into the United Nations. North Korea was no longer able to insist on its "one-Korea policy." Falling short of the expectations that the North's talks with Japan on normalization would be successfully concluded within six months, they hit a snag and had made no progress at all. On top of these developments, in the wake of the Gulf War, the United States had started pressuring the North, raising suspicions about the latter's nuclear development program.

Against the backdrop of these international developments, President Kim Il-sung was pushed to a point of making an important decision. At China's advice, he decided to accept the simultaneous dual entry of the North and the South into the United Nations. This meant that North Korea had given up its "one-Korea policy" in the international arena. At this time the United States announced the withdrawal of all tactical nuclear weapons deployed overseas (September 28, 1991), and the Soviet Union immediately took a corresponding measure. Soon afterwards, all tactical nuclear weapons were withdrawn from South Korea.

In this context, in a speech to the UN General Assembly, President Roh Tae-woo urged North Korea "to give up its nuclear development program," and expressed his "willingness to promote discussion of the nuclear issue between the North and the South." Until that point, South Korea had been silent on the nuclear issues due to the U.S. policy of "no confirmation, no denial" (NCND). On the other hand, this development provided a new opportunity for North Korea, which had been demanding withdrawal of nuclear weapons from the South, establishment of a nuclear-weapons-free zone in the Korean Peninsula, and suspension of nuclear war exercises. Immediately after President Bush's announcement of nuclear weapons withdrawal, North Korea welcomed it with an official comment: "Now our legitimate demands have been realized."

* * * * * * * * *

China's strong influence in allowing North Korea to return to the table for a negotiated settlement cannot be overlooked. In early November 1991 I met with a leading North Korea specialist from China during his visit to Seoul. I learned important information from him and reported it to the Blue House. According to the Chinese visitor, President Kim Il-sung visited China for ten days in early October that year (October 3–14) and toured China's Special Economic Zone. During his visit, he was advised by Deng Xiaoping and other top Chinese leaders to do three things: first, undertake opening and economic reform while maintaining a socialist system like China; second, seek an early conclusion of the North-South negotiations for inducement of foreign capital and technology, which would require an environment of peace and security on the Korean Peninsula; and third, resolve suspicions of North Korea's nuclear development program, seizing the opportunity of the U.S. withdrawal of nuclear weapons from South Korea.

According to the same specialist from China, after his return from China, Kim Il-sung immediately called a Politburo meeting on October 16 to announce his decision to reach an early conclusion of the North-South negotiations, agree on denuclearization, and establish a special economic zone. In addition, he made the so-called strategic decision to pursue normalized relations with the United States as the top priority, using the nuclear issue as the North's best negotiating leverage.

When I reported this information to the office of the National Security Advisor at the Blue House, they accepted it as "sufficiently plausible." They started to become optimistic about adopting a basic North-South agreement and resolving the nuclear issue. It took only two months to confirm the information. Toward the end of that year, the Basic North-South Agreement was adopted (December 13) and the adoption of the Joint Declaration of the Denuclearization of the Korean Peninsula was agreed upon (December 31). In addition, the North announced a plan to establish the Rajin-Sonbong Special Economic Zone (December 28).

The North's circumstances required that it expedite the North-South agreement in order to solve its economic problems and extricate itself from international isolation. The North also wanted one of the results of the inter-Korean talks to be a cessation of the Team Spirit exercise. Its domestic politics demanded that it hold a big celebration in honor of President Kim Il-sung's eightieth birthday in April of the following year.

For the South, the incumbent president only had about a year left in his term, and it was desirable that the North-South talks yield some results before the presidential election campaigns were in full swing. Negotiations with the North had been the government's top priority. The government's obsession with a summit led to a delaying tactic, which unfortunately put the talks into a deadlock. The government did not expect the deadlock to last almost a year. The South concluded that it could no longer hold on to the unlikely prospect of an inter-Korean summit.

CHAPTER 5

BASIC AGREEMENT AND DENUCLEARIZATION

How to Negotiate

Once the leaders of the North and South had decided to reach a settlement, the negotiation process began moving swiftly. At this point, determining the negotiating strategy and approach was less important than the determination to achieve a negotiated settlement itself. Once the negotiators confirmed this, they followed their leaders' wills.

After a wasteful one-year hiatus, the fourth round of the North-South High-Level Talks was held in Pyongyang at the end of October 1991. During this time, the two sides agreed upon the title and format for the North-South Basic Agreement. Subsequently, at the fifth round of talks that was held in the middle of December in Seoul, both sides agreed to announce the substance and language to be used in the historic document.

* * * * * * * * *

On the morning of October 22, our delegation was aboard a special train from Kaesong bound for Pyongyang. North Korean representative Choi Woo-jin came to my compartment, where he and I candidly discussed the issues that would be subject to negotiation when the two sides met in Pyongyang. It had been a long time since we last had a similar opportunity. Ever since we first worked together on the issue of UN admission, we had developed a useful working relationship and were comfortable expressing frank and candid views with one another. I believe both of us played the role of problem-solvers in the inter-Korean negotiations.

When Choi walked into my compartment, he began expressing his views on the withdrawal of U.S. nuclear weapons from the South:

U.S. President Bush's announcement to withdraw nuclear weapons from the South has improved the situation. We welcome his decision to withdraw all tactical nuclear weapons from the Korean Peninsula, and we want to trust his decision. After the withdrawal of U.S. nuclear weapons, we will sign a safeguard agreement with the IAEA to accept its inspections. The South would have no reason, I believe, to oppose our proposition to make the Korean Peninsula a nuclear-weapons-free zone, with the support of the surrounding nuclear states. We are going to propose a nuclear-free Korean Peninsula during this round of talks. "

If Choi was right, that meant we could look forward to discussing the nuclear issue in addition to the adoption of the Basic Agreement. Choi and I also discussed many other subjects. We promised to work together to produce an agreement this time. For the title of the Basic Agreement, we agreed that it should include "reconciliation," "nonaggression," and "exchange and cooperation."

Our candid exchange of views lasted about an hour. It was very valuable because in North-South dialogues, if one side makes a claim based on inaccurate information or lack of understanding of the other party's intent, it often became difficult to change its initial position. Frank, unofficial dialogues with Choi Woo-jin helped us gain mutual understanding, a requirement for the successful conclusion of talks.

After we arrived in Pyongyang, we checked into our lodgings, where we immediately held a delegates meeting. At the meeting, I briefed the delegation on my discussion with Choi Woo-jin on the train. I believed my briefing substantially contributed to the realignment of our position.

* * * * * * * * * *

The next day at the opening session of the fourth round of the High-Level Talks, held at the People's Palace of Culture, the North's Premier Yon proposed a joint declaration of a nuclear-weapons-free zone for the Korean Peninsula. He said that peace was the most urgent issue to resolve. He also said that when the total and complete withdrawal of U.S. nuclear weapons from the South was confirmed, the North would accept inspections in compliance with international agreements.

In addition, Premier Yon presented a proposed agenda for the fourth round, which accommodated the South's demand for a draft of a "declaration of nonaggression, reconciliation and cooperation and exchange." He expressed strong expectation for the adoption of a "new draft declaration, which reflected the North's will to find a breakthrough to the talks through concessions and compromises."

Our side in turn urged the North to "work together with the South to change the armistice into an inter-Korean peace mechanism, to promote arms reduction based on military confidence-building measures, and to make concrete efforts to realize free exchange of visits, logistics, and information." The South also asked the North "to suspend its nuclear development and accept IAEA inspections without conditions."

As for the agenda for the fourth round of talks, the South proposed a single comprehensive agreement on "reconciliation, non-aggression, and exchange and cooperation." Presenting a draft agreement, the South pressed for the adoption of the agreement during the fourth round.

Thanks to my previous discussion with Choi Woo-jin—through which both sides were able to ascertain the other's position—it was not difficult for the negotiators to agree to adopt the format of a single document during the first day. That evening, a working-level meeting was held.

For the working-level meeting, the South was represented by Senior Delegate and Vice Minister of Unification Song Han-ho, myself, and a new delegate, Lee Dong-bok. The North was represented by Senior Delegate and Cabinet Councilor Paek Nam-sun and delegates Choi Woo-jin and Kim Young-cheol. Our discussion continued until late that evening. Afterwards, the six delegates met several more times until the agreement was finally adopted.

The format of the agreement was not difficult to agree upon. The working-level delegates agreed that the title of the agreement would be "Agreement on Reconciliation, Nonaggression, and Exchange and Cooperation between the North and South," and that the structure would consist of sections in the following order: preamble, North-South reconciliation, North-South nonaggression, North-South exchange and cooperation, and amendment and implementation.

We also discussed the actual substance of the agreement, but the North adamantly opposed some of the points that were included in the South's draft. In the end, we agreed to discuss the contentious issues separately through delegates at Panmunjom.

During the plenary meeting of the fourth round of talks, we formally agreed to proceed at the working level with what had been negotiated. The plenary also discussed issues related to the declaration of the nuclear-weapons-free zone and North Korea's acceptance of IAEA inspections. However, we realized that these issues would not be resolved during this meeting.

Nevertheless, although we had not been able to produce any specific document, this fourth round was extremely valuable in that it broke the yearlong deadlock and everyone assented to the title and structure of the agreement.

* * * * * * * * *

Prior to holding the fifth round of talks, four working-level meetings were held for two weeks at Panmunjom, beginning on November 11. Three representatives from each side participated. Although mutual understanding had increased, points of dispute still remained.

For example, the North and South had different unification formulas. Yet, both sides shared the view that unification should be achieved by independence, peace, and national unity through a gradual, step-by-step approach, confidence-building, the removal of political and military hurdles, and the promotion of exchange and cooperation.

However, the North was still concerned about the South's possible absorption of North Korea, and the South was still uneasy about the North's possible communization of the South.

Regarding the issue of peace, the two sides developed a proposition that the promotion of reconciliation and cooperation and assurance of nonaggression should be pursued in parallel, and that these elements should be incorporated into a comprehensive agreement. The North raised the issue of American troop withdrawal, but they quickly dropped it as the negotiations moved forward.

During the initial phase of negotiations concerning the issue of arms reduction, the South wanted to first build confidence before reducing arms, whereas the North argued that arms reduction precede confidence-building measures. However, both sides soon agreed that both could be simultaneously pursued. The North and South also developed a common understanding that the nuclear issue should be discussed as a separate issue.

Although both sides were easily able to agree upon the basic agenda for the talks, the North firmly maintained its stance on the details of some important issues. For example, in order to adopt an effective agreement, the South attempted to push through some provisions that were not originally included in the North's proposal. However, the North would not accept them.

After the four rounds of discussions between the North and South, most provisions had been resolved, but there remained some unsettled issues, including a peace agreement, guaranteeing non-aggression, and the issue of a maritime border. It seemed that there was no way to satisfactorily resolve these issues.

The South argued that the state of armistice should be transformed into a "solid state of peace between the South and the North," while maintaining the Military Armistice Agreement until such a peace regime was established.

In contrast, the North insisted that it would not sign a peace agreement with the South, which was not a signatory to the Military Armistice Agreement and had no right of operational command over its own troops. The North maintained that it would sign a peace treaty with the United States, and only a non-aggression agreement with the South. Given that the issue of a peace agreement was vital to the success or failure of the talks, the South dedicated many strenuous hours of effort to this topic. Yet, the North would not back down on this issue.

As for a maritime border on the West Sea (the Yellow Sea), which was not defined by the Military Armistice Agreement, our side insisted that a clear borderline be fixed according to the practice of control that existed at the time. However, the North refused. They did not accept the Northern Limit Line (NLL), which had been unilaterally drawn by the United Nations Command. The North insisted on claiming a twelve-nautical-mile limit to territorial waters according the Law of the Sea Treaty.

In addition, the South insisted that provisions of military confidence-building measures and the principles of arms reduction be clearly included in the Basic Agreement. However, the North opposed this, saying that such detailed issues could be discussed at the Joint Military Commission, which would later be established.

* * * * * * * * *

Around this time, there were growing suspicions concerning North Korea's nuclear development program. Some newspapers expressed views opposing the adoption of the North-South Basic Agreement "unless the nuclear issue is resolved." Those involved in the negotiation strategy at the Ministry of Unification began to share the same views.

This group of people held the firm opinion that it was impossible to expect a change in the North's attitude, and that there was no possibility for the adoption of an inter-Korean agreement. They argued that since there was no prospect of adopting an agreement, the South should forcefully press the North on the nuclear issue. In the end, we did not fulfill the agreement at the working level "to complete the draft language for a North-South agreement."

This failure was attributed to the absence of a firm position on our side concerning those important issues in dispute, which were difficult to resolve to begin with.

First, there was the question of whether to link the issue of nuclear inspection with the adoption of the Basic Agreement or to pursue the two issues in parallel. In other words, there was a question of choosing between a "strategy of nuclear linkage" or a "parallel strategy." However, the South had failed to make the choice.

Second, there was a question of deciding whether to suspend the Team Spirit exercise for the following year. It was clear that the North could not agree to the Basic Agreement without the suspension of the combined ROK-U.S. military exercise. However, the South Korean defense minister opposed the suspension of the Team Spirit exercise. In the end, the United States held the key to this issue.

Third, there was a question of linking an inter-Korean summit to the Basic Agreement. While the North was clearly not in favor of a summit, the South's negotiating headquarters preferred that the Basic Agreement be adopted at a North-South summit meeting.

It was not until November 22, after an interagency ministers' meeting was held in advance of the fifth round of the High-Level Talks, that we fortified our position on those critical issues. On the North Korean nuclear issue, the South chose a "parallel strategy" that separated the nuclear issue from the Basic Agreement. We also decided to separate the issue of a summit from the adoption of the Basic Agreement.

Regarding the Team Spirit exercise for 1992, the United States conveyed to South Korea that it would consider cancelling the exercise. The United States had a keen interest in nuclear non-proliferation and was supportive of South Korea's efforts to have the North accept international nuclear inspections and improve inter-Korean relations.

Many insiders believe this positive development between South Korea and the United States was made possible due to Blue House National Security Advisor Kim Chong-whi's close consultation with Donald Gregg, the American ambassador to Korea.

Donald P. Gregg served in the CIA for more than thirty years and served as its station chief in Korea; he later was appointed national security advisor to Vice President George H.W. Bush for six years before serving as ambassador to Seoul from 1989 to 1993. He had a deep understanding of the issues affecting the Korean Peninsula as well as an affection for the Korean people. He supported an engagement policy toward North Korea. After retiring from government, he continued to contribute to the resolution of the Korean question as president and chairman of the Korea Society in New York.

"We Brought the Seal with Us"

The fifth round of the North-South High-Level Talks was held December 10–13, 1991, at the Sheraton Grand Walkerhill Hotel in Seoul. On the first day, I went to Panmunjom to meet the North Korean delegation, and once again rode in the same car with North Korean delegate Choi Woo-jin on our way to the hotel. We talked for about an hour and a half. Choi began the conversation by saying:

> We've brought the seal to use on an agreement. This time, we should make a final agreement. Let's do it through concession and compromise.

We touched on the points of dispute such as provisions on measures guaranteeing non-aggression, and the transformation of the Military Armistice Agreement into a peace regime between the North and the South. Once again, we realized the difficulty in resolving these issues.

I said: "On these two particular issues, there is no room for our side to compromise. It will only be possible to adopt an agreement when the North accepts our positions."

At my firm statement, Choi Woo-jin appeared uncomfortable. But he welcomed President Roh Tae-woo's November 8 declaration of denuclearization, adding that "after the adoption of the Basic Agreement, it would be possible to produce an agreement on the nuclear issue as well, and the North would be able to accept nuclear inspections."

He also alluded to a possible North-South summit. Since this was what our side wanted, if Choi's words were indeed credible, I thought we would be able to make significant progress.

After arriving at the hotel, our delegation had a meeting to consolidate and analyze the information we had collected from the North Korean delegates. I made a detailed report on my conversation with Choi Woo-jin. The deputy delegate, Kim Chong-whi, who rode in the same car with Premier Yon, the head of the North Korean delegation, also reported that Yon had said, "This time we have President Kim Il-sung's instruction to produce an agreement. Let's agree this time without fail. Let's immediately have a meeting and produce an agreement. If we do that, it would also be possible to hold a summit. Let's also hasten economic cooperation."

These advance statements and positions of the North were immediately reported to our higher office. At an inter-agency meeting held that evening, we reconfirmed our goal to adopt the Basic Agreement at the fifth round of the talks.

* * * * * * * * * *

The first plenary meeting of the fifth round was an open session at the Sheraton Grand Walkerhill Hotel. During the meeting, the South presented a proposal that addressed a few points on the issues that were still in dispute. It also introduced a written draft for a joint declaration of denuclearization. In addition, the South presented an urgent proposal for conducting simultaneous nuclear inspections in both the North and South by the end of January 1992.

According to the proposal for mutual nuclear inspections, our side would inspect the Yongbyon nuclear facilities and the Sunan airport, and the North would inspect U.S. military bases such as the air force base at Gunsan. Our proposal was made based on the advice of the United States.

In response, the North said it would be willing to compromise for the purpose of adopting a North-South agreement. The North Koreans proposed setting up liaison offices at Panmunjom instead of Pyongyang and Seoul. Also to our surprise, the North conceded on the issue of a maritime border. The North expressed its willingness to continue the discussion of the maritime border issue. Until an agreement was reached for the maritime border, both sides would honor the existing zones currently under control by each side.

The North praised South Korean President Roh's declaration of denuclearization as a step forward. It expressed its interest in adopting a joint declaration of denuclearization based on the points of Roh's declaration and the content of the North's own version of a declaration of a nuclear-weapons-free zone.

However, the North Koreans made clear they still opposed a peace agreement, insisting that the South be freed from its dependence on the United States if it wanted to gain the authority to raise the issue of a peace agreement.

* * * * * * * * *

As agreed upon by the plenary that morning, a six-member group meeting was held in the afternoon in order to negotiate the text of the Basic Agreement. At the request of the North, negotiations proceeded in the form of free discussion, with the microphones turned off and no tape recorders.

This marked a new practice since the beginning of the North-South High-Level Talks. Until that point, all North-South meetings were wired by microphones to Pyongyang and Seoul for monitoring by their negotiation headquarters.

Conscious of their monitors in Pyongyang, the North Korean delegates often seemed to make hardline statements, and frequently received new instructions from their headquarters. Therefore, having a closed meeting without the use of microphones meant that the North Korean delegation had some level of discretionary authority. This increased the prospects of a successful negotiation.

The compromise proposal for setting up a liaison office at Panmunjom, as well as the proposal for temporary agreement on a maritime border based on the existing zones of jurisdiction exercised by each side, had already been reflected in the revised proposals of both sides. This eliminated all obstacles in reaching an agreement on these issues.

However, the North Korean side was consistent at both the plenary and the six-member meeting in its adamant opposition on the issues of "guaranteeing the implementation of non-aggression" and an "inter-Korean peace regime." The North also criticized the South, saying, "Arms reduction is an urgent issue, but the South is insisting on following European-style military confidence-building measures that have taken more than ten years."

The purpose of military confidence-building measures was to guarantee the transparency of military operations and to prevent mutual suspicion and miscalculation. Yet, the North was unwilling to accommodate this, saying, "Such measures would not be significant in the area of military affairs, which require the protection of classified information more than any other area."

The first meeting of delegates adjourned before dinner-time. The South concluded that the North would make no concessions on the two issues in dispute. The South unilaterally put off the second meeting of delegates until the next day. The negotiation faced another breaking point.

North-South Basic Agreement

That night I had gone to bed early. When the phone later rang, it was an unexpected call from North Korean delegate Choi Woo-jin. He said,

> We agreed to continue our talks after dinner. How can you be in bed while we are waiting for you? Mr. Lim, I want to see you now. What's holding your side back from reaching an agreement? Did I not tell you yesterday that our side was ready to agree this time? Agreement is possible. Please come to my room now.

I was alarmed. It was late at night, but Choi wanted to see me. Since he said "agreement is possible," I assumed he must have received new instructions from Pyongyang. I told him that I would come to his room. I got out of bed quickly, put on my clothes and went to Deputy Delegate Kim Chong-whi's room and rang the bell. But there was no response. It was strange. I notified the situation room that I would be meeting with Choi. Then I went up to the seventeenth floor where the North Korean delegation was staying.

Choi met me with a smile and offered me North Korean beer he had brought from Pyongyang. That night the two of us talked for forty minutes until two o'clock in the morning, and we were able to achieve a breakthrough to the negotiation deadlock. Choi seemed to have received new instructions from Pyongyang. He reiterated that "the Basic Agreement must be adopted this time." He alluded to the North's acceptance of the provision regarding the transformation of the Armistice to a "state of peace between the North and the South," which was the most important issue to the South.

Choi also told me that the North had decided to accept our proposal to hold a working-level meeting at Panmunjom to discuss the denuclearization of the Korean Peninsula. In addition, he suggested that he and I jointly produce a mutually acceptable proposal regarding another sticking point—the implementation measures for non-aggression. He suggested that we submit this proposal to our respective superiors.

The South's proposal consisted of four military confidence-building measures (Article 12), principles of arms control (Article 13), verification methods (Article 14), and establishment and operation of a joint military commission (Article 16). On the other hand, the North Korean proposal simply stated that "military confidence and arms reduction shall be implemented," without any mention of specific measures or principles.

We agreed we would include all points of the South's proposals with adjustments that the North would be able to accept without losing face after shifting from their previous positions. The four items that were included in the South's proposal regarding the implementation of non-aggression were reduced to one provision. We agreed this provision should be carried out as a "task for a joint military commission."

Our compromise version became the basis for Article 12 in the Basic Agreement. Choi and I were confident that our joint product would be acceptable to our superiors. We shook hands to reaffirm our mission in reaching a successful conclusion at the end of the process.

* * * * * * * * *

I returned to our floor of the hotel and knocked on the door of Kim Chong-whi's room. Our delegates Song Han-ho and Lee Dong-bok were there with Kim. I briefed them on my private meeting with the North Korean delegate. I learned that while I was meeting with Choi Woo-jin, Kim Chong-whi was meeting with Northern delegate Ahn Byung-soo at the request of the North. Kim said he and Ahn "agreed to produce a final agreement this time." They also agreed to reconvene the delegates meeting soon.

The four of us reviewed the proposal formed between Choi Woo-jin and myself. Kim, Song, and Lee were all surprised and pleased with the compromised solution that Choi and I had worked out together. We agreed to report it for approval to the inter-ministerial meeting that was scheduled for 7:30 a.m. I wrote up a two-page report on the results of my midnight contact with Choi Woo-jin.

This report was immediately forwarded to the inter-ministerial meeting and the Blue House. Prime Minister Chung Won-shik told us at our 8:30 a.m. delegates meeting that the inter-ministerial meeting approved the compromise by Choi Woo-jin and myself without any revision. Prime Minister Chung ordered immediate contact with the North Korean delegates to finalize the proposal for adoption.

* * * * * * * * * *

The second day's plenary of the High-Level Talks was held on the morning of December 12 at ten o'clock for a brief twenty minutes and adjourned after confirming the mutual agreement to promptly resume the six-member working-level meeting.

That second working-level meeting lasted about seven hours, until six o'clock. Again, no microphones or tape recorders were turned on, and uninhibited free discussions unfolded in a friendly atmosphere. Now that the sticking points were resolved, our discussion focused on language and the order of provisions for a final agreement.

At last, the six-member delegate meeting finished writing the text for the Basic Agreement. The delegates were proud and pleased with their accomplishment. Thus, the negotiation of the Basic Agreement was completed thirty-two hours after it began at ten o'clock on the morning of December 11, 1991.

With seventy million Koreans and the whole world were watching, the North-South Basic Agreement was adopted at a signing ceremony at nine o'clock on the morning of December 13, 1991. It was entitled "Agreement on Reconciliation, Nonaggression and Exchange and Cooperation between the South and the North" (usually referred to as the North-South Basic Agreement) and consisted of four chapters and twenty-five articles. This historic document was signed by Chung Won-shik, Chief Delegate of the South's delegation, as the Prime Minister of the Republic of Korea, and by Yon Hyong-muk, Head of the North's delegation, as the Premier of the Administration Council of the Democratic People's Republic of Korea.

The author (*right*), as vice minister of unification, exchanges ratified copies of the North-South Basic Agreement with North Korean representative Choi Woo-jin (*left*) at Panmunjom in January 1992. Courtesy Lim Dong-won.

This was the first time since the history of the Korean division that the North and South ever printed their official titles of state in an inter-Korean agreement. With the signing of the agreement, the two sides agreed to hold delegate contacts at Panmunjom in December that year, with a shared view that the Korean Peninsula should be free of nuclear weapons.

In a concluding remark, the North Korean head of delegation declared, "Now we are on the same path to peace, reduction of tension, and unification." The South Korean chief delegate declared, "The North and South now have a common foundation to promote coexistence and co-prosperity toward peace and unification. This agreement ends an era of confrontation and division and opens a new era of cooperation and unification."

* * * * * * * * *

The Basic Agreement adopted that day recognized that "North-South relations, not being a relationship between states, constitute a special interim relationship stemming from the process towards unification," and pledged to exert joint efforts to achieve peaceful unification. The agreement contained three areas of content:

- For reconciliation between the North and South—the two sides will recognize and respect each other's systems; will not interfere in each other's internal affairs; will suspend slander and vilification of one another; will not attempt to sabotage or subvert the other; will cooperate in the international arena; and will transform the present state of armistice into a solid state of peace on the Korean Peninsula, while abiding by the present Military Armistice Agreement until such a state of peace is realized.
- For nonaggression—the two sides will not use force and undertake armed aggression against each other; will resolve disputes through dialogue and negotiation; and will maintain the current Military Demarcation Line and the areas under one another's jurisdictions. [This agreement to respect the MDL and the areas of jurisdiction has been kept to this date.] To guarantee nonaggression, the two sides will realize various military confidence-building measures and will promote arms reduction.
- For exchange and cooperation between the North and South—the two sides will carry out exchange and cooperation in various fields such as the economy, science and technology, culture, arts, health, sports and the press. The two sides will realize meetings and reunions of separated families, re-link the railways and roads that have been cut off, open maritime and air routes, and establish postal and telecommunications services.

After we concluded the signing ceremony, both delegations went to the Blue House. The main building on the Blue House compound, which had been newly built in the traditional Korean architectural style with blue roof tiles, looked reassuringly grand and refreshing. President Roh Tae-woo held a one-on-one meeting with North Korean Premier Yon Hyong-muk. This meeting was followed by a luncheon reception hosted by President Roh, who was pleased with the adoption of a "good agreement." He congratulated all the delegates on their contributions. He said, "As the saying goes, 'beginning something is halfway completing it.' From now on we should all work toward bringing about the monumental historic achievement of unification."

In response, Premier Yon said, "The adoption of this Basic Agreement, I believe, provides a new turning point towards unification. We shall do our best to faithfully carry out this agreement."

It was 4:40 p.m. when the Northern delegation returned to Panmunjom to cross the border into their side of the land. It was reported that they flew by helicopter from Kaesong to Pyongyang and were warmly received by President Kim Il-sung.

Joint Declaration of the Denuclearization of the Korean Peninsula

Right after the start of the Gulf War in February 1991, suspicions of a North Korean nuclear program surfaced. According to U.S. intelligence sources, North Korea had been operating a 30-megawatt atomic reactor (which later was confirmed to be a 5-megawatt reactor) since 1987. The reactor seemed to be for military use, "capable of producing plutonium to make a nuclear bomb in a year." The same sources claimed that the construction of a reprocessing plant that would extract plutonium from spent fuel rods was near completion.

Ever since the end of the Cold War, the United States regarded "prevention of nuclear proliferation" as one of its foreign policy's primary tasks. The United States was seriously concerned the North Korean development of nuclear weapons would lead South Korea to seek its own nuclear development program, with Japan finding a rationale to do the same. Although Japan had declared their "three non-nuclear principles" long ago, there were concerns that the situation would change if North Korea possessed nuclear weapons. Accordingly, preventing North Korea from developing nuclear weapons became a critical issue for the United States.

Most of the world's countries (as well as South Korea) had joined the Treaty on the Non-Proliferation of Nuclear Weapons (NPT), created in 1970 at the initiative of the five declared nuclear powers, including the United States and the Soviet Union. The NPT obliged its member states to receive international nuclear inspections. North Korea also joined the NPT in 1985 in return for the Soviet Union's promise for assistance to build a nuclear power plant.

However, when the outlook for Soviet assistance became unpromising after the emergence of Mikhail Gorbachev, North Korea refused to sign the IAEA Safeguards Agreements, rejecting IAEA inspections. In response to increasing international pressure, North Korea—which had been vulnerable to the nuclear threats of the United States since the Korean War—listed a set of preconditions for its acceptance of IAEA inspections. The conditions included U.S. assurance against nuclear threats, suspension of U.S.-ROK Team Spirit "nuclear war exercise," withdrawal of nuclear weapons from South Korea, and the establishment of a nuclear-weapons-free zone on the Korean Peninsula. The United States disregarded these demands.

* * * * * * * * *

Under these circumstances, there was an unexpected breakthrough regarding the withdrawal of nuclear weapons from the U.S. forces in Korea. On September 28, 1991, President George H. W. Bush announced the withdrawal and dismantlement of all tactical nuclear weapons deployed overseas.

This announcement, after which nuclear weapons were withdrawn from South Korea, was made as an emergency measure to prevent the proliferation of Soviet nuclear weapons in the midst of the crisis of the disintegration of the Soviet Union. The Soviet Union followed suit when President Gorbachev declared "the Soviet Union will withdraw all tactical nuclear weapons deployed in the republics of the Soviet Union and it will destroy them."

Nuclear weapons had existed since 1957 in South Korea, and it was known that at one time there were as many as 760 nuclear warheads there. However, the number was drastically reduced in the 1980s during the Carter administration, to about a hundred. With President Bush's announcement, approximately forty W33 artillery shells and sixty B61 bombs (designed to be delivered by aircraft) were all removed from the South.

Seizing this opportunity, South Korea shifted from its policy of NCND (neither confirm nor deny) to directly raise the nuclear issue with North Korea. President Roh Tae-woo announced a "Declaration of Denuclearization and Peace Building on the Korean Peninsula" (November 8, 1991), which read, in part, "The Republic of Korea shall not manufacture, possess, or use nuclear weapons, nor shall the ROK possess reprocessing or enrichment facilities." President Roh urged North Korea to do the same.

* * * * * * * * *

After North Korean nuclear suspicions were raised, several U.S. officials, including the director of the Arms Control and Disarmament Agency, nuclear specialists, and other members of the intelligence community, made frequent visits to Seoul to warn of the danger of North Korean nuclear development. They explained to us how we should deal with it, as though they were teaching us. As South Korean representative for arms control, I organized and participated in several meetings with them.

Through these meetings, South Korea and the United States developed common directives for the "promotion of negotiation."

First, priority was to be given to the prevention or abandonment of North Korea's reprocessing and uranium enrichment facilities. To this end, we chose to work towards the adoption of a "joint declaration of denuclearization." We decided to induce North Korea's abandonment by means of mutual abandonment between the North and the South. To obtain North Korean agreement, the South would first declare it would not build such facilities.

Second, South Korea would seek early implementation of mutual nuclear inspections between the North and the South as a test case. At this time, the United States wanted to confirm, with eyes on the ground, the information on North Korean nuclear facilities that had been collected through the analysis of satellite pictures. Verifying the reprocessing facilities solely by satellite images was difficult. The timing coincided with North Korea's interest in confirming the withdrawal of U.S. nuclear weapons from the South. We took this opportunity to propose immediate implementation of mutual nuclear inspections between the North and the South.

Third, South Korea and the United States agreed to urge North Korea to immediately sign IAEA safeguards agreements and to accept early IAEA inspections. Since this issue was to be resolved between North Korea and the international organization, and not solely with South Korea, we agreed to consider linking the issue with North Korea's demand for suspending the U.S.-ROK Team Spirit military exercise.

Fourth, with regard to an inter-Korean nuclear inspection system, the United States strongly desired "challenge inspections" to inspect undeclared nuclear facilities and materials as well as "military facilities." IAEA inspections were limited to "civilian facilities and materials" declared by a state, with no access to military facilities. Challenge inspections would complement deficiencies in the IAEA system by allowing inspectors to determine objects for inspection themselves and to inspect undeclared suspicious sites as well.

* * * * * * * * *

On December 26, 1991, one week after President Roh declared, "There is not a single nuclear weapon in our country," representatives of the North and South held a meeting at Panmunjom for negotiations on the nuclear issue. President Roh's statement directly confirmed in the name of the head of state of South Korea that the withdrawal of U.S. nuclear weapons had been completed. This provided justification for North Korea to respond to an effort to adopt a joint declaration of denuclearization.

At the meeting, each side was represented by two delegates and three assistants. As the chief delegate for the South, I was sitting across from my North Korean counterpart Choi Woo-jin. Delegate Lee Dong-bok was sitting next to me, and Delegate Kim Young-cheol was sitting next to Choi.

In my opening statement at the first meeting, I urged the North to accept international nuclear inspections as soon as possible. I told them that the South would accept inspections of U.S. military bases, and proposed that simultaneous nuclear inspections be conducted within a month between the North and the South.

In addition, I reintroduced a draft joint declaration of the denuclearization of the Korean Peninsula that was previously proposed. I refuted the North's proposal for the establishment of a nuclear-weapons-free zone based on the unrealistic nature of its content. Given the vast difference between the two proposals, I could foresee the difficulties of negotiation.

The North's Choi Woo-jin said, "In the wake of the South's 'declaration of non-existence of nuclear weapons,' the North has also issued a foreign ministry statement defining our position on the issue of international nuclear inspections." He added that since the issue was to be resolved between the North and the IAEA, the South should not interfere.

In an ensuing negotiation, the North, contrary to our expectations, withdrew its proposal for the establishment of nuclear-weapons-free zone, and presented its own draft version of a joint declaration of denuclearization, which was quite similar to our draft. Their draft said that North Korea would not produce, possess, or use nuclear weapons, and it would use nuclear energy only for peaceful purposes. It also proposed the establishment and operation of a "North-South Joint Nuclear Control Commission." The draft also accepted one of our most critical demands that North Korea not possess reprocessing and uranium enrichment facilities.

We did not expect such a change in the North's attitude. We were surprised and at the same time encouraged. However, problems still remained. The most controversial point at the negotiation was our proposal on the designation of objects for inspection, which reflected the concept of a challenge inspection. The North adamantly objected. In the end, we settled on a provision stating that inspections shall be conducted on the "objects selected by the other party and agreed upon between both parties." This compromise was Lee Dong-bok's idea.

* * * * * * * * *

On December 31, a third meeting was held at Tongilgak on the North Korean side of Panmunjom. After seven hours and thirty-five minutes of discussion, we finally arrived at a successful conclusion and produced another historic document—"Joint Declaration of the Denuclearization of the Korean Peninsula."

It took three rounds of meetings to achieve the goal of adopting the Joint Declaration of Denuclearization. In the process, our side urged North Korea to sign IAEA Safeguards Agreements and to accept IAEA inspections, while the North demanded the immediate suspension of the Team Spirit exercise. These issues had to be resolved in a package deal.

After a series of repeated arguments, the two sides agreed that their governments would announce the content of the agreement on January 7 of the following year, at ten o'clock in the morning. The South Korean government was to announce the suspension of the Team Spirit exercise, and North Korea would officially declare that it would promptly sign IAEA Safeguards Agreements and ratify them without delay through due legal procedures. The governments of the two sides made their announcements on schedule as agreed.

On December 31, at 5:30 p.m., the senior delegates of both sides signed the Joint Declaration of Denuclearization, and agreed to put the declaration into effect at the upcoming sixth round of the North-South High-Level Talks.

The news of the adoption of the Joint Declaration of Denuclearization quickly spread through television and radio to the world at the very start of 1992. It was like sending New Year's greeting cards with a message of joy and peace to the nations of the world. Reactions from the United States and many other countries to the news of the adoption of the Joint Declaration of Denuclearization and North Korea's pledge to accept international nuclear inspections were all positive. The U.S. government spoke highly of the North Korean agreement to abandon its reprocessing facilities and commented, "We are very satisfied."

South Korea and the United States had successfully secured important North Korean concessions in return for the suspension of the Team Spirit exercise. North Korea signed the North-South Basic Agreement and the Joint Declaration of Denuclearization, and made a commitment to accept IAEA inspections.

However, the North did not intend to accommodate mutual inspections between the North and the South. Although it agreed to accept IAEA inspections, the North did not want mutual nuclear inspections with the South. North Korea appeared to have thought that accepting non-challenge IAEA inspections would be easier than implementing inter-Korean inspections. In addition, North Korea may have decided that working with the IAEA would be more conducive to its interest of having direct talks with the United States to improve U.S.-North Korea relations.

North Korea wanted to use the nuclear issue as leverage to obtain security assurances from and to improve political and economic relations with the United States. The North Korean strategy of using the nuclear card was firm then, and has remained consistent.

Brinkmanship and the Agreed Framework

After President Roh Tae-woo's July 7, 1988 declaration, the United States took a "modest initiative" toward North Korea, allowing confidential meetings between a North Korean diplomat and the political counselor of the U.S. embassy in Beijing from December of that year. Through this channel, North Korea asked for a high-level meeting with the United States. The United States was known to have imposed five conditions for North Korea, including the elimination of anti-American propaganda; credible assurances of the abandonment of terrorism; return of the remains of Americans missing in action from the Korean War; progress in the North-South dialogue; and the implementation of confidence-building measures along the DMZ. It is known that thirty-four counselor meetings took place until September 1993.

As a consequence of the counselor meetings in Beijing, the United States accepted North Korea's persistent request for a high-level meeting. On January 22, 1992, such a meeting was held in New York for the first time since the end of the Korean War. In that meeting, Kim Yong-soon, the director of the International Department of the Korean Workers' Party, met with Arnold Kantor, Undersecretary of State for Political Affairs.

* * * * * * * * *

In the wake of this meeting, Robert Carlin, a North Korea analyst at the Bureau of Intelligence and Research of the U.S. Department of State, and a political counselor of the American embassy in Seoul, visited me when I was Vice Minister of Unification, to brief me on the result of the Kantor-Kim meeting. I was informed that Kim Yong-soon made it clear that "North Korea had neither the intent nor the capability to develop nuclear weapons. North Korea will sign IAEA Safeguards Agreements and ratify them within one or two months, and therefore there will not be a problem accepting IAEA inspections."

I was further informed that Kim Yong-soon had said, "Now that the North-South Basic Agreement and the Joint Declaration of Denuclearization have been adopted and North Korea has decided to accept IAEA inspections, it is time to improve relations with the United States through the holding of high-level talks."

According to the American briefers, the United States responded with three conditions for the North to meet: first, signing and ratification of the IAEA Safeguards Agreements; second, implementation of a first IAEA inspection; and third, the carrying out of mutual nuclear inspections between the North and the South.

It was clear to me that while publicly welcoming North Korea's decision to accept IAEA inspections, the United States was not interested in high-level talks with North Korea. Also, it was expected that North Korea would take a delaying tactic in carrying out its commitments. That would create more difficulties. At Robert Carlin's request, I expressed my view:

According to what I have sensed from my contacts with the North Koreans, they are pursuing a "survival strategy" amidst the crisis of their system. Their most important foreign policy objective is clearly to end the hostile relationship with the United States and normalize diplomatic relations. North Korea is delaying the implementation of IAEA inspections in order to induce direct talks with the United States for the purpose of receiving legal assurance that the United States will not threaten North Korea with nuclear weapons. North Korea will use its nuclear card to improve its relations with the United States.

The United States once proposed the idea of "cross recognition between the four powers." It seems that it will only be possible to resolve the nuclear issue when the United States improves relations with North Korea. It would be easier for the United States as a superpower to engage North Korea and resolve the nuclear issue through improvement of relations rather than pur pressure on the North. The first and second conditions that were imposed by the United States will likely be met by North Korea sooner or later, unless there is an unexpected turn of events. But, it is my judgment that North Korea will not carry out your third condition that mutual nuclear inspections be carried out between the North and the South. Therefore, if the United States insists upon the third condition, it will be difficult to make progress in negotiations with North Korea.

North Korea's nuclear diplomacy became active after the Supreme People's Assembly ratified the IAEA Safeguards Agreements signed by the North Korean government. North Korea stated that it was possible for Pyongyang to accept IAEA inspections because the fundamental obstacles had been removed by the announcement of the U.S. withdrawal of nuclear weapons, the suspension of the Team Spirit exercise, the declaration of the non-existence of nuclear weapons in South Korea, and the Joint Declaration of Denuclearization. Through its state-run television, North Korea also made the bold move of showing its nuclear facilities at Yongbyon.

On May 4, 1992, North Korea submitted a detailed 150-page initial report to the IAEA for nuclear inspections. The report said North Korea was operating a 5-megawatt experimental reactor and it was building two atomic power plants and a nuclear reprocessing facility (a radiochemical laboratory).

What was surprising about the report was its revelation that about ninety grams of plutonium had already been extracted. This revelation was a shock to the United States because it had not been able to predict North

Korea's capability to reprocess nuclear materials. This report led the United States to suspect that "in that case, they may have produced enough kilograms of plutonium to manufacture a nuclear bomb."

From May 14 to May 16, IAEA Director General Hans Blix and his party visited North Korea and inspected its nuclear facilities at Yongbyon. The inspection report prepared by Blix's team stated,

> The construction of a reprocessing plant, which was the focus of IAEA's interest, was approximately 80 percent completed; the installation of the equipment inside the plant was only 40 percent completed, and the construction work was suspended; the plutonium that North Korea had extracted was too small an amount to manufacture a bomb, and it would take several more steps in terms of equipment and technology before the North would be able to manufacture a nuclear bomb.

In conclusion, the IAEA report said, "There was no clear evidence that North Korea was developing nuclear weapons."

At the end of May, the IAEA confirmed the substance of its first inspection, verifying that spent fuel rods had not been unloaded. The IAEA sealed all the facilities.

However, the situation deteriorated when the United States made an allegation:

> An analysis of the ninety grams of plutonium that was extracted by North Korea showed there was output from three times of reprocessing which amounted in total to an estimated one hundred and forty-eight grams. There is serious discrepancy between this and North Korea's declaration.

In response, North Korea requested direct talks with the United States to resolve this issue, but the request was rejected.

At that time, President Bush was occupied with his reelection campaign. The Bush administration maintained the hardline position that there should be no reward for fulfilling international obligations under the NPT, and it would not have bilateral talks with North Korea until complete transparency was guaranteed.

＊　＊　＊　＊　＊　＊　＊　＊　＊

In March 1993, North Korea announced its intent to withdraw from the NPT, demanding a political solution through direct negotiations with the newly-inaugurated Clinton administration. This was an exercise of North Korea's brinkmanship tactics.

In the end, the Clinton administration decided to conduct a comprehensive give-and-take negotiation through high-level U.S.–North Korea talks. At one point, in spring 1994, the first nuclear crisis almost developed to the brink of war, but a breakthrough was achieved when former president Jimmy Carter met with President Kim Il-sung in Pyongyang.

Consequently, the Agreed Framework was signed in Geneva in October 1994. In compliance with this agreement, North Korea would freeze all its nuclear activities and permit themselves to be monitored by IAEA inspectors. The United States would provide light water reactors (LWR) with a total generating capacity of 2,000 megawatts. The nuclear facilities would be completely dismantled by the time the LWR project was completed in the estimated ten-year time frame. The United States would supply 500,000 tons of heavy fuel oil annually to make up for energy deficit incurred by North Korea before the LWRs came into operation. The United States would provide formal assurances against the threat or use of nuclear weapons against North Korea, and lift various sanctions and move toward full normalization of relations.

With the Agreed Framework in place, the process of North Korean denuclearization started moving forward. However, this agreement would be nullified eight years later by the neoconservatives of the George W. Bush administration.

Dialogue with Kim Il-sung

The historic documents of the "Agreement on Reconciliation, Nonaggression and Exchanges and Cooperation between the South and the North" and the Joint Declaration of the Denuclearization of the Korean Peninsula went into effect at the sixth round of the North-South High-Level Talks held in Pyongyang on February 19, 1992.

After a brief session of the sixth round of talks, we visited North Korea's Presidential Palace, where President Kim Il-sung welcomed the delegates of the South with individual handshakes. "Since His Excellency President Roh Tae-woo issued a special statement regarding the enforcement of the North-South agreement yesterday," said the North Korean president, "I have also made a statement."

The day before, President Roh had said in a special statement,

> The government of the Republic of Korea solemnly declares to the nation and the world that it will faithfully implement with utmost effort the content of the agreements that went into effect this time. At the same time, I ask that the highest leader of the North Korean authorities also declare his will to the nation and the world to sincerely carry out the content of the agreement.

Now it was President Kim Il-sung's turn. In a thick voice, but with clear pronunciation of each word, President Kim read his statement:

> The documents that went into effect at this time are a pledge that the responsible authorities of the North and the South have made to the Korean nation. The government of the Democratic People's Republic of Korea considers these historic documents of agreement to be a valuable result of efforts toward independent, peaceful unification of the fatherland. The government will exert all of its effort to carry out the agreements. Now our Korean nation has taken a precious step towards the independent and peaceful unification of the fatherland. This journey must not stop or slow down but must lead to tomorrow's unification. To do this we should not depend on foreign forces, but thoroughly maintain our independent position, stop the arms race, and realize arms reduction. It is time to determine our position on the issue of foreign troop withdrawal. And we must resolve the nuclear issue as well.

After reading his statement, he led us to the central hall to take pictures with him. The photo session was followed by a luncheon hosted by President Kim on the third floor. The lunch was served on a large round table four meters in diameter.

Kim Il-sung showed great manners as a host who knew how to smoothly lead the conversation. Every time a new dish was served, he provided interesting details about it; for example,

> This fish is raw *sogari*. *Sogari* only live in the cold upper streams of the Daedong and Cheongcheon Rivers. It does not exist in Japan. We mainly serve it to foreign guests. My Japanese friend, parliamentarian Utsunomiya Dokuma, loves it. He says its taste is unmatched. When he comes to Pyongyang, this fellow first asks for *sogari*. But the Chinese do not eat raw fish. Was it the Koreans or the Japanese who started eating raw fish first? Maybe the Japanese learned it from Koreans. Is there *sogari* in the South?

Offering us *duljuk-sool*, a North Korean wildberry wine, he went on:

> *Duljuk* look similar to berries. It is a plant native exclusively to Korea, and only grows on the high zone of our side of Mount Baekdu. This *duljuk-sool* is naturally brewed and has no alcoholic content. No extra alcohol was added to it.

The North Korean leader elaborated on each dish that came to the table and he brought up other subjects as well. He even made a comment on white rice:

> I heard Prime Minister Chung's hometown was Jaeryong, Hwanghae Province. Jaeryong's rice is famous. It is the best rice in our country.

The royal families of the Yi dynasty were known to have brought Jaeryong rice to Seoul for food. Jaeryong is known as the first place in our
country where people started growing rice. All Korean people wish to
eat white rice with meat soup, live in a tile-roofed home, and wear silk
clothes. The desire for white rice was considered most important.

The moment I heard his comment on rice, I could not suppress my bit-
terness. The North Korean leader knew so well of the people's desire to eat
white rice, and the North emphasized the importance of rice as seen in their
slogan, "rice is communism." Why, then, were people struggling so desperately that they could not even eat corn, let alone rice?

Somebody brought up the topic of air pollution and talked about the
clear air in Pyongyang and the polluted air in Seoul. Kim Il-sung intervened:

In the South every individual has a vehicle that emits carbon dioxide.
I think it is bound to pollute the air. According to my Japanese friend,
pollution is so bad in Tokyo that many people who live above the third
floor suffer from tuberculosis. For the sake of the people's health and
the beauty of Pyongyang, I oppose the use of gasoline automobiles. I
want to develop battery cars that people can drive. Premier Yon, how
much progress have we made in the development of battery cars?

Yon simply answered, "We are making good progress." It was not convincing to me that North Korea, which had not even reached the stage of
producing regular automobiles, was developing battery-powered vehicles
out of concern over pollution and the health of the people.

Prime Minister Chung said he wished to visit Mount Baekdu and the
North Korean leader responded: "If you want to visit Mount Baekdu, you
should go in August. Weather is capricious on the mountain. You have the
best chance to see the Crater Lake in August. I don't know where you are
going to meet for your next prime ministerial talks. How about holding the
talks on Samjiyon Lake at Mount Baekdu?"

President Kim was informed that the seventh round of High-Level Talks
would be held in Seoul, but the eighth round could be held at Mount Baekdu.
"Well, then," Kim said, "you meet there in August. You have to get there by
airplane. I think there should be sufficient hotel facilities."

The next day on our way back by train to Kaesong, the North Korean
delegates suggested that the seventh round be held at Mount Halla on Jeju
Island, in advance of holding the eighth round at Mount Baekdu. They said,
"We are going to promote tourism by the instruction of the president, and
we want to see the tourist facilities on Jeju Island." Our side welcomed the
proposal for alternating between the two highest mountains on the penin-

sula as venues for the North-South talks. We thought it would have great symbolic significance.

However, the North told us "as a result of investigation, we found that the facilities at Samjiyon Lake at Mount Baekdu are not suitable for the High-Level Talks." This ended the idea of splitting the talks between the two mountains.

✳ ✳ ✳ ✳ ✳ ✳ ✳ ✳ ✳

Turning back to Kim Il-sung's luncheon comments, he expressed a great interest in tourism.

> I hear that many people of the South come to see Mount Baekdu by way of the northeast region of China. The Chinese are busy collecting dollars spent by South Korean tourists. Why don't we have them go to Mount Baekdu through North Korea? It is desirable that the North and the South start their cooperation in tourism. There are great mountains in the North. Great Monk Seosan listed the five great mountains in Korea, including Baekdu, Kumgang, Myohyang, and Guwolsan. Of the five, four are located in the North, except Mount Chirisan, which is in the South. We have not developed Mount Guwolsan for tourism yet. But Mount Kumgang and Mount Myohyang are fully developed, and many tourists come there. Foreign visitors who see Mount Kumgang say they want to come back to see it again.

He continued, "I know in the initial stages of its economic development, when the South did not have much foreign exchange, that it started tourism to earn it." It was obvious that he was interested in investment by South Korean businesses in North Korean tourism, and had even considered the designation of a special tourist zone at Mount Kumgang. He wanted to attract a large number of South Korean tourists to North Korea.

President Kim also talked about economic cooperation between the North and the South.

> Since the North-South dialogue has been going well, I have heard that those South Koreans who have money are becoming interested in making investments in the North. I hear that Chairman Kim Woo-jung of Daewoo Corporation also wants to invest in tourism for Mount Kumgang. That's a good thing. Chairman Kim Woo-jung is a capitalist, but he is working harder than laborers, and he spends most of his time living abroad for his business. His wife's story is interesting. She was unable to see her husband, so she started playing golf. I was told that whenever she hits the ball, she pretends she is hitting her husband's head. You cannot say that Chairman Kim Woo-jung who works to the point of neglecting his family is a capitalist who exploits his workers. South

Korean businesses are growing because of the hard-working capitalists. If we only had five people like Chairman Kim Woo-jung, we of the same people could catch up to the South. . . . Is it true that Chairman Chung Ju-young quit business and got involved in politics? Is doing politics better than doing business? Playing the head of a party will not be as comfortable as running a business. . . . He will learn that there are a lot of difficulties in politics."

He also mentioned a Korean-American pathologist, Dr. Sohn Won-tae, who recently visited Pyongyang:

Dr. Sohn is the younger brother of the former defense minister of South Korea, Admiral Sohn Won-il. He and I were like brothers when we were in middle school in North Manchuria. Dr. Sohn's father was Minister Sohn Jeong-do, a Protestant church minister who rescued me from jail when I was a youth. He was my benefactor. Even today, I cannot forget his love. Anyway, Dr. Sohn came here without warning this time. He said he wanted to eat "twisted crackers." About sixty years ago, I bought him twisted crackers on the street. That night I called my chef and taught him how to cook "twisted crackers." The next day, we had them together as we reminisced about our old days of friendship. It was a touching moment.

The last course for the luncheon was roasted *supjoge* mussels. President Kim again made an introductory comment: "Help yourselves. *Supjoge* mussels are good for longevity. They cultivate them in North Hamgyong Province."

Kim Il-sung's last words at the lunch that day were about oxbone soup. "I understand Seoul *seolnongtang* tastes great. . . ." Although he had a problem with his hearing, he looked quite healthy for an eighty-year-old man. The luncheon lasted an hour. This turned out to be the last time we saw him. He never had a chance to taste Seoul *seolnongtang*. He died in July 1994, two years after that luncheon, at the age of eighty-two.

* * * * * * * * *

One of the things I learned from the luncheon conversation was that the North Korean leader was relatively well-aware of what was happening in the South. It seemed that his frequent contacts with Japanese politicians and South Korean businessman like Kim Woo-jung had made a strong impact on his thinking. I realized how important it was to bring a change to the North Korean leader's mind through such contacts. I was convinced such change would help North Korea to take a path to opening and reform.

In his public statement, President Kim Il-sung mentioned arms reduction, withdrawal of U.S. troops, and that there was no need to make nuclear warheads, perhaps as part of a propaganda campaign. But, during the closed luncheon, I noted that he mainly talked about inducement of investment, tourism, and inter-Korean economic cooperation.

With the North-South Basic Agreement in effect, North Korea became proactive for the improvement of relations with South Korea in an attempt to overcome its economic difficulties. During 1992, the North sent an emissary to propose a summit in Pyongyang in April. In May, North Korea accepted an IAEA nuclear inspection. In July, North Korean Deputy Premier of Economic Affairs Kim Dal-hyun visited Seoul to promote a model case of inter-Korean economic cooperation. In addition, North Korea proposed holding meetings of members of separated families on Liberation Day and adopting the protocols of the Basic Agreement.

CHAPTER 6

COLD CURRENTS FOR INTER-KOREAN RELATIONS

Emergence of Opposition

The first phase of North-South High-Level Talks began in September 1990 and was characterized by a year of exploration. The second phase began in October 1991 during the fourth round of talks; this time was marked by active negotiation and the successful adoption and enforcement of the North-South Basic Agreement.

In the third phase of the talks (beginning February 1992), the two parties began negotiating the "protocols of the Basic Agreement." After this, we were scheduled to move into the fourth phase of talks and establish joint commissions to implement the agreement. However, due to a delaying tactic made by the South, this did not come to fruition.

1992 was a presidential election year in South Korea and various domestic politics affected the progress we had made. As the campaign warmed up, the view emerged that the North-South dialogue need not be expedited. At the same time, the presidency was in its lame-duck phase. Under these circumstances, the North-South negotiation lost momentum. In the end, it took seven months before we were able to produce the protocols of agreement in September 1992.

According to the North-South agreement, three joint committees—political, military, and exchange and cooperation—were to be set up. In addition, it was agreed that four Joint Commissions for the implementation of the agreement would be established within three months after the Basic Agreement went into effect. The three joint committees were tasked with completing the protocols of agreement by May 18 and defining the missions of the Joint Commissions.

The three joint committees met for the first time in mid-March and agreed to expedite negotiations in order to meet the deadline for the completion of the protocols of agreement. However, at the political committee meeting, our side began employing a delaying tactic by insisting that "unless the nuclear issue is resolved, we cannot expect reconciliation and cooperation between the North and the South." The North felt this attitude demonstrated our "unwillingness to implement the agreement by using a delaying tactic under the pretext of the nuclear issue."

* * * * * * * * *

Since the beginning of the presidential election campaign, South Korea's conservative press had created a negative atmosphere for North-South dialogue. They espoused that "no inter-Korean relations should be improved without the resolution of the nuclear issue." Conservative opinion leaders alleged that North Korea had already developed nuclear weapons and that they would use them to attack the South.

On March 9, 1992, a daily newspaper reported that 74 percent of South Koreans were "convinced of North Korea's possession of nuclear weapons." According to the same paper, 51 percent believed that the North "did not intend to accept nuclear inspections." At that time, the U.S. intelligence community was focusing on a suspected nuclear reprocessing plant in Yongbyon, without concluding that North Korea actually possessed nuclear weapons.

It was around this time that people began saying a "South-to-South dialogue" within the South was more difficult than a North-South dialogue. We were internally split between proactive engagement and negative opposition regarding North-South negotiations. Consequently, even after the meetings of the three joint committees, no further progress was made.

The critics of dialogue advocated a delaying tactic, arguing that the South should take "a slow and cautious approach to the North-South dialogue, while being mindful of the political environment at home and abroad." The rise of criticism was somewhat related to the departure of the director of the National Security Planning Agency (NSPA), Seo Dong-gwon, who had been strongly pushing the process of dialogue with the North.

The new NSPA director who replaced him was more interested in domestic politics. He claimed his mission was to assist "the governing party to reinvent a new regime through elections." Soon after Mr. Kim Young-sam became the presidential candidate of the ruling party in the middle of May, people in government circles began talking openly about "regime reinvention."

Nevertheless, the proponents of engagement maintained their position that North-South negotiation should be aggressively pursued as had been agreed upon, so that the joint implementation commissions could carry out the protocols of agreement.

This group argued, "Since the North is forthcoming on economic cooperation, our side should seize this opportunity to improve inter-Korean relations. The North-South dialogue should not be cannibalized by the pursuit of domestic politics."

Prior to the scheduled holding of the seventh round of the North-South High-Level Talks, we held a strategy meeting of senior officials on April 30. At that meeting, the chairman of the Political Committee, who was the special assistant to the NSPA director and who was spearheading the negative campaign against inter-Korean dialogue, said,

> According to information we have recently collected, North Korea is completely reconsidering its policy toward the South in view of the presidential election campaign taking place here. It is clear that the North is going to nullify the North-South Basic Agreement and deal a blow to the High-Level Talks. Therefore, we have no reason to further North-South relations."

In short, he was calling for a delaying tactic in light of the development in domestic and international politics.

As these negative assessments were made by NSPA officials supposedly in control of information about North Korea, others did not have much to say. Yet, they did not seem to believe what they had heard.

✳ ✳ ✳ ✳ ✳ ✳ ✳ ✳ ✳

The North Korean delegation arrived in Seoul as scheduled on May 3, 1992, to attend the seventh round of the talks. Unlike on previous occasions, the North Korean delegates looked relaxed and more positive. By this time, the Team Spirit exercise had been suspended. They had successfully celebrated the eightieth birthday of their leader Kim Il-sung. They had signed the IAEA Safeguards Agreements, and they seemed confident in the prospect of nuclear resolution. They had revealed their nuclear facilities at Yongbyon on television, suggesting their willingness to reach a resolution to the nuclear issue.

The first day's session was held at Shilla Hotel. Premier Yon, head of delegation for the North, said in a casual conversation that several big projects had been completed in honor of President Kim Il-sung's eightieth birthday. He boasted of the completion of a housing project on Tongil Street in Pyongyang that would provide 50,000 homes and a 156 kilometer-long, four-lane highway from Pyongyang to Kaesong. Yon said: "The next time you come to Pyongyang for a meeting, you can come by the new highway. It will only take two hours."

In their keynote statements that day, both sides revealed contrasting views concerning the adoption of the protocols of agreement. The South argued that the Joint Implementation Commission should be established before May 19, but that sufficient time should be taken to discuss the protocols of agreement, since there was no deadline for adopting the protocols.

The North side responded, "It was the fault of both sides that we did not set a deadline for the protocols. However, since the Joint Implementation Commission cannot function without the protocols, the two sides should adopt them before the Joint Commissions start working on May 19."

In addition, the North made a surprising proposal for an "exchange of visits between separated family members, as the first gift to the South for implementing the Basic Agreement." They suggested, in celebration of the August 15 National Liberation Day, that one hundred elderly people from each side visit their separated family members, and seventy performing artists from each side visit and perform for the other side.

At the seventh round of the talks, the two sides agreed to establish the Joint Implementation Commission on May 18 and to exchange a list of each side's members for the Commission that day as well. As for the protocols of agreement, the North conceded to the South and agreed to adopt them by September 5. The proposal for exchanged visits between the elderly and artists was also agreed to take place both in Seoul and Pyongyang around August 15. The Red Cross societies of both sides would be responsible for carrying out the actual exchanges.

Such positive cooperation by the North Korean delegation discredited the NSPA's fabricated and false intelligence assessment that "North Korea would not comply with the Basic Agreement and it would 'blow up' the High-Level Talks."

Aborted Repatriation of Long-Term Prisoner Lee In-mo

As President Roh sank into his lame-duck status and the presidential campaign heated up, North-South relations that had somehow been kept afloat began to sink as well. Ultimately, the exchange visits of separated families for the August 15 National Liberation Day—which had been proposed by the North and supported by President Roh Tae-woo—were hindered and ultimately aborted by the South.

When Kim Young-sam was nominated as the presidential candidate of the ruling party in May, senior government officials began rallying behind him in pursuit of their personal interests. Even the existing senior secretaries of the Blue House pledged their loyalty to the promising presidential candidate. President Roh was utterly powerless.

Leading the supporters for the governing party's presidential candidate was the director of the NSPA and his close associates, who voiced their frank and open views that "the improvement of North-South relations was not desirable." They abandoned the "parallel strategy" that the Roh Tae-woo government had maintained, and instead, insisted "real progress is not expected unless the nuclear issue is resolved."

* * * * * * * * *

Following the adoption of the Basic Agreement, North Korea was determined to accept economic cooperation with the South in order to revive its deteriorating economy. The North was very eager to carry out pilot projects such as the Nampo industrial complex they had been discussing with Chairman Kim Woo-jung of the Daewoo Group.

The North's economic interests motivated it to accept the South's long-time desire to hold exchange visits by separated family members, prompting it to hasten the visits by aging parents to National Liberation Day on August 15. In addition, the North had another ulterior motive: it was hoping for the repatriation of Lee In-mo, a long-term North Korean prisoner who had refused to renounce communism.

There was something noteworthy happening inside the North Korean regime. Pyongyang's pragmatic proponents of engagement were promoting the exchange visits by separated family members in order to promote economic cooperation with the South. At the same time, their political hardliners wanted to exploit Lee In-mo's loyalty to the North as a tool to raise the morale and solidarity of the North Korean people.

It was around this time that the Human Rights Committee of the Council of Korean Churches gathered signatures, in the Busan area where Lee In-mo lived, for a petition for his repatriation, and submitted it to the government. The petition stated, "In consideration of the poor condition of the prisoner's health, such as his inability to physically move around, and the lack of relatives upon whom he could depend, he should be returned to his family in the North as soon as possible."

Up until this time, law enforcement agencies had always opposed the repatriation of Lee In-mo. They had several concerns:

His repatriation would serve no good purpose but only cause harm. It would merely provide an excuse for other former long-term prisoners who have refused to renounce Communism to ask for repatriation. In addition, Lee In-mo's repatriation would encourage pro-North Korean activities in the South. Lastly, the North Korean regime would treat the prisoner as a national hero for political propaganda.

However, the Blue House and the Ministry of Unification both now held the view that "we should repatriate Lee In-mo on humanitarian grounds, to clean up the legacy of the Cold War and move forward to the improvement of North-South relations."

* * * * * * * * *

The division of views concerning the repatriation of Lee In-mo persisted with no hope of resolution. In the end, the decision was left to the president. After a careful review of both the humanitarian and political views, on May 23 President Roh Tae-woo instructed that officials "positively consider the repatriation of Lee In-mo, and review the possible repatriation of all other former long-term prisoners who wish to return to the North." There were 175 former long-term prisoners who had violated the national security laws and who had refused to renounce Communism.

President Roh's instructions reflected his strong political will to do away with the past legacies of the Cold War and to realize the exchange visits of separated family members. In order to comply with the president's instructions, Prime Minister Chung Won-shik summoned a meeting of senior officials at the prime minister's residence on the morning of June 1. In deference to the president's decision, the meeting overrode the NSPA's opposition and agreed to carry out the "unconditional unilateral repatriation of Lee In-mo" to North Korea. However, the opposition group managed to successfully thwart the implementation of the president's political decision. It leaked the information to the press so that it could actively manipulate public opinion to oppose Lee In-mo's repatriation. In the end, both the repatriation of Lee In-mo and the proposed exchange visits by separated family members were frustrated by the obstructive manipulation of the opponents. This failure demonstrated both the difficulty in making progress in North-South relations and the ease with which any progress made could be destroyed. It also showed how little influence a lame-duck president could exercise on inter-Korean relations.

* * * * * * * * *

Less than six months later in March 1993, newly-inaugurated President Kim Young-sam repatriated Lee In-mo to the North. This was his first decision on inter-Korean affairs. Lee's return was not linked to the issue of exchange visits by separated family members. It was an unconditional repatriation based on humanitarian grounds, which was carried out after an outpouring of petitions from human rights organizations as well as Cardinal Stephen Kim's petition for an unconditional, immediate repatriation.

About-Face on Economic Cooperation

Near the end of July 1992, North Korean Deputy Premier for Economic Affairs Kim Dal-hyun came to Seoul to discuss the details of economic cooperation between the North and South. However, we failed to make the best use of that opportunity to improve North-South relations. The timing of his visit coincided with the presidential campaign and the atmosphere of a hardline attitude toward the North Korean nuclear issue. Thus, the top North Korean economic official returned empty-handed to Pyongyang.

Kim Dal-hyun's delegation had been the first of its kind to be comprised of economic specialists who were emerging as technocrats of the North Korean government. But they quickly lost their roles because of their unsuccessful visit to the South.

On the first evening of their visit, the North's economic delegation attended a dinner reception hosted by Deputy Prime Minister for Economic Planning Choi Gak-kyu at the Hyatt Hotel. Before this reception was held, there was a high-level economic meeting, attended by six senior officials from the South—Deputy Prime Minister Choi Gak-kyu, Blue House Security Advisor Kim Chong-whi, myself as Vice Minister of Unification, and a few officials from the Economic Planning Board—and six counterparts from the North, including Deputy Premier Kim Dal-hyun, Lee Song-dae, and Chung Woon-up.

At the meeting, Kim Dal-hyun said, "We have not come here to simply tour industrial facilities. We have come to discuss realistic projects of economic cooperation." He added, "Let's undertake some economic cooperation pilot projects even before the adoption of the Economic Exchanges and Cooperation Protocol of the Basic Agreement. We propose that we agree on three projects and announce them."

The first project was to construct a natural gas pipeline that linked Siberia and the two Koreas. The North informed us that North Korea and Russia had signed a memorandum a month earlier concerning the construction of a pipeline that would pass through North Korea. Realizing such a project would take a long time, the North proposed to conduct a feasibility study, whereas several South Korean businesses had already been interested in the venture.

The second project was the joint construction of LWR nuclear plants for shared use of electric power. North Korea suggested that a suitable site should be selected along the northern side of the Demilitarized Zone. Under this plan, the South would provide most of the capital and technology and the North would operate the plants to provide power to both economies. The decreasing output of hydroelectric plants in the North during the winter and the increasing demand for electricity during the summer in the South seemed to have been taken into account. The South Korean government also was studying a similar project.

The third project was related to the joint construction of a light industrial complex in Nampo, in which the Daewoo Corporation was interested. The North requested immediate approval by the Seoul government of Daewoo's participation. Daewoo had been promoting this project even before the adoption of the North-South Basic Agreement. The North Korean delegation argued,

> The North and South have taken different economic paths. By undertaking a pilot project in advance of the active implementation of inter-Korean economic cooperation, both sides would learn a lot from this new experiment. This would help the North make necessary preparations for the future.

Kim Dal-hyun then concluded the three-project proposal:

> Economic cooperation should not wait until all the other issues have been resolved. If we cannot even jointly construct a small factory, what reconciliation or cooperation will we be able to achieve? I am confident that if we agree and carry out these projects, it will have a positive impact on the development of other issues.

Earlier that year, in an effort to allow a "limited opening" to revive its deteriorating economy, North Korea had revised its foreign investment law and other laws governing economic activity. Watching the formerly Communist European states' continuous transformation to a market economy, North Korea had started seeking its own way out from economic deterioration.

However, all Deputy Premier Kim Dal-hyun was able to achieve from his Seoul visit was a modest agreement that the South would dispatch a technical team to study the feasibility of a Nampo industrial complex, and that South Korean Deputy Prime Minister Choi Gak-kyu would visit Pyongyang at the invitation of the North. The South firmly expressed its policy of linking the nuclear issue to economic cooperation ("resolution of the nuclear issue first, economic cooperation afterwards"). The North's request for the initiation of pilot projects had been virtually rejected.

* * * * * * * * *

After a troublesome internal debate, the South did send a study team for the construction of a Nampo industrial complex, but no subsequent progress was made. The planned visit of the South Korean deputy prime minister was aborted by the announcement of the so-called South Korean Workers' Party spy incident. As time passed, it became more apparent that Kim Dal-hyun's visit to Seoul had been a complete failure.

The hardliners in the North waged an attack on Deputy Premier Kim Dal-hyun's "rosy illusion" and he was dismissed at the end of that year. Along with Kim Dal-hyun, other pragmatic technocrats, including Kim Jong-woo, Deputy Director for External Economic Affairs, disappeared one by one from the political scene in the North. It is unfortunate that we missed the opportunity to work with Kim Dal-hyun and the others. With their dismissal, we lost hope of economic cooperation between the North and South, and invariably delayed the emergence of pragmatic forces in North Korea for a long time. Eight long and wasteful years later, inter-Korean economic cooperation became possible.

Success of Principled Negotiation

For three months following the seventh round of the High-Level Talks, no progress was made on the drafting of the protocols of the Basic Agreement for both the Political and Military Committees. Nevertheless, we were able to hold an effective and relatively smooth discussion in the Exchange and Cooperation Committee, of which I was in charge. Based on the spirit of the Basic Agreement and in compliance with our basic negotiating strategy, I did my best. I believe I was able to contribute to the creation of a new negotiation model between the North and the South.

My committee was responsible for four areas: economic, social and cultural, traffic and communication, and exchange visits of separated families. Each area was headed by an assistant minister or director general level official from the relevant ministries.

We conducted several meetings to develop a negotiating strategy and method. We agreed upon the method of establishing a set of principles for resolving issues. In short, we would employ the method of "principled negotiation," which had been developed by a Harvard University research team and was being widely used in international negotiations. This method was different from the method of "positional bargaining." Our approach was to focus on interests, not positions; invent options for mutual gains, not one-sided gains; and insist on using objective criteria, rather than one's position.

As a negotiating strategy, we would respect the "face" and self-esteem of the North; we would induce agreement by way of persuasion and a learning process. We wanted to develop objective criteria and principles to produce reasonable mutual gains. In the strategy meeting, I emphasized:

> We should remember that inter-Korean negotiation is not a zero-sum game. It should create a satisfactory resolution for both sides to assure common interests between the North and the South. The goal of negotiation is not victory but the creation of the means to produce a wise outcome through efficiency and amicability. Although the North Korean delegates are distrustful of us and confrontational, if we make efforts to understand them and maintain the posture of "problem solvers" rather than "adversaries," we can build mutual confidence and resolve the issue. This is what I have learned from my experience. This is my conviction. Please, trust me and let us try to apply my experience and conviction.

Of course, I did not think it would be easy to promote exchange and cooperation between a market economy system and a rigid system of command economy—between an open, diverse society and a closed, collective society. The implementation of exchanges and cooperation was a risky political burden on North Korea. It would likely lead to the opening of its closed society and might result in a system transformation.

Yet, it was my judgment that North Korea was in urgent need of South Korean investment and inter-Korean economic cooperation, as it was diplomatically isolated and its economy was increasingly exacerbated after the fall of the communist camp. In a single-party dictatorial state, the top leader often turns the impossible into the possible. For example, the North Korean leader accepted the simultaneous entry of the North and the South into the United Nations, which the North had adamantly opposed in the beginning. North Korea had also accommodated Article 5 of the Basic Agreement, which stipulated transformation of the "present state of armistice into a solid state of peace between the North and the South"; and it had accepted the Joint Declaration of the Denuclearization of the Korean Peninsula.

These sudden developments had only been possible because of the rapid decisions made by North Korea's highest leader, who had responded pragmatically to the reality of circumstances. By the same token, instead of insisting on our positions, we needed to understand the other party's difficulties and consider their peculiar circumstances. This was the only way we would be able to build mutual trust and dependence.

* * * * * * * * *

At the first meeting of the Joint Exchanges and Cooperation Committee on March 18, I introduced four principles that would aid the efficiency of negotiation in my keynote statement. These principles were reciprocal exchanges and cooperation on the basis of common interest; exchanges and cooperation towards unification; exchange and cooperation to create an institutional mechanism between the North and the South; and exchange and cooperation to resolve urgent issues first. I presented draft copies of protocol of agreement for each of the four sectors of the Committee.

The principles adopted by the Exchange and Cooperation Committee were thus different from those used by my fellow South Koreans in the Political or Military Committees, who argued over the nuclear issue to delay the negotiation. I was determined to uphold that the nuclear issue be addressed by the Joint Nuclear Control Committee, while the other committees concentrate on the writing of the protocols of agreement by the deadline.

In our committee, the North also stressed the importance of meeting the deadline for the protocols of agreement. It presented its own draft protocol of agreement for the committee. While the North's version was comprehensive, it only had thirty provisions, compared to ours, which had more than ninety. Fewer than twenty items were similar in content between the two draft versions.

The two sides held committee meetings to discuss and negotiate the essential aspects of the issues. We met once a week on average and each side presented its proposed amendments three times. With each revised proposal, the number of provisions in the North's version increased, in the end to a total of fifty, while ours decreased. Through this kind of process, our Joint Committee was ready to adopt the "protocol of exchange and cooperation" at any time.

* * * * * * * * *

On September 8, newspapers printed the following front-page headline, "Complete Resolution of Protocol of North-South Exchange and Cooperation." It featured a large picture of the North's Kim Jong-woo shaking hands with me. The reports said that the Exchange and Cooperation Committee had successfully adopted a complete protocol of agreement that included seventy provisions.

The press welcomed the latest agreement but it also treated the news as an unexpected surprise, reporting, "The adoption of the protocol of North-South exchange and cooperation has raised positive expectations for the upcoming eighth round of the High-Level Talks. It will revitalize the deadlocked negotiations at the Political and Military Committees."

The success of the Exchange and Cooperation Committee was largely attributed to the North Korean decision to expedite the negotiations in light of its difficult economic situation. At the same time, I am confident that our negotiators' resolve and effective negotiating approach contributed to the success as well.

Obstruction from Within

An internal preparatory meeting for the eighth around of the High-Level Talks was held on August 11. At this meeting, the chairman of the Political Committee who was the special assistant to the NSPA director said,

> There is no way for us to expect the adoption of the protocol of agreement for the political sector. And since the North maintains its principle of a simultaneous package solution, the protocols of agreement for other fields should not be adopted without the political protocols. Therefore, it is more important to consider domestic political needs, and we should focus on our public relations.

His intent was clearly to create tension in inter-Korean relations and use it for the presidential campaign.

In a subsequent high-level strategy meeting to prepare for the eighth round of the High-Level Talks, we decided to follow a "principle of accumulative solution" if the simultaneous package solution failed. If the Political Committee failed to adopt its protocol, the other two committees would proceed and adopt the protocols and immediately implement the agreements for the two joint commissions first.

The meeting also decided again to promote the exchange visits of the separated family members on a new date. The South side would link the North's request for the repatriation of Lee In-mo to the issue of exchange visits of separated family members.

President Roh Tae-woo approved this strategy, emphasizing that all protocols of agreement be adopted at the eighth round. He also instructed us to resolve the exchange visits of separated family members. President Roh strongly desired to implement at least exchange visits among the separated family members as part of the Basic Agreement.

I was on my fourth trip to Pyongyang on September 15. This time, I rode in a Mercedes-Benz that was waiting in front of the Tongilgak at Panmunjom instead of going by train. The automobiles carrying us ran on a new highway connecting Kaesong to Pyongyang, which after four years of construction was completed before the eightieth birthday of President Kim Il-sung. I was told that the new four-lane highway was 156 kilometers long with 18 tunnels and 84 bridges. But I did not a see single car running on the highway until we arrived in Pyongyang two-and-a-half hours later. The trip would have taken four hours by train.

* * * * * * * * *

We started our negotiations that evening as soon as we arrived in Pyongyang. We successfully concluded the negotiation of the protocols of agreement for the Exchange and Cooperation Committee and the Military Committee. But the Political Committee failed.

The first day's plenary was held the next morning. We were supposed to attend the second day's plenary meeting at ten o'clock the following morning as normally scheduled. However, we had to first discuss what to do about the Political Committee's failure to reach its protocol of agreement. After receiving the report from Lee Dong-bok that agreement for the political sector was impossible, Prime Minister Chung Won-shik revealed what he had been told by the deputy head of the North Korean delegation, Ahn Byung-soo. On their way to Pyongyang in the same car, Ahn had told the prime minister, "The North side will do its best to agree on protocols for all three fields. But if the Political Committee fails, the North side will be flexible to adopt just the two protocols of agreement this time."

Prime Minister Chung expressed a firm position, saying "even if the Political Committee fails to adopt its protocol, we will still adopt the protocols of agreement for the Exchange and Cooperation Committee and the Military Committee."

Lee Dong-bok seemed to be shocked at the prospect of adopting the protocols for the two other committees. He must have realized that his prediction had been off the mark: the North side, which had called for a simultaneous package solution, was indeed willing to accommodate the results of the two committees by themselves.

Because of the problem with the Political Committee, the plenary meeting scheduled for the morning of September 17 was postponed until the afternoon. Due to the adjusted schedule, our delegation was able to go and see the West Sea sluice gate at Nampo. Just before our departure, however, we were surprised to hear that the Political Committee had agreed on its protocol. Lee Dong-bok, who had been obstinately against the agreement, must have changed his mind and abandoned his delaying tactic.

After seven months, the negotiation of the protocols of agreement was finally concluded. It would have ended four months earlier as agreed if there had not been a delaying tactic by the Political Committee. In the final analysis, one of the primary reasons for the failure to implement the Basic Agreement is that we wasted four valuable months.

* * * * * * * * *

At approximately five o'clock that afternoon, the plenary of the eighth round adopted the three sets of protocols for the implementation of the Basic Agreement and put them into force. It was also agreed that the four joint implementing commissions would hold their first meeting beginning on November 5, with weekly follow-up meetings at Panmunjom. The two sides accepted the North Korean proposal to hold a ninth round of the North-South High-Level Talks in Seoul from December 21. This was beyond our expectations. However, the issue of an exchange visit of separated family members, which had been a special order by President Roh Tae-woo, was not resolved due to fabricated instructions to ignore the president's orders.

Fatal Blow to Inter-Korean Dialogue

With the final adoption of the three sets of protocols for the Basic Agreement, we entered the phase of implementing the agreements through the activity of the joint commissions. However, beginning in October, the domestic political situation in the South deteriorated.

On October 6, the NSPA announced that North Korean agents had been operating to organize a South Korean base for the Workers' Party through a massive spy operation in the South. With the presidential election only three months away, this immediately created a tense situation in political circles. The announcement claimed,

> Lee Seon-shil, a female candidate for the North Korean Workers' Party Politburo, and more than ten other high-level spies have been dispatched to the South. They have been working underground for the past ten years to organize a local branch of the South Korean Workers' Party for the central region, while carrying out other illegal activities of espionage, such as recruiting four hundred individuals as supporting members from across the fields of politics, academia, the press, culture, labor and social circles. The NSPA has confirmed that these individuals were involved in attempts to communize the South, and sixty-two of them have been arrested.

In addition, this shocking announcement was followed by rumors that some opposition politicians were involved in the case. The NSPA announcement triggered the rise of a strong conservative, anti-North Korean atmosphere in the midst of the presidential campaign. In short, an anti-Communist, anti-North Korean Cold War atmosphere started dampening public support for reconciliation and cooperation between the North and South.

North Korea confronted this incident by issuing a series of statements. In the name of the Committee for the Unification of the Fatherland, the North claimed, "This incident is a fabrication and the North has nothing to do with this." The statement also called for the dismantlement of the NSPA and the abolishment of the National Security Law. North Korean Premier Yon Hyong-muk sent a letter to the South in which he said, "The so-called South Korean Workers' Party Incident is a political scheme carried out by the NSPA, and we demand the South's frank admission and apology."

* * * * * * * * *

In Washington, on October 8, two days after the NSPA's announcement, the ROK-U.S. Security Consultative Meeting (SCM) issued a joint statement, saying that unless significant progress such as the implementation of North-South mutual nuclear inspections was made, preparations for the 1993 Team Spirit exercise would continue. This joint statement became a major cause of the eventual suspension of North-South dialogue.

The ROK-U.S. combined Team Spirit exercise first began in 1976, and the number of participating soldiers grew every year. By 1988, with the participation of 218,000 troops, including 78,000 U.S. soldiers, the Team Spirit exercise became the world's largest joint military field exercise. An aircraft carrier loaded with nuclear weapons also participated in the exercise. North Korea had strongly reacted to this exercise, calling it a "nuclear war exercise." During each season of the Team Spirit exercise, North Korea recalled all military troops that had been assigned to economic construction, and mobilized all reservists for three months. It imposed a great economic toll on the North.

In a May 31 interview with the *Stars and Stripes*, General Robert RisCassi, then commander of U.S. Forces Korea, had alluded to the preparations in progress for the 1993 Team Spirit exercise. The military and hardline conservatives of South Korea and the United States were in favor in resuming the exercise, which had been suspended in 1992. They argued that the exercise should be used as a stick to pressure North Korea.

The premature announcement for the exercise in early October, almost three months earlier than normal, provided sufficient grounds for suspicion. In previous years, exercise announcements had been made in late December. It was a shared view among observers that the early Team Spirit announcement was a political manipulation to influence the presidential election that year and to stall the meetings of the Joint North-South Commissions that were scheduled for November.

Contrary to public perception, the resumption of the Team Spirit exercise had not been discussed within the South Korean government before it was agreed upon at the SCM. The ROK side is said to have insisted that the joint statement express a hardline position that the Team Spirit exercises would resume if no mutual nuclear inspections were conducted. It was learned that the United States had accepted Korea's position, under the conditions that South Korea would reimburse $2,580,000 if the exercise was cancelled by the end of December and $5,560,000 if it was cancelled by the end of January 1993.

* * * * * * * * *

North Korea's response to the announced decision to resume the Team Spirit exercise was remarkable. The North sustained its effort to abort the decision in three phases. In the first phase, they demanded an unconditional reversal of the decision. In the second phase, they demanded a reversal by the end of November. And in the third phase, they made their final efforts to revert the decision by mid-January 1993.

A series of North Korean statements began with a foreign ministry spokesman's statement of October 23, stating, "the decision to resume the Team Spirit exercise is a criminal act that blocks the implementation of the provisions of the Basic Agreement and drives the North-South dialogue into a crisis." The statement called for the unconditional reversal of the Team Sprit decision, fiercely criticizing the decision linked to the nuclear issue as a "declaration of total confrontation to give up the Basic Agreement and the joint declaration of denuclearization."

On November 2, a foreign ministry spokesman warned: "If the South and the United States carry out the Team Spirit exercise, it will create a new obstacle to the enforcement of the nuclear Safeguards Agreements." This was an indication that the North might reject IAEA inspections. On November 3, the North demanded that the South announce a decision to cancel the resumption of the Team Spirit exercise in any form by the end of November so that the Joint Commissions could meet in December.

The deadline for the end of November passed, but on December 4, the North sent a telephone message, requesting that the South make an announcement of reversing the Team Spirit exercise decision by December 15 so that the ninth round of the High-level North-South Talks could be held on schedule on December 21. The deadline was extended by fifteen days. However, North Korea did not meet our government's condition that mutual inter-Korean nuclear inspections precede the resolution of the Team Spirit exercise issue.

* * * * * * * * *

Under these circumstances, Robert A. Scalapino wrote in an Asia Foundation report, "The decision to resume the 1993 Team Spirit exercise was a mistake," and called for an indefinite postponement of the exercise. Scalopino alleged that "since the meaning of the Team Spirit exercise has been politicized, it would be a great obstacle, instead of contribution to the peace and stability of the Korean Peninsula."

Later Donald Gregg, former American ambassador to South Korea, recalled the Team Spirit exercise decision was "the most serious mistake in Korea policy" while he was in office. Back in Washington, the administration did not have time to reconsider the decision because of the ongoing presidential campaign. On November 3, Bill Clinton was elected as U.S. president, but his administration did not review the issue in its early months.

In Korea, the presidential candidate of the governing party and his assistants welcomed the decision to resume the Team Spirit exercise, and after he was elected, showed no interest in reversing the decision. As the possibility of reversing the decision evaporated, North Korea issued a statement to declare the suspension of all North-South talks. The progress of the High-Level Talks, which had been so painstakingly made, had finally come to an end.

* * * * * * * * *

The North-South High-Level Talks began with a preparatory meeting in February 1989 and ended with a Nuclear Control Committee meeting held in January 1993. During these four years of activity, the talks went through eight rounds of plenary meetings, holding a total of more than one hundred and thirty meetings of various types within the framework of the High-Level Talks, including working-level meetings and joint committee meetings. The North and South adopted the Basic Agreement and its protocols that promised to "oppose war and make peace through reconciliation, exchange and cooperation in a new post-Cold War era." The High-Level Talks also agreed on the denuclearization of the Korean Peninsula. The talks successfully set a new direction for the development of inter-Korean relations.

However, because there was no improvement in relations between North Korea and the United States, the improvement in North-South relations consequently suffered a fatal blow. Entering a new post-Cold War era, South Korea normalized its relations with China and Russia, but the U.S. administration of the senior George Bush showed no interest in improving relations with North Korea. Even the North Korean attempt to play a nuclear card failed to work. Under these circumstances, the agreements of the North-South talks were not carried out due to the emergence of the conservative Kim Young-sam administration and its lack of understanding of inter-Korean relations and the national issue.

*   *   *   *   *   *   *   *   *

It turned out that I was the only delegate of the South who participated in the North-South High-Level Talks from the very beginning to the very end. There was no change in the composition of the North Korean delegation, but the South Korean delegates were frequently different due to changes in their assignments.

I personally participated in more than sixty negotiation meetings for the goal of ending the Cold War on the Korean Peninsula and improving inter-Korean relations, and it is a privilege and a matter of pride for me to have done it. With the inauguration of the Kim Young-sam administration in February 1993, I stepped down as Vice Minister of Unification, completing forty years of public service. I was sixty years old.

III SUNSHINE POLICY

CHAPTER 7

MEETING KIM DAE-JUNG

Sincere Recruiting Efforts

About a week before Christmas 1994, Chung Dong-chae, a former reporter who had covered the Ministry of Unification, wanted to meet me at a hotel coffee shop in Seoul. He introduced himself as chief secretary to Kim Dae-jung, then chairman of the Asia-Pacific Peace Foundation. He said he was meeting me at the chairman's request. Chung got straight to the point:

> After failing in the last presidential election, Mr. Kim Dae-jung established an institute for unification studies called the Asia-Pacific Peace Foundation. He is currently searching for someone who can run the institute. You have been recommended by several people, and Mr. Kim Dae-jung would like to offer you the job—I hope you will accept.

This came as a surprise. I knew little about Kim Dae-jung because I was not interested in politics. Everything I had heard about him from the military government and the conservative media had all been negative. I remembered phrases such as "Kim Dae-jung has impure political thoughts. He is a red. He is a radical. He is a liar."

I knew Kim Dae-jung was interested in unification, because about five years earlier, I had obtained a copy of his unification proposal for a "confederation system." I read it with interest. It was true that I was interested in his unification design after I learned that the government's "National Community Unification Formula" had accommodated much of his unification design. This happened at a time when the people had a rising interest in democratization and unification. In all honesty, that was all I knew about him—nothing more, nothing less.

Working with someone who had long been an opposition leader was unimaginable. I cordially declined, saying, "I appreciate the offer, but I have no intention or ability to work for the gentleman."

However, as if he had already been anticipating my refusal, Kim Dae-jung's chief secretary said, "Your ability has already been proven. Take your time to consider his offer. I hope you will give us a positive answer later."

One week later on Christmas Eve, I met with him again. He had called me a number of times. He brought me a written message from Kim Dae-jung. "Judgment of one's ability is for others to make. You should not be so humble. I expect your positive decision."

But I declined again for health reasons. I said I had just had a full medical examination. "I have worked forty years in government. I am now sixty. I don't want to work at a stressful job. I need rest."

Chung Dong-chae advised that I meet with Kim Dae-jung before I decide. I told him there was no need to do so. He then complained that I was not being responsive, "whereas many people were waiting in a long line to see Mr. Kim."

I turned down the offer twice, but I could not reject it completely without further consideration. I asked for my wife's thoughts. She said, "You have done enough for the country and the nation. Now it is time to enjoy a restful life." I also solicited advice from my old military academy classmates. They were all against me taking the job, saying, "You would be considered a turncoat by most of your military colleagues, seniors and juniors alike. It would tarnish your good reputation. You should not be taken advantage of by a politician who has presidential ambitions."

* * * * * * * * *

In the new year, there were two developments that influenced my wife and me. The first one was that while we were engaged in prayer, we were reminded of our minister's sermon on the first Sunday of the new year. He had said, "Take the opportunity to become a winner." This gave us a sense of mission. The minister continued, "Free yourself from the past. Have a vision for the future. Lead a positive, proactive life, not a negative and passive life."

Second, I received a positive report back from the results of my medical exam. I had no serious health problems other than some normal geriatric symptoms that could be treated with medication and caution. Medically speaking, I would have no trouble working a normal job. This coincided with Chung Dong-chae's third visit.

My wife then changed her mind. "The results of your medical exam seem to show the Lord's will for you to continue working. We should humbly accept it." Then Chung conveyed Kim Dae-jung's message once again. "Mr. Kim sent me again to persuade you to meet with him," he implored, "so please meet him once."

At last, I accepted his request to meet with Kim Dae-jung. Chung wanted me to see Kim immediately, but I told him I would see him after my planned visit to Washington toward the end of January. In Washington, I attended a seminar that was jointly sponsored by the Sejong Institute and a university in Washington, DC; I also visited four research institutes to assess U.S. policy on North Korea in the aftermath of Kim Il-sung's death and the signing of the U.S.-DPRK Agreed Framework.

While visiting Washington, I was informed by the Korean embassy of press reports claiming that I had been selected as secretary general to the Asia-Pacific Peace Foundation. I was bewildered by the reports since the matter had not yet been settled.

I asked three scholars with whom I was travelling to Washington what they thought. They were split. One welcomed the news. The other advised against it. And the third person said it would be an adventure worth taking.

First Meeting

On January 23, 1995, I met Kim Dae-jung, chairman of the Asia-Pacific Peace Foundation, for the first time. He received me in a small reception room in his house in Donggyo-dong, Seoul. Our meeting lasted two hours and included a luncheon. Our dialogue that day turned out to be another turning point in my life. Someone later said that "joining Kim Dae-jung with Lim Dong-won at this meeting would change the fate of the Korean Peninsula." He was right.

Chairman Kim explained in detail his perspectives and what he had been doing regarding the North Korean nuclear issue. He believed the issue should be resolved "through a give and take" between North Korea and the United States in a "package solution" and with "simultaneous implementation." He advocated the same view he had made earlier in his speech at the National Press Club in Washington.

In that speech, Kim Dae-jung had also asserted that "the United States should talk to Kim Il-sung to resolve the nuclear issue. And to this end, the United States could consider sending a respected elder statesman like former president Jimmy Carter to Pyongyang." In our meeting, he said he was pleased to see Carter eventually go to Pyongyang to achieve a breakthrough in U.S.-North Korea relations.

On the unification issue, he said,

As we see an emerging era of historic transformation with the end of the Cold War and the development of democracy and the market economy among the nations of the former Communist block, we should undertake our initiative to end the Cold War on the Korean Peninsula as well.

He added that implementation of the North-South Basic Agreement would be key to such efforts.

He also told me that a year earlier he had given a speech entitled "Sunshine Policy from a Position of Strength" at the Heritage Foundation in Washington. The concept of his "Sunshine policy" was borrowed from the Aesop's fable in which the Sun removes a traveler's cloak. This was the first time I had heard of the Sunshine policy.

Chairman Kim Dae-jung suggested we continue our conversation over lunch. We were joined by his wife, Lee Hee-ho, and his chief secretary, Chung Dong-chae. The chairman kindly briefed me on the purpose, programs, and management of the Asia-Pacific Peace Foundation. He emphasized, "The world is now entering an era of the Asia-Pacific. I am glad to have successfully held the Asia-Pacific Democratic Leaders Conference at the end of last year. Together, let us make this Asia-Pacific Peace Foundation into a world-class research institute."

* * * * * * * * *

At my first meeting with Kim Dae-jung, I was impressed by his acute analysis, judgment, and unmistakably clear approach to the nuclear issue. His deep insights were above the level of any specialist. It surprised me and may have even triggered a sense of fear within me. I admired him for the conviction in his philosophy of unification; his grand vision for the future; and his logical way of thinking.

What's more, he recognized the value of the North-South Basic Agreement, for which I had worked so hard. Later, President Kim Dae-jung stated in his inauguration address, "The path toward the resolution of the North-South conflict was paved by the implementation of the North-South Basic Agreement adopted on December 13, 1991. If we carry out this agreement, we can successfully resolve inter-Korean problems."

It occurred to me that if this man was elected president, we could make good progress in inter-Korean relations. I also realized that the prejudice I had against him was dissipating.

Until that first meeting, I had not known that Kim Dae-jung had lived as a man of conscience in action. He had upheld his strong conviction in democracy and peaceful unification throughout a tortuous political life, during which he survived five brushes with death, six years in prison, ten years under house arrest, and two exiles abroad.

I recalled he was portrayed as a Communist when he spoke of peaceful unification, a radical when he spoke of democracy, and a liar when he spoke of politics. However, this same man whom people called a Communist was speaking of unification before me; this so-called radical was advocating the merits of democracy to me. I, too, had been deceived by these rumors, and now felt ashamed. I summed up my response: "I shall respect your leadership and shall do my best to help your research." That was my acceptance of the position as the secretary general of the Asia-Pacific Peace Foundation.

Three-Stage Unification Formula

On February 2, 1995, I officially took the job as secretary general at the Asia-Pacific Peace Foundation. The inauguration ceremony was presided over by Chairman Kim Dae-jung and one month later the foundation held a reception in honor of my inauguration at the Lotte Hotel's Crystal Ballroom. National Assembly members, academics, and many Kim Dae-jung supporters attended the reception.

In a welcome statement, Chairman Kim Dae-jung said I was a native of North Korea, formerly a soldier, diplomat, and a lead delegate to the North-South High-Level Talks. He said I was a "unique individual, well-versed in theory, and long experienced in practice on the issues of national security, diplomacy, and unification."

He went on to say that I was "a public servant who has a reasonable way of thinking and a strong sense of responsibility; a good honest man with unswerving conviction; a man who has presented a vision of unification for the nation." He concluded, "Now that he has joined us in the study of unification, in which I have had a lifetime interest, I feel like I have gained the support of one million troops."

I began my inaugural address by saying,

> I join the Asia-Pacific Peace Foundation with a sense of calling to march on the path towards unification under the leadership of Chairman Kim Dae-jung.
>
> Unification will not happen on its own. Unification is something we must work to achieve. Therefore, a leader's role is vital in setting the right goal and direction and getting the support of the people for unification. I am ready to support Chairman Kim Dae-jung and his firm philosophy and clear grand vision for peaceful unification. We cannot separate the issues of national security, diplomacy, and unification. We need bipartisan, pan-national efforts for unification. I shall use my knowledge and forty-year experience to build national consensus.

During the time when I had accepted the position, my wife and I were harassed by an endless barrage of phone calls. Most of them were negative. They said things like, "Is the rumor true?" "I can't believe it!" "Are you out of your mind?" and "They will only take advantage of you." Some called me a traitor, saying that they would never see me again. Yet, there were some who encouraged me, saying, "Do your best."

* * * * * * * * *

The Asia-Pacific Peace Foundation had been established by Kim Dae-jung in January 1994. Its three goals were peaceful unification of the Korean Peninsula, democratization of Asia, and realization of world peace. Its programs included research, education, and public affairs.

I became the foundation's secretary general and director of the Asia-Pacific Peace Academy. I was put in charge of all of the foundation's programs. My specific assignments included organizing and implementing academic symposiums and speaking tours at home and abroad as part of our effort to develop the foundation. Most importantly, however, the task Chairman Kim had given me as soon as I took the job was to complete and publish a "three-stage unification formula" for the fiftieth anniversary of liberation. He said, "I have pushed this project for a year. But so far, we have only produced an unsatisfactory draft formula that reflects plenty of academic theories but not enough realistic applicability." He also said he had learned a lot from visiting Germany and studying German unification. He suggested that studying unification in Germany and Yemen would be helpful.

I reviewed the draft carefully and found ten problem areas. I discussed these problems with the writers of the draft formula several times before submitting my review and an alternative formula. Chairman Kim suggested that he and I discuss the problems one by one. We had an animated discussion over a few days.

Through this discussion, I was once again surprised by his superb insights and scholarly attitude. He enjoyed debates through which he would defend his points of argument and persuade his listener. At the same time, he was a good listener and very receptive to others' ideas if they made sense.

Regarding the draft formula, I believed that we should first clearly define the concept of a "North-South confederation," which would be the first stage of unification. Then we should list tasks to accomplish during this phase. A "North-South confederation" should be a cooperative system between the two governments that peacefully manages the state of division toward unification. This is not a form of unification but a form of cooperation for peaceful coexistence before unification.

The goals of this stage should be to induce North Korea to change; build political confidence; restore the national integrity; construct an inter-Korean economic community; realize arms reduction; and transform the armistice into a durable peace regime.

After the confederation, the second stage towards unification is "federation." Kim Dae-jung's federation model, however, was different than the "Koryo Federation" advocated by North Korea. Chairman Kim's concept of a federation was similar to the federal systems in countries like the United States, Germany, and Switzerland. Under his system, there would be one state, one system, and two local governments. In contrast, North Korea's federation formula advocated one state, two systems, and two local governments. However, it is impossible to incorporate two different systems into a single federation. I argued that until North Korea became a market economy like the other democratic countries in Eastern Europe had, we would need a confederation formula to manage North Korea in consideration of its stage of development

I believed the first stage would be reconciliation and cooperation; the second stage would be the North-South confederation; and the third stage would be a unified federation. Chairman Kim, however, believed it should be confederation, federation and complete unification. He would not modify the three-stage unification formula he had been advocating for so long. He was reluctant to accept my idea of the stage of reconciliation and cooperation. He thought that if the North and South agreed, it would be possible to establish a confederation without the stage of reconciliation and cooperation. However, after becoming president, he realized the impossibility of jumping to confederation without reconciliation and cooperation. Consequently, he started a policy of active reconciliation and cooperation. He also realized that the reconciliation and cooperation stage was equally as important to the unification process as the confederation stage.

President Kim realized once more at the June 2000 summit in Pyongyang that it was not easy to enter directly into a state of confederation. In fact, the summit declaration of June 15 was an acknowledgement of entrance into a stage of reconciliation and cooperation, transcending distrust and confrontation.

     *   *   *   *   *   *   *   *   *

Through the course of our discussion, I was able to clearly discern Chairman Kim Dae-jung's philosophy of unification and his concrete policy toward North Korea. Based on our discussion, I drastically revised and rewrote an initial draft report, and Dr. Park Geon-young reconstructed the unification formula in a final draft. In early July, Chairman Kim, Dr. Park, and I met for two days at a hotel for a final reading and review of the draft. Chairman Kim shared his unique, meticulous insights and his consideration of readers' concerns. With a sincere and thorough attitude, he read aloud every word in every line of the report.

On the evening of September 14, 1995, a public reception was held at the Lotte Hotel's Crystal Ballroom to celebrate the publication of *Kim Dae-jung's Three-Stage Unification Formula: Centered on a North-South Confederation*. The reception was a big success, with more than 1,300 people attending from various realms such as politics, academia, and the arts.

This book was published in English by the University of Southern California Press in early 1997. It was also published in Japanese by the *Asahi Shimbun* in the beginning of 2000. While President Kim Dae-jung was in office, the book served as the bible for North Korea policy.

I did my best to contribute to the publication of the book. On several occasions, I had open and uninhibited discussions with Chairman Kim Dae-jung, through which I was able to ascertain in detail his thoughts on unification, diplomacy, and national security. Working so closely with him on these matters was extremely significant and worthwhile for me. Yet, I did not know then that because of my work for the Asia-Pacific Peace Foundation, I would assist him closely during the five years of his presidency.

Keeping Distance from Politics

In mid-July 1995, Chairman Kim Dae-jung announced his return to politics and his plan to organize a political party. In early September, the National Congress for New Politics was established. He assured me that his new party had nothing to do with the foundation, and asked me to continue vitalizing its activities. He appointed me vice chairman and I became busier, working even harder for the foundation.

At that time, National Assembly elections were scheduled for the following spring and election politics were fully underway. Before the general elections, the National Congress for New Politics recommended several times that I run for the National Assembly in a Seoul district, but I firmly declined the recommendations. The press then reported that I was to be placed high on the party's list of proportional candidates as a unification and security specialist on behalf of the National Congress for New Politics. Party Chairman Kim Dae-jung also offered me the chance to join the National

Assembly to work in the field of unification and national security as a proportional list member. He was going to put my name within a safe range of electability on the party's list of proportional candidates. I politely declined his kind offer, saying, "As I told you in the beginning, I am not interested in politics. I am not suitable to be a national assemblyman. Please don't be concerned about me. I will continue to work for the Asia-Pacific Peace Foundation."

Seeing my firm resolve, he got up to shake hands with me and said, "Many people are doing all kinds of things to become national assemblymen. You, however, are declining a free, unsolicited offer that would surely make you a member. I really admire your integrity. Thank you."

When the list of candidates for proportional members was announced, my friends commented: "You have surprised us twice. The first was when you joined Kim Dae-jung. The second is when you turned down the offer to be a proportional member. Once you partnered with Kim Dae-jung, you should also have joined his politics. It does not make sense."

* * * * * * * * *

In May 1997 Kim Dae-jung was nominated as the presidential candidate of the National Congress for New Politics, running for presidency for the fourth time after failing in 1971, 1987, and 1992. I did not directly participate in or contribute to his campaign. I simply continued my work at the foundation.

The 1997 presidential election was a three-way contest among Kim Dae-jung of the National Congress of New Politics, Lee Hoi-chang of the New Korea Party, and Lee In-je, who had hurriedly established a party after he was defeated in a primary of the New Korea Party. In early November, a "DJP coalition" (Kim Dae-jung–Kim Jong-pil) emerged between Kim Dae-jung's National Congress for New Politics and Kim Jong-pil's United Liberal Democrats.

When the election was over, Kim Dae-jung was elected with 40 percent of the vote. Lee Hoi-chang received 38 percent, and Lee In-je, 19 percent. This was the first peaceful power transition from a governing party to an opposition party in the history of Korean politics. For thirty-six years until that time, conservative parties from the Gyeongsang region had ruled South Korea. For the first time ever, a democratic reformist government led by people of the Jeolla region had emerged.

CHAPTER 8

BREAKING NEW GROUND

Reconciliation, Cooperation, Change, and Peace

In early February 1998, President-elect Kim Dae-jung sent me a message saying he wanted me to assist him closely as Senior Presidential Secretary for National Security and Foreign Affairs. I had to think it over for a while. Before receiving the message, I had thought that I would help President Kim indirectly by concentrating on developing the Asia-Pacific Peace Foundation into an outstanding think tank. However, I soon decided and conveyed to him my willingness to do whatever he wanted me to do. He was very pleased with my decision:

> I know you were a vice minister six years ago. I feel bad asking you to take a vice minister-level position again at the age of sixty-five. But I appreciate your acceptance.

Two weeks prior to the presidential inauguration, I started preparing for my new assignment as soon as my appointment as senior presidential secretary was announced.

Starting from day one after the election, the president-elect began working day and night to deal with the nation's financial crisis. He could not afford to recuperate from his long exhausting campaign. Korea's national debt to foreign investors exceeded $150 billion but its foreign exchange holdings were only $3.7 billion. To make matters worse, sixty percent of the foreign debt was due within a year.

Korea accepted an IMF rescue package under the stern conditions that Korea would reform its economic policy to undertake an "acceleration of market opening," "abolishment of preferential policy for conglomerates," "lifting of restrictions on foreign equity ownership," and various other measures likely to slow economic growth to three percent. President-elect Kim would have to focus on economic issues for the foreseeable future.

With the goal of small government in mind, the new administration carried out a massive structural reform by reducing and integrating its ministries and agencies, enforcing a thirty percent personnel reduction. My office was also affected by the structural reform, but I was able to keep four secretaries. The reform guidelines also advised replacing all secretaries and most staff with new people (who presumably would be more beholden to the new administration), but I did not accept any infusion of new people from the outside and instead simply retained all of those who professionals who had been dispatched from the relevant ministries. They were all outstanding public servants from whom I received valuable support.

* * * * * * * * *

President Kim wanted me to assist him in the areas of national security, foreign affairs, and North Korean policy. I first identified pending issues that required immediate attention. I called a working-level coordination meeting attended by assistant ministerial officials to prepare the new government's positions and to report them to a Standing Committee meeting of the National Security Council (NSC). I focused on three task areas and came up with appropriate positions for them.

* * * * * * * * *

The first task was to establish a foundation for the new government's North Korea policy, which was introduced during the campaign. The second task was to revise our strategy for the Four-Party Talks scheduled for Geneva in April. The third task was to set up an institutional mechanism through which the president could comfortably make the right decisions on the issues of national security, foreign affairs, and unification. Namely, the task was to establish an NSC Standing Committee (the NSSC) that could effectively and reasonably coordinate and integrate positions of the agencies concerned.

To establish the foundation of the new government's North Korea policy, I first reviewed and supplemented President Kim's North Korea policy design, the "Three-stage Unification Formula" that he introduced to the public during his campaign. I then wrote a draft report and sent it to the Ministry of Unification for its review. I asked the ministry to write a final report and submit it to the next NSSC. The ministry's final report was almost a carbon copy of my original draft. The report was finally approved at the second meeting of the NSSC. The elements of the policy foundation were announced as described below.

There were three possible policy options to consider in connection with the unification issue. One of them was to carry out a "confrontation policy" to precipitate a North Korean collapse. However, this option was excluded because of the likelihood of precipitating a war. The second option was a "policy of malign neglect" until North Korea collapsed, but this option was unattractive since this policy might contribute to either an explosion (eruption of war) or an implosion (due, for example, to internal insurrection or the massive exodus of people from the North). Therefore, the only viable option should be an "engagement policy" through the patient pursuit of reconciliation and cooperation that could induce change in North Korea for opening and economic reform.

The official title of the engagement policy was the "Policy of Reconciliation and Cooperation." However, this policy was better known as the Sunshine policy at home and abroad, a term that President Kim was fond of using. As I explained before, the term "Sunshine policy" came from the Aesop's fable in which the warmth of the Sun, not the strength of the wind, took off the traveler's cloak. The intent of the Sunshine policy was for both the South and North to stop the cold wind of the Cold War and exude the warm sunshine of reconciliation upon one another. The Kim Dae-jung administration pursued a consistent engagement-based policy towards North Korea for five years.

* * * * * * * * *

The goal of the Sunshine policy was to induce incremental change in the North for opening and reform towards a market economy, and to establish peace on the peninsula to create a state of *de facto* unification first. To induce change, it was necessary to improve relations with the North through reconciliation, cooperation, and peaceful coexistence, a climate in which people could travel between the North and the South and help each other by sharing their resources.

The four key words in our North Korea policy were reconciliation, cooperation, change, and peace. This policy was not based on an "imminent collapse theory." Rather, it was based on a "theory of gradual change" that North Korea too should change slowly and gradually as China and Vietnam had.

This policy also aimed to realize a process of détente on the Korean Peninsula, as it had taken fifteen years of effort to end the Cold War in Europe. Thirty-five nations of the free camp and the Communist camp in Europe had signed the Helsinki Accords in 1975 to start a process of détente through exchange, cooperation, and arms control. Ten years afterwards, Mikhail Gorbachev emerged as a reformist Soviet leader, declaring a policy of *perestroika*, *glasnost*, and a foreign and national security policy of "new thinking" for opening and reform. As a result, systemic transformations from Communism to democracies and market economies took place, ending the Cold War between the two camps. In this process, the Berlin Wall crumbled and German unification was achieved.

President Kim outlined three fundamental principles of North Korea policy in his inauguration speech: "No armed provocation of any kind will be tolerated that destroys peace; no unification by absorption will be pursued; instead, reconciliation and cooperation will be actively pursued."

The major operating principles of this North Korea policy were

> to maintain a strong security posture while improving North-South relations through exchange and cooperation; to create conditions and an environment for North Korea to change by itself through increased contact and dialogue, exchange and cooperation; to promote the establishment of an economic community to increase economic interdependence; to implement arms control for tension reduction and the establishment of peace; and to promote a consistent North Korea policy based on the support of the people.

In conclusion, the Kim Dae-jung administration would deter war through a peacekeeping effort via the ROK-U.S. alliance and a self-reliant national defense, while establishing peace through cooperation with North Korea. We wanted to keep peace by maintaining the armistice system that manages the state of the division, while trying to transform the armistice into a peace regime in order to dismantle the Cold War system.

As Europe built the European Union (EU) for political integration through the European Economic Community (EEC), we thought it would be desirable to build an inter-Korean economic community for economic integration, which would serve as a base for political integration. To implement our policy, we would carry out the North-South Basic Agreement; support private business to work with the North based on the principle of separation of politics and economy; place a priority on the resolution of the issue of separated families; provide humanitarian assistance at the governmental and civilian levels; reduce tension and build military confidence; secure international support for ending the Cold War; and support the implementation of the Agreed Framework to resolve the nuclear issue.

I believed that in consideration of the North Korean system, it would be prudent to effect change at all levels of their society. I thought we should have high-level contacts and persuade the North to effect change from above; at the same time, we should provide more aid and promote increased contact and exchange with the people in the North, so that they would change their thinking, leading to change from below. I also believed we should pursue a functional approach through economic cooperation on the one hand, and arms control on the other.

* * * * * * * * *

Engagement policy is neither an appeasement policy nor the policy of the weak. In fact, it is an offensive strategy and proactive policy that only a strong party can employ. I held the view that we should be confident and shed past concerns of victimization by the North. In order to win the battle without a fight, I advocated promoting the engagement policy. However, there was a widening disparity between the North and the South in terms of economic, military, and diplomatic capabilities. The competition of systems between the North and the South had ended in a total victory for the South. In the wake of the end of the Cold War, the international environment developed in favor of South Korea. As the Communist system lost its grounds for existence, democracy and the market economy were spreading to the world, driving the North into deeper isolation.

Until the mid 1970s, the North had surpassed the South in terms of per capita income. However, by 1997 the South's per capita income had reached $10,000, about twenty times as much as that of the North. According to statistics that the North submitted to a UN organization, the North's per capita income was $1,013 in 1990, which was recorded as the North's best economic year. By 1997, it had fallen by more than half, to $464. That year the size of South Korea's economy was $476 billion, whereas North Korea's was only about $10.3 billion. South Korea's volume of trade was $280 billion, while the North's was $1.4 billion, a ratio of 200 to 1.

As the old Communist bloc transformed into a market economy, the North Korean economy became isolated and the operating rate of their plants fell below thirty percent. On top of this economic decline, the natural disasters of 1995 and 1996 caused a severe food shortage and hundreds of thousands of people died of starvation, which resulted in many residents defecting from the North to China. North Korea had no foreign currency with which to import food, not to mention any strategic resources, such as fuel for energy. North Korea had no choice but to depend upon humanitarian aid from the international community. It was around this time that predictions of an imminent North Korean collapse were emerging again in Seoul and Washington.

Militarily speaking, the North was more powerful than the South. In 1997, the South had 700,000 troops and the North had 1,100,000; the South had 2,200 tanks and the North 3,800; the South had 5,200 artillery pieces and the North 12,000, and the South had 550 aircraft fighters and the North

850. However, most of the North Korean military equipment had been acquired in the 1960s and 1970s and was more than thirty years old. About half of the North's weapons—40 percent of the tanks, 50–60 percent of the artillery guns, and 70–80 percent of the aircraft fighters—were considered outdated and ineffective, compared to South Korea's military equipment, which had been introduced in the 1980s and 1990s. In terms of defense expenditures, South Korea's economic growth had allowed it to increase its spending each year, reaching $16 billion (less than three percent of GDP), as the North was spending $2 billion (twenty percent of its GDP) while its economy kept shrinking. Nevertheless, the North Korean military, especially with its long-range artillery and missiles, posed a great threat to our security. On the other hand, South Korea had a strong military alliance with the United States, the only superpower in the world, and U.S. troops were stationed in South Korea for deterrence. The South was maintaining diplomatic relations with most nations in the world, including China and Russia. Korea became the 12th or the 13th largest export country, with growing stature in the international arena.

* * * * * * * * *

Gaps in power between the North and the South were widening in favor of the South. However, in the worst-case scenario, if the North were cornered into an inescapable dead end, it might launch a suicidal attack in desperation and trigger a war of destruction. If a war broke out, there was no doubt that we would win. However, it was crucial to prevent a national calamity that would kill a great number of people and destroy everything we had built—including industrial facilities. We needed a policy to manage the North Korean challenge—to deter provocation and adventurism, and to tame and bring the North into the international community.

The essence of the policy of reconciliation and cooperation was to prevent war with a strong deterrent; at the same time, it was intended to establish peace by inducing North Korea to change. Last, it involved managing the division toward the realization of *de facto* unification through peaceful coexistence.

Theories of Imminent Collapse

My first practical task was to prepare for the second round of the Four-Party Talks, which were scheduled for the middle of March. After I took my job as Senior Presidential Secretary of National Security and Foreign Affairs, my first guests for policy discussion were the U.S. delegate to the Four-Party Talks, Charles Kartman, who was also deputy assistant secretary of state; Ambassador Stephen Bosworth of the U.S. embassy in Korea; and Jack Pritchard, White House NSC Director of Asian Affairs.

Their interest was to learn about the new government's position on the upcoming Four-Party Talks, which were scheduled to take place in ten days. I had already prepared our new government's position after my discussions with Deputy Foreign Minister Song Young-shik, our representative to the talks. President Kim had approved it as well. Based on the new unification policy, the new administration's position was different from that of the previous administration. The most significant change to the North Korea policy was that the new government dismissed the "imminent collapse theory" and replaced it with a "gradual transformation theory."

President Kim Young-sam's administration had pursued a policy of denuclearization first and improvement of inter-Korean relations later under the premise of North Korea's imminent collapse. This policy had aggravated inter-Korean relations, forcing the previous administration to deal with North-South relations within the context of the Four-Party Talks.

Through the so-called strategy of 4 minus 2, the Kim Young-sam administration sought dialogue with the North in order to manage a process of North Korean collapse within the framework of the Four-Party Talks. In other words, they had tried to integrate inter-Korean relations with international relations.

Former Senior Presidential Secretary of National Security and Foreign Affairs Yoo Chong-ha claimed he had persuaded Anthony Lake, the White House national security advisor, to agree to hold Four-Party Talks. Yoo said, "He was convinced that North Korea would collapse in a few years and that it was necessary to prepare for it through such talks."

Anthony Lake wrote in his book *Six Nightmares* that the North Korean economy was going down the path to deterioration, and he believed "the collapse not only of the regime but of the system itself could come in a few years." He said he promoted the Four-Party Talks based on the judgment that "the weaker the North Korean economy, the more likely the collapse of the regime will be sudden and violent, and the greater the costs of eventual unification."

Although President Kim and I did not exclude the possibility of a North Korean collapse—and recognized a need to prepare a contingency plan—we regarded it as wishful thinking. Realistically, collapse was not probable. Accordingly, the new administration rejected the previous administration's policy of linking inter-Korean dialogue to international relations in anticipation of an imminent North Korean collapse. We decided to keep the Four-Party Talks separate from the North-South dialogue. We determined that it was still too early to expect progress from the Four-Party Talks but we should proceed with the second round since talks had already begun.

We decided to discuss tension reduction on the Korean Peninsula and replacement of the armistice agreement with a peace regime during the Four-Party Talks; we would pursue North-South dialogue as a separate channel to improve inter-Korean relations through reconciliation, exchange and cooperation. Our position was to continue the Four-Party Talks in parallel with the North-South dialogue, each acting independently and complementing the other at the same time.

* * * * * * * * *

I explained in detail to Bosworth and Kartman the new government's view of the North Korean situation and its North Korea policy, as well as its position on the Four-Party Talks. Fortunately, they said they understood the policy and the position of the new administration, and promised to cooperate closely with it. This was the first policy discussion between the Kim Dae-jung and Clinton administrations.

After my first meeting with Ambassador Stephen Bosworth that day, over the next three years, until his departure, he and I maintained a close working relationship to develop ROK-U.S. relations.

In our first meeting, we recalled that eight years earlier, the CIA had predicted that North Korea would suddenly collapse within a few years like Romania, and that even three years prior, the same agency had predicted that the North would collapse within two to three years at least. We both shared the view that the worst may have been averted now.

Intelligence judgments are always made for worst-case scenarios to warn policymakers and enable them to plan countermeasures. Neither an explosion due to a suicidal attack by North Korea nor an implosion that would force the people to flee en masse was desirable.

At that meeting we agreed to develop a policy that would prevent the occurrence of either scenario and to dispel the vague hope of an imminent collapse of North Korea.

Ambassador Bosworth was a professional diplomat who started his career in 1961. He was ambassador to Tunisia, director of policy planning at the State Department, ambassador to the Philippines, president of the U.S.-Japan Foundation (1988–1995), and executive director of the Korean Peninsula Energy Development Organization (KEDO) from 1995 to 1997. In November of 1997, he came to Seoul as the U.S. ambassador. He was a superb diplomat who was reasonable and had an outstanding ability to deal with complex issues.

---

* * * * * * * * *

The North-South Basic Agreement of 1991 had paved a path toward improved inter-Korean relations. But the North-South relationship had deteriorated during the five-year period of the Kim Young-sam administration (1993–1997). This was a consequence of the flawed judgment regarding the imminent collapsibility of North Korea and the linkage of the nuclear issue to inter-Korean relations.

North Korea, which had long sought to improve its relations through high-level talks with the United States, resorted to brinkmanship tactics to draw the attention of the new Clinton administration when it announced on March 11, 1993, that it would withdraw from the Nuclear Non-Proliferation Treaty (NPT). Accepting North Korea's wish for dialogue, the Clinton administration held U.S.–North Korea high-level talks in June to start negotiating a package deal for the resolution of the nuclear issue and the possibility of normalizing U.S.–North Korean relations.

In response, President Kim Young-sam declared a nuclear linkage strategy by saying, "We will not shake hands with someone who has a nuclear weapon in hand." Subsequently, the South also gave up efforts to improve inter-Korean relations. It became impossible to implement the North-South Basic Agreement that had taken so much effort to adopt. This marked the beginning of five wasted years.

In November 1993 President Kim Young-sam derailed the U.S.–North Korea negotiation process by strongly opposing the Clinton administration's inclination to accommodate a "package solution" proposed by North Korea. The North, in turn, attempted to unload the spent fuel from its 5-megawatt reactor in defiance of the United States. In a chain reaction, the United States planned to launch a military attack, putting the Korean Peninsula on the brink of war. This was the first nuclear crisis, erupting in the spring of 1994.

At that time, former president Jimmy Carter visited Pyongyang and met with North Korean leader Kim Il-sung. Carter's visit successfully averted the crisis and provided new momentum for a "give-and-take" negotiation between the United States and North Korea in Geneva.

In an interview with the *New York Times* in mid-October 1994, President Kim Young-sam again expressed his intent to reject the negotiations in Geneva, which were near a conclusion. President Kim told the *Times* that "to reach a compromise with North Korea—which faces the danger of imminent collapse—will only help prolong its survival. The United States, having less experience than South Korea in negotiations with Pyongyang, was being deceived in Geneva."

In the Agreed Framework adopted in Geneva on October 21, 1994, North Korea agreed to immediately freeze its nuclear activities, gradually dismantle all its nuclear facilities, and receive IAEA inspections.

* * * * * * * * *

Upon Carter's return from Pyongyang, President Kim Young-sam accepted his proposal for an inter-Korean summit, which was never realized due to North Korean leader Kim Il-sung's sudden death. At the news of his death, President Kim Young-sam issued an emergency order putting all armed forces on maximum alert, thus driving the North Koreans into a state of fear of an invasion from the South. North Korea responded with denunciation and condemnation of the South.

Following their leader's death, North Korea was hit by natural disasters and famine. People died from starvation in increasing numbers and others defected from the North. The Kim Young-sam administration again relied on the prospect of an imminent collapse, and the South's relations with the North continued to deteriorate, while Kim Young-sam continued to disagree with the United States over how to resolve the nuclear issue. Thus, the subsequent Kim Dae-jung administration first needed to normalize the traditionally cooperative ROK-U.S. relations and thaw the frozen inter-Korean relations.

NSC Standing Committee

When North-South relations emerged as an important issue in the early 1990s, ministers of the related ministries met frequently. However, these meetings were not institutionalized and were held on an ad hoc basis; they produced no binding decisions and members were not responsible for the outcome of their meetings. Although the issues discussed were actually under the jurisdiction of the National Security Council, there was no designated sponsoring agency at the time. Furthermore, no minutes of the meetings were kept despite the fact that important issues of foreign affairs, national security, and North Korea were being discussed.

The new government needed a system to coordinate and synthesize differing positions among the relevant ministries to formulate and implement effective policies. Some experts held the view that similar to the U.S. system, operation of the NSC should be placed directly under the control of the Senior Presidential Secretary of National Security, who assists the president in the areas of unification, foreign affairs and national security.

Encouraged by these views, immediately after I was appointed as the senior presidential secretary, I designed a plan to establish an NSC Standing

Committee (NSSC) and an NSC Secretariat. Ministers of unification, foreign affairs, and national defense, the director of the National Intelligence Service, and the senior presidential secretary of National Security and Foreign Affairs would attend the NSSC. The presidential secretary would concurrently head the NSC Secretariat, and the standing committee would meet regularly once a week.

The committee would produce concerted policy through coordination and cooperation, and would prepare a meeting report, which would include minority views, for the president's approval. Once approved, the report would be distributed to the members of the committee for thorough implementation. To support effective committee operation, a working-level meeting would review in advance agenda and issues for the committee meetings, and the working-level meeting would also conduct situation assessments on a periodic basis.

For the secretariat, I would have a deputy director and twenty staff members whose responsibility would be to provide staff support for the standing committee. I was conscious of the new government's policy of "small government."

These ideas were incorporated into a document called a "Proposal for Improved Operation of the National Security Council," which was reviewed and adopted by the first meeting of the NSC Standing Committee. In the meantime, President Kim had instructed us to include the director of coordination (from the office of the prime minister) as a member of the standing committee; he would be able to voice his views but would not participate in votes of decision. The president's decision was made in consideration of the fact that his administration was a coalition government with the United Liberal Democrats, whose chairman was serving as the prime minister.

The first meeting of the NSSC was held on March 7 in the conference room of the Office of North-South Dialogue. At this meeting I presented six agenda items, which were the fruit of three weeks of preparation and the results of the preparatory working-level coordination meeting.

* * * * * * * * *

The first item concerned the sharing of the cost for light water reactors (LWR). In a letter to the U.S. president, former president Kim Young-sam had promised, "South Korea will pay for seventy percent of the cost of the LWR, which will be constructed in North Korea in accordance with the U.S.-DPRK Agreed Framework." The U.S. government wanted the new administration to honor the previous administration's pledge.

Of the total cost estimate of around $5.2 billion (later re-estimated at $4.6 billion), South Korea and Japan were committed to pay $3.6 billion and $1 billion, respectively. It was not determined who would pay the remainder. The policymakers of the previous administration had thought that North Korea would soon collapse, and when it did, that the South would naturally have ownership of the light water reactors.

In the committee meeting, there were objections to assuming seventy percent of the burden, regardless of the imminent collapse theory. According to them, the financial burden was simply too costly. Yet, the majority supported the view that agreements between governments ought to be honored even after a change of administrations. This view also took into account that the Agreed Framework was adopted with the agreement of the South Korean government to stop North Korea's nuclear development.

At the end of the discussion, subject to approval by the National Assembly, we agreed to reconfirm South Korea's financial commitment and to pay South Korea's share in Korean currency and materials. The unresolved remainder of the cost should be the responsibility of the United States. The committee decided that the new administration should inform the United States of its reconfirmation, as well as the terms of payment and our government's position on the unresolved portion of the cost.

* * * * * * * * *

The LWR project began with the establishment of the Korean Peninsula Energy Development Organization (KEDO) and the participation of 200 workers each from the North and South, undertaking the basic groundwork in the Kumho area of North Hamgyeong Province, North Korea in August 1997.

According to the Agreed Framework, the construction of the LWR was to be completed by 2003, but it seemed that even if everything went smoothly, the first reactor would not be completed before early 2008—a delay of five years from the original plan.

When the Republican administration of George W. Bush—which had opposed the LWR project—was inaugurated, the project suffered severe blows. The hard line "neocons," including Vice President Dick Cheney, attacked the LWR project as a "symbol of diplomatic humiliation" and also opposed the provision of heavy fuel oil to North Korea. They did not hide their intention to abolish the Agreed Framework.

Ultimately, at the end of 2002, the Bush administration, raising suspicions of a North Korean highly enriched uranium program (HEUP), suspended the LWR project, which had been approximately thirty-five percent completed. About $1.5 billion, to which South Korea contributed $1.1 billion, had been spent for the project at the time of its suspension.

＊　＊　＊　＊　＊　＊　＊　＊　＊

The second agenda item for the NSSC was the Four-Party Talks. The committee meeting confirmed the principle of parallel promotion of the Four-Party Talks and a separate channel of North-South dialogue, as previously agreed upon by the United States when I discussed the issue with its representatives. At the first round of the Four-Party Talks in December 1997, our side raised the issue of the improvement of North-South relations. However, the North had objected, saying that the Four-Party Talks were not the venue to discuss the North-South issue. For the North, it was rather a forum to discuss a U.S.–North Korea peace treaty to replace the Military Armistice Agreement and U.S. troop withdrawal from South Korea.

During the second round of Four-Party Talks in Geneva in mid-March 1998, North Korea proposed a revised agenda for "Change in the Status and Role of U.S. Forces in Korea," instead of the withdrawal of U.S. troops from Korea. However, the United States rejected the proposal, arguing that the issue of U.S. forces in Korea should be discussed along with all other military issues during the final stage of building a peace regime on the peninsula.

The Four-Party Talks had begun as the result of a U.S.-ROK summit agreement on Jeju Island in April 1996. A preparatory meeting in New York in August 1997 preceded the talks. The four parties met for six rounds over the course of two years until August 1999. The parties agreed to set up and run two subcommittees. But they did not make any progress due to the North's insistence that the issues of U.S. troop withdrawal and a peace treaty with the United States be treated as the main agenda for the talks. In the end, the Kim Young-sam administration's "4 minus 2 strategy," aimed at internationalizing the inter-Korean issue based on the assumption of an imminent North Korean collapse, had failed.

＊　＊　＊　＊　＊　＊　＊　＊　＊

The third agenda item was adjusting defense burden sharing with the United States. Korea began sharing the defense burden with the United States in 1989 with its first payment of $45 million, increasing its share each year according to the principle of paying one-third—$400 million of the total cost. However, it was financially difficult for South Korea to pay as agreed upon due to a foreign exchange crisis that had precipitated the IMF's intervention. The won-dollar exchange rate had fallen from 900 to 1 to 1,900 to 1.

Noting that our share of the defense burden was mostly used to pay the wages of Korean workers employed by the U.S. military forces, in addition to construction costs payable to Korean contractors, the committee agreed that it would be more reasonable and practical to pay Korea's share at the previous exchange rate. The committee decided that the Ministry of National Defense should negotiate with the United States regarding the application of this matter. Fortunately, this was later settled through a process of negotiation.

* * * * * * * * *

The fourth agenda item was the provision of food aid to North Korea. In response to the fourth call of the UN World Food Program (WFP), we decided, as did the previous administration, to provide humanitarian assistance of 30,000 tons of corn and 10,000 tons of wheat flour ($11 million worth of aid). The previous administration had also sent 50,000 tons of corn to the North through the UN Food and Agriculture Organization (FAO).

However, we decided upon a new principle of food assistance in which we would provide food directly to the North in our name. We also decided to encourage non-governmental organizations (NGOs) to provide humanitarian assistance to the North Korean people. We believed this would help foster a sense of national community between people in the North and South. This would also help facilitate the resolution of the issue of separated families and contribute to improved inter-Korean relations.

During the five years of the Kim Dae-jung administration, we directly provided 700,000 tons of rice, 430,000 tons of corn, and 915,000 tons of fertilizer to the North, and NGOs shipped 80,000 tons of corn and 30,000 tons of wheat flour directly to North Korea.

The fifth agenda item for the NSSC was the foundation of North Korea policy, which was prepared by the Ministry of Unification, based on my initial work mentioned earlier. This policy foundation was later adopted at the second NSSC meeting.

* * * * * * * * *

The sixth item was my proposal for improved operation of the National Security Council. The committee approved this proposal as I presented it, without revision. The National Assembly approved an amendment to National Security Council law in May. Rules for NSC operation were proclaimed by presidential decree, and on June 5 the Secretariat of the National Security Council was established.

* * * * * * * * *

The first meeting of the NSSC was successful. The committee decided to meet at four o'clock every Thursday afternoon. Prior to committee meetings, a working-level coordinating meeting would be held with the participation of assistant minister-level officials every Tuesday afternoon to discuss the agenda for the upcoming meeting to ensure its efficient operation.

To guarantee the freedom and confidentiality of committee discussions, the only other person allowed at the committee meetings was one note-taker. After the president's approval, copies of a report of each meeting were distributed to members the following morning. This rule was observed from the first meeting.

I suggested that the members should have dinner together after each meeting, and all of them welcomed the idea. My intent for these dinners was for members to have an opportunity to exchange information and views that may not have been covered during the official meetings, to build a spirit of teamwork, and to enhance mutual understanding and friendship. These post-committee meeting dinners were observed until the end of the Kim Dae-jung administration.

The NSSC deliberated many important policy issues that greatly contributed to the president's decision-making during his five-year tenure. President Kim frequently spoke highly of the activities of the NSSC at the State Council conferences and at the meetings of the senior presidential secretaries. He thanked the NSSC for assisting him to make the right decisions with comfort and confidence in the area of foreign affairs, national defense and unification. The meticulous President Kim approved almost one hundred percent of the recommendations by the Standing Committee.

During the five years of the Kim Dae-jung administration, beginning with its first meeting on March 7, 1998, until its last meeting on February 20, 2003, the NSSC held a total of 229 meetings. The committee met almost every week with the exception of those times when the president traveled overseas and required two committee members to accompany him. The president made twenty-five such overseas trips.

During its five-year operation, the NSSC reviewed 708 agenda items in total. Of these, 39 percent were related to North Korean issues, 28 percent to foreign affairs, and 19 percent to national defense. The National Security Council meeting was presided over by the president three or four times a year.

As the Senior Presidential Secretary of National Security and Foreign Affairs, Minister of Unification, Director of National Intelligence Service, and Special Assistant to the President for Unification, Foreign Affairs and Security, I attended all the standing committee meetings with the exception of one. President Kim Dae-jung wanted me to contribute to the consistency of policy by attending the meetings without fail.

Open Panmunjom

In order to find the thread that would unwind the spool of inter-Korean relations, I believed we needed to make multidimensional efforts. During the early period of the Kim Dae-jung administration, I focused on four areas of interest regarding North Korea. One of the urgent tasks lying before us was the restoration of dialogue between the North and South authorities.

I also thought it was important for private businesses to actively engage in trade with the North and to promote economic cooperation. We needed policy measures to encourage contact and exchange with the North on the private business level, which had previously been avoided. It was also urgent to restore in any form the military armistice meetings, which had been dysfunctional for the previous seven years.

* * * * * * * * * *

The first task was to begin a dialogue between the authorities of both sides. In early April 1998 the North proposed to hold a vice-ministerial meeting to discuss matters of mutual interest, including the provision of fertilizer.

Prior to this proposal, a North-South Red Cross meeting had been held in Beijing toward the end of March. At that meeting, the North Korean Red Cross requested that the South provide the North with 200,000 tons of fertilizer. The South Korean Red Cross told its counterpart that such a large amount of fertilizer aid could not be handled through the Red Cross channel, and suggested this matter be dealt with by the governments.

On April 11 a vice minister-level meeting was held in Beijing. The South was represented by Vice Minister of Unification Chung Se-hyon, and the North by Chun Gum-cheol, DPRK Cabinet Councilor. Our side proposed a "principle of reciprocity," linking fertilizer aid with meetings between separated family members. The North side turned it down, and the meeting ended without results.

The Kim Dae-jung administration placed high priority on the issue of separated families. This issue was pushed personally by President Kim, who regarded it as the responsibility of the government to realize the passionate desires of separated families and find out whether their family members were still alive, so they could meet them even once before they died. There were more than 100,000 people who had registered in the hope of meeting their family members in the North.

We made it clear that we would link a gradual provision of fertilizer to the issue of separated families. Our side proposed that the South would provide 200,000 tons of fertilizer on humanitarian grounds in return for the North's equally humanitarian cooperation to resolve the issue of separated families. The North side responded that applying the principle of reciprocity to a humanitarian issue was inhumane. The North insisted on provision of fertilizer first, and discussion of issues of mutual interest later. Although the North had great expectations for the new Kim Dae-jung administration, it did not show any interest in compromising its position throughout the week-long talks with the South in Beijing. Thus, the talks that had been resumed after a lapse of four years were ended unilaterally by the North.

After the failure of the talks, the North began launching an offensive campaign to denounce the Sunshine policy. During the same period, the provocative incident of a North Korean submarine infiltration occurred. The domestic press criticized the Sunshine policy for its failure to resolve the issue of separated families. This was the beginning of our attempt to apply the "principle of reciprocity."

However, a lesson we learned from our failed talks was to give first and take later, since we had resources to help the North. This would protect the North Koreans' pride and help us pursue our goal. The question was how to enlist the support of the opposition party and the conservative press, which were strongly advocating the "principle of reciprocity." A year later, in May 1999, inter-Korean talks resumed as the result of secret contacts between the authorities of both sides.

* * * * * * * * *

At the end of April 1998, in accordance with its policy of reducing tension and improving North South relations, the Kim Dae-jung administration announced "Measures to Vitalize Economic Cooperation between the North and South." Based on the principle of "separation of politics and economy," the government decided to allow business people to travel to North Korea, to approve the free provision or leasing of production facilities to the North, and to lift the $1 million limit on loans to the North. To allow South Korean businesses to invest in all areas, the new measures switched from a "positive system" that permitted certain investment areas on a list to a "negative system" that imposed no restriction on investment areas, except for some sensitive areas. The government also took the bold move of imposing no restrictions on the amount of investment. In conclusion, businesses were now free to make their decisions in economic cooperation with the North according to the principles of a market economy.

After the government's new measures were announced, business people, through contacts with the North, studied the economic feasibility of investing in the North. But the dominant assessment was that it was too early to invest in the North due to the lack of infrastructure and legal assurances, as well as the uneasiness of an unstable situation. As time passed, it turned out that "processing-on-commission trade" was the safest form of business that would allow South Korean companies to take advantage of cheap North Korean labor. As this type of processing-on-commission trade increased in volume, more South Koreans traveled to the North to provide technical assistance and quality control. Under such an adverse business environment, Hyundai Chairman Chung Ju-young actively sought to explore a tourism project at Mount Kumgang and other avenues of business cooperation. Through business, he contributed greatly to the improvement of relations between the North and South.

* * * * * * * * * *

Allowing private sector exchanges and dialogue was also an urgent task for the improvement of inter-Korean relations. To celebrate the August 15 Liberation Day, some civil organizations were planning to propose to the North the joint holding of an "August 15 North-South Unification Festival." It was time for the government to cease monopolizing the issue of unification and to encourage a civic unification movement, and assist it in the right direction. The government recognized a need to help establish an NGO to promote civilian contact and exchange with the North.

Until this point, North Korea had waged a political offensive against the South each year as part of its "united front tactics," calling for a "pan-national North-South rally of the masses representing all social walks and ranks," or a "national conference of political negotiation." North Korea also asserted that North-South dialogue for unification of the fatherland should not be a monopoly of the Northern and Southern authorities, and that the people should get together in one place to discuss the issues of unification, including U.S. troop withdrawal and abrogation of the National Security Law.

* * * * * * * * * *

The Kim Dae-jung administration did not wish to maintain the past policy of disapproval of civilian contacts between the North and the South. We thought it was desirable to initiate proactive proposals with confidence in dealing with the North. Even if the North would demand the withdrawal of U.S. troops or the abrogation of the National Security Law, we thought we should confront the North up front and aggressively argue our positions.

As discussed earlier, with the changed international environment and the widening disparity in economic capabilities between the North and the South, we now had the resources and political confidence that we could persuade the North and gradually lead them in exchange and cooperation. To do this, I felt we needed a civilian national organization that would voice concerted views.

The South is a diverse, liberal democratic society. Regarding the North Korean issue, it was necessary to establish a dialogue between the liberals and conservatives to coordinate their views and resolve their conflicting positions. I had the conviction that the sound conservatives (not the extreme rightists) and the healthy liberals (not the extreme leftists) could work together, and that national issues such as unification and inter-Korean relations should be pursued from a balance between the conservatives and liberals.

In early June, President Kim Dae-jung instructed me to undertake a positive review of the issue of holding a joint North-South civilian unification festival. In response, I stressed the need for a pan-national council for reconciliation and cooperation. This issue was reviewed by the relevant agencies and approved by the NSSC meeting held in early July.

The recommendation was to support the establishment of a pan-national organization that would include political parties and unification movement organizations to carry out campaigns to integrate public opinion, minimize internal conflicts within the South, and promote inter-Korean exchange and cooperation. If realized, this new organization would also lead the North-South dialogue on the civilian level.

Political parties and unification movement organizations supported this proposal. In early September 1998, the Korea Council for National Reconciliation and Cooperation was officially founded with some 120 affiliate civilian organizations.

* * * * * * * * *

Another urgent task for improvement of relations was the re-opening of Panmunjom as a location for inter-Korean discussions—it had been closed to talks for the past five years. Panmunjom served as the venue for the negotiation of the armistice in the 1950s, Red Cross talks and other North-South contacts in the 1970s, and for working-level contacts for the North-South High-level Talks in the early 1990s. It also served as a passing point for travel between Seoul and Pyongyang.

However, Panmunjom had again turned into a place of tension with the suspension of the Military Armistice Commission's (MAC) function. For North-South reconciliation and peace, I thought we should open Panmunjom for inter-Korean liaison, dialogue, and meetings of separated family members. It should also serve as a corridor for exchange of visits and transport of goods. For this to happen, I knew that the MAC should first resume meetings at Panmunjom. I had first to find out what was preventing the MAC from holding meetings.

In 1991, the United Nations Command (UNC) appointed a South Korean general as its senior representative for the MAC. In response, North Korea ignored the MAC for seven years. In 1994, the North declared the UNC–North Korea MAC meeting ineffective and demanded it be replaced by a "North Korea–U.S. General Officers Meeting." The intent of the proposal was clearly to exclude South Korea, which was absolutely unacceptable to the South.

After the start of the Kim Dae-jung administration, North Korea revised its proposal to hold a "General Officers Meeting between the Korean People's Army and the UN Forces." This proposal did not make any progress due to some objections that were raised by our Ministry of Defense (MND). The MND insisted that the meeting should be held within the framework of the Military Armistice Commission: all participants including the ROK representative should have equal voice and the meeting should be operated with the notion of a "main speaker" rather than "a senior representative."

Neither the North Koreans nor the UNC appreciated the MND's position. I advocated that it was important to manage the armistice system and also open Panmunjom for improvement of North-South relations. I advised that the MND seek pragmatic interests rather than sticking to its position. The specific point of my advice was that we should revise the MND proposal from the "framework of the Military Armistice Commission" to the "framework of the Military Armistice Agreement," which reflected a higher concept.

As for the right of voice, I suggested that a senior representative exercise the right of voice according to international practices, provided that other representatives also have the right to speak at the meeting.

American Ambassador Bosworth and General John H. Tilelli, the commanding general of the UNC, supported my suggestion and also held the view that North would accept it. I referred this issue to the NSSC, where the MND conceded to my suggestion.

Toward the end of May, the UNC presented this revised proposal to the North Korean side and succeeded in getting its acceptance. In June, the first meeting of the Panmunjom General Officers Talks was held, restoring the mission of the Military Armistice Commission that had been suspended for seven years. The Liaison Office of North-South dialogue also reopened. Panmunjom was open again after four years.

In mid-June that year, Chairman of Hyundai Chung Ju-young staged a spectacular event when he led a convey of trucks carrying 500 head of cattle through Panmunjom. This impressive event, which led later to the opening of tourism at Mount Kumgang, provided a turning point for the people's perspectives on North-South relations. It was the opening signal of a new era of reconciliation and cooperation between the North and the South. Such an event would have been impossible without the May agreement between the UNC and North Korea.

Mount Kumgang Tourism

Honorary Hyundai Chairman Chung Ju-young (1915–2001) was the first person who proactively responded to the announcement of the government's "Measures to Vitalize Economic Cooperation between the North and South." At the beginning of 1989, nine years before the start of the Kim Dae-jung administration, Chung had visited the North and reached an agreement with the North Korean authorities that Hyundai would carry out economic projects, including a tourism business at Mount Kumgang. However, he had been unable to carry out the projects. Chairman Chung wanted to undertake these projects again after the new administration was inaugurated.

Chung showed enthusiasm for the tourism project. He firmly believed in reducing tension on the Korean Peninsula and contributing to peaceful unification. He said, "To live mutually helping each other between the North and the South amounts to unification. Development of Mount Kumgang, which is my hometown, is the last wish of my life."

I believed actively supporting Chairman Chung's projects, based on the principle of separation of politics and economy, was a shortcut to the success of our policy for reconciliation and cooperation. I took the lead in encouraging the relevant government agencies that were still skeptical, to cooperate with and assist Chairman Chung.

When Chung visited the North on June 16, 1998, taking with him 500 head of cattle through Panmunjom, he earned the North's permission to develop Mount Kumgang and carry out tourism business by using tourist cruise boats from the South. In October, Chung took another herd of cattle—501 head this time—to North Korea and met with Chairman Kim Jong-il. The two agreed that Hyundai would start the Mount Kumgang tourism business beginning November 18 of that year.

The first meeting between Chairman Chung Ju-young and Chairman Kim Jong-il took place at the Baekhwawon Guest House, where they had a broad discussion of economic cooperation beyond the Mount Kumgang tourism project. The topics of their discussion were known to include oil exploration in the West Sea; automobile assembly and production; the doubling of the Seoul-Shineuiju railway tracks; and construction of a thermal power plant in Pyongyang.

Once he confirmed Kim Jong-il's ardent interest in economic cooperation, Chung asked for long-term exclusive business rights to carry out those projects. In the pursuit of mutual interests, he proposed the construction of an industrial complex on the north side of the DMZ to utilize South Korean capital and technology with North Korean labor. (Chung had in mind Haeju, located on the west coast.) Kim Jong-il accepted Chung's proposals in principle.

* * * * * * * * *

The NSSC reviewed whether to approve the Mount Kumgang tourism project at the recommendation of the Ministry of Unification, which reported that Chairman Kim Jong-il issued a special order to override North Korean law and systems in order to promote the tourism project. Apparently, the North had decided to open the Mount Kumgang area, which was North Korea's front-line area, as well as the Jangjeon port, which was a naval base. We had thought it would be difficult for the North to open Jangjeon port because it served as an important front-line base for the North Korean fleet and its submarines.

At Hyundai Chairman Chung's prodding, the North had initially decided to open the Wonsan port located further in the north, instead of the Jangjeon port, due to the military's strong opposition. We learned that Chairman Kim personally decided to open the Jangjeon port. The members of the NSSC were not fully convinced of the veracity of the unification ministry's report. However, they all agreed that if the report was true, it would be an important first step toward the reduction of military tension.

According to the agreement between the Hyundai chairman and the North Korean leader, the North would guarantee safe passage for the tourist cruise ship along a route five miles from the coastline. A comprehensive memorandum of understanding to assure the personal safety and the safe return of tourists would be issued by the Ministry of Social Safety. Neither side should recognize escapees or defectors to the other side. In addition, they agreed on a mechanism to resolve disputes that might arise once tourism began. The agreement also included a provision that North would provide Hyundai with a certain area for the development of a tourism complex, as well as an exclusive right of development for thirty years—all of which Hyundai would pay for in cash.

Later it was learned that in a confidential deal, for the price of its thirty-year exclusive business rights, Hyundai had agreed to pay the North $942 million in monthly installments of $12 million over six years and four months, until May 2005. We were astonished to hear of the large $12 million per month amount. However, we heard that Hyundai was satisfied with the negotiated deal. This agreement was soon revised based on the number of tourists.

On the basis of the principle of the separation of politics and economy, at the recommendation of the Ministry of Unification, the NSSC approved granting a permit for the Mount Kumgang tourism project. The committee wanted to see Hyundai carry out the tourism project as a purely private business matter according to the principles of a market economy. With this decision, the Ministry of Unification was tasked to come up with proper measures for the personal protection of tourists and to prepare an educational tourism program. For the form of payment for Hyundai's long-term business rights, the government decided to recommend payment in goods since we were concerned that cash might be used for military purposes. Our intelligence organizations were instructed to follow the flow of cash from the deal and to plan an initiative to prevent the military's use of the funds. An intelligence research report confirmed that North Korea was spending more than $100 million a year on importing construction equipment for national land development and parts for aged plant facilities. The report estimated that some of the cash the North received from the South was spent on those payments.

* * * * * * * * *

On November 18, in a festive atmosphere with fireworks that lit the night skies, the first cruise tourist ship, with 826 tourists and Chairman Chung Ju-young aboard, left Donghae port for Mount Kumgang. This historic and emotional scene was broadcast to all corners of the world.

Two days later, President Clinton arrived in Seoul and from his hotel room watched the departure of the second tourist cruise on television. At the press conference following a summit with President Kim Dae-jung the next day, President Clinton described his impression of the scene. He said he was moved by the festive atmosphere of peace in which the cruise boat left, carrying over 600 tourists. He said it was "a very inspiring and beautiful scene."

Clinton's comment on this scene of inter-Korean exchange and cooperation, a scene of the reduction of tensions, and an example of the success of
the Sunshine policy, was televised worldwide. This helped subdue the hardliners' outcries regarding security crises and to resolve the concerns of business investors who had been worried about security risks in Korea.

* * * * * * * * *

The opening of the Mount Kumgang tourism project was undertaken
during a period of several critical events, including suspicions that North
Korea had built an underground nuclear weapons complex at Kumchangni,
and the North's test launch of the three-stage Taepodong-1 ballistic missile
that flew over the skies of Japan in August. There were demands from the
hardliners at home and abroad to launch a "precision attack" to take out
the North Korean nuclear facilities, creating the atmosphere of a security
crisis. At a time when South Korea needed to induce foreign investment to
overcome its "IMF financial crisis," foreign investors became reluctant to do
business in South Korea for fear of the possibility of war.

After eight months in office, the Kim Dae-jung administration, which
started with a promise to search for reconciliation and cooperation, had not
been able to find a starting point to improve its relations with the North. At
the same time, the government was confronted with difficult challenges from
the financial crisis and security crisis.

It was under these circumstances that the luxurious tourist cruise boat
began its operation, carrying full loads of South Korean tourists to the
North, tearing down the barrier of the division. This was significant in several ways. The tourism provided an opportunity to reduce tension on the
peninsula and to improve inter-Korean relations. It provided a good opportunity for both sides to turn around their economies.

Since we were in a difficult security situation, it was not easy for the
government to approve the Mount Kumgang tourism project. I had recommended to the president that despite some concerns and lack of assurance
for success, he needed to approve the launch of the Mount Kumgang tourist project, as an effort to resolve the double crisis of finance and security.
The president fully supported my view and accepted my recommendation.
Nevertheless, this was an adventure.

A Hero's Welcome in the United States

President Kim Dae-jung's early diplomacy was focused on gaining the support of the international community for South Korea's efforts to avert the
economic crisis and for its Sunshine policy toward North Korea.

The United States, Japan, and China welcomed President Kim Dae-jung as a "state guest" to show him their highest courtesy. Before he became the president, Kim Dae-jung was already an international hero who had suffered imprisonment, house arrest, and political exile throughout his lifelong struggle for democracy and human rights. Now he was recognized as the first Korean president who had accomplished a democratic transition of power from the ruling party to the opposition party. For this reason, he was truly respected and well-treated wherever he went. He also was highly praised as a president who was pursuing aggressive economic reforms based on democracy and the market economy in order to overcome the difficulties of the financial crisis. In addition, his diplomatic skills were outstanding.

* * * * * * * * *

In early June 1998, President Kim embarked on a nine-day state visit to the United States. On June 9, the national anthems of the two countries were played on the White House lawn, accompanied by a 21-gun salute at a grand official arrival ceremony, which was followed by an honor guard review, welcome remarks by President William Clinton, and return remarks by President Kim.

In his welcome remarks, President Clinton expressed his sincere respect and admiration for President Kim:

> Kim Dae-jung is here today as president, after the first-ever democratic change of power from the governing party to the opposition in the fifty-year history of the Republic of Korea. . . . The irresistible longing for freedom, human rights, and democracy has carried Kim Dae-jung to the presidency of the country, and now back to America, where he once lived in exile . . .

Clinton called Kim, who had long been unjustly politically persecuted and even sentenced to death, "one of the heroes of freedom," along with South Africa's Nelson Mandela, Czechoslovakia's Vaclav Havel, and Poland's Lech Walesa.

The arrival ceremony was followed by a serious summit in an atmosphere of mutual respect at the Oval Office. The 65-minute summit meeting was attended by Minister of Foreign Affairs and Trade Park Chung-soo, Ambassador Lee Hong-koo, and myself from the Korean side; and Vice President Al Gore, Secretary of State Madeleine Albright, and National Security Advisor Samuel Berger from the U.S. side.

At the summit, President Clinton did not spare his praise for President Kim. He said many people were encouraged by President Kim's generosity, conviction, and vision. He also spoke highly of President Kim's accomplish-

Korea-U.S. summit at the White House on June 9, 1998. From left: the author; Korean Ambassador to Washington Lee Hong-koo; Foreign Minister Park Chung-soo; Kang Kyung-hwa, interpreter; President Kim Dae-jung; President Bill Clinton; Tong Kim, interpreter; and Vice President Al Gore. Courtesy Lim Dong-won.

ments during the first hundred days, including economic reforms, noting that democracy and the market economy in Korea was a model for Asia, with a positive impact on other countries. The American president also expressed a strong commitment to support President Kim's efforts to revive the economy.

Then Clinton asked Kim to explain his North Korea policy. As if he had been waiting for this moment, President Kim explained the policy for thirty minutes in an upbeat tone, beginning with an assessment of the North Korean situation. Having listened to President Kim seriously, Clinton agreed with Kim's approach and said, "In view of your stature and experience, I would like you to lead on the issue of the Korean Peninsula. You take the driver's seat and I will take the seat beside to help you."

At this moment, I was touched and unable to control my joy. This was the moment of change in the Clinton administration's view of North Korea.

In the arena of international diplomacy, personal friendship and trust between heads of state become assets for both countries. In practice, President Clinton faithfully lived up to his word throughout his presidency to jointly pursue an engagement policy towards North Korea. The ROK-U.S. relationship during the Kim Dae-jung and Bill Clinton era was the best it had ever been.

In advance of President Kim's visit to the United States, the *New York Times* reported that on his visit President Kim would ask that the U.S. government end economic sanctions on North Korea. The *Times* editorial said, "President Kim knows well that the best way to bring change to North Korea is not to sanction it but to expand economic and diplomatic relations with the North. The United States should listen to him."

The Clinton administration was not ready to lift the sanctions, and President Kim was employing the diplomacy of taking the initiative through the press to build a favorable atmosphere.

* * * * * * * * *

That evening, 200 politicians, businessmen, human rights activists, and successful Korean-Americans attended a state dinner at the White House. The guests were ushered by junior military officers as the United States Marine Band played music to create a friendly and relaxed ambiance. I was particularly impressed by the performance of soprano Hong Hye-gyong, a graduate of the Julliard Music School, who started performing in New York six years earlier. She performed two songs and received thunderous applause from the audience. The first song was "The Great Lord," as a symbol of the path of life President Kim had traveled, and the other was "Longing for Mount Kumgang," reflecting wishes for unification. Before singing, Ms. Hong said, "My mom loves President Kim so much, we call him 'Mom's boyfriend' at home." Everybody laughed and applauded.

Another memorable event during President Kim's visit to Washington was his speech before a joint audience of both chambers of the U.S. Congress. The House chamber was filled with senators, congressmen, senior administration officials, ranking military generals and members of the diplomatic corps in Washington. They all stood up to welcome "the hero from Korea" upon his entrance into the chamber. During his speech, President Kim received sixteen standing ovations.

The mass media of newspapers and television welcomed "the hero from Korea who has championed democracy and human rights" in their competitive coverage of President Kim's visit to the United States. The visit was a big success.

A New Era of Cooperation between Korea and Japan

President Kim visited Japan for four days from October 7, 1998. Twenty-five years earlier he had been kidnapped from Tokyo as a dissident by the military regime in Seoul. Many years later, he was now returning to Japan as a state guest and the president of the Republic of Korea. I could well imagine how difficult it must have been for him to convey his sentiments. The Japanese had a great interest in President Kim's visit. Newspapers and broadcasts all welcomed his visit, covering it for days in advance.

Unlike his visit to the United States in June, which we had predicted would be successful, we were not sure how the president's Japan visit would go. The most difficult and important question was how we were going to discuss and resolve the issue of the past, which had been the cause of emotional conflict between the two peoples. The immediate issue of economic cooperation was also important. There were three additional issues that were difficult. They included conclusion of a fishery agreement, opening the cultural market to Japan, and the issue of comfort women from World War II.

* * * * * * * * *

The itinerary for the first day of President Kim's visit to Japan was to attend an official welcome ceremony at the Guest House, pay a courtesy call on the Japanese emperor, and attend a welcome dinner at the royal palace. On the second day, the president met with Prime Minister Obuchi Keizo for a summit in the morning, and delivered a speech at the Diet in the afternoon before attending a dinner hosted by the Japanese prime minister in the evening.

At every opportunity during his visit to Japan, President Kim stressed, "Let's clear up the unfortunate past history of the twentieth century and develop our partnership for the future in this threshold of the twenty-first century." He said, "The past is not overcome by forgetting it, but will be overcome by remembering it." He was mindful of the importance of the accurate teaching of history. Moving towards the creation of a new partnership for the future, he signed a joint statement that reflected this idea. Korea and Japan also adopted an "action plan" that consisted of forty-three items across five fields.

In the joint statement, Prime Minister Obuchi Keizo said, "Japan humbly accepts the historical fact that by its colonial domination of the past, it caused great damage and pain to the Korean people. And for that, Japan has deep remorse and apologizes (*owabi*) from the bottom of our heart."

President Kim responded, "I accept and value the expression of the Japanese prime minister's recognition of history. Now the times call for us to overcome history's unfortunate past and develop a new future-oriented relationship based on reconciliation and cooperation."

The two leaders agreed "to open a new era of exchange and cooperation between the peoples of their countries with fully-open hearts." Korea agreed to gradually open itself to Japanese popular culture and promote the exchange of youth and people in all fields.

As part of the agreement on economic cooperation, Japan promised that its Export/Import Bank would give a $3 billion loan to South Korea. Other pending issues such as a fishery agreement and a dual taxation prevention agreement were also resolved through President Kim's visit. The two leaders agreed to strengthen cooperation on security and other global issues. To his special credit, President Kim secured Japan's support for his engagement policy towards North Korea.

*　*　*　*　*　*　*　*　*

The climax of President Kim's Japan visit was perhaps reached during his speech at the Diet, at which the president addressed to an audience of 600 legislators. His delivery was interrupted by applause ten times. The speech was simultaneously televised in Japan and Korea. Many Japanese viewers were impressed by it, and several Diet members commented, "It was a moving speech that touched me."

In the speech, President Kim Dae-jung said:

> There is a clear contrast between pre- and post-war Japan. By choosing imperialism and war, Japan caused great pain and sacrifice both for the Japanese people and people of other Asian nations, including Korea. However, after the end of World War II, Japan changed. The Japanese people achieved parliamentary democracy and economic growth, upholding the principle of non-nuclear pacifism. Yet, there are many people in Asia who still cannot discard their suspicions of and their concerns about Japan. This is because they believe Japan has not done enough on its own to correctly understand and humbly reflect upon its past. This is very unfortunate not only for Japan but also for all the countries in Asia.

In a follow up to this acute assessment, he continued:

> It now is time for our two countries to look squarely at our past and forge a future-oriented relationship. Japan needs genuine courage to look at the past squarely and respect the judgment of history. Korea should also rightly evaluate Japan in all its changed aspects, and search with hope for future possibilities.

According to opinion polls, 81 percent of Koreans and 78 percent of Japanese said they believed President Kim's visit had greatly contributed to the improvement of ROK-Japan relations.

Upgrading Korea-China-Relations

After his visits to the United States and Japan, President Kim Dae-jung visited China in November 1998.

Having gone through the normal protocols for a summit visit—including a 21-gun salute and an honor guard review—President Kim had a summit meeting with Chinese president Jiang Zemin in the East Hall of the Great Hall of the People in Beijing.

The two leaders agreed to expand the relationship between China and Korea, which had been focused on economic and trade relations for six years since its normalization, into all other areas of political, security, social and cultural affairs. They also upgraded the diplomatic stature of their relationship from a "neighborly friendly relationship" to a "cooperative partnership," and agreed to actively promote exchanges and cooperation in various fields.

A joint statement was adopted to reflect the summit agreement. It consisted of twelve paragraphs with specific agreement on thirty-four projects. Included in the joint statement were expanded exchange between the governments, parliaments, and political parties of the two countries; efforts to increase trade in view of China's persistent trade deficit; Korea's loan of 7 billion won to China; and the active participation of Korean corporations in the construction of infrastructure in China.

President Jiang expressed enthusiastic support for South Korea's Sunshine policy, and he gave this advice: "If a cold wind blows to the North, they will hold their cloaks more tightly. In contact with North Koreans, you need patience and restraint. It is important not to hurt their pride but to build a generous environment." He added, "President Kim's support for an improvement of relations between the United States and North Korea is very wise."

However, when President Kim asked him to exercise China's influence on North Korea to improve North-South relations, the Chinese president declared, "China has no influence on North Korea." He said, "The Chinese ambassador in Pyongyang does not even know whether Chairman Kim Jong-il is a person who can speak or is a mute." Jiang probably meant to say that his ambassador could not meet with Chairman Kim Jong-il.

President Jiang also said that the North Koreans even rejected his proposed visit to Pyongyang. This was a period of a strained relationship between North Korea and China. His discontent and distrust of the North was understood in that context. However, China–North Korea relations were restored by Kim Jong-il's visit to China in May 2000.

*   *   *   *   *   *   *   *   *

The next day there was a welcome dinner hosted by Chinese Premier Zhu Rongji. There, President Kim recollected his past hard days in comparison with Zhu's own ordeal during the Cultural Revolution, thereby building personal human relations. The Korean president and the Chinese premier also discussed a number of specific projects for economic cooperation.

President Kim asked for favorable consideration for South Korean companies to participate in a high-speed rail construction project, the automobile industry, commercialization of code division multiple access (CDMA) in wireless communications, the financial sector, and the construction of atomic energy reactors in China. After the exercise of President Kim Dae-jung's effective salesmanship, Premier Zhu explained China's situation, promising his generous support for the accommodation of South Korea's proposals.

CHAPTER 9

PEACEMAKING

Hole in the Ground

In early August 1998, the press started covering leaked reports concerning suspected underground nuclear facilities at Kumchangni. The reports alleged that North Korea was digging a large underground tunnel as part of building suspected underground nuclear facilities. In short, North Korea was allegedly continuing to develop a secret nuclear weapons program in violation of the Agreed Framework.

In early- to mid-July, the U.S. Congress released a report on the "Threat Assessment of Long-range Ballistic Missiles to the United States." The report was prepared by a commission headed by Donald Rumsfeld (who later became secretary of defense). It concluded that "rogue states like North Korea, Iraq, and Iran would be able to develop and possess long-range ballistic missiles within five years that could threaten the security of the continental United States, if they chose to do so." The report recommended the development and deployment of a missile defense system against missile threats.

The report's assessment differed from that of an earlier CIA report that these countries would take more than fifteen years to possess such missiles. In the beginning, the Rumsfeld report did not draw much attention, even within the United States.

ROK and U.S. intelligence agencies had been working together on Kumchangni for years by this time. They followed a policy of collecting evidence first and planning countermeasures later. The North Koreans had begun the Kumchangni underground project ten years earlier. The information we had then was that "large amounts of dirt were coming out from the digging of a big tunnel, and two huge dams and a bridge were being built in the adjacent valley." The number of army troops that were employed in this large construction project were comparable to the strength of a brigade. Yet, there was no sign that they were attempting to hide the project.

According to the U.S. Defense Intelligence Agency (DIA), the North Koreans had started installing a nuclear reactor and a reprocessing plant in the tunnel, and the two dams under construction would support a reservoir that would supply cooling water to the nuclear facilities in the tunnel. The DIA estimated that the North could start operating the nuclear facilities in as soon as two years. In view of the scale of the tunnel—190 meters in length and six stories high—the facilities would be able to produce enough plutonium to make "8 to 10 nuclear bombs a year."

When the DIA intelligence assessment on the North Korean underground nuclear facilities reached the U.S. Congress, its members and staff were alarmed and upset. This information was first published in a headline story in *Time* on August 10, and then by the *New York Times* on August 17. However, the CIA was known to be raising questions regarding the credibility of the DIA's unconfirmed intelligence.

Some of our people who were directly involved in dealing with North Korea wondered what could have been the reason behind the circulation of such unconfirmed information. There were suspicions that some hardliners in the DIA were creating an issue with the suspicious underground nuclear facilities in an effort to support the Rumsfeld recommendation for a missile defense system.

After a careful study, the NSSC announced,

> We have confirmed that a large-scale excavation project was in progress but its use is not clear at this point. There is no evidence to conclude that it was related to a nuclear weapons program. This is the shared assessment of the Republic of Korea and the United States.

Nevertheless, the conservative press continued to sensationalize the "suspected underground nuclear facilities at Kumchangni." The press accused the Kim Dae-jung administration of taking a lukewarm response to the North Korean nuclear issue because of its Sunshine policy.

* * * * * * * * *

A few days prior to a scheduled August 21 U.S.-DPRK high-level meeting in New York, Dick Christenson, the Deputy Chief of Mission at the U.S. embassy in Seoul, came to my office to listen to my views. He said that for the upcoming meeting the United States was considering raising the issue of the suspected underground nuclear facilities at Kumchangni. Christenson was an able diplomat, fluent in Korean, and had accompanied former president Jimmy Carter on a trip to Pyongyang.

Before he asked me a question, I said, "There has been no information showing that steel structures were transported into the underground site. There is no evidence showing the construction of a nuclear facility. Is it not premature to raise the issue at this point?" I also warned, "If you do not handle this carefully, it might backfire. What if the North Koreans demand compensation for the price of showing the underground site?" I suggested, "If the United States must raise this issue for some unavoidable reason, it would be better to discuss it as a supplementary agenda in a side discussion, not as the main topic for the talks."

My prediction turned out to be right. It was learned that the North demanded payment of $300 million for the price of allowing visits to the underground site. After providing the North with 600,000 tons of food in the form of humanitarian assistance, a U.S. inspection team was allowed to visit the suspected site. The team found that it was not being used for nuclear development. In the meantime, the Korean Peninsula was thrown into a security crisis because of the DIA's distorted and overblown intelligence. Consequently, the international credibility of the U.S. intelligence community was damaged.

When the truth came out, people became angry at the press. However, the press scarcely even reported on the results of the Kumchangni site inspection.

* * * * * * * * *

At the end of August, North Korea fired a Taepodong-1 missile. Since early August, I had carefully followed the preparations for the missile launch, receiving a daily intelligence report through the combined ROK-U.S. intelligence channel. We traced the progress for the preparation work at the missile test firing site in Taepodong, Hwadae-gun, North Hamgyung Province.

Finally on August 31, I received a report that the Taepodong-1 missile had been launched and had fallen into the Pacific Ocean, 500 kilometers east of the Japanese islands. The missile launched at 12:07 p.m. and it flew 1,550 kilometers in 4 minutes and 53 seconds before landing at 12:12 p.m.

North Korea did not make an official announcement until September 4. The announcement claimed that North Korea had "successfully launched a three-stage rocket to put a satellite into orbit." It called the three-stage rocket satellite "Gwangmyongseong-1," claiming that "it was circling the earth every 165 minutes and 6 seconds, transmitting signals and songs of Generals Kim Il-sung and Kim Jong-il."

The size of the satellite was very small—only 20–30 kilograms. The United States seemed to have failed to trace the trajectory of the rocket, prejudging it as a missile from the early stage of its launch. However, the collective judgment based on several circumstantial pieces of evidence, including a lack of signal transmissions from the alleged satellite, was that the North Koreans had succeeded in launching a satellite delivery system but had failed to put a satellite into orbit.

* * * * * * * * *

The motivation of the North Korean rocket launch seemed related to the celebration of the fiftieth anniversary of the North Korean regime, which had announced an "era of Kim Jong-il" toward a "strong and prosperous country." Attracting the world's attention, the rocket launch would be used as propaganda, portray itself as Kim Jong-il's achievement. The regime needed some good news for its people, who had been undergoing the hardship of the so-called arduous march for a number of years. It would serve to change the subdued social mood to a festive atmosphere.

On September 5, a day after the announcement of the satellite rocket launch, North Korea held the first session of the 10th Supreme People's Assembly, which adopted a constitutional revision to reorganize the governing structure and introduce some elements of a market economy. The constitutional revision abolished the position of State President (that was held by Kim Il-sung) and designated the President of the Presidium of the Supreme People's Assembly (Kim Young-nam) as the head of state. It also stipulated that the chairman of the National Defense Commission was the most powerful state position. It guaranteed the supreme authority of Chairman Kim Jong-il, who concurrently occupied the positions of the General Secretary of the Korean Workers' Party, the Chairman of the Central Military Commission of the Korean Workers' Party, and the Supreme Commander of the Korean People's Armed Forces.

This constitutional change symbolized the end of a period of "rule by the bequest" of Kim Il-sung, and the beginning of a period of "Kim Jong-il rule," four years after Kim Il-sung's death in July 1994.

* * * * * * * * *

In the wake of the Taepodong-1 missile launch and the emerging suspicion of underground nuclear facilities at Kumchangni, the Rumsfeld report gained more support from hardliners. Yet, a noted American North Korea specialist sarcastically commented, "It was fortunate that North Korea's launching of the Taepodong-1 missile resolved the question of a rationale for developing and deploying a NMD system against China. North Korea's missile capability is militarily insignificant but it may have a great psychological value." In a sense, Chairman Kim Jong-il and the American hardliners were maintaining a "partnership of mutual hostility."

In any case, the suspicions about North Korea's continued nuclear weapons program, on top of its development of long-range ballistic missile capability that could carry a nuclear warhead, provided hardliners with a good opportunity to alarm the U.S. Congress. The North Korean missile launch provided the Republican members of Congress, who disliked the U.S.-DPRK Agreed Framework, a basis to demand abrogation of the agreement. They cut the budget for the provision of heavy fuel oil to the North. Some of them demanded that the United States suspend talks or contacts with the untrustworthy North Koreans, and that the United States undertake a total review of North Korea policy. They also called for a precision military strike on the North Korean nuclear facilities.

The Taepodong-1 missile also had shocking reverberations in Japan. The Japanese government cancelled its commitment to contribute $1 billion to the construction of the light water reactors as agreed in the Agreed Framework. It also suspended humanitarian aid to North Korea and cancelled normalization talks with the North. This incident provided the right-wing Japanese nationalists with an excuse to advocate the strengthening of Japan's military capabilities.

*　*　*　*　*　*　*　*　*

Now the Clinton administration's forward-looking North Korea policy faced pressure for an overall review and revision. In mid-November, at the request of the opposition-dominated Congress, President Clinton appointed former Secretary of Defense William Perry as North Korea Policy Coordinator. Perry's mission was to undertake an official policy review and submit a final report to the Congress within five months.

I was shocked to hear the news that the former secretary of defense was appointed as the North Korea Policy Coordinator. He was known as a hardliner secretary of defense who pushed for a military attack during the so-called first nuclear crisis in the spring of 1994. This fact alone was enough to arouse my concerns that the Clinton administration's policy was already leaning towards a hard line.

All of a sudden, the "nightmare of June 1994" was revived. At that time, after the failure of a "package solution," the North Koreans started unloading spent fuel rods in disregard of a U.S. warning. Having judged that diplomacy had failed, the Pentagon rushed to plan an aerial strike on the nuclear facilities at Yongbyon.

Although the military attack plan was limited to destroying key components at the reactor site with precision bombs, it raised new concerns. Given the unique situation in the Korean Peninsula, such a military attack would inevitably lead to an all-out war. At the time, the Pentagon estimated that if war were to break out, it would inflict enormous damage. In the first three months, it would claim 52,000 U.S. military casualties, as well as 490,000 South Korean military casualties, and one million civilian casualties. Such a war would destroy most of the industrial facilities on the peninsula.

Nevertheless, then-Secretary of Defense Perry insisted that the United States should wage a preemptive strike on the nuclear facilities at Yongbyon, while preparing for an all-out war. He believed that since the North Koreans had crossed the line, they should be attacked unless they immediately ceased nuclear activities. Perry submitted "three military options" to a National Security Council meeting presided over by President Clinton. It seemed that war was unavoidable.

While the NSC meeting was being held at the White House, the telephone rang. Former president Jimmy Carter was calling from Pyongyang, saying he had helped avert the crisis through his talks with North Korean president Kim Il-sung. A miracle had prevented war at the last minute.

Remembering this 1994 nightmare, I said to President Kim Dae-jung, "We must take proactive action to come up with our own strategy." I recommended that we make active diplomatic efforts to persuade the Perry team to accept our strategy.

Even before this development, I had completed creating a "comprehensive approach strategy for the dismantlement of the Cold War structure on the Korean Peninsula," which was approved by President Kim.

Comprehensive Approach

The concept of a comprehensive approach strategy for the dismantlement of the Cold War structure on the Korean Peninsula was later incorporated into Dr. Perry's North Korean Policy Review to serve as the basis of trilateral policy coordination among Korea, the United States, and Japan. The concept was as follows:

The cause of North Korea's development of nuclear weapons and missile programs could be attributed to the Cold War structure on the Korean Peninsula. Therefore, an "allopathic treatment" would not be effective on all the developments of such a structural problem. When a big rock obstructs your view, you cannot see the mountain behind it. But the rock is only a part of the mountain. Just as you have to climb over the rock to see the mountain, the fundamental resolution to the North Korean nuclear and missile issues would only be achieved through the application of a comprehensive approach designed to dismantle the Cold War structure on the peninsula, while resolving each of the pending issues in dealing with North Korea.

The Cold War structure on the Korean Peninsula consists of six closely-related and interdependent elements: distrust and confrontation between the North and South; a hostile relationship between the United States and North Korea; the closed and intransigent nature of North Korea; weapons of mass destruction; military confrontation and an arms race; and the military armistice.

* * * * * * * * *

I believed that the North and the South should first overcome their half-century of distrust and confrontation and reconcile with one another. They should develop a relationship of exchange and cooperation in various fields to build reconciliation and mutual confidence through peaceful coexistence. Also, through economic cooperation, they should build and develop a North-South economic community, while realizing arms control. These would be essential to dismantling the Cold War structure. If we took these measures, we would be able to reach the state of *de facto* unification allowing free travel and mutual aid between the North and the South.

In addition, the United States and North Korea should end their hostile relationship and normalize relations. Russia and China had already normalized relations with South Korea. North and South Korea were members of the United Nations, and the international community recognized the two states that exist on the Korean Peninsula.

Yet, the United States and Japan still did not recognize North Korea, maintaining the hostile relations of the Cold War on the Korean Peninsula. Due to its fear of security threats, North Korea would find it difficult to give up the temptation to develop nuclear weapons. The United States and North Korea needed to carry out mutual threat reduction and build mutual confidence through a process of give-and-take.

For the peace and stability of the peninsula, the United States should engage North Korea and normalize relations, rather than letting it be influenced by another power. Normalization should be preceded by the lifting of economic sanctions and the end of hostile relations. This would provide prime motivation to transform the military armistice agreement into a durable peace regime.

At the same time, North Korea should open up and change its command economy into a market economy, as did China and Vietnam. It should become a responsible member of the international community. It was not possible, nor desirable, to bring down North Korea from the outside. Gradual change of North Korea through opening and economic reform would not only enable the North to recover its economy but also help eliminate its military adventurism. It would contribute to an eventual transformation of the North Korean system. If more containment pressure and sanctions were applied to North Korea, it would be more difficult for it to change. If the international community created the right atmosphere and conditions under which the North felt safe to open and reform, quantitative changes could bring about qualitative changes.

* * * * * * * * *

It was necessary that weapons of mass destruction be removed and denuclearization be realized on the Korean Peninsula. North Korea's possession of nuclear weapons might have the perilous result of spurring South Korea and Japan's nuclear armament. In order to remove the threats of North Korea's nuclear weapons and missile programs, the United States should first address North Korea's security concerns. The North wanted to use its nuclear development program for deterrence and as negotiating leverage for normalization of relations with the United States. The process of normalization between North Korea and the United States would amount to a process of dismantlement of North Korea's weapons of mass destruction. The key to the resolution of the nuclear issue lay in the creation of an environment favorable to building mutual confidence, in which there would be no need for nuclear weapons. Without building mutual confidence, complete verification would be impossible.

For forty years, the North and the South were engaged in a fierce arms race to amass excessively formidable military power. The two sides should build mutual military confidence and reduce their conventional arms, while maintaining a military balance in the direction of further reductions. This would contribute to the maintenance of stability and peace on the peninsula. One reason for North Korea's concentration on nuclear development might have had to do with the expensive cost of maintaining a conventional forces arms race. Therefore, the process of denuclearization should be accompanied by a process of conventional arms reduction.

If we replaced the Military Armistice Agreement with a peace regime, we would be able to end the Cold War on the Korean Peninsula. The transformation of the Military Armistice Agreement into a peace regime would be achieved through the resolution of the issue of weapons of mass destruction, normalization of U.S.–North Korea relations, and conventional arms reduction. The status and role of foreign forces in Korea would have to be resolved, and this would require arms control measures to prevent war and to guarantee peace.

*　*　*　*　*　*　*　*　*

The basic position of our government was to ban North Korea's nuclear development and realize the denuclearization of the peninsula. However, we would not seek a military solution, but instead prevent war and achieve a peaceful solution. We would seek a fundamental solution in terms of the dismantlement of the Cold War structure. Our stance was anti-nuclear weapons and anti-war, pro-peace and in support of ending the Cold War.

From this position, we needed to recognize the North Korean regime as it was and negotiate with it based on our engagement policy, seeking "gradual change" in the North instead of an "imminent collapse." We decided that our approach to the final resolution should include the following:

- We should recognize North Korea's perceived security threats from the United States and the South, as well as the security threat from North Korea, to seek steps to mutual threat reduction.
- As we saw in the European process of dètente based on the 1975 Helsinki Accord, we should take a comprehensive approach on the Korean Peninsula that would include normalization of relations; military confidence-building and arms reduction; economic, trade and scientific technology cooperation; and cultural, educational, and information exchange. We should give and take from them as appropriate. We should build mutual confidence by pursuing a package settlement through gradual and simultaneous action.
- We should cooperate with the United States and Japan, which were yet to resolve hostile relations with North Korea. We should also seek the cooperation and support of China and Russia. Our negotiations with North Korea should be carried out on the basis of the strong deterrent of the combined U.S.-ROK forces. For negotiating tactics, we should use both "sticks and carrots." Our posture in dealing with the North Koreans should reflect confidence, patience, consistency, and flexibility.

*　*　*　*　*　*　*　*　*

The comprehensive approach strategy to the dismantlement of the Cold War structure on the Korean Peninsula was fixed by the approval of the NSSC in early December, 1998. At an NSC meeting in the beginning of the new year, President Kim said:

The unstable security environment on the Korean Peninsula is fundamentally related to the Cold War structure that has continued for the past half-century. We should dismantle this Cold War structure. To this end, it is very important for us to develop trilateral cooperation with the United States and Japan, while promoting a cooperative relationship with China and Russia as well. In parallel with international cooperation to deal with the pending issues of North Korea's nuclear and missile development, we should exert our diplomatic efforts to secure international support for a fundamental resolution of the Korean question through a dismantlement of the Cold War structure.

Perry's Visit to Seoul

North Korea Policy Coordinator William Perry visited Seoul in early December on an Asia trip that included Seoul, Tokyo, and Beijing. He was accompanied by members of the North Korea Policy Review (NKPR) team, including Ambassador Wendy R. Sherman, a State Department counselor, and Ashton B. Carter, a professor at Harvard University and former Assistant Secretary of Defense for International Security Policy.

William J. Perry, seventy-one years old at the time, had worked over twenty years as a contractor in the defense industry before he was appointed as the Assistant Secretary of Defense for Research and Technology. After that assignment, Perry became a professor at Stanford University. Later he served as Deputy Secretary of Defense (1993–1994) and Secretary of Defense (1994–1997). Before he was appointed as North Korea Policy Coordinator, Dr. Perry had returned to be a professor at Stanford.

The first appointment on his Seoul itinerary was to meet with me to get briefed on our government's position before his meeting with President Kim Dae-jung. I hosted a working breakfast for two-and-a-half hours at the Lotte Hotel to speak with Dr. Perry and his party. From the U.S. side, Ambassador Stephen Bosworth and Wendy Sherman came with Perry. Presidential Secretary of Foreign Affairs Song Min-soon joined the meeting from our side.

Perry said he came to Seoul to update himself on the current military situation with the U.S.-ROK Combined Forces Command (CFC) and to listen to the views of the ROK government and South Korean experts. He said he would listen rather than talk. He listened attentively to my explanation and asked many questions.

I started our discussion by saying that there were three possible options on North Korea, including an "engagement policy," a "containment policy," and a "policy of neglect." I focused on explaining why we should pursue an engagement policy, analyzing the intent behind the North Korean development of weapons of mass destruction. I briefed him on the comprehensive approach strategy to the dismantlement of the Cold War structure on the Korean Peninsula (discussed earlier). I told him that it was the official position of our government to seek a resolution to the North Korean issue within that framework.

* * * * * * * * *

That afternoon, Dr. Perry called on President Kim and they spent more than an hour discussing the issue. The president recalled the Korean Peninsula situation during the first nine months of his presidency. As he discussed the North Korean issue, he referred to the European détente process and emphasized the need for a package solution through a process of give-and-take.

Perry explained his assessment as defense secretary during the "first nuclear crisis" of 1994. He said the military pressure on the North, which did not exclude a preemptive attack, was inevitable. In response, President Kim said Dr. Perry reminded him of the advice he had given in his speech at the National Press Club in Washington that former president Jimmy Carter be sent to Pyongyang.

Dr. Perry's questions were specific. He asked what sticks or carrots could be used in negotiations and what specific options were available to us. President Kim replied that the carrots should include, in addition to food assistance: lifting sanctions; removal of North Korea from the list of state sponsors of terrorism; allowing the North's access to international financial institutions; compensation for the suspension of missile exports; normalized relations with Japan; and compensation from Japan for the past. On the other hand, sticks should include cancellation of the light water reactor project, suspension of Chinese assistance, and military pressure, if necessary.

Perry said he had been assured by General John Tilelli—then Commander of the U.S.-ROK CFC, who was supportive of the Korean government's engagement policy—that "the situation on the Korean Peninsula has fundamentally changed since 1994, and any North Korean invasion would end in defeat in several weeks." Perry added that his visit to Seoul was very helpful in understanding the situation in Korea, but he never revealed his own views during the visit.

Eight months later, I met him again at Stanford. At that time, Dr. Perry was candid and said, "When I first heard President Kim's and your argument in Seoul, it was so different from what I was thinking that I was literally flabbergasted." He also told me that he decided to accept our argument after we discussed the issue again in Washington at the end of January 1999.

Coordination in Washington

After Dr. Perry and the NKPR team left Seoul, I recommended to President Kim that we "capture this opportunity and send our diplomatic team to Washington to persuade the NKPR team regarding our North Korea policy. We should cooperate with the United States to reflect our position in U.S. policy to the maximum extent possible."

The president accepted my recommendation and instructed me to go to Washington myself to persuade them. I tried to decline the president's suggestion because I believed it was the foreign ministry's job. But, reminding me that I had worked on the comprehensive approach strategy, he said I should go to Washington and persuade them with conviction. The president said I could take foreign ministry personnel as needed.

Based on the perspectives of the views expressed in the press, the Korean embassy in Washington suggested that my visit would be risky. The embassy recommended that we talk to Dr. Perry in Seoul, as he was likely to return again in February. On the other hand, Ambassador Bosworth encouraged my visit, saying, "Your visit will be welcome any time; you should talk to other people in addition to Perry and persuade them."

I left for a five-day visit to Washington at the end of January 1999, taking with me Secretary of Foreign Affairs Song Min-soon (later senior delegate to the Six-Party Talks and Minister of Foreign Affairs during the Roh Moohyun administration), who had been assisting me for some time, and Office Director Wi Sung-lac (later Director General for North American Affairs and Minister for Political Affairs at the Korean embassy in Washington). Before our departure, I emphasized a few principles for our Washington consultation.

> We are the masters and party directly responsible for the Korean Peninsula. We should lead the situation with our firm stance to gain the support of the great powers. We should never give up our position or accept what the United States decides simply because the United States has decided everything in the past. Now, given the national strength of our country, we should be able to do what is right for us. The great powers will respect our position. If we succeed this time, we will have established a precedent for Korean leadership in policy coordination with the

United States for the first time in the diplomatic history of the ROK. I want you to bear this sense of mission.

I decided to maintain the principle of confidentiality for our consultation. The content of consultation would not be transmitted through the Ministry of Foreign Affairs diplomatic communications network. As a result, secrecy was effectively protected. On the other hand, it is regretable that the consultation was not included as a part of the diplomatic record.

* * * * * * * * *

We went to Washington during a time when the U.S. Congress was in turmoil because of the Monica Lewinsky scandal, which had erupted the previous summer. Based on the special prosecutor's charges, the House of Representatives had impeached President Clinton, and the Senate was conducting proceedings for voting for or against conviction.

The Clinton administration also had difficulties because the Congress, controlled by the Republicans, had opposed the Agreed Framework and refused to approve the budget for the provision of heavy fuel oil to North Korea, demanding "cancellation of the light water reactor construction plan." To make matters worse, in the aftermath of North Korea's firing of the Taepodong missile and the emergence of suspicions concerning the underground nuclear facilities at Kumchangni, the Republican Congress decided to include $13.3 billion in the 1999 fiscal year budget as part of the financial requirement for the development of the national missile defense (NMD) system that was recommended by the Rumsfeld report.

On the evening of January 27, I was sitting across from Dr. Perry and his NKPR team again at the Watergate Hotel, where I was staying. This meeting took place a month and a half after we met first in Seoul. Perry flew in from Stanford University. He was accompanied by Ambassador Wendy Sherman, Harvard professor Ashton Carter, and the State Department's Philip Yun. On our side, we had Secretary Song Min-soon, Office Director Wi Sung-lac, and Minister Yu Myung-hwan (later Vice Minister of Foreign Affairs) from the Korean embassy in Washington.

I first handed over to Perry a paper that I had prepared in Seoul, and I explained its contents. This was followed by a serious discussion. The paper included an assessment of the North Korean situation, our view of the North and engagement policy, immediate issues to address, the strategy of the comprehensive approach to dismantlement of the Cold War structure on the Korean Peninsula, and a road map showing a list of action steps that Korea, the United States, and Japan should respectively take at each stage. The paper also contained a series of countermeasures to possible North

The author explaining the South Korean government's proposal to U.S. North Korea Policy Coordinator William Perry (*left*) in Washington, January 27, 1999. Courtesy Lim Dong-won.

Korean negative responses to our initiatives. What I explained to Dr. Perry in Seoul was an outline of our conceptual plan, but this paper provided a detailed action plan.

Dr. Perry welcomed it as "a creative and bold architecture." He valued the report, saying that the gradual promotion of a fundamental and comprehensive approach was the right direction. He thanked me for "Korea's timely initiative in creating a framework." Dr. Perry assured me that U.S.–North Korea policy could not be carried out without South Korea's agreement, welcoming again our voluntary visit to Washington for consultation. At that meeting, Dr. Perry said he would accept our proposal in principle under the condition that both sides supplement and refine it together. For example, we would further study countermeasures to North Korea's rejection of our proposals. We would define "red lines" the North must not cross, and we would develop countermeasures to take in case the North violated those limits.

Fortunately, Dr. Perry seemed to fully understand and concur on the points of my explanation. Stressing the importance of cooperation with China and Japan, he supported my plan to visit those countries. He said he was considering a visit to North Korea and asked me whether South Korea would agree to it. I responded, "President Kim would also wholeheartedly encourage such a visit."

I welcomed Dr. Perry's suggestion that he would continue to supplement and develop our proposal and use it to persuade Congress and to apply it to U.S.–North Korea policy. Dr. Perry said his team would write up a report of core concepts and he would bring it to Seoul for discussion. We thought our discussion produced satisfactory results.

＊　＊　＊　＊　＊　＊　＊　＊　＊

On the same trip, I also met with National Security Advisor Samuel Berger as well as Undersecretary of State for Political Affairs Thomas Pickering, and explained our proposal to them to ask for their cooperation. Berger said, "On top of the mutual respect and trust between Presidents Clinton and Kim, and because of your close cooperative relationship with Ambassador Bosworth, U.S.-Korea relations are reaching their best state ever."

However, Berger questioned whether our proposal would work well. He said, "To realize Korea's proposal, multiple visits to Kumchangni and a process of resolving the missile issue should begin first." I replied that if the United States accepted our proposal and promoted coordination between the United States, South Korea, and Japan, we would be able to move North Korea toward a resolution of those issues.

At the meeting with Undersecretary Pickering, whom I knew well from Nigeria when he and I were ambassadors during the same period, he said our proposal was "constructive and useful and that it would be a good basis for further discussion." Pickering highly valued Korea's posture of taking the initiative. He stressed the importance of "planning a long-term strategy at least for the next ten years." He said, "We will review Korea's comprehensive strategy to end the Cold War, to reflect it in U.S. policy." This meeting, too, ended on an encouraging note.

On the second day of my visit, former Assistant Secretary of Defense Richard Armitage (later deputy secretary of state under the Bush administration) came to see me. After listening to my statement, he too agreed in principle with the proposal from President Kim and our government. Then he added, "I praise Korea for its proactive diplomacy." Armitage said he was working on a report, reflecting the views of some the Republican experts, which would be similar to South Korea's architecture for a comprehensive engagement policy. This report was later titled "A Comprehensive Approach to North Korea" and became known as the Armitage Report. It was submitted to Congress separately from the Perry Report.

＊　＊　＊　＊　＊　＊　＊　＊　＊

While in Washington, I had luncheons, dinners, or interviews with more than twenty Korea specialists, including Arnold Kanter, Richard Solomon, Selig Harrison, and Don Oberdorfer, explaining to them our perspectives and strategy for their understanding and support. I also listened to their views. Most of them made favorable comments to the effect that our long-term comprehensive strategy was a "new desirable paradigm" for North Korea policy. Some of them noted the significance of our initiative, saying, "it was the first time that Seoul presented policy options on its own in the history of Korea-U.S. relations." They also provided me with a variety of useful information and views.

One frank view I heard was, "For its interests in Northeast Asia, the United States needs to maintain its military presence on a long-term basis. If the Cold War ends and peace is settled on the Korean Peninsula, it is feared that the American people would call for pulling troops from Korea. Therefore, we should not rush in carrying out the process of ending the Cold War. We should start it very slowly."

In response, I explained President Kim's position that U.S. troops would be needed in Korea beyond unification to serve as a "stabilizer" and a "balancer." I reminded him of the continued U.S. military presence in Europe after the end of the Cold War. I also emphasized, "The United Sates, which was partially responsible for the division of Korea and the Cold War on the Korean Peninsula, should assist to relieve the pain of the Korean people from the Cold War. This would also contribute to the furthering of U.S.-Korea relations."

Consultation with Tokyo, Beijing, and Moscow

After my return from Washington, I continued the work of introducing our strategic design to Japan, China, and Russia in order to enlist their support. As I became busy travelling to these countries, the press portrayed me as the "architect of peace on the Korean Peninsula." The *Korea Times* published a lengthy article under the title of "Lim Dong-won Gets Nicknamed Korea's Henry Kissinger."

In early February I went to Japan on a two-day trip, and met with Foreign Minister Komura Masahiko, Chief Cabinet Secretary Nonaka Hiromu, Vice Foreign Minister Yanai Shunji, and North Korea experts Professor Okonogi Masao and Professor Izumi Hajime. I explained to them our comprehensive engagement policy and how my discussions in Washington had gone. I proposed that Japan join Korea and the United States in developing a coordinated approach.

The impression I received from the Japanese was that although they wanted to partake in the issue of the Korean Peninsula, they preferred to wait for a clear American attitude. Nevertheless, they all stressed the importance of the three countries—Japan, the United States and Korea—pursuing the same goal in North Korea policy and cooperating closely to achieve their goals.

The Japanese emphasized that a second North Korean missile launch must be prevented in order to create the right environment to promote our comprehensive engagement policy towards North Korea. They were skeptical about a positive response from North Korea. In Japan, I repeatedly heard that the Japanese had not yet recovered from the shock of the first North Korean missile test.

Regarding the issue of normalization with North Korea, they said,

> Japan contacted the North through several channels. But, there was no progress because of the abduction issue and the missile launch. Japan would not consider "reparation" or "indemnity" to pay the North. Japan would only recognize the North's right to property claims for the period of colonial rule, as was the case in the Japan-South Korea normalization agreement of 1965.

In contrast, North Korea claimed that since it had fought a war with Japan, it was entitled to "reparations." North Korea also demanded "indemnity" for Japan's responsibility of the division of Korea after World War II, Japan's participation in the Korean War, and Japan's hostile policy.

※　※　※　※　※　※　※　※　※

After my trip to Japan, I flew to Beijing on February 11. It was a three-day trip that turned out to be very useful. In Beijing, I met with ranking officials of the Chinese government and the Chinese Communist Party as well as Korea experts involved with the North Korean issue. I introduced to them our strategy of a comprehensive approach to dismantle the Cold War structure on the Korean Peninsula. Then I asked them to cooperate on three things, including China's understanding and support of our strategic design, its exercise of influence on the North to stop its nuclear program and prevent another missile firing, and its advice to the North Koreans to engage in dialogue with the South.

Party Director for External Relations Dai Bingguo, a former diplomat, and Party Director for External Affairs Liu Huaqiu gave high praise to our design, saying, "President Kim's approach to the Korean issue from a practical and strategic perspective is full of imagination, and it is the best approach we have seen so far."

At a lavish three-hour dinner in my honor, I shared my candid views with Foreign Minister Tang Jiaxuan, who praised our comprehensive strategic design as a "development of the Sunshine policy" and a "practical and concrete design." He summarized China's basic position:

> The Korean issue should be resolved directly between the North and the South through dialogue; China regards it important that peace and stability is maintained on the Korean Peninsula; and China supports the denuclearization of the Korean Peninsula.

Regarding the U.S. national missile defense (NMD) system, he expressed serious concerns, saying, "Some people in the United States are using North Korea's missile launch as an excuse to raise tensions and to develop the NMD, but it is obvious who the target is." He did not hide his displeasure at Japan's participation in the construction of a missile defense.

The dinner was hosted by Foreign Minister Tang in the ballroom on the eighteenth floor of the newly-finished foreign ministry building. Attending the dinner were Ambassador Kwon Byung-hyun, Secretary Song Min-soon, and Director Wi Sung-lac from our side; and Assistant Minister Wang Yi (later deputy foreign minister and ambassador to Japan), and Deputy Director General for Asian Affairs Ning Fukui (later ambassador to Korea) from the Chinese side. We enjoyed our conversation in a good friendly atmosphere.

The executive members of the Chinese Communist Party as well as Chinese government officials all highly praised our efforts to improve relations with North Korea, and told us that it was most important to reduce the concerns of the North Koreans, who were facing a difficult situation. They said we should pursue and develop the Sunshine policy, which would help reduce tension and promote exchange and cooperation between the North and the South.

They cited an old adage, "It is difficult to pile up rocks, but easy to make them fall." Despite how few the accomplishments in inter-Korean relations might have seemed, they advised that we pursue and build upon them.

* * * * * * * * * *

In Beijing, I also invited a group of ten Chinese experts in Korean affairs to a luncheon meeting. The group included Tao Bingwei, who had been involved in Korea affairs for a long time and who was fluent in Korean. Again, I explained to them our strategic design. I used sixteen Chinese characters to define the approach to the Sunshine policy:

先易後難　Easy tasks first, difficult tasks later
先民後官　Private channel first, government channel later
先經後政　Economy first, politics later
先供後得　Give first, take later

* * * * * * * * *

Next, at the end of March I flew over snow-covered Siberia to travel to Moscow. There, I met with Presidential Assistant for Foreign Affairs Sergei Prikhodko; Deputy Foreign Minister Gregory Karasin, on behalf of the foreign minister, who was traveling; and some Korean affairs experts. As I had in the other countries, I explained our strategic design and asked for their understanding and support. I also asked that Russia exercise its influence on North Korea and persuade it to give up its weapons of mass destruction.

The Russians also said our government's comprehensive engagement policy was "very constructive and realistic." They promised that, if we asked, Russia would do its best to play a role. They added, "Russia will cooperate with the South Korean government to prevent a second North Korean missile launch. Since pressure has not resolved the issue, the Korean government's approach is desirable."

Deputy Minister Karasin hosted a luncheon in my honor at his foreign ministry's beautiful guesthouse. He confided to me some positive information about what was happening in the North. He said, "I have recently returned from Pyongyang. I was able to detect a small but important change beginning to take place there in response to the Sunshine policy. The Sunshine policy is definitely the right approach. But we should not be in a hurry to press North Korea. It would be better to steadily carry out that policy as a long-term goal."

Karasin also opined that it was especially important for South Korea to exercise its sovereign leadership for the resolution of the Korean issue. "If South Korea's policy is not taken as a 'tactical ploy,' it has a good chance to succeed."

Pleasant Plagiarism

On the afternoon of March 9, William Perry and his NKPR team visited with President Kim Dae-jung to brief him on a "Tentative Review of U.S. Policy Towards North Korea." Before starting his briefing, Perry said he had briefed President Clinton on the same subject, and the president had instructed him, "Any U.S.–North Korea policy should be in harmony with South Korea's policy. Report your review to President Kim first and seek his advice."

With that introduction, Dr. Perry began his briefing with a chart titled "A Comprehensive Approach for an Engagement Policy." Attending the briefing were Ambassador Stephen Bosworth and Professor Ashton Carter from the U.S. side, and myself, Assistant Minister Chang Jae-ryong, and Secretary Song Min-soon on the Korean side.

The briefing lasted one-and-a-half hours.

Dr. Perry first compared the situation on the Korean Peninsula in 1999 to that of 1994 and presented an approach that the United States would prefer to take in this new situation. He also had an alternative path, should North Korea reject the approach. His presentation was as follows:

> Since 1994, North Korean military capabilities have relatively weakened, whereas the deterrence of the U.S.-ROK Combined Forces has been strengthened. The Republic of Korea has aggressively and confidently embarked on a policy of engagement with the North, despite the North's limited response. Although North Korea is undergoing terrible economic hardships, there is no evidence these are undermining the regime. We must deal with the North's regime as it is, not as we might wish it to be.
>
> The Agreed Framework froze plutonium production at Yongbyon and put North Korea's nuclear facilities under international inspections. Yet the Agreement is now at risk because of the suspicions raised concerning the Kumchangni site where the North might be constructing underground nuclear facilities, and because of ballistic missile-related activities.
>
> Under this situation, there are five policy options that the United States should consider, including "accept the status quo," "buy our objectives," "attempt to reform North Korea," "attempt to undermine the regime," and "offer mutual threat reduction talks." Of these five options, the first four would be unrealistic and should be rejected. Therefore, "offer mutual threat reduction talks" would be the only practical option.
>
> The United States should propose comprehensive engagement with the North to negotiate mutual threat reduction. There are two conditions for such engagement, including a moratorium on North Korea's ballistic missile launches and access to the suspected underground nuclear facility at Kumchangni. When these conditions are met, the U.S. should be able to actively engage the North in dialogue and negotiations.
>
> If the North accepts these two conditions, the United States should be able to reduce or resolve North Korean nuclear and missile threats through a "comprehensive engagement." The United States would ease economic sanctions, increase humanitarian assistance, and end the

hostile relationship to move to normalization of relations. As part of a normalization process, we could recommend that the Secretary of State visit Pyongyang. Japan would also move to normalize relations. In the meantime, the South could enhance engagement to promote reconciliation and cooperation with the North. The approach, mutual threat reduction leading to peaceful relations with the North Korean government, could eventually proceed to ending the Cold War on the Korean Peninsula.

The United States would propose its comprehensive policy, but it should implement it on a gradual step-by-step basis in accordance with the North Korean response. If the North rejects the mutual threat reduction approach or crosses a "red line" and our engagement fails, the necessity for "crisis management" would emerge. A series of engagement activities would have to be reduced and economic sanctions against the North will be intensified. To contain the North Korean threat, the United States would have to strengthen its military posture. Consequently, the Agreed Framework would be endangered and in peril of abrogation. To prevent war, the United States should reinforce its deterrence, and in coercive diplomacy the United States should take extraordinary measures to isolate the North.

When Dr. Perry finished his briefing, President Kim was very pleased and said, "Your ideas are incredibly similar to mine. I think the North Koreans would accept this proposal." Dr. Perry responded, "This is not different from your formulation of ideas. We received a lot of good ideas from Senior Secretary Lim Dong-won. Shamefully, we stole and plagiarized his strategic design. We only reconstructed it in American expressions."

A pleasant burst of laughter erupted in the room. I later learned that the Perry team used the January presentation of our strategic design, which was presented verbally and on paper, as the base for building their proposal. In fact, Dr. Perry's "Tentative Policy Review" was no different in any significant way from our comprehensive strategic design. However, there was a slight degree of difference, as Ambassador Bosworth pointed out, in terms of "extraordinary measures" to take in case the North rejected the offer, as well as in the application of reciprocity.

President Kim appreciated the concept of mutual threat reduction in a give and take negotiation process. He highly praised Dr. Perry's remarks that even if a crisis was created by the North's negative responses, the United States would take strong measures to prevent war. President Kim also said, "Instead of being overly concerned about failure, we should confidently focus our efforts on persuading the North Koreans. Confidence can produce better results." He went on:

It is key to our work that we get international support and cooperation for this policy that Korea and the United States have agreed upon. With Japan, we should establish a trilateral system of coordination with the United States and Korea. We should also closely cooperate with China and Russia to gain their support. We should cooperate with the EU. And I think if Dr. Perry visits Pyongyang and explains this proposal directly to them and invites them to join us, it would be helpful in moving and persuading them.

Dr. Perry agreed with the president, saying, "I will work on my trip to North Korea."

* * * * * * * * *

On March 16, after a long negotiation at the U.S.–North Korea talks (a.k.a. the Kartman-Kim Gye-gwan talks) in New York, the North agreed to U.S. visits to the Kumchangni site. Two months later, a U.S. team visited it. In addition, near the end of March, a U.S.–North Korea meeting was held in Pyongyang to negotiate the missile issue. At this meeting, North Korea is known to have said that although it was impossible to give up missile development as long as the United States maintained its hostile policy, it would suspend missile exports if the United States paid $1 billion. Due to a lack of practical international measures to control missile sales, the North was able to engage in missile exports and ask for cash compensation for suspending its sales. (North Korea was not a member of the Missile Technology Control Regime [MTCR]).

Perry's Visit to Pyongyang

In mid-April, Dr. Perry called a trilateral high-level meeting between Korea, the United States, and Japan in Honolulu, Hawaii to finalize his tentative North Korea policy review as a coordinated policy. This meeting was seen as a necessary step before Dr. Perry's visit to Pyongyang.

Attending the meeting were Assistant Foreign Minister Chang Jae-ryong, Secretary Song Min-soon, and myself from the Korean side. The Americans in attendance were Policy Coordinator William Perry, Ambassador Sherman, and Professor Carter. Japan was represented by Director General for Policy Integration Kato Ryozo of the foreign ministry (later ambassador to the United States) and six others.

At the meeting, the three countries agreed to pursue a coordinated and integrated policy, which would be in support of a comprehensive approach to engagement. The policy goal was to reduce the threat of the North Korean nuclear and missile programs, looking toward the eventual dismantlement of the Cold War structure on the Korean Peninsula.

The meeting accepted the U.S. proposal to carry out "Mutual Threat Reduction Leading to the End of the Cold War on the Korean Peninsula." To this end, the three countries would produce a roadmap for consultation on the means for coordination of specific measures that each country should take at appropriate stages. They also discussed possible countermeasures to manage a crisis that might be created if North Korea crossed a "red line."

The three countries further agreed to institutionalize trilateral coordination and cooperation in order to pursue a closely coordinated and effective North Korea policy. They agreed to set up a Trilateral Coordination and Oversight Group (TCOG) that would meet at least once every quarter. As reflected in this joint trilateral approach, the Perry Report had adopted our concept of a comprehensive approach strategy for the dismantlement of the Cold War structure on the Korean Peninsula.

Before I left Hawaii, I had an opportunity to meet with Admiral Dennis Blair (Commander in Chief, U.S. Pacific Command) and his staff, and I was briefed on the military situation on the Korean Peninsula. Blair said,

> North Korean conventional forces have been at a standstill for the past few years. North Korea's long-range missiles, artillery fire, and chemical weapons are threatening, but the North Korean forces as a whole are like a wounded tiger. The combined U.S.-ROK deterrent forces are the strongest in history and they are able to cope with any contingency.

On the flight from Hawaii to Seoul, I relished a sense of accomplishment. I felt that I had achieved my historic mission. I recalled the 1970s during the peak of the Cold War when I worked on the ROK's first military strategy, and on the "Yulgok Project" to build a self-reliant defense capability, and on other tasks to develop a peacekeeping strategy. In the 1990s, in the wake of the end of the Cold War, I had proposed the engagement policy and the strategy to end the Cold War on the Korean Peninsula. I was at the center of developing a peacemaking strategy. As the protagonists of the Korean Peninsula, we had persuaded our neighboring countries to support our initiative to resolve the problem.

* * * * * * * * *

The remainder of our work was to persuade the North to accept our proposal and to undertake a process of mutual threat reduction. Toward the end of April, North Korea sent positive signals. North Korea accepted a visit to Pyongyang by Ambassador Kartman's delegation (May 14–15), a U.S. inspection team's visit to Kumchangni (May 18–25) and a visit to Pyongyang by Dr. Perry (May 26–28). We were expecting May 1999 to be a historic month and were optimistic about improved U.S.–North Korea relations.

Dr. Perry took off from Tokyo by a U.S. Air Force plane to head for Pyongyang on the afternoon of May 25. He was leading a seven-member delegation, which included Ambassador Sherman, White House NSC Senior Director for Asian Affairs Kenneth Lieberthal, and Korea Desk Director Evans Revere (later president of The Korea Society). Before Perry's departure, I went to Tokyo for another trilateral meeting.

Dr. Perry told us that he wanted to hear directly from North Korea its perspectives before making final recommendation in his North Korea policy review. He then confirmed that he would tell the North Koreans what we had agreed upon in our trilateral meeting in Honolulu. He would also tell them his proposal had the support of South Korea and Japan. Dr. Perry informed us of the main points of a letter from President Clinton that he was carrying to the North, which essentially proposed a "fundamentally new relationship." He also said an inspection visit to Kumchangni had been satisfactorily completed with the North's cooperation, and the visiting team was now on its way back home. He said this was a good omen. This meant one of the two urgent issues was being resolved.

* * * * * * * * *

After spending three nights and four days in Pyongyang, the Perry team arrived in Seoul on the evening of May 28. The next morning I was briefed by Dr. Perry on his Pyongyang visit. I also attended a trilateral meeting at the official residence of the foreign minister, during which the results of the Perry visit were explained.

The Perry team seemed to have been satisfied with the overall atmosphere in which they were received. The North was cordial and hospitable and had provided heavy press coverage for U.S. Presidential Envoy William Perry. There was a welcome luncheon hosted by President Kim Young-nam of the Presidium of the Supreme People's Assembly, and an elaborate dinner hosted by First Vice Foreign Minister Kang Sok-ju. Many North Korean members of the party, military, and government attended these events. American music, including "Oh My Darling, Clementine" and "Oh! Susanna," was played for the pleasure of the American visitors.

Perry's North Korean counterpart was First Vice Foreign Minister Kang Sok-ju, who was Chairman Kim Jong-il's most trusted official on foreign affairs and who had direct access to the chairman. It was learned that they had almost nine hours of discussion over three meetings.

Dr. Perry summarized the substance of his discussion with the North Koreans as follows:

He told them, "As a Pacific power, the United States has a role to play in Asia." After reviewing the historic tragedies that the Korean Peninsula has suffered as a result of competitive struggles among neighboring powers, Perry suggested, "For Korea to survive, prosper, and develop among neighboring competitors, it would be wise to establish a good relationship with the United States, which is located on the other side of the Pacific. This would serve the interests of both countries."

Dr. Perry also emphasized U.S. willingness to form a fundamentally new relationship with North Korea, fully explaining the concept of the comprehensive approach through mutual threat reduction. Dr. Perry said he asked North Korea first to abandon its nuclear development and to stop developing mid- and long-range ballistic missiles. In the interest of building a new relationship, there should not be a second missile launch, which would close the window of opportunity. Perry emphasized the need for a moratorium on missile launches. The issue of the suspected nuclear facilities at Kumchangni, which was resolved by the experts' visit, was not discussed during the Perry visit.

However, as the North Koreans were not ready for such a dramatic proposal by the U.S., Kang Sok-ju only reiterated Pyongyang's principled position that they had previously mentioned. Kang said that North Korea had given up its nuclear sovereignty to comply with the Agreed Framework. He demanded that the United States more faithfully comply with the Agreed Framework. Kang further told Perry that North Korea was willing to negotiate the issue of missile exports. However, the North would continue its rocket launches for a peaceful satellite project. In response to Perry's proposal, Kang said, "If the United States withdraws its hostile policy and shows it through action, North Korea will take corresponding measures."

Kim Young-nam, President of the Presidium, who served as the symbolic head of state, hosted a luncheon for the Perry team. Kim welcomed Perry's visit as "historic" and a "heroic action." He was quoted as saying, "Yesterday's enemy can be tomorrow's friend." He said he hoped Perry's visit would become an epoch-making turning point in U.S.–North Korea relations. Kim asked that the United States carry out its commitment to respect the North Korea system, its sovereignty and the principle of equality, and withdraw its hostile policy.

North Korean domestic television revealed Pyongyang's hope for improved relations with the United States when it reported, "Talks with the U.S. presidential envoy were serious and candid and proceeded in an atmosphere of mutual respect."

On the other hand, the Perry team as a whole seemed to have been somewhat disappointed in that there had been no meeting with Chairman Kim Jong-il or any definitive North Korean response to Perry's proposal. However, some members of the team thought that Perry's trip produced some positive results, including the warm hospitality provided to the visitors; the demonstration of North Korea's keen interest in the Perry proposal; the serious and candid discussions that took place; and the confirmation that communication would continue through the existing channels. They seemed optimistic about the possibility of a positive response from the North.

*   *   *   *   *   *   *   *   *   *

At the trilateral meeting in Seoul, I had characterized the results of the Perry visit as the "beginning of success." I reasoned that the North Koreans, who had long distrusted the United States, needed time to seriously review such an important proposal. I said that if Kim Jong-il had shown up to meet the U.S. presidential envoy, he would probably not have been ready to make a bold response on the spot. Nevertheless, I pointed out the positive aspects of the Perry visit that revealed North Korea's expectation of improved relations with the United States: Perry's long discussion with Kang Sok-ju, who had direct access to Chairman Kim Jong-il; North Korea's warm hospitality; and the big press coverage. Now that we could begin the peace process to end the Cold War on the Korean Peninsula through mutual threat reduction, I concluded that the three countries—South Korea, the United States and Japan—should work even more closely.

On May 25, the State Department announced that a team of fourteen experts had completed its first visit to the Kumchangni site and confirmed that it contained no nuclear-related facilities, such as a reactor or a reprocessing plant in the underground tunnel that was under construction, and that the tunnel was not designed for such facilities. A second visit to the same site was carried out the following year, but the result was the same. Contrary to the expectation of the hardliners, the visits proved that the DIA had been misinformed.

Regarding the missile issue, the United States and North Korea held several rounds of negotiations in Berlin until mid-September, when the North accepted a moratorium on missile launches "as long as and while the two sides are engaged in missile talks." In return, the United States promised to lift its economic sanctions and provide food aid.

Thus the two conditions to the Perry process—Kumchangni and the missile launch—had been removed, providing a turning point to start the comprehensive process of improving relations between the United States and North Korea through mutual threat reduction.

This was the beginning of a process for ending the Cold War and starting peacemaking on the Korean Peninsula. On September 14, the Perry Report that had been submitted to the Congress was released to the public.

Around the time of Perry's visit to Pyongyang, North Korea increased its efforts to improve relations with the United States as well as with China, Russia, and Japan. In May 1999, Chairman Kim Jong-il met with the Chinese ambassador in Pyongyang, and in November, he received Russian Foreign Minister Igor Ivanov. In December, Kim Jong-il allowed a Japanese parliamentary delegation led by former prime minister Murayama to visit Pyongyang.

Overcoming Evil with Good

At the end of May 1999, I was inaugurated as Minister of Unification. President Kim Dae-jung said, "We have made a good basis for trilateral cooperation with the United States and Japan, and there has been progress in U.S.–North Korea talks. I think we should now facilitate North-South dialogue." With that, he asked me to focus on inter-Korean relations.

Returning to the unification ministry, where I had served as vice minister six years earlier, was emotional, but I felt a stronger sense of grave responsibility with the new assignment. When I was vice minister, I played the role of a midwife to the birth of the North-South Basic Agreement and the Joint Declaration of the Denuclearization of the Korean Peninsula. These had set the direction of inter-Korean relations.

Now my job was to make up for the "five lost years" by revitalizing exchange and cooperation and building mutual confidence between the North and the South. In other words, it was my job to remove the legacies of the Cold War one by one. To do this, I would actively persuade the opposition party and the hardline conservatives who opposed the Sunshine policy to build a national consensus on our policy. I would carry out a consistent and practical policy to keep engaging the North Koreans.

* * * * * * * * *

When the Kim Dae-jung administration started, North Korea was in crisis. North Korea had insisted that the socialist countries of the old Soviet and Eastern European camps had crumbled because they had embraced pluralism such as freedom of thought, multiple political parties, and economic privatization. North Korea chose to preserve and strengthen its *juche* ideology and collectivism through focused implementation of a "human reform program."

However, refusing change and reform had led to its international isolation and its economy had reached the point of bankruptcy. Its economic strength shrank by half in the wake of the disintegration of Eastern Europe. To make things worse, North Korea was hit by natural disasters in 1995 and 1996. It suffered a severe food shortage, which led to widespread famine and refugees fleeing the country. It was a national disaster.

In a desperate attempt at survival, North Korea forced its people to endure an arduous march of austerity. To manage the crisis, the North Korean military was given a new mission in addition to their original duty of national defense. The additional duty was to suppress social instability, protect the leadership, and participate in economic construction projects. This was the beginning of "military-first politics," which had been designed to manage such national chaos.

※　※　※　※　※　※　※　※　※

The deteriorating economic situation in the North gave the hardliners in the United States and South Korea the expectation of an imminent collapse of the North Korean regime. The conservative press in the South relentlessly reported that North Korea would soon collapse. It insisted that in order to expedite North Korean collapse, the South should contain the North, instead of assisting it. They alleged that the Sunshine policy was unrealistic. The conservative press also determined that the North Koreans were not trustworthy and their regime should be brought down. Nevertheless, some specialists warned that North Korean collapse could bring national disaster. However, there was no serious audience for that warning.

History shows that a regime or a state system does not collapse solely due to economic trouble. The Soviet Union under Joseph Stalin did not collapse although millions of people died of starvation. The great starvation of 1958–1962 in China, which killed tens of millions of people, did not destroy the Chinese Communist regime. History shows instead that regimes have collapsed due to dissident coups, mass revolt, and outside military intervention.

In the case of North Korea, despite its deteriorating economic situation, intelligence authorities reported there were no signs of an emerging dissident force or an organized movement of the people whose discontent might lead to social instability. To bring down the regime by military intervention meant risking war. War was never considered as a solution. The most desirable and realistic judgment was that North Korea, like China and Vietnam, would also undergo a process of gradual change.

* * * * * * * * *

Contrary to the conservative view, members of the Unification Board of Advisers said a lesson should be learned from the 1992 Koreatown riots in Los Angeles, California. The cause of this incident was negligence and indifference on the part of the privileged for their less privileged neighbors. They were concerned that North Korea, which was in a desperate situation of despair and hardship—but still had formidable military capability—might be tempted to attack the South in a do or die suicidal attempt. They reasoned that we should carefully and wisely deal with the North Koreans, while proactively helping any North Korean compatriots with humanitarian assistance. They all supported the Sunshine policy.

As Minister of Unification, I did all I could to explain the Kim Dae-jung administration's North Korea policy—in speeches, in interviews with journalists, and on panel discussions with academics, the clergy, retired generals, and civic leaders.

When speaking to church leaders, I quoted the Bible to explain that the Sunshine policy was designed to induce change in the North through reconciliation and cooperation, and making peace on the peninsula. Paul's Letter to the Romans (12: 17-21) has the four following messages: "Never take your own revenge, for vengeance is mine, I will repay"; "If your enemy is hungry, feed him; if he is thirsty, give him a drink"; "Do not be overcome by evil, but overcome evil with good"; and "Do everything possible on your part to live in peace with all men." I claimed these words were the Biblical basis for the Sunshine policy. I said to them:

> The North and the South became enemies through a fratricidal war and the Cold War. However, there has been an earth-shattering change in the international environment. Our way of defeating the enemy is by befriending him and instilling in him love for the future of our nation.
>
> We are economically stronger and should aid our weaker brother through humanitarian assistance and economic cooperation. As the winner in system competition, we should have confidence in our ability to create an environment for the North to transform itself towards opening and a market economy. This will be the best way to achieve our goal and to overcome evil with good without fighting. Removing the legacies of the Cold War and making peace are the best ways to national prosperity, development, and unification. This is what the Sunshine policy is about. Jesus said, "Blessed are the peacemakers, for they shall be called children of God." Let us all become peacemakers.

Yeonpyeong Naval Clash

Upon inauguration, the Kim Dae-jung administration proclaimed its policy of reconciliation and cooperation and pursued a dialogue with North Korea. In his inaugural speech, President Kim also proposed an exchange of special envoys, but the North did not show interest. Eventually, the North participated in an inter-Korean meeting to receive fertilizer and food assistance. However, this meeting failed when the North rejected the "principle of reciprocity" by which the South linked fertilizer assistance to the reunion of separated families. No further progress had been made between the authorities of the North and South in the first year of the Kim Dae-jung presidency.

Yet, civilian humanitarian assistance to the North continued to grow modestly. Several civilian organizations—including Christian, Catholic and Buddhist groups; Inter-Korean Sharing Movement; Mutual Compatriot Assistance; Good Neighbors; and World Vision—were at the forefront giving assistance to the North. The Eugene Bell Foundation, established by Stephen Linton and his brother John in memory of their grandfather, an early Presbyterian missionary, launched a campaign to help tuberculosis patients in the North.

Also, in accord with the principle of "separation of politics and economy," economic cooperation on the private level was actively sought. It was very fortunate that the North opened its frontline area and approved the Mount Kumgang tourism project, although its purpose was to earn foreign currency. This was seen as a green light to reconciliation and cooperation, and tension reduction.

Taking a lesson from the failure of its first year, the government decided to take a new approach of "give first" to the North the following spring, as it could afford to do so. This new approach began with the unconditional humanitarian provision of 50,000 tons of fertilizer through the Red Cross channel to the North, which needed it badly.

The North sent messages to the South through several channels that it was interested in meeting with the South on the government level. Consequently, three closed working-level meetings were held from May 12 to June 3 in Beijing. At these meetings the North—which was in dire need of fertilizer—practically pleaded for the timely provision of fertilizer from the South. The North side said, "If you give us fertilizer, we will respond to the issue of separated families." To discuss details, the North proposed to hold a vice minister-level meeting.

* * * * * * * * *

President Kim Dae-jung was departing for Mongolia after finishing a state visit to Russia; at his request, on May 30 I flew to Ulan Bator to meet with him. There I briefed him on the result of Perry's visit to Pyongyang and obtained his approval to send urgent instructions for the North-South Talks that were being held secretly in Beijing. I also reported to him the North's changed attitude as confirmed at the Beijing talks:

> North Korea has gone through five years of an arduous march and the shock of Kim Il-sung's death. Now with the Kim Jong-il system firmly in place, the North seems to have established a decision-making process. North Korea has considerable confidence in, and is appreciative of, our government's consistent policy of reconciliation and cooperation.

Our proactive exercise of influence on Dr. Perry and his NKPR team's review of the United States' North Korea policy; our advice to the United States and Japan to improve relations with North Korea; approval of payment for investment in the development of the Mount Kumgang tourism complex project; unconditional provision of 50,000 tons of fertilizer; and the encouragement of private level humanitarian assistance—all greatly contributed to an atmosphere of confidence-building.

On June 3, I announced the content of the agreement reached at the Beijing talks: "The South will provide 200,000 tons of fertilizer to the North on humanitarian grounds. On June 21, we will meet with the North Koreans at a vice minister-level meeting to primarily discuss the issue of separated families."

* * * * * * * * *

On June 15, six days prior to the scheduled North-South vice minister-level meeting, an exchange of fire broke out between North and South navy vessels near Yeonpyeong Island in the West Sea. The clash resulted in the sinking of one North Korean torpedo boat with an estimated twenty sailors on board and severe damage (half destruction) to a patrol boat that had barely been able to flee the scene. In contrast, the damage to the South side was minimal.

For the first time since the military armistice, the South retaliated against a North Korean provocation from a position of superiority. The South's response reflected the first of the "three principles" of President Kim Dae-jung's North Korea policy, which clearly stated there would be "no tolerance of armed provocation of any kind."

Every June, North Korean fishing boats intruded south of the Northern Limit Line (NLL) to harvest crabs, and usually scurried north of the line when warned by South Korean patrol boats. But in June 1999 they did not do so. Starting from June 4, crab-fishing boats stayed south of the NLL to fish every day under the protection of five or six North Korean navy patrol vessels. To make it worse, the North Korean ships did not respond to the warning of South Korean patrol boats approaching close to the Northern boats.

We held frequent NSSC meetings to deal with the situation. In the initial phase, the committee focused on determining the North's possible intentions. According to all available information, there was no sign of unusual North Korean military movements—nor was there any sign of even limited provocation around the five islands close to the NLL. The only abnormal situation was at the crab-fishing grounds.

It was possible that the North Koreans were going too far in violation of the NLL in order to meet their target of earning foreign currency through crab fishing. We had information that the North Korean Navy was responsible for catching crabs on the west coast and that its mandatory quota for crab fishing had doubled from the previous year. Areas north of the NLL had been almost completely depleted of crabs and the buffer zone south of the line was rich crab-fishing ground. Besides, the North never recognized the NLL, claiming a 12-nautical-mile territorial sea.

The NSSC decided on a position demanding "North Korean compliance with the NLL and an immediate withdrawal from south of the NLL," and we warned that "the North side is responsible for any consequences of violating the NLL." The NLL was not an extension of the Military Demarcation Line (MDL). That line was unilaterally set up by the United Nations Command to control ships and airplanes under its jurisdiction. The NLL was fixed before the revision of the Law of the Seas, when a 3-nautical mile territorial sea had been accepted. Yet, the NLL had served as an "effective borderline on the sea" since the Korean armistice. For this reason, both sides agreed in the protocol to the North-South Basic Agreement (1992) "to continue to observe the currently existing jurisdictions until a maritime borderline is established."

When the North continued to defy our warnings, the NSSC accepted Minister of Defense Cho Seong-tae's recommendation "to push the North Korean vessels back to north of the NLL." The South Korean Navy would bring up large naval gunships from the Jinhae Naval Base to the troubled area. The committee made sure that the South Korean Navy would not open fire first under any circumstances and would observe all rules of engagement.

Upon hearing Defense Minister Cho's report of his planned strong response, President Kim issued appropriate instructions: "Hold the NLL through all means. But do not fire first. If the North Koreans open fire first, resolutely crush them. At the same time, prevent escalation under all circumstances."

On June 15 at around 9:30 a.m., our navy started "Operation Push Back" against the North Korean vessels, which had been defying our orders to go back above the NLL. Perhaps surprised at an unexpected operation, a North Korean torpedo boat started firing at a South Korean patrol boat. The South's better-armed vessels immediately responded with a hail of fire from behind. A fierce exchange of naval gunfire lasted for fourteen minutes. According to reliable information, the North side suffered heavy losses, with more than thirty casualties.

The naval incident demonstrated at home and abroad that the Sunshine policy was not an "appeasement policy" but a "policy of the strong." Nevertheless, our immediate task was to contain and isolate the incident to prevent escalation and to secure the personal safety of those South Koreans who were staying in the North on business as part of civilian economic cooperation. Our government issued an alert to all armed forces, while quickly cooperating with the United States and informing China and Russia of the incident through diplomatic channels.

＊ ＊ ＊ ＊ ＊ ＊ ＊ ＊ ＊ ＊

This incident posed three difficult issues which I as unification minister had to resolve. These included the safety and protection of our people staying in the North, the question of whether to continue the Mount Kumgang tourism project under such circumstances, and whether to suspend delivery of the fertilizer that we had promised to provide.

At the time of the exchange of fire on the west coast, there were about 2,000 South Koreans staying in the North, including 1,500 at the Mount Kumgang tourism complex. The first priority was to secure their safety. We did have an emergency plan to evacuate them. Those who were in the Mount Kumgang area would have to use the sightseeing cruise ship. Also, about 200 workers employed in site preparation for light water reactors in the Kumho area would have go to the nearest port to wait for an emergency evacuation ship that we would send from the South. However, we did not have any means to bring back South Koreans visiting the Pyongyang area. If the situation deteriorated, it would be possible for the North to detain them. We could not afford to let this happen. We tried to think of all means possible, but we agreed mostly that there was no good solution, except to ask China for assistance.

＊ ＊ ＊ ＊ ＊ ＊ ＊ ＊ ＊ ＊

The only available channel of communication with the North under these circumstances was Hyundai. I asked Hyundai to contact the North immediately. Hyundai soon came back to me with a message that the North side had said, "Mount Kumgang tourism was undertaken as a national project, and should be continued without interruption." I interpreted this message to mean that the North felt the naval incident occurred accidentally, that they were humiliated, and that they did not want an escalation. This report was a big relief to me.

Now I had to decide urgently whether to authorize or suspend the departure of that evening's tourist cruise ship to Mount Kumgang. I felt we must stabilize the situation as quickly as possible. To this end and based on Hyundai's message, I reasoned that my approval of the departure would be essential to the safety of our people staying in the North. I tried to persuade the related agencies to agree with my decision.

However, all of those agencies withheld their support. None of them expressed their views one way or the other, but it was clear they were negative. There was no time to wait. I had to be bold. I called the president and reported to him that I was going to authorize the departure of the tourist cruise ship, taking sole responsibility as unification minister. With my authorization, the tourist ship with a full load of passengers left for Mount Kumgang that evening. To my surprise, all tourists who had made reservations that evening showed up to board the ship. Just the same, our navy and coast guard on the East Sea were put on special alert.

* * * * * * * * *

Another issue was whether to continue fertilizer assistance in this situation. Five cargo ships carrying 50,000 tons of fertilizer had already left their ports for North Korea to make delivery before the opening of the North-South vice minister-level meeting in Beijing, as we had promised. The cargo ships would arrive at North Korean ports in a day or two. Therefore, I had to decide whether to recall them.

The relevant agencies overwhelmingly held the view that we should recall them. They were most concerned about the expected criticism from the opposition party and the conservative press. On the other hand, I was more concerned about the safety of our people in the North than the opposition's criticism or attack. I was the one who was responsible for immediately making a decision on this issue.

For the personal safety of these people, I thought it would be the right thing for us as the stronger nation to maintain a consistent position. To prevent escalation of the incident and restore normality quickly, I determined that the operation of the cruise ship and fertilizer assistance should continue. Perhaps due to my agonizing decision, or my hard efforts, the South Koreans who were visiting Pyongyang fortunately all returned safely.

* * * * * * * * *

However, trouble really began at the National Assembly. On the afternoon of June 16, a special session of the National Assembly was convened, at which Minister of Defense Cho Seong-tae reported on military operations during the incident and their consequences. Next, as the minister of unification and chairman of the Standing Committee of the NSC, I reported on the measures that we would take as decided by the NSSC.

I emphasized, "We will strongly respond to any further provocations. However, at this point the safety of the 2,000 South Koreans in the North is at stake." I told the National Assembly that our government would continue a consistent policy of engagement with North Korea. The opposition Grand National Party (GNP) strongly resisted.

GNP hardliners charged, "Providing fertilizer while we are exchanging fire is an act of helping the enemy." They demanded the immediate suspension of assistance, shouting, "Stop this wrongheaded policy! Apologize for this wrongheaded policy!" More than fifty GNP members made a scene and walked out of the chamber. I learned later that before coming to the chamber, they had held a representatives meeting and decided to call for the "abrogation of the Sunshine policy," "suspension of the Kumgang tourism project," and "upholding the policy of reciprocity." The GNP had planned to harshly attack the government.

While the people felt a sense of security after the first South Korean military victory over the North since the military armistice, the opposition party had decided to use the incident for its own political tactics. The press reported that some opposition members were flabbergasted at what was happening. They were quoted as saying, "It is really strange that war broke out, but stock prices are going up. The boat to Mount Kumgang is full of tourists. South Korean citizens staying in Pyongyang have all safely returned. It is a completely different situation from what should have been expected." They even speculated that some secret deal had been made between the North and the South. Such speculation was called the "new North wind deal," as there had been allegations in years past that South Korean conservatives had made secret deals with the North Koreans to say or do things to benefit the conservatives in South Korean election campaigns.

* * * * * * * * *

When the vice ministerial meeting was held in Beijing on June 22–26, the North refused to discuss the issue of separated families. Instead, the North demanded a South Korean apology for and an assurance against a recurrence of the naval incident, which it alleged was "a premeditated, deliberate armed provocation committed by the South." It seemed to me that the North was caught between the military hardliners, who were obstructing the dialogue with the South after suffering serious damage from the naval clash, and the cold reality of its need for fertilizer. I decided to pull out our delegation from the Beijing talks and wait for the North's next move.

In the meantime, the UNC–North Korea General Officers Talks at Panmunjom were held. There the North demanded the South's acceptance of responsibility for an armed provocation, punishment of those responsible, and an assurance against a recurrence of such conflict. The North also offensively called for the abrogation of the NLL and the observance of a 12-nautical-mile territorial sea in accordance with the United Nations Convention on the Law of the Sea.

Just as in its first year, North-South talks did not yield results during the second year of the Kim Dae-jung presidency, either. It was another bitter disappointment for the administration, which had concentrated its efforts on addressing the pain of separated families.

CHAPTER 10

POST-SUMMIT DEVELOPMENTS

A Small but Valuable Beginning

In early June 2000, I visited Pyongyang as President Kim Dae-jung's special envoy to discuss with Chairman Kim Jong-il the proposed agenda for a North-South summit meeting. That successful, historic inter-Korean summit and the adoption of the June 15 North-South Joint Declaration were described in the first section of this book.

Following the inter-Korean Summit, the task that lay ahead of us was how to implement the summit agreement to build mutual confidence. As soon as the summit meeting was over, I utilized secret North-South working-level contacts to consult the North on the implementation of the summit agreement.

The most urgent task was to establish an "emergency communication network" as agreed upon by the two leaders. With the North's cooperation, we set up and opened a hotline within two weeks of the summit. This hotline remained available for use by the two leaders until the last day of the Kim Dae-jung administration. It played a great role in the development of inter-Korean relations.

In addition, there were a number of other urgent inter-Korean tasks to carry out. I carefully handled them one by one. They were related to reunions of separated family members on the occasion of Liberation Day on August 15; a first North-South ministerial meeting; a visit to Pyongyang by a group of heads of news media organizations; and a visit to Seoul by the Pyongyang Symphony Orchestra for a joint performance with the South side. I also worked on Secretary Kim Yong-soon's return visit to Seoul, according to a previous agreement.

In compliance with the June 15 summit accord, North Korea had totally suspended its slanderous loudspeaker broadcast along the DMZ and stopped its radio broadcasts targeting a South Korean audience. The North's annual "anti-American struggle" event that lasted from June 25 to July 27 had disappeared. The North also suspended its annual anti-South Korean agitation program, which called for a "joint August 15 Pan-National Conference at Panmunjom." In an unusually positive action, the North returned to the South a South Korean fishing boat that had crossed the NLL into the north due to a mechanical problem. The North Koreans had rescued and repaired the boat before returning it. These were small but valuable developments in North-South relations.

* * * * * * * * * *

After the summit at the end of June, Hyundai Chairman Chung Ju-young and his party met with Chairman Kim Jong-il at Wonsan to discuss economic cooperation. At this meeting, Chairman Kim made a bold decision to designate the Kaesong area for the construction of an industrial complex, whereas Hyundai had originally been interested in another area in Haeju. Chairman Kim was quoted as saying, "Kaesong used to belong to the South before the war. Now it is as if I am returning this land to the South. I designate Kaesong for the development of an industrial complex. This will be acceptable if we can earn foreign currency."

I also learned that Chairman Kim promised Hyundai that he would remove military troops from the Tongcheon area, near the Mount Kumgang tourism complex, to construct a light industrial complex. Chairman Kim had already made a bold decision to open the Mount Kumgang area and the Jangjeon Navy Base near the DMZ.

I was surprised to receive this incredible report. I had dealt with the subject of military strategy for a long time in the past. Kaesong was the North's utmost frontline strategic point, one it they could not easily open. Located close to Seoul, Kaesong was linked to what would be the main route of attack in the event of war. In the forward area of Kaesong, a large number of long-range artillery guns, capable of striking Seoul, were deployed.

If we had been in their position, we would have never given up such an important strategic point. The North had previously refused our request for opening even Haeju, due to its military's opposition. I repeatedly asked if Hyundai had misunderstood what the North Korean leader said. For us, the Kaesong area was better than any other area for the development of an industrial complex. If what I heard was true, we would certainly welcome it.

* * * * * * * * * *

Two months later, Hyundai presented its master construction plan for the Kaesong Industrial Complex to Chairman Kim Jong-il and received his approval. When I was briefed on Hyundai's plan, I was impressed by its ambitious magnitude. The complex would take up an area of sixty-six square kilometers, which included a supporting city area of forty square kilometers. This enormous project would be completed in three phases over eight years.

Hyundai estimated that when the project was complete they would need 350,000 workers to work in the complex. They were concerned about whether the North would be able to supply that many people. Chairman Kim was said to have relieved Hyundai's concerns, saying, "By then, we should live in peaceful coexistence and undertake arms reductions. We will cut our military troops to provide young people for labor." After I heard this report, I sincerely wished that the project would be realized. I felt that we should do our share to make the project succeed.

With the promulgation of the North Korean Law for the Kaesong Industrial Zone in 2002, the first phase of the construction project, for a 3.3 square kilometer area, was undertaken. To prepare for the first phase, North Korean troops and long-range artillery guns were moved from their frontline bases to the rear area.

With the Kaesong project underway, we were in a position to promote our long-term strategy to build a "North-South economic community." To realize this strategy, we would reconnect the railways and the roads through the DMZ on both coasts, which would serve as a "peace corridor," while doubling the railroad tracks between Seoul and Shinuiju. The railways would be linked to China, Russia, and Europe to develop the Korean Peninsula as a logistics hub. We would build communication networks between the North and the South to modernize the communication system in the North, and construct power generation facilities in the North near the DMZ, which would supply electricity to both sides of the peninsula. We would carry out these projects in support of our strategy of building a "North-South economic community."

Gateway to Exchanges and Cooperation

On July 10, Secretary Kim Yong-soon sent a reply to my earlier message. In it, he proposed to hold a first North-South Ministerial Meeting at Mount Kumgang at the end of that month, with each delegation consisting of five members. He also extended an official invitation to a group of heads of South Korean news media organizations.

I immediately responded and informed him that his proposals were acceptable, except for my counter-proposal that the North-South Ministerial Talks be held alternately in Seoul and Pyongyang.

In the meantime, we had contact with the North to ask for the repatriation of 73 South Koreans who had been kidnapped or detained in the North. We provided the North Koreans with a list of 34 abductees and 39 prisoners of war. We made a request for reciprocal action before we repatriated former long-term prisoners who had refused to renounce Communism.

* * * * * * * * *

At the end of July, the first round of the North-South Ministerial Talks was held in Seoul. The two sides agreed to reopen the Panmunjom Liaison Office, relink the North-South railways, and hold a joint festival on August 15, Liberation Day, to support and celebrate the June 15 Joint Declaration.

One month later, at the end of August, a second round of the North-South Ministerial Talks was held in Pyongyang. At that meeting, the North appealed to the South for one million tons of food aid, saying that it was suffering from a severe food shortage "due to a terrible drought." The North accepted the request of Unification Minister Park Jae-kyu, who was serving as our senior delegate, for a meeting with Kim Jong-il.

Minister Park traveled all night with Secretary Kim Yong-soon by train to Gangae in Jagang Province near the Yalu River, where he had a breakfast meeting with Chairman Kim. At their meeting, Chairman Kim responded positively to the proposals that our side had made. Minister Park and Chairman Kim agreed to hold two additional exchanges of separated family members within the year, and to convene the North-South military talks. They also agreed that the two sides would hold a groundbreaking ceremony in September to reconnect the Seoul-Shinuiju railway line, and that the next round of the North-South Ministerial Talks would be held on Jeju Island at the end of September.

As agreed, the third round of the ministerial talks was held on Jeju Island at the end of September. In the middle of December, the fourth round of the talks was held in Pyongyang. By that time, the North-South Ministerial Talks had become a routine event. At these talks, we agreed to resolve the issue of allowing separated family members to meet, as well to agree on the organization and operation of an implementation committee for North-South economic cooperation. We also agreed on four documents to establish an institutional mechanism for economic cooperation.

* * * * * * * * *

On August 5, a group representing the heads of news media organizations embarked on a weeklong visit to North Korea. The forty-eight members of the group including Choi Hak-rae, chairman of the Korean Newspaper Association, and Park Sang-kwon, chairman of the Korean Broadcasting Association. Minister of Culture and Information Park Ji-won accompanied them. However, the *Chosun Ilbo* and the *Dong-A Ilbo* refused to join the group.

The members of the visiting group were given a tour of the North Korea Central Broadcasting Agency, the daily newspaper *Rodong Sinmun*, and the city of Pyongyang. They also visited the scenic mountains of Baekdu and Myohyang. On the last day of their visit, they attended a luncheon hosted by Chairman Kim Jong-il, which lasted three-and-a-half hours. The transcript of all the luncheon conversations was released to the press.

In those conversations Chairman Kim made a number of remarkable comments:

> I have decided to give Kaesong to Hyundai for the development of an industrial complex.
> I will open a direct North-South air route.
> I will set a date for a groundbreaking to reconnect of Seoul-Shinuiju railway line.
> I will extend an invitation to opposition leader Lee Hoi-chang.
> I request that the South send a congratulatory delegation on the occasion of the founding anniversary of the Korean Workers' Party.
> I will suspend rocket launches.
> If the United States removes us from its list of terrorism-sponsor states, we will immediately normalize relations with the United States.

* * * * * * * * *

After years of fervent wishes by so many people on both sides of the land, meetings of separated family members were at last held simultaneously in Seoul and Pyongyang on August 15, 2000. That morning, one hundred separated family members and a support staff of fifty-one people arrived at Gimpo Seoul International Airport aboard a North Korean plane. In the afternoon they met 750 South Korean family members at the Coex Convention Center.

This was the first time these separated family members had met in a half-century, during which they never knew if the other were dead or alive. The meeting place instantly turned into a sea of tears, and these moving scenes were quickly broadcast around the world. It was an emotional and dramatic scene, hard to watch without tears. 1,400 reporters, including 360 foreign journalists, competed to cover the event.

The North Korean families were selected from those who had been kidnapped or who had defected to the North during the Korean War. They represented natives of the South who had succeeded in life in the North. At these meetings, Southerners who had hidden the fact of the defection of their family members to the North emerged into the light of day to see their Northern relatives. This event virtually abolished the South Korean "linkage system" under which those citizens whose family members had defected to the North received unfavorable treatment.

When speaking of separated families, many people had only thought of those who had come to the South from the North. However, the reunion meetings made them realize that separated families also included those who had gone to the North from the South. The meetings of the separated family members showed the world the emotional and political maturity of our society, which had suffered an enormous national tragedy.

That afternoon, one hundred separated family members and a support staff of fifty-one people went to Pyongyang aboard the North Korean airliner. In Pyongyang they met 217 members of their families. On August 18, a South Korean airliner took the North Korean visitors back to Pyongyang and brought the South Koreans back to Seoul.

The North and South thus celebrated the fifty-fifth anniversary of the August 15 Liberation Day—the first of the twenty-first century—with the reunions of separated families. It was a "day of national reconciliation"—the first visible result of the June 15 Joint Declaration. It gave hope to other separated families, and it gave hope to the nation for improved inter-Korean relations. Externally, it demonstrated the positive prospects for inter-Korean reconciliation and peace on the Korean Peninsula. Another meeting of separated family members followed three months later in November, and again, three months after the second reunion, in February the following year.

In early September, after the first separated family exchange meetings, our government unconditionally repatriated all sixty-three former long-term prisoners who had refused to renounce communism. The repatriation reflected a mature posture of respect for the human rights of victims of the division.

Of course, there were objections to the repatriation from hardliners, who wanted to maintain the Cold War structure. These conservatives tried to steer public opinion on grounds such as "concerns of confusing values" and "the possibility the North would use the repatriation for political propaganda." The hardliners also demanded that we should have "linked the repatriation of prisoners with the return of South Korean prisoners of war and those who were kidnapped by the North." They repeated the same logic that they used when they had opposed the repatriation of Lee In-mo seven years earlier.

* * * * * * * * *

Around August 15, the Pyongyang Symphony Orchestra came to Seoul for a joint performance with the KBS Symphony Orchestra. The Pyongyang orchestra played five pieces of Western music, including Rossini's "Prelude" to *The Barber of Seville*, and ten North Korean tunes, including "Good Harvest on Pungsan Field," and "My Sweet Hometown."

During the performance, a duet by world-famous South Korean soprano Jo Soo-mi and North Korean tenor Lee Young-wook singing the "Drinking Song" from Verdi's *La Traviata* drew special applause from the audience. To conclude their performance, the KBS and Pyongyang orchestras played "Arirang" and "Unification."

The performance was a significant event, attended by President Kim Dae-jung, the First Lady, and many leaders from various fields. After the performance was over, the director of the North Korean orchestra, Huh Yi-bok, came to me and cordially thanked me for inviting the Pyongyang orchestra to Seoul. He said he was very happy that my promise had been realized. He said, "When I reported your invitation to Chairman Kim Jong-il, he granted me permission on the spot. I am deeply moved by the realization of my life-long dream." It was touching to see his genuine expression of emotion. I felt good that I was able to contribute to the North-South cultural exchange.

Special Envoy's Chuseok Present

On September 11, while we were in the middle of the Chuseok harvest holiday season in the South, North Korean Secretary Kim Yong-soon came to Seoul. When I previously went to Pyongyang as a presidential envoy, I had invited him to Seoul. He came by an airplane that carried gifts from Chairman Kim Jong-il.

Kim Jong-il sent 300 ten-kilogram boxes of caulicolous mushrooms (*matsutake*) as a Chuseok gift to the South. The person in charge of transporting this gift was none other than General Park Jae-kyong, Deputy Director of the General Political Bureau of the Ministry of the People's Armed Forces. According to General Park, caulicolous mushrooms were a special product native to North Korea and had been collected from Mount Chilbo. North Koreans were proud of this product, and the entire harvest was usually exported to Japan.

Kim Jong-il sent one box each to President Kim Dae-jung, every member of the presidential delegation on the June 15 visit to Pyongyang, every news media organization head who visited Pyongyang, each former South Korean president, other leaders of the three branches of government, and political party leaders.

I hosted a welcome luncheon at the Shilla Hotel to thank General Park and Secretary Kim Yong-soon. I also invited Minister of Defense Cho Seong-tae to the lunch to provide them with an opportunity for conversation. Minister Cho had a separate meeting with General Park and asked him to convey a message to Minister of People's Armed Forces Kim Il-chol that he wanted to have a defense ministerial meeting as soon as possible.

* * * * * * * * *

Kim Yong-soon was Party Secretary for South Korean Affairs, who also was serving as Director of the United Front for the Korea Workers' Party. His areas of responsibility included intelligence, operations, psychological warfare directed toward the South, inter-Korean negotiations, and exchange and cooperation. In short, it was as if he was doing the two jobs comparable to those of the South Korean National Intelligence Service director and the unification minister.

Among the six members of the North Korean delegation were First Deputy Director of the United Front Lim Dong-ok, who was virtually in charge of all inter-Korean affairs; and Division Director Kwon Ho-woong, who four years later served as the head of the North Korean delegation to the North-South Ministerial Talks.

Prior to Secretary Kim's visit to Seoul, he had informed me of his wish "to go to Mount Halla on Jeju Island, and Gyeongju, the old capital city of the Silla dynasty, and also see some industrial facilities." At his request, I planned to hold our first meeting in Seoul, and our meeting on the following day on Jeju Island to make the best use of our time.

On the morning of Chuseok, I took the North Korean delegation to Jeju Island aboard a ROK Air Force plane, and we visited the Folklore and Natural History Museum and a few other points of interest. After that we went up to the midpoint of Mount Halla (about 1,128 meters above sea level) and we came down to check into the Shilla Hotel. At the hotel, we had a working dinner for the second day's meeting, which lasted more than five hours until one o'clock in the morning. The atmosphere was good and we were able to talk frankly to one another.

Early the next morning, I returned to Seoul to report to the president the content of our discussion the night before, and I consulted with the relevant ministers. In the meantime, I had arranged tours of Gyeongju and the Pohang steel plant for Secretary Kim Yong-soon and his party to visit before their return to Seoul.

✻   ✻   ✻   ✻   ✻   ✻   ✻   ✻   ✻

Our interest was focused on Chairman Kim Jong-il's return visit to Seoul; connection of the Seoul-Shinuiju railway; construction of a "peace corridor" in the DMZ; finding a fundamental solution to the issue of separated families, abductees and prisoners of war; and establishing an institutional mechanism for economic cooperation. In contrast, the North was interested in securing the one million tons of food assistance and inviting a large South Korean delegation to participate in the festivities in Pyongyang celebrating the fifty-fifth anniversary of the founding of the Workers' Party.

Regarding Chairman Kim Jong-il's return visit to Seoul, we agreed that it would take place during the the the "flower blooming spring months" of April and May of the following year. The North proposed that President Kim Young-nam of the Supreme People's Assembly (SPA) Presidium visit Seoul in December, before Chairman Kim's visit. This proposal did not require additional discussion since it had been raised by Chairman Kim when I met with him as the president's envoy.

The next issue was the holding of a defense ministerial meeting. Exchange and cooperation required tension reduction and military assurance. Military cooperation between the North and the South was essential particularly to the opening and use of the DMZ, without which it would be impossible to reconnect the rail tracks. Our position was to hold a defense ministerial meeting in Seoul and resolve the issue from above, because working-level military talks making recommendations from below would take much more time. This would also be militarily symbolic and meaningful for the implementation of the June 15 Joint Declaration.

However, Secretary Kim reiterated his position of holding working-level military talks in another country, as Chairman Kim had suggested to our senior delegate Park Jae-kyu. I emphasized that the defense ministers, responsible for military affairs, must meet on the peninsula as soon as possible. I strongly requested that my message be conveyed to Chairman Kim.

Later Kim Yong-soon received instructions from Pyongyang to propose holding a North-South defense ministerial meeting on Jeju Island. Accordingly, the historic first meeting between the defense ministers of the North and the South was held on Jeju Island on September 24–26, 2000.

The defense ministerial talks succeeded in resolving a few important issues. The North agreed to open the DMZ to construct a "peace corridor," the control of which would be turned over to the militaries of the North and the South. This transfer of control was later agreed upon at the UNC–North Korea General Officers Talks. The agreement made it possible to reconnect the railway between the North and the South.

In the meantime, I made a fundamental proposal to Kim Yong-soon concerning separated families:

> There are more than 90,000 people who have applied for meetings with separated family members. If we only allow a hundred reunions every few months, we cannot resolve the issue. I suggest that within this year, we at least find out whether or not those relatives are still alive. Thereafter, we can gradually move to exchanging letters and more reunion meetings.

However, the North would not budge. "It would be unrealistic at this point," said Kim Yong-soon, "Let's review your proposal after about two more meetings of separated families before the end of the year and see how it goes."

Later, after receiving more instructions from Pyongyang, Kim Yong-soon agreed to my proposal in principle. We further agreed, "Both sides will begin determing the life or death statuses of the separated families in September and expeditiously finish the project in the near future; we will also promote the exchange of letters between them."

I also raised the issue of South Koreans abducted to the North and prisoners of war. I insisted, "Now that the South has unconditionally returned all former long-term prisoners, we should also resolve the issue of those South Koreans abducted to the North and prisoners of war." But my North Korean counterpart's response was, "We have voluntary defectors to the North and we have no abductees from the South. And the defectors do not want to go back to the South." He also alleged that it was inappropriate to discuss prisoners of war, because the issue had been settled for good by the exchange of prisoners of war upon the conclusion of the Military Armistice Agreement in July 1953. He asked, "Do you want to reopen the discussion of the 27,000 'anti-Communist prisoners of war' who remained in the South?"

In response, I revised my proposal: "What if we first undertake the task of finding out the names and addresses of those who are still alive and have them meet their separated family members on a humanitarian basis?" Perhaps for a lack of justification for turning down my proposal, Secretary Kim said, "I will report it to my superiors for review." Although his acceptance was not fully satisfactory to me, I still took it as a positive step.

In a follow-up action, out of the list of 198 men we provided to the North Koreans, they confirmed fifty-nine South Korean prisoners of war.

And in the second round of meetings of separated families, one former prisoner of war and one kidnapped fisherman showed up to meet their South Korean family members. In the third meeting, the North included two former prisoners of war and one former South Korean flight attendant to meet their South Korean relatives. Over the course of seven years, thirty-six families—totaling 150 family members—met fourteen defectors and eleven former prisoners of war through the meetings arranged by the authorities of both sides.

Secretary Kim and I also discussed the establishment of a legal mechanism to carry out economic cooperation. We had previously presented the North with four draft documents of agreement, including an "agreement on investment protection," with the objective of reaching agreement on all four documents. To solve this particular issue, we agreed to have contacts at the working-level in Seoul in September. We also agreed to have a groundbreaking ceremony for the connection of the railroad on September 25.

* * * * * * * * *

In return, the North requested that the South dispatch a group of representatives of political parties and civic organizations to join the celebration of the anniversary of the Workers' Party on October 10. I told the North that to accept such a request would be in violation of the National Security Law and against the sentiments of the South Korean people. I asked the North not to make such a request. Instead, I suggested that we start with exchanges between political parties and civic organizations.

Some time afterwards, a group of forty-two individuals and leaders of civic organizations, headed by former unification minister Han Wan-sang, went to Pyongyang aboard a plane provided by the North. The group's visit was dubbed an "observation trip" for the anniversary festival for the founding of the party, not as a "congratulatory group."

The North's invitation was declined by all South Korean political parties. Subsequently, the North sent me a message of complaint that said, "The invitations were extended directly by Chairman Kim Jong-il, but even the governing Democratic Party did not send its representatives. We feel betrayed and humiliated." I replied, "We should promote exchanges between political parties and civic organizations." But this incident strained the North's attitude towards the South.

* * * * * * * * *

In my meeting with Secretary Kim Yong-soon on September 12, mentioned earlier, he requested one million tons of emergency food assistance, saying, "Our people are facing starvation due to the worst drought in a hundred years." The request for food assistance had already been raised at the second round of the North-South Ministerial Talks.

Through interagency coordination, we had considered a plan to purchase 600,000 tons of food from abroad and provide it to the North on a loan basis. However, we had internally decided to link food assistance to a negotiation of a fundamental resolution of the separated family issue and the holding of defense ministerial talks.

The chronic food shortage in the North had become dire. North Korea needed 5.5 to 6.5 million tons annually to feed its people, but its production was only about 3.6 to 4.2 million tons, resulting in an annual shortage of about 1.5 million tons.

Without foreign exchange to buy food, the North depended entirely upon foreign assistance, and adjusted the people's daily ration according to food availability. North Korea had been going through the so-called arduous march of a food shortage.

In our fifth meeting, held in Seoul after Secretary Kim Yong-soon returned from touring Gyeongju and Pohang Steel, we clashed over the issue of food assistance and Secretary Kim walked out. Later, Kim returned to the meeting with the following instructions: "If the South provides one million tons of food, the North will be willing to hold a defense ministerial meeting on Jeju Island and also to review a fundamental resolution of the issue of separated families."

Kim's statement proved the efficacy of our linkage strategy. I coordinated with Unification Minister Park Jae-kyu on a plan to purchase 400,000 tons of corn from overseas, in addition to 600,000 tons that the government had already planned to secure for provision to the North. I then called the president and got his approval for the new plan. Now the North would receive the food assistance it so desperately needed.

The North and the South eventually announced their agreement on seven items, including Kim Jong-il's return visit, President Kim Young-nam's visit to Seoul before the chairman's visit, the holding of defense ministerial talks, of the issue of separated families, connections of the railways and roads between the North and the South, and the establishment of an institutional mechanism for economic cooperation.

During the Kim Dae-jung administration, the South provided the North a total of 950,000 tons of fertilizer, beginning with 150,000 tons in 1999, and then 200,000 to 300,000 tons each successive year. We provided an average of almost 200,000 tons a year. For food assistance, we provided a total of 1.14 million tons, beginning with 40,000 tons of corn in 1999; 300,000 tons of rice and 200,000 tons of corn in 2000; 100,000 tons of corn in 2001; and 400,000 tons of rice and 100,000 tons of corn in 2002.

* * * * * * * * *

After all pending issues were resolved before noon that day, Secretary Kim Yong-soon and his party paid a courtesy call to President Kim Dae-jung, who hosted a welcome luncheon for them. In his opening remarks, the president said: "I thank Chairman Kim Jong-il for his kindness in sending the caulicolous mushrooms to us." Emphasizing his joint responsibility with Chairman Kim for the fate of the nation, he said they should implement the June 15 Joint Declaration. He explained: "The South is a diverse society. The opposition party is in control of the National Assembly. Therefore, the North should understand that we have to persuade the opposition party and gain the support of the people for all things and gradually carry them out." He also added, "I missed meeting President Kim Young-nam in New York because he was not there as we had agreed. President Clinton felt very sorry about the incident in Frankfurt."

The incident in question occurred when Kim Young-nam was about to board an American airliner in Frankfurt on September 4. He had been leading a fifteen-member delegation to New York, where he was scheduled to attend a new millennium conference of heads of state at the United Nations. In compliance with its rules, the airline conducted a stricter security screening of the North Koreans and their baggage since the travelers were from a "rogue state." In the midst of the North Korean delegation continuing protest, the plane had taken off.

The North Koreans were a legitimate diplomatic delegation, but they had been denied boarding by an airline and were unable to catch their flight on time. After this incident, the North Korean delegation planned to proceed to New York the next day on a Lufthansa flight. However, Pyongyang instructed them to return home, and they went back to North Korea through Beijing. It was learned that North Korean Foreign Minister Paek Nam-sun also cancelled his planned visit to New York in protest against the U.S. government.

As soon as the National Intelligence Service collected relevant information regarding the incident, as the NIS director I passed it along to the U.S. government through the American embassy in Seoul. The U.S. State Department seemed very confused and asked for my cooperation. It asked me to convey an urgent message to the North that the State Department was sending a message of regret to the North, asking the delegation not to return home but to come directly to New York from Beijing to attend the new millennium conference of heads of state. I immediately took the necessary action. But it was too late for the North Koreans to reverse their plan.

According to Secretary Kim's account of the Frankfurt Airport incident involving President Kim Young-nam, the North was infuriated by what they perceived as a "deliberate action by the United States." Only after the North received my urgent notice and a message of regret from the American secretary of state did they accept that the incident did not take place at the direction of the U.S. government. The urgent message sent by the South became a good example of preventing misunderstanding and miscalculation.

Call for "Adjustment of Speed"

In the wake of the June 15 Joint Declaration, North-South relations made impressive progress, and the seventy million Korean people on the peninsula were filled with excitement and joy, believing that an era of reconciliation had finally come. Not just the people in the North and the South, but the entire world showed interest in the remarkable changes taking place on the peninsula.

On September 15, wearing the same uniforms and carrying the "Peninsula Flag" in the name of "Korea," the members of the North and the South teams entered hand in hand at the opening ceremony of the Sydney Olympics to the applause of viewers around the world. Following the moving meetings of separated families and the repatriation of former long-term prisoners, the simultaneous entry of the members of the North and South teams touched the world again.

At the end of August 2000, the midpoint of the five years of the Kim Dae-jung administration, opinion polls conducted by the news media found approximately 75 percent of respondents agreed that "President Kim Dae-jung was doing generally well." An overwhelming majority of 80 to 90 percent said the best area of the president's performance was the improvement of North-South relations through the Sunshine policy, followed by his successful management of the financial crisis.

On October 13, the Norwegian Nobel Committee announced its decision to award the 2000 Nobel Peace Prize to President Kim Dae-jung. The announcement said the prize was awarded to Mr. Kim Dae-jung "for his work for democracy and human rights in South Korea and East Asia in general, and for his successful efforts to eliminate hostile relations with North Korea, to remove the Cold War legacies through reconciliation and cooperation, and to make peace."

One week after the announcement of the Nobel Peace Prize, Seoul hosted an Asia-Europe Summit Meeting (ASEM), a forum where twenty-six heads of state from Asia and Europe gather to discuss mutual cooperation.

This was the first time in history that the Republic of Korea invited so many heads of state to Seoul to host such a meeting, a diplomatic celebration for Korea. At the meeting, President Kim Dae-jung even encouraged the participants to normalize their relations with North Korea. Afterwards British Prime Minister Tony Blair made a surprise announcement in Seoul normalizing relations between the United Kingdom and North Korea.

Since the North-South summit meeting, events related to inter-Korean relations were taking place as if floodgates had opened. Related stories were published on the front pages every day. Polls showed a support rate of 70–80 percent for our North Korea policy. Here is a list of some front-page headlines during the post-summit period:

June 15–16	North and South Cease Mutual Slander along DMZ
June 28–30	Chairman of Hyundai and Chairman Kim Jong-il Meet in Wonsan, Kaesong Area Designated for Industrial Complex
July 26	North Korea Joins U.S.-DPRK Foreign Ministers Meeting at ARF (Bangkok)
July 29–31	First Round of North-South Ministerial Talks (Seoul)
August 5–12	Heads of News Media Organizations Visit North, Meeting with Chairman Kim Jong-il
August 15–18	First Meeting of Separated Families (Seoul and Pyongyang)
August 22–23	Pyongyang Symphony Orchestra Performs with KBS in Seoul
August 29–September 2	Second Round of North-South Ministerial Talks (Pyongyang)
September 2	Repatriation of 63 Former Long-term Prisoners
September 11–14	Secretary Kim Yong-soon Visits South, Agreement on 7 issues
September 12	U.S.-DPRK Talks in Berlin Agree on Moratorium on Missile Launch and the Lifting of Sanctions
September 15	North and South Enter the Sydney Olympics Together
September 18	Groundbreaking for Railway to Connect North and South
September 22–28	109 South Korean Tourists Visit Mount Baekdu via Pyongyang
September 24–26	North-South Defense Ministers Meeting on Jeju Island
September 25–26	First Working-level Talks for Economic Cooperation (Seoul)
September 27–30	Third North-South Ministerial Talks (Jeju Island)
September 28	Announcement of 500,000 tons of Food Assistance
October 6	U.S.-DPRK Joint Statement on Anti-Terrorism
October 9–13	North Korean Special Envoy Jo Myung-rok Visits Washington, Meets with President Clinton
October 12	Announcement of U.S.-DPRK Joint Communiqué
October 9–14	South Korean Observer Group Visits North on 55th Anniversary of Workers' Party
October 13	Kim Dae-jung Announced as Nobel Laureate
October 23–25	Secretary of State Albright Visits Pyongyang, Meets with Chairman Kim Jong-il

Despite this atmosphere, the conservative press and the opposition Grand National Party were still critical of the administration's policy. They made charges, such as: "it confuses values"; "the government is being manipulated by North Korean tactics and trick"; "the North does not change, but we change"; "we are concerned about national security." They were stirring up a divisive controversy within the South, which was sometimes called a "South-to-South conflict." They wanted to put the brakes on the rapid development of North-South relations. They claimed there was a need for "a speed adjustment."

Jo Myong-rok in Washington, Albright in Pyongyang

While supporting improved inter-Korean relations, the Clinton administration maintained close coordination with South Korea and Japan in a concerted effort to resolve pending U.S. concerns. The U.S. inspection team's visit to the suspicious Kumchangni underground site had confirmed that since it was not related to nuclear activity, and thus that the North was still abiding by the Agreed Framework. North Korea's nuclear program was no longer an issue at that point.

In September, the U.S.-DPRK missile talks in Berlin produced a North Korean moratorium on missile launches and an agreement that the United States would ease economic sanctions. The moratorium agreement averted a missile crisis, enabling the United States to move toward active negotiations on the missile issue. The United States seemed to have found a path to a resolution of its two biggest concerns—Kumchangni and missile development—and it seemed to move in the direction of discussing improved relations with North Korea.

Upon the successful realization of the historic inter-Korean summit, the United States quickly supported the June 15 Joint Declaration, and it announced measures to ease economic sanctions on the North on June 19. Meanwhile, President Kim Dae-jung sent Hwang Won-tak, Senior Secretary for National Security and Foreign Affairs, to the United States to brief President Clinton on the results of the summit.

On June 23, Secretary of State Albright came to Seoul and congratulated President Kim on his successful summit. The president personally briefed her on his summit, and she discussed what measures the United States might take. The president emphasized, "It is important to talk directly to Chairman Kim Jong-il." On September 7, President Kim met with President Clinton for close policy coordination. This took place on the sidelines of the first UN Millennium Summit, which brought together many heads of state in New York.

Against the backdrop of these developments, at a bilateral meeting in New York on September 27 the DPRK's Vice Foreign Minister, Kim Gye-gwan, informed his U.S. counterpart, Ambassador Charles Kartman, that

North Korean special envoy Vice Marshal Jo Myong-rok (*left*) paying a courtesy call on President Clinton at the White House, October 10, 2000. Courtesy Lim Dong-won.

North Korea was ready to send a special envoy to Washington; it also agreed to issue a joint communiqué afterwards. Prior to this development, the first U.S.-DPRK foreign ministerial meeting had been held at the end of July during the ASEAN Regional Forum in Bangkok. At the meeting, Secretary Albright asked North Korean foreign minister Paek Nam-sun to reciprocate Special Envoy Perry's visit to Pyongyang by a DPRK envoy's visit to Washington. The North was known to have responded positively. Afterwards, the United States was surprised to hear that the North was ready to send Vice Marshal Jo Myong-rok, the First Vice Chairman of the National Defense Commission, to Washington as its special envoy. Jo Myong-rok was also the director of the General Political Bureau of the Korean People's Armed Forces. He was one of the few close confidants to Chairman Kim Jong-il and a powerful individual in the military.

Special Envoy Jo Myong-rok and his party arrived in San Francisco, where he was given a tour of Silicon Valley by former defense secretary and special envoy William Perry. First Vice Foreign Minister Kang Sok-ju and ten other officials accompanied Special Envoy Jo. On October 10, Vice Marshal Jo met with Secretary of State Albright for talks, and then he changed into his military attire to pay a visit to President Clinton at the White House.

The next day the U.S.-DPRK Joint Communiqué, expressing the two nations' will to improve mutual relations, was announced. The communiqué was an epoch-making statement. It said,

> Recognizing the changed circumstances on the Korean Peninsula created by the historic inter-Korean summit, the United States and the Democratic People's Republic of Korea have decided to take steps to fundamentally improve their bilateral relations. . . . The two sides agreed there are a variety of available means, including the Four-Party Talks, to reduce tension on the Korean Peninsula and formally end the Korean War by replacing the 1953 Armistice Agreement with permanent peace arrangements.

The communiqué promised that the countries would harbor no mutual hostile intent; they also agreed to eliminate mistrust and build mutual confidence; respect each other's sovereignty and not interfere in each other's internal affairs; develop economic cooperation and exchange; and resolve the missile issue. The agreement further mentioned support for anti-terrorism, humanitarian cooperation, and the strengthening of inter-Korean relations. The communiqué stated that Secretary Albright would visit North Korea "to prepare for a possible visit by the president of the United States."

* * * * * * * * * *

In early October, Ambassador Stephen Bosworth had notified me in advance that "North Korean special envoy Jo Myong-rok would visit the United States on October 9–12 to meet with Secretary Albright and to pay a courtesy call on President Clinton." On the morning of October 11, I was informed of the results of the Jo-Clinton meeting. Special envoy Jo was quoted as saying, "If the people and the military of North Korea are certain that there is no threat to our security, it would be possible to address the security concerns of the United States." He conveyed a letter from Chairman Kim Jong-il expressing his desire to improve relations with the United States and inviting President Clinton to visit Pyongyang. Jo was also said to have emphasized how the inter-Korean summit had made it possible to pursue an improvement of relations with the United States.

Vice Foreign Minister Kang Sok-ju, who accompanied the special envoy, had a separate meeting with North Korea Policy Coordinator Ambassador Wendy Sherman. Kang said, "The North is ready to discuss the proposals that were made by Dr. Perry during his visit to Pyongyang last May. Let's resolve the missile issue in a package solution and move toward full-fledged normalization of relations."

According to Ambassador Bosworth, after meeting with special envoy Jo, President Clinton had said, "I also hope to meet Kim Jong-il, perhaps in Pyongyang or a third country. The timing would probably be around the Asia-Pacific Economic Cooperation forum (November 14–16) or in December. Please find out President Kim Dae-jung's view on this soon as possible."

President Kim instructed me to convey the following views to President Clinton:

> Chairman Kim Jong-il wants to meet with President Clinton to resolve pending issues between North Korea and the United States. Kim Jong-il is the only person in the North who can make decisions on these matters, and I gladly welcome a U.S.-DPRK summit. President Nixon went to China when the United States had no diplomatic relationship with that nation. I hope President Clinton can see the big picture and visit Pyongyang for a successful meeting. After the Pyongyang visit, it would be good if you dropped by Seoul to have a trilateral summit with South Korea and Japan to demonstrate our close cooperation.

Within two hours after I received the request from Ambassador Bosworth, President Kim's views were conveyed to the United States.

* * * * * * * * * *

On October 13, Ambassador Bosworth informed me, "President Clinton, with the agreement of President Kim, has decided to accept Chairman Kim Jong-il's invitation to visit Pyongyang. Secretary Albright is planning to travel to Pyongyang to prepare a visit by President Clinton." With that, Ambassador Bosworth requested that I come to San Francisco, saying, "Ambassador Sherman would appreciate it very much if you would come to San Francisco and meet her there. She needs your advice and consultation, but she cannot come to Seoul due to time constraints." Sherman had succeeded Dr. Perry as North Korea Policy Coordinator.

Since President Kim had instructed me to fully cooperate with the United States, I took Director General of North American Affairs Song Min-soon of the Ministry of Foreign Affairs with me to San Francisco. Ambassador Bosworth also accompanied us on this two-day/one-night trip. We arrived in San Francisco on Saturday, October 14, to meet Sherman and Ambassador Kartman, who had flown in ahead of us from Washington.

The first agenda item was what kind of security assurance the North had in mind and how we should deal with it, since the North had said it would be willing to address U.S. security concerns if it was convinced of the removal of security threats to North Korea. My advice was that the United

U.S. North Korea Policy Coordinator Wendy Sherman (*left*) consults with the author in San Francisco on October 15, 2000, prior to Secretary of State Albright's visit to Pyongyang. Courtesy Lim Dong-won.

States should be prepared for a list of North Korean demands, including the general concept of respect for sovereignty (which the United States was considering offering), no hostile intent, non-use of force, and non-interference in internal affairs. In addition, it might be possible that the North would raise specific issues such as suspension of combined U.S.-ROK military exercises, change in the status and role of U.S. forces in Korea, dismantlement of the UNC, removal of the DPRK from the list of terrorism-sponsoring states, and transformation of the Military Armistice Agreement into a peace regime.

The second topic on the agenda was how to conclude a peace agreement. The U.S. side asked what President Kim Dae-jung's intent was when he mentioned the conclusion of a peace agreement during his term in a recent interview with the *New York Times*. I provided the following answer:

> What President Kim said simply reflected the basic position that he wants to take measures to end the state of war and start a peace-making process. Between the North and the South, there is already a declaratory "agreement of non-aggression." A peace agreement should not be declaratory but practical in nature. To this end, we should take substantive and physical measures to guarantee non-aggression and peace, includ-

ing the denuclearization of the peninsula, military confidence-building measures, and achievement of a military balance of power through arms reduction.

You should be conscious of the fact that a peace agreement is related to several difficult issues, including the dismantlement of the UNC and a change in the status and role of the U.S. forces in Korea. Therefore, you can work on the process of normalization of relations, independent of the transformation of the Armistice Agreement into a peace agreement. As the United States normalized its relationship with China, against which the United States had fought in the Korean War, the United States could normalize its relations with North Korea, even before abolishing the Armistice Agreement.

My analysis provoked a lot of discussion. The third topic was where South Korea stood on the idea of a trilateral summit amongst the two Koreas and the United States. The United States seemed to be considering the possibility of a trilateral summit in which Chairman Kim Jong-il would come to Seoul. I expressed a cautious view, saying, "That idea is not realistic at this point because the United States and South Korea should first thoroughly discuss three issues in advance—U.S. troops in Korea, arms control, and a peace regime." I also said that I suspected that given the tragic outcome of the trilateral meeting over Vietnam, negative responses to such an idea in South Korea were possible.

Aborted U.S.-DPRK Summit

U.S. Secretary of State Madeline Albright arrived in Pyongyang at seven o'clock on the morning of October 23 for a three-day visit. She was the first U.S. secretary of state to visit North Korea. The visit took place less than ten days after Special Envoy Jo Myong-rok returned to Pyongyang from his trip to the United States.

Accompanying the secretary of state to Pyongyang were: North Korea Policy Coordinator Wendy Sherman, Assistant Secretary of State for East Asia Stanley Roth, Assistant Secretary of State for Proliferation Robert Einhorn, Ambassador for Peace on the Korean Peninsula Charles Kartman, White House National Security Council director of Asian affairs Charles Pritchard, fifty members of the advance team, and fifty-seven reporters. Including other support staff, more than 210 people from the United States went to Pyongyang.

On the morning of her first day in Pyongyang, Secretary Albright visited Geumsusan Memorial Palace. In the afternoon, she delivered President Clinton's letter to Chairman Kim Jong-il at the Baekhwawon Guest House before she had her first three hours of talks with him. That evening after the meeting, Secretary Albright was guided by Chairman Kim to the May Day Stadium to watch an hour-and-a-half long culture and arts performance called the "Invincible Korean Workers' Party." The show involved 100,000 performers engaged in group gymnastics and card-turning displays.

Through the performance, Chairman Kim seemed to indicate that the United States was not a permanent enemy and that relations with the United States were improving. The same evening, Secretary Albright attended a welcome reception hosted by Chairman Kim.

The next morning, the secretary of state had a meeting with Foreign Minister Paek Nam-sun and paid a courtesy call on the President of the SPA Presidium, Kim Young-nam. After attending a luncheon hosted by Vice Marshal Jo Myong-rok, she had another three-hour meeting with Chairman Kim Jong-il. That evening, Secretary Albright hosted a return dinner at a place called Magnolia Hall, which was the last event of her itinerary in Pyongyang.

On the morning of October 25, Secretary Albright arrived in Seoul directly from Pyongyang to pay a courtesy call on President Kim Dae-jung and to discuss the results of her visit. After that, she hosted a trilateral foreign ministers' meeting with her South Korean and Japanese counterparts.

At the press conference she said, "We made important progress," expressing her satisfaction with the talks with Chairman Kim Jong-il. When asked for her impression of Chairman Kim Jong-il, she said, "He is a good listener and a good party for dialogue. He gave me the impression that he is pragmatic and decisive." (On another occasion, she had described Chairman Kim as "surprisingly well-informed, knowledgeable and good-humored.")

Secretary Albright's assessment implied that Chairman Kim Jong-il was ready to make concessions if North Korea was assured of its security and provided economic assistance, and that he was a leader whom the United States could deal with. After her assessment, the American press reported that the Western perception of North Korea as a "rogue state" and Kim Jong-il as a "crazy person" was wrong.

* * * * * * * * *

I invited Ambassador Sherman to breakfast to listen to her own assessment of Secretary Albright's visit. We were joined by Ambassador Bosworth and Director General Song Min-soon. Sherman first thanked me by saying: "Director Lim, the judgment and advice you provided me in San Francisco was very accurate and useful."

She went on to say, "North Korea expressed its willingness to resolve U.S. concerns about the missile issue." Then she told me a few things about North Korea's position. For example, "Chairman Kim offered to give up his long-range (more than 500-kilometer) missiles, if the United States will agree to launch civilian satellites for Pyongyang."

Chairman Kim agreed that North Korea would observe the guidelines of the Missile Technology Control Regime (MTCR). He also indicated that he was willing to halt all missile exports, including equipment and technology. Originally, the North had asked for cash payment in compensation for the suspension of missile exports. Now, Chairman Kim said the North was prepared to accept non-monetary assistance such as food. Ambassador Sherman said, "We made big progress. But there are still several details of this issue that will have to be resolved, such as verification and the implementation schedule for the elimination of missiles."

Just before Kim Dae-jung's summit with George W. Bush, the contents of these negotiations were reported in detail in a March 6, 2001 *New York Times* article entitled, "How Politics Sank Accord on Missiles with North Korea." The article and its interview with Ambassador Sherman disclosed the substance of the Clinton administration's negotiations on the North Korean missile issue, which had been kept confidential until then.

According to Ambassador Sherman, Secretary Albright's visit narrowed the gap with North Korea and made important progress. Chairman Kim offered several important concessions during the six hours of talks. "Chairman Kim proposed to immediately open an ambassador-level diplomatic relationship and earnestly hoped for President Clinton's visit." She also told me her personal view that "President Clinton also wants to visit Pyongyang, but because of rising Republican criticism, he will be cautious. He will probably make a decision after the presidential election is over."

* * * * * * * * *

I watched the November 7 U.S. presidential election with great interest, as it would have a great impact on the fate of the Korean Peninsula. The election was a critical juncture for determining whether President Clinton would go to Pyongyang to bring about a new turning point in U.S.-DPRK relations that would facilitate the process of ending the Cold War on the Korean Peninsula.

Charges of irregularities involved in vote-counting in Florida created confusion, and the matter was eventually taken to court. After thirty-five days of judicial litigation, in a close vote of five to four the U.S. Supreme Court ruled in favor of George W. Bush as the president-elect. The U.S. Senate was split fifty-fifty between Democrats and Republicans, but the House majority went to the Republican Party with 221 seats, over the Democratic Party's 212 seats.

The Republicans had opposed President Clinton's visit to Pyongyang, arguing that the president should not carry out such a sensitive task at the end of his term. They also said, "We cannot trust North Korea. The United States should not be fooled by North Korean tricks regarding the missile issue." The hardliners frankly revealed that they preferred to take advantage of the missile issue as an opportunity to develop and deploy anti-ballistic missiles (ABM), instead of resolving the issue through negotiation.

* * * * * * * * *

On December 21, President Clinton called President Kim Dae-jung to inform him of his decision not to visit the North. On December 29, the White House released a statement that President Clinton had given up on a visit to Pyongyang due to a lack of time. President Clinton added that his decision was not influenced by the opposition of the Republican Party. He explained that because of the eruption of violent clashes between the Israelis and the Palestinians, it had become difficult to find time for a trip to the North.

Later, Ambassador Wendy Sherman said to me, "It is too bad that President Clinton's trip was aborted." She blamed Chairman Kim Jong-il's insensitivity to timeliness. "If Kim Jong-il had moved up sending Special Envoy Jo to Washington by one month, history would have turned out differently." It seemed that Kim Jong-il had deliberately chosen the special envoy's visit one month before the election for political impact. That had been a miscalculation.

I fully agreed with her view. North Korea had summits with China in May, with South Korea in June, and with Russia in July, to improve relations with these countries. If Special Envoy Jo Myong-rok had visited Washington one or two months earlier in August or September, the fate of the Korean Peninsula would certainly have turned out differently.

On the other hand, if the U.S. presidential election had turned out differently, a turning point in relations between the United States and North Korea would have been reached, moving toward the end of the Cold War on the Korean Peninsula. Five years later, former president Clinton told former president Kim Dae-jung in person in Seoul, "If I had had one more year in office, the fate of the Korean Peninsula would have been different."

Debate at Langley

Three weeks after President George W. Bush's inauguration, on February 11, 2001, I went on an official one-week visit to Washington at the invitation of CIA Director George Tenet. This invitation was originally extended to me in September of the previous year, to promote cooperation between the agencies of the two allies. But it had been put off due to my heavy schedule in Seoul.

In Washington, I followed an itinerary prepared by the CIA. My schedule included a meeting with senior members of the CIA, a discussion with intelligence analysts of East Asia and Korean affairs, and appointments with the director of the Federal Bureau of Investigation (FBI) and director of the National Security Agency (NSA) Michael Hayden, who was in charge of collecting signal intelligence throughout the world. Hayden was an Air Force Lieutenant General, a former Deputy Chief of Staff at UNC, and later CIA director. The purpose of these meetings was to strengthen cooperation between these agencies and our own.

In addition, I was scheduled to meet with Secretary of State Colin Powell, National Security Advisor Condoleezza Rice, Deputy Secretary of State Richard Armitage (then in process of confirmation), and Assistant Secretary of State for East Asian and Pacific Affairs James Kelly (also awaiting confirmation at that point). I would also meet with think tank personnel in the private sector.

Upon my arrival at the CIA Headquarters Building in Langley in the suburbs outside of Washington, Director Tenet greeted me cordially and pointed to the marble wall in the foyer that was decorated with about seventy stars. "This is the monument in memory of those members of the CIA who gave their lives in the service of their country," the director explained.

Director Tenet said, "My senior members and analysts would like to hear your views of the situation in North Korea and East Asia. Would you make time to do that?" He also said modestly, "The most vulnerable area of the CIA is intelligence on North Korea. My people know you have visited Pyongyang many times, you had long hours of dialogue with Kim Jong-il, and you have lots of experience negotiating with the North. They all want to meet with you." Director Tenet also said it has been difficult to organize my schedule of appointments, because so many senior officials in the new administration wanted to see me.

He gave me a "heads-up" about what might be coming from the new administration. He said, "The leaders of the new administration do not trust North Korea. They demand surveillance, verification, and transparency.

Unless the North Koreans take visible action on the issues of U.S. concern, the new administration will not negotiate with them."

This meant that the Bush administration was different from the Clinton administration in terms of its priorities and approach. Tenet also told me that in order to remove North Korean threats to the U.S. forces in Korea, the Department of Defense was advocating that North Korea be called on to move its forward-deployed offensive forces, including long-range artillery guns, farther north of the DMZ.

I explained to him what the core problem of the Korean Peninsula was and why the dismantlement of the Cold War structure was important; I also described in detail the reconciliation and cooperation policy of our government. Having listened to my explanation, Tenet said, "In order to understand the Korean Peninsula, an objective analysis of the pending issues alone is not enough. I've learned that we should consider the people's attitudes to their internal national issue as well as human factors to fully understand the entire situation." He sincerely thanked me for sharing my views with him.

With the idea of a Korea-U.S. summit in mind, I asked him what President Bush was like. Tenet said he gave a thirty-minute intelligence briefing to President Bush every morning; unlike President Clinton, President Bush liked listening more than reading. After the briefing was over, President Bush would ask, "What's the main point?" or "So, what's the bottom line?"

* * * * * * * * *

Following my conversation with Director Tenet, I was given a CIA briefing on the strategic situation surrounding the Korean Peninsula. After the briefing, I participated in a two-hour discussion with strategic intelligence analysts. Director of Operations for East Asia Joseph DeTrani (who later moved to the State Department in 2004 to serve as ambassador to the Six-Party Talks) and about twenty other people participated in the discussion, during which many questions were asked and several comments made.

Knowing that intelligence reports produced by these people would be provided to the president and policy makers as a basis for their policy decisions, I thought it was a good opportunity to have a serious exchange of views with them. I tried my best to create a productive and useful discussion.

They asked questions like, "Could North Korea change without collapsing?," "Don't you think that the symptoms of change in the North are a tactic for survival?," "Isn't it more urgent to remove North Korean threats than wait for gradual change?," "What's your assessment of the North Korean military threat?," and "What are your thoughts on neighboring countries' positions on Korean unification?"

* * * * * * * * *

I started answering these questions by reminding them of 1990 and subsequent CIA assessments that had all been off the mark; they predicted that
"North Korea would suddenly collapse within a few years like Romania
did," and "North Korean collapse is imminent, or it will change suddenly
[another term for "collapse"]." I said, "By the yardstick of Western reason,
North Korea should have already collapsed." I argued, "We should analyze
and judge an Asian country like North Korea, one with a Confucian tradition and a patriarchal system, by the North Korean yardstick, and we should
think in an Asian way." I said:

> Asian countries like China and Vietnam are different from Russia and
> Eastern European countries in their historic and cultural backgrounds
> and in their stages of economic and social development. These coun-
> tries are now promoting opening and economic reform towards gradual
> change, while maintaining political stability under a system of one-par-
> ty dictatorship. I think North Korea, too, will pursue gradual change
> following the Asian model. North Korea will have no other choice but
> to gradually open itself and pursue a market economy to survive. Quan-
> titative change will lead to qualitative change. However, North Korea
> needs an external environment or conditions in order to move in that di-
> rection. If threatened from the outside or constantly contained, North
> Korea will find it difficult to open up and reform.
>
> When I hear that the symptoms of North Korean change are "tac-
> tical" or a "trick," I am reminded that when Gorbachev was bringing
> change to the old Soviet Union, Western specialists of Soviet affairs said
> it was a "trick," "breathtaking but unworthy of trust."
>
> There is one problem for those who support the theory of an im-
> minent collapse to consider. I can think of three possibilities. The first
> one is the possibility of chaos or internal conflict. If an internal conflict
> breaks out in the North, people would flee to China and the South. That
> may create a situation in which South Korea, the United States, and
> China might find it necessary to intervene.
>
> The second possibility is war. If North Korea were cornered and
> felt it had no way out but the collapse of its regime and system, it might
> choose war out of desperation in a "do or die" suicidal attempt. That
> of course would lead to its self-destruction. It would also bring about a
> national disaster on the peninsula.
>
> The third possibility is political transformation that might lead to
> unification as in the case of East Germany.
>
> We should develop and maintain a contingency plan for any emer-
> gency development. However, the first two possibilities are undesirable
> and too costly to bear. The third possibility, similar to the East German

model, would be the most desirable. However, German unification was made possible after more than twenty years of "change through rapprochement," exchange and cooperation promoted by West Germany.

In contrast, we have fought a war in Korea, and we are only at the beginning stage of exchange and cooperation. We have to prevent a undesirable situation through our policy of reconciliation and cooperation. We should induce change in North Korea and manage it peacefully.

After expounding on these premises, I discussed our government's North Korea policy:

President Kim Dae-jung's Sunshine policy aims at creating the right conditions and environment for North Korea to change, and at establishing peace on the Korean Peninsula. We are pursuing a policy of maintaining "negative peace" through strengthening our security posture, and at the same time, are making "positive peace" by inducing change in North Korea.

We oppose war. We do not want a sudden collapse of North Korea, either. In order to earn foreign currency, North Korea opened its frontline military fortress in the Mount Kumgang area and its naval base at Jangjeon on the east coast. It opened the Kaesong area on the west coast, which was a critical forward strategic point where its long-range artillery pieces were deployed in concentration for a possible attack on Seoul.

All these were made possible due to the efficacy of the Sunshine policy. In the future, the Sunshine policy will continue to contribute to tension reduction and military confidence-building on the peninsula. When the Kaesong Industrial Complex is completed, it will need a labor force of 350,000 workers. When Chairman Kim Jong-il was asked whether he would be able to supply that many workers, he said he would reduce the number of his military troops to meet the demand for labor. Of course, we will have to see if that happens. But I think it is important that we made him think of such a possibility. During his recent visit to Shanghai, Kim Jong-il expressed deep interest in the Chinese model of reform and opening. This is the very process of gradual change that the Sunshine policy is seeking.

Next, I gave my views on the question of whether the Sunshine policy was too defensive or constituted appeasement:

Our government does not believe that the North Koreans will abandon their military posture against the South unless their system changes. Since we judge that there are constant security threats, we maintain a strong deterrence. It is true that, as they have deployed their offensive forces forward close to the DMZ, they pose a threat to the South.

However, unlike in the 1970s and 1980s, there is a military balance between the North and the South. In particular, due to its disastrous economy, North Korea's economic strength has been reduced by half and its military capability has not increased. More than two-thirds of its military equipment is seriously outdated. Unlike during the Cold War period, it cannot expect military assistance from China or Russia. North Korea may still be capable of starting a war, but it would not be able to sustain its war efforts very long. North Korea should know that war would bring about self-destruction.

Their nuclear program and missile development are for deterrence and negotiation. North Korea's ultimate goal is normalization of relations with the United States. They are trying to use the development of weapons of mass destruction as a means for coping with U.S. security threats and as a negotiating card for the normalization of relations.

Therefore, only when their security environment is improved and relations with the United States are normalized will North Korea abandon its nuclear and missile development programs. As long as there is mutual distrust, North Korea will not give up its weapons first. To eliminate the threat of the North, the United States should change North Korea's threat perception based on the principle of mutual threat reduction. Through this process, we could end mutual hostility, eliminate North Korean weapons of mass destruction, and move towards the normalization of relations.

It is not a simple issue at all—as some in the Bush administration may think—to demand unilateral withdrawal of the forward-deployed North Korean military forces to the rear area. It should be no surprise that the North Koreans would also demand redeployment of U.S. military forces, which are deployed just south of the frontline.

Force redeployment would be equally difficult for both sides. Redeployment is the most difficult part of the so-called three R's—reduction, restructuring and redeployment. It would involve enormous cost. Therefore, it would be wise to resolve this issue through mutual force reduction.

Lastly, I explained our government's perspective on the roles of East Asia and the United States.

Our North Korea policy is to prevent the North from launching a suicidal attack and to create conditions for the North to change. Through reconciliation and cooperation, we are going to induce North Korea to change, and build a North-South economic community, and realize arms control.

In this way, we want to realize *de facto* unification first, under which the North and the South can exchange visits and help each other in peaceful coexistence, before we can achieve a *de jure* unification that may take decades. There is no other way.

Our neighboring countries have no reason to oppose our efforts for such a goal. For economic development, China and Russia seem to view it as in their interests that the Korean Peninsula and the region should be stable and at peace. I believe that the United States should not fear the economic rise of China but should play a role in integrating the Chinese economy into the global system, and guide China towards peaceful modernization. The United States should also play the role of a balancer and stabilizer in East Asia, restrain China and Japan from hegemonic competition, and promote cooperation for peace and the common prosperity of the region. To this end, establishment of an East Asian security and cooperation organization, similar to the Organization for Security and Cooperation in Europe (OSCE), would be a good idea.

The audience was attentive, serious and academic. They said my talk was "clear, moving and thought-provoking." They repeated, "Fantastic!" They all thanked me and said, "It will be greatly helpful to situation analysis and writing reports."

IV UNFINISHED MISSION

CHAPTER 11

HEADWINDS AGAINST INTER-KOREAN RELATIONS

Conversation with Colin Powell

On January 20, 2001, George W. Bush was inaugurated as the forty-third president of the United States. On that same day, Chairman Kim Jong-il completed a six-day visit to China. Kim Jong-il was surprised to see Shanghai's tall skyscraper buildings when he toured the Pudong Industrial Development Zone and other industrial facilities. The old Shanghai he had seen eighteen years ago was nowhere to be found. The words Chairman Kim reportedly used to describe the change were: an "epochal transformation" and "beyond imagination."

Chairman Kim had studied the Chinese market economy, observing Chinese businesses in joint ventures with foreign companies. He determined that "China's policy was right," suggesting that he would follow a pragmatic policy line through "new thinking." The world press focused its attention on whether North Korea would follow the Chinese model towards aggressive opening and reform. In fact, Chairman Kim Jong-il seemed to send a message to the new American administration that "North Korea was willing to go for opening and reform."

For twenty-four days, from July 26 to August 19, 2001, Chairman Kim visited Russia by train. He saw the transformation of Russian industries to the market economy. At his summit with President Vladimir Putin, they discussed economic cooperation for projects such as connecting the relinked railroad of the Korean Peninsula to the Trans-Siberian Railway and constructing a gas pipeline from Russia to Korea.

The steps taken by Chairman Kim were seen as an effort to restore relations with China and Russia, securing their diplomatic support and economic assistance before engaging the new administration in Washington.

* * * * * * * * * *

During my visit to Washington in February, I met with several principal members of the new Bush administration. My conversation with Secretary of State Colin Powell was particularly useful. Korean Ambassador to the United States Yang Sung-chul and Acting Assistant Secretary of State for East Asian and Pacific Affairs Thomas Hubbard, who was designated as the next ambassador to Korea, both joined us at this meeting.

Powell and I had a common military background, and we talked very candidly and frankly to one another for about an hour in a State Department reception room. He said he had served as an infantry battalion commander with the 2nd U.S. Army Division in Korea (1973–74), adding "I have affection for Korea." This was his opening statement for our conversation.

He then asked what I had been doing in the military when he was stationed as a lieutenant colonel in Korea. I replied that I had been working on strategic planning at the Joint Chiefs of Staff (JCS) as an army colonel. He then gave a quick military salute, showing his military comradeship. He impressed me as a friendly and likable person.

He asked me to share my views on a range of subjects, including the North Korean situation; the Kim Jong-il regime's view of the United States; the North Korean position on U.S. forces in Korea; the inter-Korean summit and progress in North-South relations; and U.S.-DPRK relations. In response, I started with the basic premise that North Korea was seeking a normalized diplomatic relationship with the United States for survival. I emphasized that this was their most important priority, and that they recognized the need for the U.S. military presence in Korea to maintain stability and peace in the Korean Peninsula and the region. Then I reminded him of the major progress that had been made in the resolution of security issues between the United States and North Korea.

I also advised him that the new administration should capitalize upon this good opportunity and utilize the momentum to complete negotiations on the missile issue. I explained to him in detail the peace process on the Korean Peninsula, and asked the new administration to proactively contribute to the facilitation of that process.

Secretary Powell said he was well-informed about the U.S.–North Korea negotiations, as he had been briefed by personnel from the previous administration. He said, "I agree with the efforts of the Kim Dae-jung government to end the Cold War, and I support the Sunshine policy."

In addition, Powell said, "I clearly recognize that a historic opportunity has arrived to end the Cold War on the Korean Peninsula. I will be seeking an appropriate role to support it." I had the impression that he correctly understood the core of the problem on the Korean Peninsula and that he was a superb strategic thinker. He said,

> The new administration will continue to observe the Agreed Framework. We will give an opportunity to the North Koreans to resolve the hostile relations with the United States. We are prepared to pick up where the Clinton administration left off in negotiating with North Korea.

However, he added,

> We are now studying how to re-approach contacts with North Korea. We are not in a hurry. We will not pay them to gain any results. We will not yield to any North Korean blackmail. If they are serious about removing their missiles and the conventional forces threat, the United States will provide many things to help the people of North Korea.

He also said that the new administration was very suspicious of the North and that it would seek surveillance and verification. I responded by citing arms control theory:

> In the absence of mutual confidence, complete verification is impossible, and it would take a long time to resolve the issue. The fundamental solution to the issue is to first create the conditions and environment under which the North Koreans feel they do not need to develop weapons of mass destruction. This is something the new administration should remember.

Secretary Powell said in response, "I agree with the importance of confidence-building. However, there is an expression, 'trust but verify.' Is this not the question of how we should build confidence with North Korea?"

I replied that there was no other way to build confidence than by way of dialogue and implementation of agreements. For example, I shared that the projects of reconnecting the railways and roads through the DMZ and constructing the Kaesong Industrial Complex were not simply for economic cooperation, but were an important confidence-building measure for us. We reconnected the railways not because we trusted them, but because we wanted to build mutual confidence.

It was beneficial to have had such a candid and frank conversation with Secretary of State Powell, who was in charge of U.S. foreign relations. It was important to increase the new administration's understanding of North Korea and to gain support for our policy when the new American administration was still formulating its own. As a result of our meeting, we came to share the same perspective regarding the need to end the Cold War on the peninsula. The meeting was effective and a good opportunity.

Secretary of State Colin Powell (*left*) has a serious discussion in Minister Lim's office at the Ministry of Unification on July 27, 2001. Courtesy Lim Dong-won.

I was encouraged that the American secretary of state seemed to have the correct perspective and a reasonable approach to the issue of the Korean Peninsula. Colin Powell and I met again to continue our important discussion when he visited me in Seoul in the summer that year. I was then the Minister of Unification for the second time.

* * * * * * * * * *

However, the so-called neoconservatives (neocons), led by Vice President Dick Cheney and Secretary of Defense Donald Rumsfeld, resisted Secretary Powell and his State Department's rational and realistic engagement approach to the North. Instead, they supported a hostile policy against North Korea.

Throughout the first Bush administration, U.S. North Korea policy underwent a season of conflict and confrontation due to internal division. There were two distinct camps within the administration. As President Bush listened to Vice President Dick Cheney, U.S.–North Korea relations deteriorated more and more.

The Bush Administration's "ABC" Mindset

With the exception of Secretary Powell and career diplomats in the State Department, most of the officials whom I met from the Republican administration had a negative view of North Korea. These people would say things like, "North Korea is a single-party dictatorship. It is unpredictable and suspicious"; "Kim Jong-il is failing to feed his people and infringing upon human rights"; "Their recent move towards opening is a trick and a magic show to gain economic assistance"; "North Korean missiles and conventional arms impose a serious threat to the United States."

I was shocked by the hostile and hardline attitudes towards the North, which were quite a departure from the policy of the Clinton administration. They called for "regime change in North Korea to remove the security threats," rather than "inducement for change." They strongly called for "containment" and "pressure" on North Korea, which they called a rogue state. They strongly held onto the position that the "United States would never give in to blackmail or pay rewards to the North. It would not be dragged along by the North anymore."

They claimed that Secretary Albright's visit to the North and President Clinton's consideration of a visit to Pyongyang were examples of lowering the U.S. diplomatic posture, hurting the pride of the United States, the world's sole superpower. They said, "The Clinton administration's North Korea policy was wrong. We pursue a policy opposite to Clinton's." Thus, a new term—ABC (Anything But Clinton)—was coined.

Saying that they were not in a hurry, the hardliners began a slow and long process of policy review. They showed no interest in continuing the progress that had been made on the missile issue through the expeditious efforts of the Clinton administration. They argued, "Developing and deploying a missile defense (MD) system to protect the United States from the threat of the North Korean ballistic missiles is more important than negotiation." Nevertheless, they recognized the importance of the ROK-U.S. alliance.

The last appointment on my Washington visit was a meeting with National Security Advisor Condoleezza Rice, who later became Secretary of State for President Bush's second administration.

After I came to Washington, I heard three things from senior members of the new administration: "North Korea is not trustworthy"; "North Korea will not change, but will collapse"; "We have to remove the North Korean threat first." In my dialogue with Dr. Rice, I started by saying that a more balanced view was needed. I said, "Our Sunshine policy was modeled after the dètente process in Europe to induce North Korean change through reconciliation and cooperation."

I explained that like China, North Korea's gradual change was inevitable. As I had said to Colin Powell, we should engage the North Koreans not because we trust them but because it was essential to build mutual confidence. Since the inter-Korean summit, we had made a good progress in North-South relations. I told her that to resolve the issue of weapons of mass destruction, South Korea and the United States should take a mutually reinforcing approach.

In response, Rice said, "I fully appreciate the successful results of the Sunshine policy, and I have no disagreement with South Korea's policy on North Korea." She promised closer cooperation with South Korea. However, she said that the new administration was skeptical of North Korea's intent to change. She said, "We should seek North Korean change not through the leader's change of belief but through a collapse of the failed system." She added, "If the North Korean dictator really wants to seek change, he should first take positive action on the issues of U.S. concern."

She said, "Our new government will engage North Korea, but we will not start where the previous administration ended. We will probably go through a thorough review for a considerable period of time." Her view was contradictory to what Powell had told me and was a reflection of the "ABC" mindset.

In response, I said, "You should not pass up on this valuable opportunity to resolve the question of the Korean Peninsula. South Korea and the United States should cooperate to end the Cold War in Korea. The forty-first president, George H. W. Bush, successfully helped contribute to the end of the international Cold War to expand democracy and the market economy. However, he did not end the Cold War on the Korean Peninsula. I hope that the forty-third president, George W. Bush, will end the Cold War in Korea as one of his great legacies. In this context, our government expects you to do a lot of important work."

When I finished, she broke into hearty laughter. I was not sure whether that meant she agreed with me.

Those Who "Need the Bad Guys"

From February 26 to 28, Russian president Putin visited Seoul for a summit with President Kim Dae-jung. A joint summit statement was issued afterwards, which brought trouble to President Kim's diplomatic efforts. The

White House protested our government's joint statement. This occurred a week prior to a scheduled meeting between Presidents Kim and Bush.

Paragraph 5 of the joint statement reflected our understanding of U.S. policy under the Clinton administration—policy that the new Bush administration wanted to change. The paragraph said, "The Anti-Ballistic Missile (ABM) Treaty (1972) is a cornerstone of strategic stability, and it should be reserved and strengthened." The joint statement also mentioned "an early effectuation and implementation of the Strategic Arms Reduction Treaty (START II)," and also called for "ratification and enforcement of the Comprehensive Nuclear-Test-Ban Treaty (CTBT)." This was the source of the White House's dissatisfaction.

The problem surfaced with the American press coverage of the joint statement. The *New York Times* reported, "President Kim publicly sided with Russia in the controversy over the U.S. national missile defense (NMD) system," and the Russian daily *Izvestia* reported, "the Korean president's public expression of opposition to the U.S. missile defense policy was a great diplomatic fruit for President Putin."

The White House protest was rough. The Bush administration had been planning to abrogate the ABM treaty to clear the way for the development of an NMD system, while the Republican-controlled Congress refused to ratify START II and CTBT. The White House said it could not overlook how the South Korean government, a U.S. ally, had publicly joined Russia to challenge the United States.

Only after this mishap occurred did we hold an NSC Standing Committee meeting to blame the foreign ministry for its diplomatic misstep. According to the foreign minister's explanation, it had nothing to do with the ministry's pursuit of independent diplomacy. The minister said he did not think the ROK-Russian joint statement would create a problem since a year earlier, the United States had held the same position at the G8 summit in Okinawa. Nevertheless, the foreign ministry was responsible for failing to discern that the old American administration's policy had been replaced by the new administration's, which had decided to negate the ABM treaty in order to develop an NMD system.

This incident inflicted serious damage to President Kim's image as a "diplomacy president." The incident also became a big burden for the president, who was scheduled to go to Washington soon. He had to express his regrets a few times. After his visit to Washington, he replaced the foreign minister.

* * * * * * * * *

The day before the ROK-U.S. summit, Secretary of State Colin Powell held a press conference, through which he spoke highly of President Kim's Sunshine policy and said the United States would closely cooperate with the ROK. He also clearly stated that if North Korea took constructive action toward reducing the threat of proliferation of weapons of mass destruction and missiles, the United States would also take commensurate action.

Concerning the pending issue of missile negotiation, he announced: "We do plan to engage with North Korea to pick up where President Clinton and his administration left off," expressing a policy of proactive engagement with the North. Powell's press conference was similar to what he and I had discussed a month earlier. That was very encouraging to us.

On March 8, President Kim had a breakfast meeting with Secretary Powell in Washington. The breakfast was followed by an hour-long Korea-U.S. summit and twenty-minute press availability. President Kim also attended a luncheon hosted by President Bush at the White House. During the summit, President Kim explained the Sunshine policy and its effectiveness to President Bush, and proposed "developing inter-Korean relations and U.S.–North Korea relations to complement each other." He also asked that the new administration seize the momentum to negotiate the missile issue and play a proactive role in the ending of the Cold War on the Korean Peninsula. However, Bush said, "Verification is important because I don't trust North Korea." Bush did not show an interest in an early resolution of the missile issue.

During the press conference, President Bush candidly revealed his negative attitude to North Korea, using unrefined diplomatic language. His statements included:

> I do have some skepticism about the leader of North Korea.
>
> We're not certain as to whether or not they're keeping all terms of all agreements.
>
> I am concerned about the fact that the North Koreans are shipping weapons around the world . . . we wanted to stop their ability to develop and spread weapons of mass destruction . . . and we can verify that . . . they have stopped it.

In short, by saying that he needed a fundamental review of North Korea policy, President Bush showed no intention of facilitating contacts with the North any time soon.

Bush had accepted the neocons' view that instead of negotiating the missile issue, the development of an NMD system should be his policy priority. As a result, Secretary Powell was forced to leave in the middle of the summit to awkwardly tell the press that he wished to retract the statement he had made the day before. This incident was symbolic proof that the neocons, led by Vice President Dick Cheney, were in control of U.S. Korean Peninsula policy at the White House.

The American press reported that the hardliners, including Vice President Cheney and Secretary of Defense Donald Rumsfeld, saw North Korea's development of long-range missiles as the perfect justification for development of the NMD system. According to the press, the Neocons thought any diplomatic effort on North Korea was meaningless and believed they should build a nuclear missile defense to take a strong military posture against North Korea. In May that year, President Bush actually announced a new security strategy that included the construction of a NMD system.

*　*　*　*　*　*　*　*　*

In advance of the Korea-U.S. summit, the *New York Times* published an article by Ambassador Wendy Sherman titled, "Talking to the North Koreans." She urged President Bush to seize every opportunity to reduce or eliminate the missile threat through the less costly means of arms control negotiations. Sherman asserted that missile negotiations with North Korea and development of an NMD system could be pursued in parallel. She stressed, "President Bush can move forward on both strategies without foreclosing any options." In the same day's edition, a *New York Times* editorial commented that the Sunshine policy had contributed to considerable progress in the thaw between the North and the South, and the Bush administration should not miss the good opportunity to end military confrontation on the last battlefield of the Cold War.

Secretary Powell and moderate career diplomats at the State Department were known to hold the view that the United States should continue the missile negotiations, which were in the final stages. Since success of the missile negotiations would take a long time to verify, it would not interfere with the ongoing NMD development. This was the basis of the moderates' argument for parallel pursuit of missile negotiations and development of the NMD system. In reality, there seemed to not be many Americans who believed that the purpose of NMD was to deal with the North Korean threat.

In fact, the Bush administration was not the first to promote a missile defense program. The concept of missile defense was "hit a bullet with a bullet." A series of missile defense programs, including the Reagan administration's Strategic Defense Initiative (SDI), widely known as "Star Wars," were attempted in the past. The Bush administration's missile defense was the sixth U.S. attempt. Its proponents seemed to think even if pushing the NMD system would become "a rush to failure," it would unquestionably contribute to scientific development and the defense industry.

* * * * * * * * *

In the wake of the Korea-U.S. summit, most reports by the American media expressed concerns about President Bush's attitude toward North Korea. In "Losing Momentum on Korea," the *New York Times* reported that Bush had not listened to President Kim, and despite the importance of timing, Bush supported the hardliners' position. The article went on to say, "Regrettably, President Bush has decided for the time being not to renew discussions with North Korea aimed at shutting down Pyongyang's development and sales of long range missiles." Under the headline of "Bush Korea Policy: The Hawks Have It," the weekly magazine *Time* wrote that Bush bluntly rejected President Kim's proposal and had missed a good opportunity because of the NMD project. *Time* added that Bush displayed uncoordinated diplomacy, creating internal division in his administration.

The British daily *The Guardian* published a column under the headline of "Why Bush Needs the Bad Guys." The column argued that the Bush administration was seeking a rationale for the NMD from rogue nations. It further criticized the hawks for relishing the linkage of the North Korean nuclear and missile development programs with the rationale for the NMD system. "Because Bush wants to get his missiles, the president needs rogues."

President Bush poured cold water on the great progress that had been made in inter-Korean relations and abandoned the Korea-U.S. joint efforts that had begun to facilitate a peace process on the Korean Peninsula. For six years (2001–2006), the Bush administration implemented a hardline hostile policy of seeking the collapse of the North Korean regime. However, his policy failed and only brought about a North Korean nuclear test.

These six years were a very difficult period for the South Korean government, which had to simultaneously maintain the ROK-U.S. alliance and manage inter-Korean relations. Shortly after the nuclear test, and from early 2007, President Bush suddenly turned his policy around to engage and negotiate directly with North Korea.

North Korea angrily reacted to the result of the Kim Dae-jung–Bush summit. Bush's personal characterizations of Kim Jong-il as a "dictator," "distrustful," and a "spoiled child" were insults to the North Koreans and they resented them. They suspended dialogue with the South on the grounds that "President Kim Dae-jung had failed to persuade President Bush."

North Korea took a series of wrong steps in violation of the spirit of the June 15 Joint Declaration by deciding to independently resolve the national issue. They broke off inter-Korean talks, further straining relations between the North and the South. This was their biggest mistake. On the morning of

March 13, the North notified the South that it could not send a delegation to the fifth round of the North-South Ministerial Talks, which were scheduled to meet in Seoul that afternoon. The North's unilateral decision to avoid dialogue put inter-Korean engagement on hold for a year.

In retrospect, the North should have pursued a "South-first policy" rather than a "U.S.-first policy." In straining North-South relations, the North inadvertently reinforced the negative image the Bush hardliners were trying to create. In contrast, the North should have more proactively carried out inter-Korean relations and delivered a blow to the hardliners' perceptions and allegations. In the end, the North Koreans and the American hardliners had entered into a relationship of hostile coexistence. The North had made a critical mistake.

After the June 15 Joint Declaration, the North and the South had produced valuable results in various fields—to the extent that some conservatives were calling for a slowdown. We had reached the point where we could push our fundamental discussions harder for more results. Unfortunately, we ended up wasting a precious year with the deadlock of our dialogue. The restoration of inter-Korean relations was made possible only after I visited Pyongyang as a presidential special envoy again and reached agreement with Chairman Kim Jong-il in April of the following year.

Back to the Ministry of Unification

On March 26, 2001, President Kim Dae-jung reshuffled his cabinet members in an effort to re-innovate the government. Ten cabinet ministers out of the total nineteen were replaced, and I returned to the Unification Ministry as the minister.

Prior to the cabinet reshuffle, I was in a meeting with President Kim to present my weekly intelligence report, during which he asked me to take the position of Unification Minister again. I first declined the offer, saying, "I would like to take some time to rest." However, the president would not accept it. He said, "We held a summit. Now is the time to proactively carry out the agreement of the June 15 Joint Declaration. As the NIS director, you have constraints and restrictions running and controlling North-South relations from the top. I want you to openly negotiate with the North and persuade the public and the United States from the forefront. It's important for you to maintain consistent control over inter-Korean relations. I will instruct the new NIS director to make sure that you can still oversee the areas of inter-Korean relations." I could not decline the president's earnest request.

* * * * * * * * *

The Republic of Korea's Ministry of Unification was established in March 1969, based on the spirit of Article 4 of the Constitution that stipulates, "The Republic of Korea seeks unification . . . and formulates and carries out a policy of peaceful unification." The ministry began with a fixed number of people, forty-five, to work in research, education, and public affairs. It was a small ministry headed by a cabinet minister. However, its symbolic significance was great.

The responsibility for inter-Korean dialogue was transferred to the ministry from the Korea Central Intelligence Agency (KCIA) in 1980. When the post-Cold War era began in 1988, the unification ministry's role expanded to produce unification policy, carry out contacts and dialogue with the North, and control some functions of other ministries.

When I reassumed my position as the unification minister, the ministry was getting busy with various kinds of meetings between the authorities of the North and the South, social and cultural exchanges, economic cooperation and humanitarian assistance, as well as education and public affairs programs.

Upon my return, my concerns were focused on how we should meet the challenges of the new difficult environment that was being created at home and abroad. The American hardliners, led by President Bush and Vice President Cheney, had expressed their hostile policy toward North Korea and were going to force North Korea to surrender. On the other hand, recalcitrant North Korea would undoubtedly react by raising tension on the peninsula. I was also concerned about the conservative Cold War supporters at home, who were collaborating with the Bush administration's hardline policy.

At this time, our government was interested in realizing Chairman Kim Jong-il's visit to Seoul; removing landmines from the DMZ, undertaking the project to connect the railways; promoting the construction of the Kaesong Industrial Complex; supporting continued operation of Mount Kumgang tourism; and sustaining the efforts for more reunions of separated families. In reaction to the Bush administration's hostile posture, the North had suspended inter-Korean dialogue. Under these circumstances, we had to continue our efforts to induce a positive response from the North.

We decided to complete our portion of the railway and road project south of the DMZ and to repair the temporary road on the east coast by the end of September. In addition, we provided 200,000 tons of fertilizer to the North in their time of need. Despite strained North-South relations, we did our best to implement the June 15 Joint Declaration. While exerting efforts to persuade the opposition party and to gain the support of the people, we also tried our best to persuade the United States.

A Neocon Trap

In the meantime, our government exerted efforts to persuade the Bush administration, which was reviewing its North Korea policy. In mid-May 2001, Deputy Secretary of State Richard Armitage visited Seoul to explain President Bush's "new strategic initiative." I wanted to use this opportunity to discuss with him the coordination of North Korea policy between our two countries. He and I had a friendly relationship. When I met him in Washington in January 1999, he had described his study of North Korea policy. In addition, when he was nominated as deputy secretary of state the previous February, I met with him again in Washington to discuss North Korea.

During his visit, I explained to Armitage the NSSC's recommendations. I conveyed that while we understood the United States needed to cope with the new security environment, we hoped that the U.S. development of a NMD would not play an adverse role in tension reduction on the Korean Peninsula. I told him my views:

> The United States says it is developing an NMD system to deter the North Korean missile threat. But, it is hard to understand why the United States has suspended missile negotiations with the North that would essentially remove the missile threat. Our government's position is that while you develop your NMD, you should continue U.S.–North Korea negotiations on the missile issue. Since North Korea wants normalized relations with the United States, you should not make a mistake by pushing it into a different sphere of influence. Engagement with the North would be beneficial to the U.S. strategy for East Asia. As you said before, I hope that the United States will contribute to ending the Cold War on the Korean Peninsula through a "comprehensive approach." Inter-Korean relations and U.S.–North Korea relations are inseparable. Therefore, our two countries must closely coordinate our policies on the Korean Peninsula issue.

In response to our recommendation, Armitage said, "We respect South Korea's position." Yet, this kind of positive response was limited to the State Department. It did not contribute to changing the negative attitudes of the neocon hardliners.

* * * * * * * * *

On June 6, President Bush announced that his administration had completed its North Korea policy review. He said the United States was now ready "to undertake serious discussions with North Korea on a broad agenda to include improved implementation of the Agreed Framework relating to North Korea's nuclear activities; verifiable constraints on North Korea's missile programs and a ban on its missile exports; and a less threatening conventional military posture." It was an open proposal for dialogue with the North.

On the other hand, North Korea immediately reacted through its foreign ministry spokesman by saying, "President Bush's proposal for the resumption of negotiations is a U.S. attempt to achieve the goal of disarming us, and is an utterly unacceptable agenda. We cannot help but assess the U.S. proposal to be unilateral and preconditioned, and in intent, hostile." The North Korean statement included, "In particular, the issue of conventional forces cannot be a subject of discussion before the withdrawal of U.S. troops from Korea."

The North further charged, "If the United States really has the will to end its hostile policy and to engage us in a genuine dialogue, the agenda for dialogue should be implementation issues for the Agreed Framework and the DPRK-U.S. Joint Communiqué of 2000." In short, North Korea was in favor of dialogue but not under the agenda unilaterally set by the Bush administration.

North Korea had determined that the Bush administration would not try to improve relations and had thus overreacted to Bush's proposal by turning it down. Regardless of the prospect of success or failure, the North should have proactively responded to Bush's proposal for dialogue. In a sense, the North Koreans had fallen into a trap set up by American hardliners.

Due to North Korea's rejection, the United States was able to take the diplomatic offensive. In contrast, the North was driven back into a defensive position. Three months later, the 9/11 terrorist attacks took place and the United States took an even harsher position on the North. The North lost the window of opportunity to engage the United States for a long time to come.

The North Koreans should have begun talks with the United States when the opportunity was available. North Korea had made another big mistake.

The Pyongyang Festival and its Aftermath

On National Liberation Day the following year after the inter-Korean summit, representatives of civilian organizations from both sides of Korea gathered in Pyongyang for the first time in the history of Korea's division to hold the 2001 festival for national unification. More than 300 South Korean civilian representatives went to the North for a weeklong visit.

This event was the first of its kind, because it had been forbidden to South Koreans for a half-century. Carried away by emotion and excitement, some South Korea visitors behaved in violation of their agreement with the government. The conservative press was displeased with the South Korean group's visit to the North from the beginning. Therefore, when they got wind of some violations, the conservative press reported them daily in big headlines with distortions and exaggerations.

The opposition Grand National Party did not miss this opportunity to attack the administration, and it re-submitted to the National Assembly a bill to recommend dismissal of the unification minister who had authorized the group's visit to the North. This time the bill passed. It was passed with the support of the United Liberal Democrats (ULD), who had "big hope for the next presidency" for their leader Kim Jong-pil. They thought a hardened conservative image of Kim Jong-pil would be helpful to increase his chances of winning the presidency. When the bill passed, the coalition government between the Democratic Party and the ULD collapsed, and the ULD deteriorated to the point of no recovery.

*　*　*　*　*　*　*　*　*

The background to this incident: the Kim Dae-jung government had professed that it would not monopolize the affairs of unification but would encourage unification movement on the civilian level. This policy was based on our judgment that more contact and more exchange with the North would contribute to encouraging change in the North and the process to end the Cold War.

Our government determined it was time to shake off its inferiority complex and fear of victimization towards the North. We wanted to extricate ourselves from a defensive position, and thought it was time to be confident in the strength of liberal democracy and our superiority in national power over the North. It was time to take a proactive approach. The competition between systems was over, and now was the time to change the North and manage that process.

With this perspective, the Kim Dae-jung administration established and supported the National Council of Reconciliation and Cooperation, gradually taking measures to promote and expand civilian contact and exchange. In the Mount Kumgang tourism complex, a "North-South Workers

Meeting" and a "North-South Farmers Discussion" was held. In June, a large conference on the "North-South Unification Debate" was also held at Mount Kumgang. This debate was attended by 420 representatives from South Korean civilian organizations and 740 North Korean representatives. They were assigned to ten subject areas to engage in free debate.

At the debate, the North Korean representatives expressed their stereotypical arguments, whereas the South Korean representatives freely presented diversified and animated views. In some cases, the South's debate, characterized by harmony in diversity, pushed the North Korean representatives to a defensive position. The August 15 joint civilian festival that would be held two months later in Pyongyang was also discussed at the debate.

* * * * * * * * *

However, the unification ministry had to be cautious in permitting South Korean groups to visit the North; it was not a matter for it to solely decide. The consensus of the relevant agencies, including the NIS, was to disapprove the application of civilian visits to the North on the grounds that the groups would not behave uniformly. It would be difficult to control 300 individuals representing over one hundred progressive and conservative organizations, and it was unpredictable how everyone would behave.

President Kim Dae-jung instructed me to approve the group's visit. I realized that the president's thinking was beyond the level of those in charge of the relevant agencies, and his will was firm. I determined the president was right and decided to take every preventive caution against any undesirable behavior. However, if anything went wrong, I, the unification minister, would take all responsibility for it.

* * * * * * * * *

Around noon on August 15, the South Korean delegation of 337 people (including 26 reporters) left for Pyongyang on two airplanes on a direct route over the West Sea. Before their departure, although we were under time constraints, we conducted an education program for them regarding a code of conduct during their stay in the North.

The North postponed the opening ceremony from ten o'clock that morning to seven o'clock that evening in order to wait for the arrival of the South's delegation. This was the beginning of the problems. In violation of their agreement with the government, and against the discouragement of the festival promotion headquarters, about eighty members of a progressive organization had joined the ceremony at the newly-built "Memorial Monument of the Three Charters."

The following day, the visiting group viewed an "exhibit of atrocities under the Japanese imperial rule, and distortions of history." Later the delegation was divided into ten small groups in the categories of businessmen, religious people, journalists, writers, artists, laborers, farmers, women, and youth to participate in discussions between the two sides. At the Jangchoon Catholic Church, they had the first inter-Korean Mass since the division of Korea. The South Korean visitors did not participate in the closing ceremony, but some members of the progressive organization joined in outdoor festivities after the closing ceremony.

The conservative newspapers disregarded any positive aspects of the August 15 joint event, such as its significance and accomplishments, and only highlighted the negative outcomes. The negative reports were printed on the front and inside pages under headlines such as "Visiting Group Violates Agreement, Wrong Permission for the North Visit Backfires" and "Pyongyang Festival a Shame to the ROK."

The South Korean delegation was given a tour of Mangyungdae (Kim Il-sung's birthplace), the Tomb of Emperor Dangun, Pyongyang City, as well as Mount Baekdu and Mount Myohyang. For this, the conservative press focused on criticizing a professor who had written, "In the spirit of Mangyungdae, let's succeed in achieving unification" in the visitor's book at Mangyungdae, and a woman visitor who had shed tears before a wax figure of Kim Il-sung. The conservative press wrote inflated stories out of such cases with big, agitating headlines. The press effectively portrayed these isolated incidents from an ideological angle in order to arouse negative public opinion.

* * * * * * * * *

When the visiting group returned to Seoul after their seven-day trip, the atmosphere was cold. Seven of them were arrested. Yet the conservative press's ideological arguments would not subside. The criticisms by the press continued: "GNP Wants Minister Lim's Resignation, the ULD Wants to Hold those Responsible Accountable," and "Strain in the DJP Coalition Detected." In the midst of these reports, the GNP defined the August 15 joint festival as a "mad, frantic show."

The GNP declared that the Sunshine policy had totally failed and pledged to hold the unification minister accountable for that failure. It also said it would seek the cooperation of the ULD to secure enough votes to expel the unification minister.

Following the return of the visiting group, and after the arrest of some of its members, I had a one-on-one meeting with President Kim. I said, "I am sorry that I've failed to assist you well. I will resign so that the DJP coalition will not face more difficulties." I earnestly asked him once again to accept my resignation.

The president replied, "I told you to send them, and I am sorry that it created a difficult situation for you. This is not something for which you should take the responsibility. This is not your personal matter. The opposition party is going to submit a bill of recommendation for dismissal. I will respond to it appropriately. I sent a message to the ULD through the chief of staff and asked whether they want to quit the coalition government. Don't let yourself be shaken. Minister Lim, you should continue implementing the Sunshine policy. Forget these other things, and please concentrate on your work." That was his wish.

* * * * * * * * *

On August 24, the ULD officially decided to cooperate with the opposition party Grand National Party to hold the unification minister accountable for the failed Sunshine policy. Public attention was focused on whether the DJP coalition would crumble as well as what would happen to me as unification minister.

After the Blue House released a statement that the president was not considering changing the unification minister, and that the individual behavior of the visiting group had nothing to do with maintaining the Sunshine policy, the press shifted the trajectory of its reporting to the fate of the DJP coalition.

The National Joint Event Promotion Committee issued a statement on August 28 at a press conference regarding the "2001 National Unification Festival." The committee apologized for the unexpected behavior. Then it detailed the positive things that had resulted from the event. The committee expressed deep regrets about the exaggeration and distortion by some news organizations, as well as the tactical maneuvering of some politicians. The committee accused them of agitating an internal ideological conflict within the South.

The statement also said, "It is not right for Minister Lim Dong-won to resign. The demand for the unification minister's resignation because of some mishaps in the civilian exchanges is simply a ploy of the opposition party to take advantage of the North-South issue for its political gain."

Kim Jong-pil—"JP"—continued to press the case, saying, "If Minister Lim resigns, everything will be smoothly resolved." Until recently, he had been the Kim Dae-jung administration's prime minister, carrying out the Sunshine policy. He was closing his eyes to the polls, which showed that

70–80 percent of the people supported the Sunshine policy, and more than 90 percent opposed his presidential aspirations.

In the meantime, I had already clarified my position at the National Assembly Committee on Unification, Foreign Affairs and Trade:

> I apologize to the people for the unexpected behavior of the civilians during their North Korea trip. However, we have successfully carried out the Sunshine policy of reconciliation and cooperation. I disagree with the allegations that we have failed. Therefore, concerning the issue of my resignation, I believe it is my moral obligation to leave it to the presidential authority.

On September 1, the National Assembly convened, and a bill recommending dismissal was submitted. Before the vote, Representative Chung Beom-gu of the Democratic Party took the floor and said, "In the promotion of *Ostpolitik* that led to the successful Basic Agreement between West and East Germany, Chancellor Billy Brandt had his right-hand man, Egon Bahr, who pursued 'change through rapprochement.' In Korea, we have Lim Dong-won. The opposition GNP and the ULD are trying to victimize Minister Lim, who has pursued a consistent peacemaking policy." He then emphasized, "Politics are finite, but the nation is infinite." He appealed, "I ask you all to make the right judgment, one for which you can be responsible in the eyes of history."

Nevertheless, the National Assembly passed the bill of recommended dismissal by a vote of 148 to 119. Fifteen ULD members and one independent member joined the GNP in voting to pass the bill. This ended the DP-ULD coalition government.

* * * * * * * * *

As Kim Jong-pil's presidential ambitions grew and were encouraged by the ULD, he said, "I will win in the next year's presidential election." However, the Democratic Party made it clear that it might support him as their party chairman if the two parties were to combine into one, but not as their presidential candidate. The Democratic Party asked, "How could we support someone who only has five percent of popular support?"

Some newspapers commented that the "sudden change in JP's attitude was attributable to his uneasiness with his age and to 'old man's greed,' which led to the demise of the DJP coalition." They commented that he had been encouraged by the conservative press, which had attacked the government's North Korea policy like in a witch hunt, and he had miscalculated his political gain from the Lim Dong-won case. Others also commented that "JP had erroneously thought that DJ (Kim Dae-jung) would concede to him in the end, as he did before, if he kept pressing."

Consequently, JP's presidential ambitions were shattered, and the ULD started a rapid decline. After gaining forty-nine seats in the National Assembly from the general elections of April 1996, the ULD had successfully participated in a coalition government with the Democratic Party (according to its prior agreement with the DP) as the result of President Kim Dae-jung's 1997 election, which had been a mutual victory for both parties. However, the ULD, which had tried to break the coalition in early 2000, failed miserably in the next general elections. Labeled as an "ultra-conservative party," it could not even gain the minimum of twenty seats to become an independent legislative group in the National Assembly. Even worse, JP lost his seat as the ULD's number one proportional candidate in the April 2004 general elections.

After the fateful vote on the bill of recommended resignation, all members of the cabinet submitted their resignations. On Friday, September 7, a new cabinet was announced. When I left the unification ministry, some of the reporters described me as the "the Sunshine policy martyr."

Pyongyang's Three Mistakes

On the morning of Monday, September 10, 2001, I received a call from President Kim Dae-jung. After asking me about our preparations for the fifth round of the North-South Ministerial Talks, he said,

> We are in the same boat. We should go together to the end. I will appoint you as Special Advisor to the President for National Security and Unification. So, return to work right away. I know you worked hard for the holding of the fifth round of the suspended North-South Ministerial Talks. I would like you to manage everything so we can accomplish our goal.

I again accepted the president's offer. I felt bad for my wife at that moment, because we had planned to go on an overseas trip as free citizens for a change. Now I had to cancel our plans.

There were three possible reasons I could guess for appointing me as his special advisor. First, he wanted me to directly assist him in the areas of national security and unification to continue carrying out the Sunshine policy. Also, he wanted me to continue to exercise overall management of inter-Korean dialogue, maintaining my line of contacts with the North. And, the president wanted me to coordinate the issues of national security, foreign affairs and inter-Korean relations to come up with better alternatives, and supervise their implementation. To this end, he wanted me to continue to lead the NSC Standing Committee effectively and consistently.

On the morning of September 12, I received from the president a letter of appointment with my new title of Special Advisor. The appointment ceremony was held in an unsettled atmosphere because barely twelve hours had passed since the 9/11 attacks.

At 8:45 p.m. local time in Seoul on the previous night (8:45 a.m. in New York City) the World Trade Center, the symbol of American capitalism, was attacked and burnt to ashes by the deliberate crashing of two civilian airliners that had been hijacked by suicidal terrorists from the Middle East, killing thousands of people. Shortly afterwards, the Pentagon (Department of Defense) in the Washington area, the headquarters of America's control of the world, was also attacked. It was the first time in the fifty-seven years since Pearl Harbor that the continental United States, known as a safe fortress, had been attacked.

Despite the frenzied atmosphere caused by the 9/11 attacks, the North Korean delegation arrived in Seoul on schedule on September 15 to participate in the fifth round of the North-South Ministerial Talks. Our government's strategy was to connect the disconnected railways and roads to promote economic cooperation; to reduce tension and build military confidence through peaceful use of the DMZ; and to simultaneously push economic and military cooperation.

At the talks, we agreed to undertake the project of connecting the Seoul-Shineuiju railways at an early date; to hold a working-level meeting to discuss the realization of tourism to Mount Kumgang by a land route and the construction of the Kaesong Industrial Complex; and to hold the fourth round of exchanges between separated families on Chuseok. The talks produced agreement on thirteen different issues.

However, we failed to adopt a joint anti-terrorist declaration, which was the subject in which the president had been particularly interested. The president had hoped to win President Bush's heart by adopting a joint anti-terrorist statement.

The North did not accommodate our side's proposal, saying that it had issued a joint anti-terrorist statement with the United States in October 2000, and that its foreign ministry's spokesman had issued an anti-terrorist statement after 9/11.

On the other hand, the Bush administration did not want to recognize a U.S.-DPRK joint anti-terrorist statement. If North Korea had accepted our proposal to oppose terrorism together, it may not have been later called a "member of the axis of evil."

* * * * * * * * * *

American Korea specialists said North Korea had missed three good opportunities. First, North Korea had sent Vice Marshal Jo Myung-rok as a special envoy to Washington too late. It should have done so at least a few months earlier. Second, realizing that it was hard to find a South Korean leader like President Kim Dae-jung, who had a vision and who would earnestly seek improved inter-Korean relations, the North should not have wasted so much time. Third, if North Korea had proactively cooperated with U.S. efforts to fight terrorism in the wake of the September 11 attacks, it would have been possible to find an opportunity to improve relations with the United States. I fully agreed with the view that North Korea had missed these three opportunities.

Due to his wounded pride and anger that had turned into hatred by the September 11 attacks, President Bush declared a "war on terror" and initiated military action to search and punish terrorists throughout the world. The first target for attack was Osama bin Laden's al-Qaeda, and then its protector, the Taliban government in Afghanistan. President Bush gave the countries of the world two choices: side with "good" and stand by the United States to fight terrorism, or side with "evil" and help the enemy.

On October 7, the United States began waging an attack on Afghanistan and the Taliban government. President Bush declared that the United States would not hesitate to attack any area that supported the terrorists.

Our government took emergency steps to protect the U.S. forces in Korea and major strategic facilities from a possible terrorist attack. These steps were met by an immediate, strong protest from the North, charging "In a hostile act against the North and in violation of the June 15 Joint Declaration, the South took emergency alert measures and publically stated that it would watch North Korea's movements." The North Koreans were particularly disturbed by the U.S. Defense Department's announcement that it would deploy additional military aircraft to Korea. They seemed to take the U.S. action, in conjunction with our emergency security measures, as a preliminary military step for a possible U.S. attack on the North. The North Koreans were seriously wary of this development.

Consequently, the North notified the South of their decision: "Since the South is introducing another country's issue into internal national affairs, smooth North-South dialogue and exchange have become impossible. In this tense atmosphere in the South, we cannot send a group of separated families to Seoul." In addition, the North suggested changing the venue of other meetings, which we had agreed would alternate between Seoul and Pyongyang, to Mount Kumgang because, they said, that location would have no security problems.

Our side immediately rejected the North Korean suggestion. We urged the North to carry out the agreements without fail and without change. We insisted the sixth round of the North-South Ministerial Talks be held in Pyongyang as agreed upon. In order to decide upon the venue for the talks, fourteen proposals and counterproposals were exchanged within a three-week period. Nevertheless, in the end, our side determined that sustaining the talks was more important than the venue. We agreed to hold the next ministerial talks on November 8 at Mount Kumgang.

*　*　*　*　*　*　*　*　*

At the sixth round of the talks, we agreed on the dates of working-level meetings in which we would discuss the details of the exchange meetings of separated families, as well the dates for the meeting of the economic cooperation promotion committee. We also agreed to hold the next round of the ministerial talks in Seoul. The talks at Mount Kumgang provided momentum to resume progress in inter-Korean relations.

However, in the last open session, the senior delegate on our side clashed with his North Korean counterpart over the dates for the next round of the North-South Ministerial Talks. When our senior representative minister Hong Soon-young walked out of the talks, everything evaporated.

The important point of discussion for the seventh round of the ministerial talks was not the dates, but the venue. The key issue was how we would successfully pressure the North to withdraw their allegation that they could not have talks in Seoul because "it was in a war-like tense atmosphere," and thus put the talks back on the normal track.

President Kim Dae-jung was greatly disappointed and annoyed. In view of the unstable security situation on the Korean Peninsula since the September 11 attacks, it was necessary for our government to make further progress in inter-Korean relations in order to gain U.S. support for our engagement policy.

President Kim's disappointment and anger was understandable since we had worked hard to hold the ministerial talks, and our own team ruined everything. Shortly afterwards, President Kim appointed Minister Chung Se-hyon to replace the unification minister.

From this incident, we again learned that when the unification minister served as the senior delegate to negotiating talks, he should follow the president's instructions. We also learned that in negotiations, it is preferable to focus on interests, not positions; to focus on substance more than procedures; and to settle for the second best option if the best is not possible.

I focused on taking the best possible steps to prevent the state of inter-Korean relations from further deteriorating. My urgent task was to correctly convey our intentions to the highest authority of North Korea and to ascertain their intentions. In compliance with the president's will, I sent a letter in the name of the president's special advisor to Chairman Kim Jong Il:

> It is very frustrating to witness how North-South relations are being affected by the international situation that recently developed due to the September 11 incident and the U.S. attack on Afghanistan. In these difficult circumstances, I believe that we should maintain the self-respect of our nation and unite our strength to turn this adverse situation into an opportunity.
>
> Under the current situation, it is particularly important that we implement the June 15 Joint Declaration and proactively promote North-South relations, which should under no circumstances be strained. I wish to visit Pyongyang for a meeting with you so that I may convey President Kim Dae-jung's words, and to listen to your views.

Four months after he received my letter, I met with Chairman Kim Jong-il.

Bush Doctrine of Preemption

In waging its attack on Afghanistan, the United States could not capture Osama Bin Laden, but had destroyed the Taliban government. By the end of November, the United States occupied 90 percent of the Afghan land.

From about this time, attention was focused on the next possible target. There were reports that the U.S. hardliners were insisting upon expanding the U.S. offensive to attack Iraq and remove Saddam Hussein's regime. Around the same period, John Bolton, Undersecretary of State for Non-Proliferation, denounced North Korea as a "country developing biological and chemical weapons" and listed it after Iraq as a "national security threat country."

The New York Times reported on the possibility of "North Korea becoming a target in the next phase of the war on terror." At a press conference, President Bush at last warned that states that were developing weapons of mass destruction would be held responsible, and that North Korea was included in those countries. The American press heavily covered the "North Korea-bashing," creating a tension that suggested an attack on North Korea was imminent.

In his January 2002 State of the Union Address to Congress, President Bush designated North Korea as a member of "the axis of evil," along with Iraq and Iran. He declared that North Korea was a target for "regime change" by a "preemptive attack." He said, "North Korea is a regime armed with missiles and weapons of mass destruction, while starving its citizens. . . . The United States of America will not permit the world's most dangerous regime to threaten us with the world's most destructive weapons. . . ." President Bush declared a "year of war" by pledging to wipe out terrorists scattered around the world.

When the long-used label of "rogue state" was replaced by a "member of the axis of evil," North Korea became one of the "three main enemies" of the United States. The message was the United States would not diplomatically engage these countries to resolve issues, but would accomplish the goal of bringing down North Korea through military "preemption" and "regime change."

The North Korean foreign ministry quickly issued a statement denouncing the United States: "This time Bush revealed his reckless attempt to attack us militarily. In recent years, no U.S. president has ever, in a policy statement, directly and frankly threatened to invade our sovereign and independent country. This is tantamount to a declaration of war against us." The foreign ministry statement also said, "Our people will never forgive the preposterous U.S. attempt to stifle us. We will ruthlessly crush the invaders."

The American press and pundits were engaged in heated discussions. The *New York Times* published a February 6 column by Michael O'Hanlon titled "Choosing the Right Enemies," which essentially made the following points, summarized below:

> Mr. Bush is wrong to lump three countries and the terrorist group together, as they are different from one another. The North Korean regime is not like Saddam Hussein's Iraq. In cooperation with the Clinton administration, North Korea closed its nuclear facilities in observance of the Agreed Framework, and imposed a moratorium on its missile testing, making progress in a process of rapprochement. There is no evidence that the regime actively supports major terrorist organizations.
>
> The Bush administration has failed to offer a serious alternative to Mr. Clinton's policy. Threatening rhetoric does not amount to a policy and actually increases the chances of war. If North Korea were willing to begin economic reform along the Chinese model, the United States should commit to providing substantial economic assistance. Kim Jong-il is no Saddam Hussein; he can possibly be coaxed, but probably not bludgeoned.

The *Washington Post* (February 11) published "Risky Rhetoric," an essay by James Laney (former ambassador to South Korea) and Morton

Abramowitz (former Under Secretary of State). The essay is partially summarized below:

> President Bush "implicitly threatened to destroy North Korea . . ." and "renewed a major debate and widened the split in the Korean-American alliance." The Republican hardliners had opposed negotiation with the North, calling for use of military force, if necessary, and opposed the 1994 Agreement, seeking North Korean collapse. The South Korean government, concerned about an outbreak of war, opposes military action. It also opposes a sudden collapse of the North, which would "produce massive instability in Korea and pose enormous economic problems for the South."
>
> South Korean President Kim Dae-jung meanwhile "began an enhanced engagement with North Korea—the so-called sunshine policy —which led to a reduction of tensions, and a summit between the two leaders and a host of bilateral agreements. . . . The Clinton administration was bought into this approach and tried to work out an arrangement to stop North Korea's missile program."
>
> "The advent of the Bush administration led to a break with Kim Dae-jung. President Bush refused to resume Clinton's efforts at missile negotiations and the normalization of relations with the North and showed little interest in the sunshine policy . . . besides putting another knife in the diminishing South Korean President, Bush's words can have dangerous escalatory consequences.
>
> "If Bush really intends to deal with North Korea militarily . . . he must weigh the massive calamity for both South (and North) Korea and the United States. . . . If he intends to try to bring the North Koreans down by isolation and withholding aid, he will have to confront China. But it would only increase tension. . . . As every government in the area wants, he has to be willing to engage North Korea seriously" to limit weapons of mass destruction.

President Bush's naming of North Korea in the axis of evil and his pronouncement to bring it down by "preemptive attack" shocked our people. A sense of insecurity and crisis quickly spread among the people, along with anti-American sentiments. To be accurate, it was not the development of "anti-Americanism," but anti-Bush sentiment.

It was the common perception of our people that if the United States took military action, North Korea would immediately launch missile attacks to turn Seoul into a sea of fire. The people of South Korea were firm in opposing war. Whether they were liberal or conservative, the people expressed their concerns in one voice against President Bush's talk of "preemptive attacks." A group of approximately 300 intellectuals who were inclined to be pro-American conservatives issued a statement expressing similar views. Even the conservative press and the opposition party, which had consistently supported President Bush, started to voice their concerns.

CHAPTER 12

RESTORATION OF
INTER-KOREAN RELATIONS

Tug of War between Kim Dae-jung and George W. Bush

Two weeks prior to his State of the Union address, President Bush announced he would visit Korea on a trip to three countries in Northeast Asia in mid-February.

President Kim Dae-jung planned to persuade Bush to support his North Korea policy during their upcoming summit in Seoul. To prepare for Bush's visit, President Kim stayed at the Walkerhill Hotel, taking advantage of his time off during the lunar New Year holidays. While working on his preparations, the president called me to the hotel, and we discussed a strategy for the summit.

President Kim's position was clear. Since we absolutely opposed war, the United States should engage North Korea in dialogue, rather than applying the Bush Doctrine to the North. He was interested in developing a logical way to persuade President Bush.

It had been the practice that whenever an American president came to Korea, he would visit a U.S. unit and a post at Panmunjom to see the military confrontation on the Korean frontline, to demonstrate "the U.S. commitment to defend South Korea." Accordingly, the American side was preparing for a visit by President Bush to the ROK Army observation post (OP).

I suggested a new idea for President Bush's itinerary, and President Kim liked it. Instead of Bush's visit to a ROK Army OP, I proposed that he and President Kim go to Dorasan Station. Dorasan Station was the last and newly-built railroad station along the railway that had been designed to connect the North and South through the DMZ. We had just completed our portion of the rail project, which included a modern station building, pending work in the DMZ to demine the area and prepare the railroad bed.

There the American president would see the railroads linking the North and the South as a symbolic place of peaceful coexistence and as an example of our policy of reconciliation and cooperation. My plan included a scenario in which the two presidents, standing on the platform of the station, would sign a railroad tie against the background of a milestone board showing the words "Seoul to Pyongyang."

This would soften the hardliner image of President Bush and send a peaceful message that would alleviate the concerns of both North and South Koreans.

Evans Revere, Deputy Chief of Mission at the American embassy, also agreed with my idea, and he recommended the scenario to Washington. The U.S. presidential advance team inspected the site in preparation for the plan.

* * * * * * * * *

On the morning of February 20, President Kim and President Bush held their meeting in the Blue House Reception Room. Their meeting lasted approximately one hour and forty minutes—nearly an hour longer than originally scheduled. The summit was attended by Foreign Minister Choi Sung-hong, myself as Special Advisor to the President for National Security and Unification, and Senior Secretary Yim Sung-joon for National Security and Foreign Affairs. Attending the meeting from the U.S. side were Secretary of State Colin Powell, National Security Adviser Condoleezza Rice and White House Chief of Staff Andrew Card.

At the meeting, President Bush said he was aware that the Korean people were befuddled by his recent, strong statements. He also said he did not want to create trouble for President Kim, expressing his support for the Sunshine policy. He defended himself, saying, "I am not belligerent, but we needed to send a firm message to the suspect North Koreans that we would not tolerate their bad behavior."

President Kim had been waiting for this moment of opportunity. He took the initiative in their discussion by presenting a logical explanation on the issue of weapons of mass destruction and missiles. He said, "The United States is concerned about the threat of North Korea's long-range ballistic missiles. For the United States, this is a threat for ten or fifteen years down the line. As for South Korea, we have been exposed to the present danger of North Korean missiles since the mid-1980s. We cannot allow North Korea to develop nuclear weapons. We must denuclearize the Korean Peninsula without fail."

President Kim told the American president that during the inter-Korean summit, he had encouraged Chairman Kim Jong-il to facilitate negotiations with the United States for an early settlement of these issues, to assure North Korea's survival and establish peace on the Korean Peninsula.

President Bush responded by saying that if North Korea launched provocations against South Korea, it would be the same as if they had done so to the United States. He emphasized that the United States would carry out its security commitment to South Korea. He said, "North Korea is the most dangerous arms seller. They export missiles to the Middle East to threaten countries friendly to us. We will never overlook this."

President Kim emphasized, "What's most important to us is our alliance with the United States." He went on to explain that our government's position was to seek early resolution, through peaceful means, to the issue of North Korean weapons of mass destruction.

In addition, President Kim provided a detailed explanation of the Sunshine policy, which was designed to encourage North Korea's reform and change. He stressed the necessity of U.S.–North Korea dialogue, assuring President Bush that he had confirmed that North Korea's top priority was to achieve a normalized relationship with the United States, for its own survival and economic recovery.

In connection with President Bush's reference to North Korea as "the most dangerous arms seller," President Kim pointed out that until the 1980s North Korea had annually earned $80 million from the sale of missiles, but since then, their sales had dropped to $20 million per year.

However, President Bush did not withhold his intense criticism and hatred for the North Korean leader: "Kim Jong-il is a vicious dictator who starves his people and violates their human rights. . . . We should send the winds of freedom to topple down the North Korean regime." He also asked, "Why didn't Kim Jong-il keep his promise to visit Seoul? Why did he suspend the dialogue with the South?"

President Kim reminded him that President Reagan had called the old Soviet Union an "evil empire," yet he had pursued dètente through dialogue, and eventually changed the Communist system toward the end of the Cold War. He added that President Nixon went to China, after terming it a "war criminal," to improve relations with China, inducing its opening and reform. "While it is easy to have dialogue with a friend," President Kim continued, "it is difficult to have dialogue with somebody you don't like. But for the sake of national interest or necessity, sometimes you have to engage that party." With this persuasive logic, President Kim recommended that the

United States, "with a magnanimous attitude as the sole superpower, unconditionally engage with North Korea."

After listening to President Kim, President Bush said, with a positive look on his face, "That is a good example. I respect President Reagan most." Then Bush turned to Secretary Powell and National Security Advisor Rice and said, "I will discuss this issue with them. But North-South dialogue should come first."

President Kim reemphasized, "We pursue our Sunshine policy based on the ROK-U.S. alliance." Then he listed the results of his policy, including the reduction of tension, the suspension of mutual slander, the prevention of infiltration and provocation, the reunions of separated families, and increasing movement of people between the South and North. He said, "70 to 80 percent of our people support the Sunshine policy."

Citing the example of the June 1999 Yeonpyeong naval clash, the first time since the armistice in which the South retaliated against a North Korean provocation, President Kim strongly emphasized: "The Sunshine policy is not an appeasement policy. It promotes détente from the basis of strength. It is an offensive policy that only the strong can carry out." President Bush responded by saying: "I understand it well," and repeated, "I support it."

President Kim went on:

> Our people think that the Korean Peninsula issue should be peacefully resolved, and they have the confidence we can do it. They are resolutely opposed to war. If the United States takes military action against North Korea, it would clearly escalate into an all-out war. The Pentagon has estimated that within three months of war, 500,000 South Korean soldiers, 50,000 American troops, and more than one million civilians would be killed or wounded, while most industrial facilities would be destroyed. We would win the war in the end. But don't you agree that we should avoid such a calamity?

President Kim also detailed North Korea's missiles and long-range artillery power, and their suicidal, bellicose "do or die" attitude. In response, President Bush said, "I have no intention of attacking or invading North Korea."

Throughout the conversation, the American president repeated, "I understand," or "It's a good policy." Bush showed an interest in the issue of separated families and food aid, asking about the number of separated families. When President Bush was getting up, he expressed his satisfaction with the meeting by saying, "It was a great debate, frank and useful."

George W. Bush (*left*) and Kim Dae-jung sign a railroad tie in front of the Dorasan Station milestone board, February 20, 2002. Courtesy Lim Dong-won.

"Will Neither Attack Nor Invade North Korea"

At the joint press conference following the summit, President Bush said, "I support the Sunshine policy. . . . We have no intention of invading North Korea, nor does America have the intention of attacking North Korea." He said that he would seek a resolution of the issues through dialogue and that he would continue food aid to the North Korean people. He seemed to have been influenced by President Kim's sincere and logical persuasion.

On the afternoon of the first day of his visit, President Kim and President Bush met again at Dorasan Station. President Bush came by van to the barb-wired station area from a frontline U.S. Army unit near the DMZ, where he had had lunch with U.S. soldiers. Kim, who had arrived by train, met Bush on site, and they were briefed on the status of progress regarding the railway relinking project.

The two presidents then walked to the Dorasan Station platform and signed a railroad tie in front of the milestone sign that read, "205 kilometers to Pyongyang; 56 kilometers to Seoul." Next, President Bush moved into the station hall to address about 300 representatives from various fields. He commented how a satellite picture of the Korean Peninsula showed the South radiating brilliant lights at night, but the North was pitch black. He added his hope that President Kim's vision would illuminate the entire peninsula. He warned again, "The threat of the world's most dangerous regime with the world's most dangerous weapons will never be tolerated." He added that the ROK-U.S. alliance is the "foundation of a stable Korean Peninsula."

* * * * * * * * * *

In the evening, a reception was held in the Sejong Room of the Blue House for political leaders of the governing and opposition parties and representatives of various organizations. The reception was followed by a private dinner hosted by President Kim in the Choongmu Room. The dinner was attended by a small group of seven participants from each side. The size and the format of the dinner had been proposed by the U.S. side for an informal and friendly conversation.

From the United States, Secretary Powell, National Security Advisor Rice, Ambassador Hubbard, and National Security Council Senior Asia Director James Moriarty attended the dinner. From the Korean side, Foreign Minister Choi Sung-hong, myself as Special Advisor to the President, Ambassador to the United States Yang Sung-chul, and Senior Secretary Yim Sung-joon attended.

When dinner began, President Kim raised his wine glass for a toast. At this moment, President Bush said, "I am a good Christian and I don't drink." He signaled to a secret service agent, who brought a can of beer to the table. "This is non-alcoholic beer," he proclaimed. Then he used it for the toast. President Kim asked him which denomination he was. He said he was a Methodist. He also shared that he used to drink a lot and misbehaved when he was young, but his pious Christian wife made him a "born again." President Kim said he was a Catholic but his wife was a Methodist. Bush then joked, "You don't have a religious war?" This provoked loud laughter at the table.

President Kim explained in detail how the Methodists influenced British society during the Industrial Revolution. President Bush and the First Lady seemed impressed by President Kim's knowledge and his logical way of talking. The dinner conversations went smoothly in a friendly atmosphere, touching on a variety of topics, including Korean baseball players and Korean women golfers who were dominating sports news. The two heads of state agreed that their summit was a big success. It was the first visit to Korea for President Bush, and he said he was most impressed by the Dorasan Railroad Station at the DMZ.

* * * * * * * * * *

Both governing and opposition political parties and the press at home and abroad showed favorable responses to the result of the Korea-America summit. The *New York Times* published a news analysis, stating that Bush confirmed that he had "no intention of invading North Korea" and had declared his support for the Sunshine policy. The article also said Bush tried to mitigate the concerns of the Korean people in the aftermath of his State of the Union address. The Bush administration also expressed its satisfaction with the summit, describing it as "successful."

The senior State Department officials accompanying President Bush commented that it was good to have learned during the trip that the Sunshine policy was supported by 70–80 percent of the people. I was impressed by their admission that they had sometimes been misled by some press reports and allegations of the opposition party.

On the other hand, some Defense Department officials complained, "Although President Bush did not compromise in principle, he went too far." Their confusion was understandable because only less than a month earlier, President Bush had designated North Korea as a "target for regime change by preemptive strike"; now in Seoul, President Bush pledged he would "neither attack nor invade North Korea."

Back to Pyongyang as Special Envoy

On April 3, I arrived at the Sunan Pyongyang Airport aboard presidential Air Force Three as presidential special envoy again to meet with Chairman Kim Jong-il. There I was met by a few North Korean officials, including Director General Choi Sung-chol of the United Front. Upon our arrival at the Baekhwawon Guest House, the first deputy director of the United Front gave me a pleasant welcome.

On the first day of my visit, I had a two-and-a-half-hour meeting with Secretary Kim Yong-soon, and in the evening, a dinner meeting. The daytime meeting was attended by five delegates from each side. In a prepared opening statement, Secretary Kim harshly criticized the United States, saying, "Due to the Bush administration's war policy, North-South relations have experienced a serious setback. And the South, which followed the U.S. policy, should bear its share of responsibility."

He said, "Before we begin our discussion of inter-Korean relations, we want to hear clear answers from the South concerning two questions. The first question is whether the South wants to respect the basic spirit of the June 15 Joint Declaration and cooperate with us, or whether the South wants to turn against us and collaborate with the foreign forces." Kim Yong-soon attacked the South Korean concept of the "main enemy" and the combined ROK-U.S. military exercise to press me on the second question, "Since the South's designation of the North as its 'main enemy' and Bush's 'axis of evil' both have similar inferences, do you wish to unite our strengths to keep the peace, or do you wish to collaborate with the foreign forces to choose war?"

When it was my turn to speak, I first explained the purpose of my visit based on a short prepared statement, presenting an assessment of the security situation on the Korean Peninsula and proposing steps to restart the process of resolving inter-Korean issues. Then, I replied to Kim Yong-soon by refuting his belligerent statements.

I had not prepared my answers in advance. Improvising, I argued: "National cooperation and international cooperation are not mutually exclusive. They are, in fact, mutually compatible." To provide the basis for my argument, I said, "The Korean Peninsula issue is both an internal and international issue. This dualistic nature of the issue is a stark reality." I further argued that international cooperation was essential to national cooperation. I continued,

> We have agreed through the inter-Korean summit meeting to resolve the question of unification on our own initiative through the joint efforts of the Korean people. We also agreed to accomplish it through peaceful means, not by force. The task lying before our nation today is to reduce tension and establish peace in advance of unification. We should share the same perspective that we need cooperation of the United States and other surrounding countries in a peacemaking process.
>
> The urgent tasks are to end hostile relations between North Korea and the United States, and to normalize their relations. As long as North Korea and the United States maintain hostile relations, we cannot hope for peace on the peninsula. This is an undeniable reality.
>
> On the issue of unification, we should pursue it on our own initiative. We must resolve the peace issue not only through inter-Korean cooperation but also through international cooperation. We do not seek international cooperation to oppose and confront the North. The international cooperation that we are seeking will help inter-Korean relations and solidify the base of peace.

During dinner that evening, Deputy Director Lim Dong-ok brought up the subject of North Korean defectors. Our conversation turned again into another heated debate. He opened his offensive: "The South Korean National Intelligence Service encourages and kidnaps North Koreans from China and then takes them to the South as though they are defectors. This is a malicious crime!"

About three weeks earlier, twenty-five North Korean defectors had entered the Spanish embassy in Beijing. It was learned that these defectors were assisted by international NGO activists working in China. This was the first in a series of incidents of North Korean defectors entering embassies in Beijing to come to South Korea.

The Chinese government refused to grant refugee status to these people but agreed to expel them to the Philippines. And we were able to bring them to South Korea after they rested a few days in the Philippines. Korean ambassador Kim Ha-joong, who had maintained good relations with high-ranking Chinese government officials, played an important role in the resolution of the defectors' plights.

To contradict the North's claim that the NIS had encouraged and kidnapped North Koreans, I said that the North Korean charges were totally ungrounded. I retorted, "Before the North criticizes the South, it should take care of its own people. The number of North Korean defectors who manage to come to Seoul increased from 70 to 150 in 1998. They have doubled in number every year since, from 300 to 600. We have many problems accommodating them. However, out of humanitarian consideration, our government cannot help but do so. And we will continue to do so in the future."

*   *   *   *   *   *   *   *   *

At six o'clock on the evening of April 4, I met with Chairman Kim Jong-il at the Baekhwawon Guest House. Chairman Kim gladly welcomed me at the entrance of the reception room. As a pleasantry, I said, "Thank you for your invitation, and congratulations on your sixtieth birthday." First, he asked me about President Kim's health and how he had been doing recently. He then said, "How is the weather in Seoul nowadays? In the North, it did not snow enough last winter, and the reservoirs are not at full capacity. And we have an electricity problem . . ."

Having heard him say that he had twice read President Kim Dae-jung's letter, I explained the three focal points that were contained in the letter, one by one. First, I explained President Kim's views on the Bush Doctrine, the changed international security environment, and North Korea–U.S. relations:

> After September 11, the Bush administration proclaimed a war on terrorism and the proliferation of weapons of mass destruction; it prefers military action over diplomatic negotiation. Following the attack on Afghanistan, Iraq is becoming the next target. You may find it disturbing, but it is true that the United States is openly talking of North Korea as the next target for preemptive attack and regime change. North Korea should correctly realize that the Bush administration's foreign policy is entirely different from that of the Clinton administration. The Bush administration is trying to unilaterally attain its goals on the basis of strong military might, rather than through international cooperation— and a military preemptive attack rather than by preventive diplomacy.

Therefore, this situation requires a new, wise countermeasure, different from before.

President Bush opposes President Clinton's approach to North Korea. He defies the U.S.–North Korea agreements. He distrusts North Korea, and he is skeptical of dialogue. The Bush administration maintains the position that there will be no rewards or compensation.

However, President Kim secured President Bush's commitment that the United States would neither attack nor invade North Korea during their summit. This is a very significant shift in U.S. policy in that it reversed President Bush's public statement on North Korea in his State of the Union address three weeks earlier. President Bush promised to resolve all the issues through dialogue and to continue food aid to the North. He also said he earnestly supports President Kim's policy of reconciliation and cooperation.

Our government is very pleased with the result of the summit, as we had him publicly state those points of importance at a press conference. Nevertheless, President Bush was displeased by the North's negative response to his proposal for dialogue last year.

Pointing out that there had been no progress in inter-Korean relations in the meantime, President Bush expressed his strong suspicions of North Korea. Under these circumstances, it would serve no good cause to avoid dialogue, either from the point of principles or pragmatic interest. President Kim advises that you engage in open dialogue to draw international attention and weaken the hardliners' opinion in the United States.

I also conveyed to Chairman Kim Jong-il the State Department message that the United States was willing to send Ambassador Pritchard to Pyongyang to explain a new road map of U.S. policy toward North Korea. After a detailed introduction of Pritchard, I said, "It would not be a wise decision to turn down the U.S. proposal because you think Pritchard's rank is not high enough."

* * * * * * * * *

In addition, I informed him that when Japanese Prime Minister Koizumi Junichiro met with President Kim Dae-jung in Seoul (March 22), President Kim encouraged him to improve relations with North Korea. I related how Prime Minister Koizumi expressed his willingness to cooperate in various areas. I told him that Koizumi had said if there were progress on the abduction issue, he would persuade his people to promote improved relations with the North.

I also delivered Chairman Kim the Japanese government's message that Japan wanted to improve relations with the North and would continue steady dialogue. Considering the Japanese provision of aid to the North so far, they expected a reciprocal response on the human rights issue. In view of public opinion in Japan, they shared it would be impossible to improve relations unless the abduction issue were resolved. I shared how President Kim advised Prime Minister Koizumi to provide food aid to the North. I said to Chairman Kim Jong-il,

> President Kim said you should avoid having something from the past become an obstacle in the future. In fact, we too know that North Korea did not invite the Yodogo kidnappers to the North aboard a Japanese airplane. More than thirty years have passed since the incident. Perhaps a solution would be to send them from the North in the form of a voluntary departure. Regarding the Japanese abductees, you could express a regret over the "misdeed of the blind radical followers" and repatriate the Japanese abductees earlier. These are President Kim's thoughts.
>
> Would it not be wise for you to receive monetary compensation through a normalized relationship with Japan and use it for your economic development? President Kim thinks if North Korea receives compensation from Japan, North Korea would be eligible for international financial assistance and loans. The issue of clearing the past should not be considered on the basis of face but pragmatic interests."

After listening quietly, Chairman Kim Jong-il reacted negatively to the use of the term "abductees." But he showed deep interest in President Kim's advice, taking a largely positive position on the Japan issue. Chairman Kim said, "To resolve the issue of the 'missing people,' we are going to resume Red Cross talks with the Japanese soon."

He went on: "I know President Bush visited Dorasan Station. Even on that occasion, did he not use his foul language of criticism, saying that he could confirm the 'axis of evil' after visiting the adjacent area? Did he not say the North Korean system must change? On the other hand, I heard that in a recent working-level contact in New York the U.S. side told us that President Bush's foul talk was not the official position of the U.S. administration, and they asked for our understanding of President Bush's personality." Chairman Kim seemed to have taken consolation from the American working-level officials. In a way, I suspected that knowing how important face was to him, face-saving might justify his attitude change towards the Bush administration.

President Bush often disclosed his distrust and hostility by describing Chairman Kim Jong-il as a "dangerous person," a "failed dictator," a "tyrant" "the axis of evil," a "spoiled child," or a "pigmy."

With regard to Bush's characterizations, an American press outlet pointed out that "President Clinton never during his term in office criticized any foreign head of state, including Kim Jong Il, not even once." There were clearly some concerns about President Bush's unrefined, undiplomatic language.

North Korea responded in kind and even more rudely. It called Bush harsh names, including a "first-class warmonger," a "monstrous head of war," an "insane belligerent," the "world's worst fascist dictator," a "tyrant of tyrants who surpasses Hitler tenfold," a "flunk in diplomacy," a "villain who does not have the composure of a normal person, not to mention that of a president," and a "morally immature boy not to be dealt with."

* * * * * * * * *

Chairman Kim expressed a feeling of regret:

> We tried hard to work well with the Americans. Secretary of State Albright visited Pyongyang and President Clinton was planning to come here. We were able to communicate well with the Clinton administration. Then, the outcome of the American election took more than a month. The results created an entirely different situation. President Bush says he wants to work with us, but doesn't he look down on us and make foul statements? However, if he stops his rude criticism, I would be willing to accept President Kim's advice and have a dialogue with the United States. If an ambassador from the U.S. State Department wants to come here, that would be fine.

Reconfirming his last sentence, I told him that I would convey that message to the United States. Chairman Kim frankly revealed that the Clinton administration was also difficult in the beginning, but that they had been able to produce agreements through engagement in dialogue and negotiation. He also said,

> What I would like to say to the United States is that if they think we are like the Taliban regime in Afghanistan, they are making a big mistake. The United States seems to be puffed up after defeating puppets like the Taliban regime. However, we are resolutely determined to fight invaders to the last and to drive them out.
>
> Since we fortified our entire country with underground facilities, I hear that the United States is developing nuclear bombs capable of destroying them and targeting us. Well, if they want to go war, let them do so. Of course, what we sincerely want is for Bush to withdraw hostilities against us and for us to coexist together.

From this visit to Pyongyang, I drew three conclusions: Kim Jong-il distrusted the United States; he feared the United States; yet he wanted badly to normalize relations with the United States. He had voiced the last point during the 2000 Inter-Korean Summit, stating that based on the North's strategic judgment, maintaining relations with the United States was in the interest of the nation, and he therefore wished to normalize relations with the United States.

It appeared clear to me that North Korea was keeping weapons of mass destruction and maintaining a strong military force because of their fear and distrust of the United States. It was clear that the North Koreans were using them as negotiation leverage.

Through my meeting with Kim Jong-il, I got the strong impression that North Korea would not give up its nuclear weapons development program and weapons of mass destruction until after relations with the United States were normalized.

Question of Sequencing: America or the South

Later in my meeting with Chairman Kim, I explained our position on the second subject of how to resolve the inter-Korean issue. I started by saying, "It is regretful that North-South relations were hit by an external headwind." Then I relayed to him President Kim's strong view that we should still continue to develop North-South relations and uphold the spirit of the June 15 Joint Declaration. I said to him,

> I personally feel bad that for the past year we have wasted valuable time. However, the eleven months that remain of our administration is not a short period. We should deploy a 'speed battle' in North-South dialogue to recover the loss. Now is the time for the North to switch from "America first and the South later" to "the South first and America later."
>
> Unlike during the Clinton administration, we may fail in inter-Korean relations if the North pursues an approach of "America first, the South later." If you turn to the "South first, America later," it will have a positive impact on North Korea–U.S. relations as well. President Kim, who has only eleven months left in his term, regards ensuring that the next administration achieves the spirit of the June 15 Joint Declaration as his most important task. To do this, we certainly need the North's cooperation. I cordially ask you, Mr. Chairman, to capture this good opportunity."

Having listened attentively, Chairman Kim explained his view of estranged North-South relations, asking the South to change its attitude:

> When you said you wanted to come here as a special envoy, my subordinate comrades opposed your visit, saying, "the situation does not

allow it," "we should resolve the issue with America first," or "timing is premature." I accepted your visit because of President Kim's strong request.

We have noted some disturbing actions on the part of the South for a while. Did we not promise that the North and the South would autonomously resolve the Korean issue? During his visit to the United States in March last year, President Kim succumbed to President Bush's pressure. Bush was insisting that "he would not allow the South to promote inter-Korean relations without U.S. approval," and that "the South should keep the policy of reciprocity."

In addition, President Kim had agreed with Russia to support the ABM treaty, but he reversed the agreement under U.S. pressure. In light of these incidents, how can you say that the South is sovereign and independent? We naturally began to suspect it would be difficult to carry out the June 15 Joint Declaration if the United States opposed it. Is it not true that under South Korea–U.S. cooperation the South would support the United States' hostile policies towards the North? If that is not the case, what is it?

I explained it was not true that President Kim yielded to President Bush's pressure. I refuted Chairman Kim's assertion, reminding him that during the past year, our government tried hard to implement the June 15 Joint Declaration and to persuade the United States in that regard.

I said to Chairman Kim that just as he had pointed out, the Clinton administration had also had a hardline policy in the beginning. Because of President Kim's relentless and successful efforts, the Clinton administration transformed its policy in favor of President Kim's comprehensive engagement policy. At that time, I had gone to Washington at President Kim's wishes to persuade the Americans. I told them that in view of the mutual threats as perceived respectively by the United States and North Korea, mutual threat reduction should be a starting point toward the resolution of the issue. Then it would require a gradual give and take comprehensive approach to include the areas of political, diplomatic, security, and economic affairs.

It was the Perry Report that reflected the U.S. acceptance of these points. I insisted that our efforts had also contributed to progress in North Korea–U.S. relations in the meantime. Our cooperation with the United States had not been "anti-North Korean cooperation," but "cooperation for peace on the peninsula." It was "international cooperation" for "national cooperation" in every aspect. I told Chairman Kim,

> Our government will continue the same kind of efforts toward the Bush administration. When President Bush came to Seoul last time, President Kim persuaded him to publicly promise that the United States would

not include North Korea as a target for the Bush Doctrine. As I stressed in my meeting with Secretary Kim Yong-soon yesterday, national cooperation and international cooperation are not contradictory but complementary.

I returned to the pending issue of North-South relations:

First, we should revitalize North-South relations so that we can mitigate the intensity of the U.S. hardline policy. To change the atmosphere, we need to expedite holding the second round of the North-South Defense Ministerial Talks. If the defense ministers of the North and South sit together to discuss the issue of tension reduction and peace, the United States will have to respect their discussion.

The defense ministerial talks will also be greatly helpful to the easing of concerns of the threat of the North Korean conventional forces. This can provide the first step to military confidence-building between the North and the South. In addition to the symbolic meaning of these efforts, we also critically need military assurance for the peaceful use of the DMZ for the reconnection of the railways on the west coast, and the connection of the roads on the east coast."

Chairman Kim retorted, "What good would the defense ministerial talks do when the United States has its grip on the sword?" I responded,

President Kim asked me to tell you that the best solution is to appeal to world opinion and American public opinion through the defense ministerial talks, and to change the atmosphere by the connection of the railways and the roads. President Bush also emphasized that there should first be an improvement in inter-Korean relations.

Regarding the pending issues, I advocated that we should immediately take steps to promote the "five core projects," which included relinking the railways and the roads; construction of the Kaesong Industrial Complex; promotion of Mount Kumgang tourism by land transportation; taking steps to build military confidence; and increasing various exchanges and meetings of separated families.

I emphasized to him that our side had completed the railroad construction up to the southern border of the DMZ and that we had been waiting for the removal of landmines and the clearing work for the railroads in the DMZ. I said, "Now is the time that we hold the defense ministerial talks and adopt an agreement of military assurance."

* * * * * * * * *

At this point, Chairman Kim Jong-il brought up the importance of connecting the railroads on the east coast. In the previous summer, he had visited Russia by train for about a month, stopping in several places in Siberia, and holding a summit meeting with Russian President Putin. It was learned that he and the Russian president had agreed to connect a Trans-Korea Peninsula railway with the Trans-Siberian Railway, and to modernize the North Korean railway system. Russia was known to have completed a survey of the North Korean rail system. Chairman Kim said he thought it would make sense to promote Mount Kumgang tourism by land transportation and proposed that we connect the railways on the east coast. He elaborated on his proposal:

> I know Busan is one of the five largest ports in the world. Would it not be great to connect the railway from Busan along the east coast to the Trans-Siberian Railway? And, to avoid the trouble of reloading, I think it would be good to construct a combined track system to allow for the compatibility of both the wider Russian tracks and our regular tracks.

I told him in response that his idea was a good one, but that we did not have railways running along the east coast in the South yet. I explained that there was no railroad between Gangnung to the DMZ—a distance of 130 kilometers. When Chairman Kim appeared surprised that there was no railway, I replied that although our government would not oppose the linking of the railway to the East Coast Line, it would take a long time to connect Gangnung to Onjeong, Mount Kumgang. Therefore, I said we should treat it as a long-term project.

At this moment, General Ri Myung-soo, Chief of Operations for the Korean People's Army, came into the room, wearing civilian clothes. This was our first introduction. We then returned to the discussion of linking railways.

General Ri opened a map and provided a briefing on the North's plan for reconnecting the railways to the east coast line and linking the roads to Mount Kumgang. He also reported that the preparation for the Seoul-Shinuiju line connection on the west coast had been completed, and that they could immediately start the work if ordered. He reported that the removal of the landmines would not take too much time. They had planned to carry out the railway connection project and the road connection project in parallel in anticipation of the development of a Kaesong Special Zone.

After the report, Chairman Kim asked me if the South genuinely had intentions of developing the Kaesong Industrial Complex. I summarized the importance of developing the Kaesong Industrial Complex and our master plan for construction that included the supply of electricity, gas and a communication network. I added that the construction of the railways and roads were vital to the project. I asked Chairman Kim to order his people to begin working on the projects as soon as the next day. At my request, Chairman

Kim ordered the KPA chief of operations to tell the minister of the People's Armed Forces to carry out the projects right away.

During my meeting with him, Chairman Kim reiterated his suggestion to construct an east coast railway line, rather than have tourists from the South try to access Mount Kumgang by land. He added that the Russians were greatly interested in container transportation, but that the North was interested in tourism as well. There were many tourist spots on the east coast in addition to Mount Kumgang, such as Wonsan beach and Chilbo Mountain.

* * * * * * * * *

It had been learned that until shortly before his death, President Kim Il-sung had planned to propose a project to modernize the Seoul-Shinuiju line on the west coast at the aborted inter-Korean summit meeting. Why was Chairman Kim Jong-il's priority placed on the east coast line? Had there been a Russian promise of massive assistance? Did Kim Jong-il really believe that Russia was economically capable of supporting the North Korean project? These and other questions were going through my head as I was listening to Chairman Kim.

Reminding him of President Kim's idea that the Korean Peninsula should become a logistic hub and major distribution center, I said that according to a study, connecting the trans-peninsula railway to the trans-Siberian railway would significantly reduce transportation time and reduce transportation costs by one-third. I reiterated that these were great projects that would help realize peace and prosperity on the Korean Peninsula. I said we should start with the DMZ projects first. I stressed that it was important that the armies on the two sides cooperate closely to remove landmines and begin the railway and road projects.

Chairman Kim said we should not focus on the Seoul-Shinuiju line only in view of China's interests, but that we should also consider the construction of an east coast line in view of our relations with Russia. He said we should take both Russia and China—the east and the west—with us. The chairman also made an impressive remark on the symbolic, historical significance of these projects:

> If we connect our railway with the Chinese railway system on the west coast, and with the Russian railway system on the east, it would create a "peace zone" on the Korean Peninsula. How could a war break out here when goods are transported from Busan to Europe through the trans-Siberian railway system and the trans-China railway system?

Restoration of the Original State

The third item on my agenda to discuss with Chairman Kim was the issue of his return visit to Seoul and the holding of a second North-South summit. I conveyed President Kim's sincere message that the president wished to have him visit the South at an appropriate time between June 15 and August 15. I underscored the significance of such a visit.

Chairman Kim responded,

> In fact I was going to visit Seoul last spring. I also want to see President Kim again as soon as possible. However, the situation changed with the election of President Bush, who is hostile to North Korea. Under the Clinton or Gore administration, I would have visited Seoul already.

He was still thinking that South Korea was a dangerous place that was carrying out Bush's hostile North Korean policy with the presence of U.S. forces. He said,

> Given that the Grand National Party and the right-wing forces are demanding an apology from us for the Korean War and the explosion of a Korean Airliner, creating opposition to my visit and threats to inflict personal harm on me, the people around me are opposing my visit. They fear that my visit might further complicate the situation. At present, I frankly do not feel like visiting the South."

I responded:

> Although it is true that some opposing forces are making noise, such a thing is quite possible in a diverse society. Please, don't be too concerned. Public opinion polls show that an absolute majority welcomes Chairman Kim's visit to Seoul.
>
> Also, in order to change the Bush administration's view of the North, it is President Kim's view that you should visit Seoul as agreed upon in the last summit. Would you please make your decision in terms of a historical and national perspective, not a political perspective?

When I said we could consider his visit to Seoul and Jeju Island, he unexpectedly said, "Let's think about holding a meeting in a third country." He said Irkutsk, Siberia would be a good place to meet. He said, "There are more than ten big hotels in Irkutsk. We could also have a trilateral summit that included Russia, to discuss the issue of connecting to the trans-Siberian railway." When I said it was not appropriate to hold a summit in a third country, he replied, "Don't decide on this matter one way or the other. You just report it to the president."

* * * * * * * * *

I still had one more item on my agenda to discuss with Chairman Kim. I proposed we resume the reunions of separated families within the month, and Chairman Kim accepted my proposal. He added, "The light water reactor team has learned a lot from their trip to the South," and he thanked the South for its warm hospitality.

Then he ordered Secretary Kim Yong-soon, "In response to the special envoy's visit, send an economic observation team to the South." He suggested to me, "It would be better if you show them small- and medium-size enterprises, more suitable to the North, than large industrial facilities. But make sure to show the Samsung Electronics company to them."

Next, I requested that the North dispatch its sports teams to the Asian Games, which were scheduled to start in September in Busan. I asked him to send to the South not just the sports teams but also cultural and arts performing groups to participate in the opening and closing ceremonies of the Asian Games. I also explained the proposal of the event organizing committee to carry a relayed torch flame from the top of Mount Baekdu in the North to the South. The chairman of the Asian Games Organizing Committee told me that he had sent invitations a long time ago, but had not heard any response from the North. He asked me to help realize his proposal. This was a subject of President Kim's interest as well.

Listening to me, Chairman Kim appeared as though he was hearing about this subject for the first time, and he asked several questions. "A torch relay would be a little difficult, but consider us sending a cultural and arts performing group with sports teams done," and he then ordered Secretary Kim Yong-soon to do so on the spot. Later, the North sent a 637-member delegation to participate in the Busan Asian Games. This set a precedent of North Korean delegations participating in international sports events held by South Korea.

During the three-week period of the games, the North Korean delegates stayed in the Mangyungbong ship anchored at the port of Busan, by which they came down from the North. During the daytime, the North Korean athletes competed against other countries in Asia. In particular, the performance of 300 "beautiful young female cheerleaders" instantly captivated the spectators at the scene as well as television viewers across the country. Positive comments from both the South Korean press and public opinion expressed that the cheerleaders demonstrated the love of Korean kinship to the world, contributing greatly to the success of the Asian Games.

* * * * * * * * *

While at my meeting with Chairman Kim, I also relayed a message from the United States: "Secretary of State Colin Powell said he wanted to meet with the North Korean foreign minister at the coming ASEAN Regional Forum (ARF) in Brunei. He hopes that North Korea will attend the ARF. I hope that Mr. Chairman will consider this."

Chairman Kim instructed Secretary Kim Yong-soon to tell the foreign ministry to positively consider the request. In fact, Secretary Powell and North Korean Foreign Minister Paek Nam-sun met in Brunei that summer.

Finally, Chairman Kim made his concluding statement:

> Please convey to President Kim that we will engage the United States without any conditions. We will resume Red Cross talks with Japan. Regarding my return visit to Seoul, tell him that I also want to see him soon, but do not wish to go to Seoul. I suggest we meet in a different place. However, you should keep it confidential until it is realized.
>
> We have frozen North-South relations due to the deterioration of our relations with the United States. Now with the special envoy's visit, North-South relations have been restored to their original state. With your visit, we have resolved all issues. Let's schedule meetings of separated families again, and let's expedite the connections of the railways and roads on the east and west coasts.
>
> Let's carry out the Kaesong Industrial Complex project, and hold North-South talks to discuss necessary steps for supporting it. Special Envoy Lim Dong-won should discuss further details with Secretary Kim Yong-soon and write up an agreement.

I thanked Chairman Kim for his "important decisions" and I got him to include specific dates of implementation in an agreement that I would work out with Secretary Kim Yong-soon.

* * * * * * * * *

The meeting lasted a total of two hours. Chairman Kim and I exchanged candid and broad views, concerning what the North referred to as "a grave situation confronting the Korean Peninsula and the Korean nation," and regarding all issues pertaining to North-South relations. In conclusion, it had been a successful meeting that led to the agreement to restore inter-Korean relations and to promote mutual interests through building mutual confidence.

Five Hours with Kim Jong-il

Chairman Kim Jong-il invited our party to a dinner after our meeting. We all moved to the dinner venue, where Chairman Kim said, "Secretary Yong-soon told me I didn't have to host a dinner this time. So I said if the United Front Department did not host a dinner, the National Defense Commission would. Now I am hosting this dinner." Everybody laughed. He seemed to be in good spirits.

We sat across from each other at the table as if we were in a meeting. Chairman Kim and Secretary Kim Yong-soon sat on one side, flanked by General Ri Myung-soo and Deputy Director Lim Dong-ok of the United Front Department. Facing them, NIS Deputy Director Kim Bo-hyun and I sat in the center with the Director-General for Exchange and Cooperation Cho Myong-kyun and Dialogue Coordinator Seo Hoon sitting on both sides of me.

At dinner, Chairman Kim again led a frank conversation on various topics. I was impressed by his deep interest in and accurate information regarding South Korean popular culture. He also showed a keen interest in the South Korean stock market and in the wide uses of the Internet and mobile communications.

Jeju Island was his first topic. "When they returned from their trips to Jeju Island, Secretary Kim Yong-soon and Minister of People's Armed Forces Kim Il-chol proudly said Jeju was so beautiful." He asked a number of questions about the island. Then, to my surprise, Chairman Kim began talking about South Korean pop music.

> By the way, is the singer Haeun, who sang the Jeju Island song "Gam-sugwang," still active? Last year, singer Kim Yon-ja did very well in Japan and she came here for a performance. She is an outstanding singer. She is coming back again. I have made a request of five South Korean songs for her to sing, including "Winter Tea House," originally sung by Cho Yong-pil, and "Galmuri" by Na Hoon-a.

I said, "This is my first return to the Baekhwawon guest house in two years and it is good to be able to watch CNN and BBC by satellite broadcast. I noted that my visit to Pyongyang as a special envoy was reported as an important new item, and that the world is paying attention to us." Chairman Kim then asked which one of the two, CNN or BBC, had more viewers.

Chairman Kim said, "When you return to Seoul, don't go by plane. You can go by land and pass through Panmunjom. Secretary Kim Yong-soon also went to the South by air, but he returned by land. We should practice the principle of reciprocity." He provoked another burst of laughter around the table. Chairman Kim continued talking:

> I frequently visit the websites of the Blue House, the National Intelligence Service, and the Ministry of Unification, through Yahoo. The Blue House site has a well-arranged history of presidents, including

President Park Chung-hee. The Unification Ministry's "window to understand North Korea correctly," I think, is a good idea. What's most
important here is to know our counterparts well.

It was a good decision to allow the people in the South to watch
Pyongyang television news. We should get to know more about each
other. When I visit military units, I stay in the local area and it is very
convenient to watch Seoul news live at night through Internet broadcasts.

I responded by asking: "What do you think of allowing an exchange of
visits between our military? They can exchange frank views concerning the
peaceful utilization of the DMZ, and increase mutual understanding between them? How about sending General Ri Myung-soo to Seoul?"

Chairman Kim rejected this saying, "General Ri has all the military operation plans in his head. So, that will be difficult." The listeners broke into
laughter again. He seemed overly concerned about a possible terror attack
from the rightists. "What do we do if I or General Ri go to the South and
get attacked by rightist terrorists? Are the South Korean gangs like Japanese
Yakuza? When I went to Russia, I heard that the Mafia was scarier than the
Russian police. Under the Soviet Union, they say the Communist Party was
scarier, but now the Mafia is."

* * * * * * * * *

He continued, "What we need nowadays is electricity. Many people say
that our economic structure is bad, but the real problem is not the economic
structure but a shortage of energy. If the energy problem is resolved and the
economy is still bad, *then* you could say that our structure is the problem."

Secretary Kim Yong-soon intervened to support the chairman: "If we
had continued with the construction of our atomic power plants as we had
planned, we would not have this current electricity problem. We suspended
the construction of the power plants in return for U.S. provision of heavy
fuel oil and construction of the light water reactors; this delay has created a
power shortage." Chairman Kim also sarcastically said, "The South talked
for a while of providing electricity to the North by direct supply. But, when
the United States opposed it for 'strategic reasons,' the South did not say a
word."

I had to provide an explanation in response:

The North side requested a supply of two million kilowatts, with an
initial supply of 500,000 kilowatts. We studied the request and concluded that it would ruin both transmission systems due to the qualitative
difference in electricity between our two systems. In order to prevent
reverse current, we would have needed to build direct current transform-

ers. This would have cost a lot and it would also have taken a long time to build them. We thus concluded that direct supply was not a good option. To help resolve the North Korean power shortage, our government has been studying a range of alternatives, including renovation and repair of the old North Korean thermal power plants, and provision of smokeless coal.

Chairman Kim said it was a source of national pride that kimchi had spread worldwide, adding:

> When I went to China, I tried South Korean kimchi. It was too salty and spicy. The best kimchi is still Kaesong's *bossam* kimchi (wrapped kimchi). But in terms of palace cuisine, I think South Korea's version is the best. For *naengmyun* [cold noodles], Pyongyang cold noodles are still the best. When Chairman Chung Ju-young comes to Pyongyang, he only eats cold noodles for his three daily meals. I remember that President Park Chung-hee told our special envoy Park Sung-cheol that he wished things would go well so that he could come to Pyongyang and eat Pyongyang cold noodles."
>
> I hear that Representative Park Geun-hye wants to leave the Grand National Party to run for the presidency. What's your take on the prospects of the presidential election? Anyway, I would like to meet Representative Park Geun-hye.

I told him that we would have to wait until November to see who would appear as a likely winner. "You never know until you count the votes," I said.

* * * * * * * * *

Then Chairman Kim switched subjects and talked about his known interest in movies—particularly South Korean movies and history dramas:

> Not too long ago, I saw the South Korean movie *JSA* (Joint Security Area), which was very well done. The casting of the characters was good, too. The movie described well how even though the young soldiers are enemies, they are able to transcend ideology and understand one another as fellow humans. The movie successfully portrayed the conflict of systems, rather than human conflicts. I showed it to the military generals and the party cadre. I thought such a movie would be fine for our people to see.

Having not seen the movie, I felt uncomfortable. I did not know how to respond to his comments. When I later returned to Seoul, one of the first things I did was to borrow and watch a tape of *JSA*.

Chairman Kim then talked about South Korean television historical dramas. He asked General Ri and Secretary Kim, "How many episodes of *Yeoinchonha* [A World Under Women's Influence] did you see?" They answered that they had respectively seen up to the thirtieth and twenty-ninth episodes. Chairman Kim commented:

> I saw up to the last episode. It is a great piece of work. I encouraged everyone to see it. The ending scenes of the heroine's expression at the end of each episode was impressive. Of course, only forty percent of the story is based on facts and the rest fiction. I admire the South Korean writers and producers who made such a great piece out of the perhaps a page or less of historic records. I also liked *The First King Wanggeon* and *Empress Myungseong*. The South definitely does a great job in producing historical dramas.
>
> When Vice Marshall Jo Myung-rok returned from a visit to the United States, he said he was surprised that the officials at the State Department were fluent in Korean—perhaps because they had served in the South for some time. In Russia, only a few interpreters can speak Korean fluently . . . it is a sharp contrast.

I said in response:

> There are many Korea specialists in the United States who have an interest and affection for Korea. I think it would be very helpful if Mr. Chairman invited them to Pyongyang and frequently exchanged views with them. The United States is a country that is susceptible to public opinion. North Korea should consider a track-two approach on the civilian level. Recently, I learned the North turned down applications from Professor Robert Scalapino and former American ambassadors to South Korea to visit Pyongyang. I think it would be beneficial to be proactive and invite them first.

"Whom would you recommend to invite?" Chairman Kim asked. In my reply, I listed about ten people, including former ambassadors Donald Gregg, James Laney, Steve Bosworth, and Morton Abramowitz, Selig Harrison, Don Oberdorfer, Leon Sigal, some members of Congress, and journalists.

Chairman Kim continued:

> It seems an ambassador, whatever his name is [it was Donald Gregg], is coming here soon. Secretary Young-soon, write down these names, inform the foreign ministry of who these people are, and ask them to study the matter. It's been a year and three months since President Bush came into power. Don't you think things should somehow change a little from now on? I am optimistic about this matter. If you scrutinize the situation, is the United States not losing credibility and being isolated around the world? Somehow, they will have to change their attitude.

His comment reflected the sincere hope that our government also had for a change in the Bush administration's hostile posture towards North Korea.

However, in less than six months, these wishful expectations on the part of the North and the South turned out to be wrong.

As dinner was ending, he said to me, "Please tell President Kim that this time I have done everything according to his wishes. Also convey to him our thanks for the president's efforts to have Western countries rightly understand North Korea."

We exchanged farewells. It was eleven o'clock at night. Just like when I first met him to prepare for the inter-Korean summit two years earlier, I had spent five hours speaking to him.

'Cold Days of the Blooming Season'

On the morning of April 6, after my return from Pyongyang, I announced an inter-Korean joint press statement at a televised press conference for domestic and foreign reporters. The statement started by announcing our agreement: "In accordance with the agreements of the June 15 Joint Declaration, the inter-Korean relations that had been temporarily suspended will be restored to the previous level." The statement also included the following: "A new east coast rail line and parallel roads, and the Seoul-Shinuiju line and parallel roads on the west, will be connected as soon as possible. . . . A fourth exchange meeting of separated families will be held at Mount Kumgang from April 28. . . . A second economic cooperation promotion meeting will be held in Seoul from May 7, and depending on the progress of the meeting, a seventh round of the North-South Ministerial Talks will be held. . . . Based on the principle of brotherly love and humanitarianism, the North and the South will cooperate with each other."

As agreed upon, the fourth meeting of the separated families was held at Mount Kumgang towards the end of April, in which 849 separated family members met. In the fifth meeting, which was held in mid-September, 875 people met their separated family members. On the humanitarian level, our side completed the delivery of 200,000 tons of fertilizer by the end of May.

However, not all the agreements were carried out. We had to overcome the "cold in the blooming season" (a traditional Korean reference to the last bout of cold weather that comes in the beginning of spring). North-South relations were again temporarily hampered by a number of unfavorable developments that involved the issue of holding a summit in a third country, and American hardliners' obstructions and delaying tactics. However, when the North announced economic reforms on July 1, 2002, inter-Korean relations picked up again.

Around that time, the South Korean press published satellite pictures, obtained from the United States, of the North Korean Kumgang Dam, which showed three cracks. Instantly, this became a major subject for news coverage, and the press exaggerated concerns that "Seoul would be buried by a flood of water." As the concerns spread, the conservative hardliners intensified their criticism of North Korea.

The North Koreans responded by saying that the South Korean press was being manipulated by an American scheme to destroy North-South relations. It took a considerable time to prove the conservative press reports were groundless.

In reaction to these developments, the North notified the South that they were not coming to attend the economic cooperation promotion meeting that had been scheduled for early May. The North again suspended the inter-Korean dialogue for two months. Nevertheless, civilian exchanges continued without interruption.

Fortunately, several private sector projects were carried out without change. These included the Mount Kumgang tourism project; a visit to the North by a group of 250 people from Jeju Island (May 10–15); a visit by National Assembly member Park Geun-hye (May 11–14), a visit by representatives of the Korean National Welfare Foundation; and a joint celebration of the second anniversary of the June 15 Joint Declaration at Mount Kumgang. From the North, twenty-five North Korean safety control specialists came to the South to attend a training program concerning the operation of light water reactors (June 2–28).

* * * * * * * * *

Regarding Chairman Kim Jong-il's proposal of a summit at Irkutsk, after a prudent review, President Kim concluded that it was not acceptable. Our government decided to propose a summit at Panmunjom if Seoul was difficult for the North to accept.

On April 22, I sent a message to Secretary Kim which in summary said we agreed to an early second summit meeting some time from late June to mid-July. For the venue, we preferred the Freedom House on our side of Panmunjom, and also pointed out that meeting in Irkutsk would betray the original agreement of a return visit to Seoul and might cause misunderstanding on the part of the surrounding countries.

Secretary Kim Yong-soon returned a prompt but negative message:

> Panmunjom is an area under the jurisdiction of the United States—a nation that threatens us as an "axis of evil." It is beyond reason to hold a summit there. Also, the number of U.S. troops threatening us militar-

ily in other areas of the South is larger now than ever. The South is in a chaotic state of instability amidst anti-American and anti-government demonstrations. It is impossible to think of our General's visit to such a place. The Bush administration's hostile attitude has radically changed the situation. Historically, summit meetings were often held in a third country. What's more, Siberia is a good choice as it is related to the issue of linking with the "silk road of steel." A visit to an area of the South is absolutely impossible.

For a while, we kept to our position of demanding a return visit to Seoul, and the North's proposal for Irkutsk remained a point of contention. Later, the North sent us a message that there was no need to further argue on the venue for a summit as it had decided to withdraw its proposal altogether.

After these exchanges, neither the proposal for a summit in a third country nor Chairman Kim's return visit to Seoul was realized during the remainder of Kim Dae-jung's term.

* * * * * * * * *

June 2002 in Korea was a time in which all the people's attention and interest was focused on the World Cup Games, co-sponsored by South Korea and Japan. The outstanding Korean team advanced to the semi-finals as one of the world's four strongest teams. The entire nation was captivated and excited. The North Korean people also watched the games through broadcasts of pre-recorded tapes.

On the morning of June 29, one day before the end of the World Cup, a North Korean patrol boat launched a surprise attack on our high-speed naval boats by firing guns near Yeonpyeong Island on the west coast. The unprovoked attack sank one of our naval boats, killed six South Korean sailors, and injured eighteen others. The damage was terrible.

Before it sank, the South Korean boat—the *Chamsuri*, a 156-ton PKM 357—had been hit right in the steering room. The crew had done its best to fight back but there had been no frigates in the range to protect it. Our navy was unable to retaliate and was unilaterally defeated.

The question that drew a lot of attention and interest was why the North Korean Navy had committed such a reckless provocation at that point. An analysis report we received raised the possibility that the North Korean naval unit (the 8th Battle Group) had deliberately launched the provocation to take revenge for their humiliating defeat near Yeonpyeong Island three years earlier. The president immediately called an NSC meeting and instructed us to issue a "strong protest against the North." At the same time, he instructed us to take steps to "prevent escalation" and take a "cool response." We asked the UNC to call a General Officers Meeting at Panmunjom and to investigate the incident.

Early the next morning, the North sent us a message via hotline to inform us, "This incident was not deliberately planned or intended. We confirm that people of lower ranks on the local level were solely responsible for this unintended clash. We regret this has happened," and they added, "Let's work together to never let it happen again." Their message was such that the high-level leaders of the North were not involved in the incident—it was a localized incident. Expressing apology, the North side did not want an escalation of the incident.

As we had decided at the NSC, we sent the North a strong reply, demanding a public apology, punishment of the responsible, and assurance against the recurrence of a similar incident. The president's decision to take a cool response was a wise one. A few days later, the commander of U.S. forces in Korea officially informed our government that there was no sign that the attack had been ordered by any command higher than the 8th North Korean Naval Battle Group.

* * * * * * * * *

The hotline between the North and the South—one of the valuable results of the inter-Korean summit—had played a truly important role. However, it was not something we could make public at the time. After this exchange of communication, President Kim decided to attend the closing ceremony of the World Cup Games in Yokohama, Japan as scheduled.

In domestic politics, the opposition Grand National Party, which had been preparing for the next presidential election, seized this naval incident as an opportunity to launch a barrage of political attacks, accusing the government of having been defeated in the sea battle with the North because of its Sunshine policy. However, the people responded to these charges with a cool, not a hyped, reaction.

Tourists went on their travels to Mount Kumgang as usual, and three professors of Hanyang University departed for Kimchaek University in Pyongyang to conduct an IT program. In addition, a group of twenty-five North Korean LWR safety control engineers arrived at Daeduk on schedule to participate in a thirty-day training program.

Amidst criticism from the opposition party and the conservative press, Defense Minister Kim Dong-shin took responsibility for the "operational failure" of the incident on the west coast and resigned.

Nevertheless, by still undertaking economic reform measures, the North showed a positive attitude to the improvement of inter-Korean relations.

North Korea's Economic Reform

On July 1, 2002, North Korea embarked on economic reform with the announcement of "economic management improvement measures." The North's new measures included price reform, raising commodity prices by more than thirty times to reflect the actual market prices for farmers; a wage reform increasing wages twenty to thirty-fold; and a foreign exchange reform that raised the exchange rate closer to the realistic market rate. The new measures were intended to gradually abolish the socialist system of the rationing of food and daily necessities with the introduction of self-sufficient corporate management, equality-minded distribution reform, and a wage system differentiated according to workers' abilities.

After the end of the Cold War in 1990, which was followed by the transformation of Communist countries to a market economy, North Korea was internationally isolated as it faced economic difficulties. North Korean attempts to break through the economic blockade by improving relations with the United States were frustrated. The operation rate of industrial plants dropped to thirty percent. In addition, an energy shortage, a backward transportation network, and a series of natural disasters aggravated North Korea's chronic food problem. North Korea's economy deteriorated to the level where it had to depend entirely on food aid from the international community.

People continued to die of starvation amidst the crumbling economic structure, and as the prospect of improved relations with the United States became slimmer, it was becoming more difficult to control the populace. Under these circumstances, North Korea chose to seek a breakthrough by its "economic management reform measures."

For some years, North Korea had been working on an economic reform plan. In September 1998, the North adopted the economic concepts of cost, price, and profit and it revised its constitution to allow private ownership. It enacted or amended fourteen laws related to economic activities. North Korea had designated the Rajin-Sonbong special economic zone to practice a limited open economy. At the same time, North Korea exerted efforts to study the market economy and capitalism by sending an increased number of economic workers on overseas education programs. In addition, to create a favorable international economic environment, the North improved its strained relations with China and Russia. Chairman Kim Jong-il himself visited the scenes of reform and opening in these countries. After his visits, he asserted the need for "new thinking." Kim Jong-il issued instructions for the improvement of economic management in October 2001 to slowly prepare for major economic reform.

Peace and stability was a prerequisite to North Korea's economic reform, just as economic cooperation was essential to inducing and expanding the supply of capital and technology. Accordingly, North Korea sought improved relations with the South through the inter-Korean summit and it continued its efforts to improve relations with the United States and Japan. When the North Koreans were challenged by the Bush administration's hostile policy, they could not afford to leave their broken economy unattended. Consequently, they took measures to reform their economy. Unlike the early stages of reform and opening in China and Vietnam, the North began economic reform in a very difficult external environment in which they could not bring in foreign capital and technology.

* * * * * * * * *

In mid-July, a working-level inter-Korean meeting was held at Mount Kumgang at the request of the North side. At the meeting, the North proposed "an early implementation of the agreements with Special Envoy Lim Dong-won on April 5."

However, as a condition to resuming dialogue, our side strongly demanded that the North first make a public apology for the North Korean provocation on the west coast and a commitment to prevent future incidents, punish the responsible, and express condolences to the victims. I also directly notified the North that they should "apologize for the west coast incident and announce their participation in the Asian Games in order to change the atmosphere."

Five days later, on July 25, the North sent a message to the South Korean unification minister in which they expressed regrets for the naval clash on the west coast as a public apology, and proposed the holding of another working-level meeting at Mount Kumgang in August. This was the first time in the history of national division that the North publicly expressed a message of regret to our government. In the past, North Korea had expressed "regrets" to the U.S. government for the "ax murder incident at Panmunjom" (1976) and the submarine incursion into Gangnung (1996)—but not to the South Korean government.

Although our government thought the North Korean expression of regret was not sufficient in view of the sentiments of the people, we decided to accept their proposal for an inter-Korean dialogue. In a subsequent working-level meeting, both sides agreed on the dates for the implementation of the agreements that were reached when I went to Pyongyang as the presidential special envoy in early April.

In August, the seventh round of the North-South Ministerial Talks was held in Seoul. This meeting was followed by an inter-Korean sports meeting and the second economic cooperation promotion meeting. Also in Seoul, an August 15 National Unification Festival was held. One hundred and ten North Koreans came to Seoul to attend this significant event—the first of its kind since the division. In the previous year, about 300 South Koreans had gone to Pyongyang to participate in the first meeting.

In the last week of August, to the excitement of those people who wished for unification, there were several events held to herald the beginning of a new movement on the peninsula. At the second economic cooperation promotion meeting, which was held on August 27 in Seoul, both parties agreed to respectively hold a groundbreaking ceremony at the same time on September 18 to kick off the railway and road connection projects on the east and west coasts.

In addition, there was an announcement that the North Korean teams and cheerleaders would participate in the Busan Asian Games. This was a time of great excitement for the 70 million people of the North and the South.

For those of us who were engaged in the promotion of reconciliation and cooperation, the following September turned out to be a month full of hope and joy with the expectation of smooth progress. On September 18, groundbreaking ceremonies were held on both sides of the divide for the re-connection of the railways and roads that had been cut off for a half-century. Landmine removal work began within the DMZ to build a "peace corridor."

On September 20, the KBS Symphony Orchestra performed in Pyongyang. During the two-week period of the Asian Games, the Korean people felt the heated enthusiasm of national reconciliation, when 630 North Koreans, including 300 "cheerleader beauties," participated in the games.

In addition, there were a series of events which demonstrated revitalized North-South relations: the fifth meeting between separated family members (September 13–18); a unification soccer game in Seoul (September 7); a Munhwa Broadcasting Corporation (MBC) pop song festival in Pyongyang (September 28); a North-South joint celebration of the founding of the nation in Pyongyang (October 1–5); a visit by a group of a hundred Catholic priests to the North (October 2–9); the eighth round of the inter-Korean ministerial talks in Pyongyang; and a North Korean economic inspection group of eighteen high-ranking officials that toured industrial facilities in the South (October 26–November 3).

Rising Above the Neocon Hindrances

On August 30, 2002, Japan announced that Prime Minister Koizumi would depart on a visit to Pyongyang on September 19 for a summit with the North Korean leader. This announcement came as a surprise to the international community, including the United States. A few days earlier, the Japanese foreign ministry's Tanaka Hitoshi, Director General of the Bureau of Asian and Oceanic Affairs, had agreed to hold the summit while he was negotiating the resumption of normalization talks in Pyongyang.

Japan and North Korea had resumed their Red Cross talks in Beijing at the end of April 2002, ending a two-year deadlock in the talks. A North Korea-Japan joint press statement said that the North had agreed to investigate and inform Japan of the results of an investigation concerning missing Japanese citizens (eleven suspected abductees and forty-nine incommunicado). The North had also agreed to allow a fourth homeland visit by Japanese wives who were married to Korean husbands. There were 1,831 Japanese wives living in the North who had gone with their Korean husbands on their repatriation to the North in the past. Only forty-three Japanese wives were known to have had a homeland visit to Japan at that time.

However, rapid developments such as Koizumi's visit to Pyongyang and the relinking of the inter-Korean railways and roads triggered a strong reaction amongst American neoconservative hardliners.

Undersecretary of State for Arms Control and International Security John Bolton, (later U.S. ambassador to the UN), who had been known as a leading advocate of a hard line, abruptly came to Seoul on the pretext of delivering lectures. On August 29, he met with the defense minister and an assistant minister of the Foreign Ministry to pronounce that "North Korea's highly enriched uranium program (HEUP), which they had pursued since 1997, has reached a dangerous level," and expressed that it would impose a major obstacle to the improvement of relations with North Korea. His statement bore the message that there was no way for Washington to allow improved relations with the North under such circumstances.

With no clear evidence presented and in the absence of a joint assessment between South Korean and U.S. intelligence agencies, it was inappropriate to give credence to the untrustworthy political statement of Undersecretary Bolton, who had frequently made hostile statements. Our government decided not to be concerned with Bolton's warning until a credible joint assessment with the support of evidence by U.S. and Korean intelligence agencies was established; instead, the South decided to continue the development of inter-Korean relations. Bearing in mind the inaccurate information from the

United States about the "Kumchangni underground nuclear facilities," we held our firm position that we should not be shaken by distorted and over-blown information.

On September 17 in Pyongyang the Japan-DPRK Pyongyang Declaration was adopted at the end of Prime Minister Koizumi's summit with Chairman Kim Jong-il. Through the declaration, both sides agreed to "resume the Japan-DPRK normalization talks in October 2002," and Japan apologized for its past colonial rule. In compensation for the damage to the North during colonial rule, Japan also promised to provide (after normalization) "economic cooperation, including grant aids and long-term loans with low interest." Regarding the issue of Japanese abductees, North Korea "confirmed that it would take appropriate measures," providing a clue to the resolution of the sensitive issue.

* * * * * * * * *

In terms of inter-Korean relations, not everything was going smoothly. The U.S. Department of Defense (DoD), which had always exercised the jurisdiction of the DMZ under the United Nations Command, tried several times to interfere with the construction of a "peace corridor" in the DMZ.

Secretary of Defense Rumsfeld and other hardliners openly tried to block the projects relinking the railways and roads between the North and the South. The North and South had agreed to hold their respective ground-breaking ceremonies on September 18. The United States had known about these projects for a long time. To undertake the construction of the east coast railway line, we needed an agreement between the UNC and the DPRK to transfer the jurisdiction of the DMZ to the North and the South.

In sharp contrast to the Clinton administration, which two years earlier actively supported the construction of a peace corridor on the west coast with its full blessing, Secretary Rumsfeld refused to turn it over to South Korea.

Determining that this issue would not be resolved between the ROK defense ministry and the U.S. DoD, we chose to utilize a direct channel between the two presidential offices, the Blue House and the White House. Senior Secretary Yim Sung-joon for National Security and Foreign Affairs talked to National Security Adviser Rice on the phone and faxed her President Kim Dae-jung's resolute position on the projects, stating that he hoped the White House would resolve the issue for him.

At the DoD's instructions, General Leon LaPorte, Commander of the U.S. Forces in Korea, asked our defense minister if we really wanted to carry out the project of connecting the railway and roads in spite of North Korea's

HEU program. The deputy chief of mission at the American embassy in Seoul was asking the Blue House the same question. It was clear they were going to resist the development of inter-Korean relations based on their suspicions of North Korea's HEUP.

Our government maintained the position that "we would deal with the HEUP issue when we obtained evidence of it." Our government firmly believed that improved inter-Korean relations could contribute to the resolution of the nuclear issue. We expressed our resolute position to carry out the projects of connecting the railways and roads without fail. We strongly urged the United States to call a meeting of the General Officers Talks at Panmunjom and take necessary steps to assure the holding of the groundbreaking ceremonies. Confirming our resolute position, the U.S. side finally informed us that it would accommodate our position.

At the subsequent fourteenth meeting of the General Officers Talks between the UNC and the DPRK People's Army in Panmunjom, they agreed "to turn over the jurisdiction of an area of the DMZ (the east coast) to North and South Korea." The agreement was followed by an inter-Korean military working-level meeting that adopted "the agreement of joint North-South management of the east and west coast zones to provide military assurances for the connections of the railways and roads." This was done barely a day before the scheduled undertaking of the projects.

We did not yield to the pressure of Defense Secretary Rumsfeld and other neocons who had tried to use the suspicious HEU program as a tool to oppose and frustrate our efforts. We succeeded in carrying out our will, for the time being. If we had yielded to U.S. pressure at that point, inter-Korean relations would have encountered another crisis and the June 15 Joint Declaration might even have been discarded. It was a very difficult task, but we carried it out successfully. However, this did not end the trouble related to the DMZ.

* * * * * * * * *

By the time the work of removing landmines had been almost completed in November, the United States raised another suspicion and demanded the implementation of mutual verification. The United States alleged that "the South has removed many landmines, but the North side's landmine removal was done at a minimal level." It was common sense that the defensive strategy of the South had led to installing more landmines and the offensive-oriented North had installed fewer landmines. Our side could not understand why the United States was raising this question at that time.

Nevertheless, the North responded to the demand for mutual verification by sending a list of its inspectors to the South. The United States refused to recognize the North's response, saying that the North should submit the list directly to the UNC. The North side opposed the U.S. intervention, arguing it was not obliged to submit the list to the UNC for inspection within the zone that was turned over to joint inter-Korean management. Then the North began accusing the South of failing to exercise its given rights. The United States insisted that it would not tolerate any action that undermined the authority of the UNC.

This strange exchange of charges led to a three-week delay in removing landmines. Having determined that we should not allow a U.S. delaying tactic to interfere, we proposed that we skip the verification step and move to the construction work. Thus, we successfully pushed through and overcame another difficult hurdle.

Nevertheless, the U.S. interference was persistent. At the end of November, Major General Soligon, Deputy Chief of Staff for the UNC, held a press conference to say, "The approval of the UNC should be obtained for both travelers and materials crossing the Military Demarcation Line en route to Mount Kumgang for tourist purposes, and ROK forces should comply with the terms of the Military Armistice Agreement." This was another clear interference.

The United States alleged that the North-South draft protocol, which defined clearance procedures for people and logistic supplies to pass through the peace corridor, was a direct challenge to the authority of the UNC and an intolerable scheme to drive a wedge between South Korea and the United States. Because of this interference, the South could not send railroad ties and other materials to the North for use in the connection of the railways. This delayed the railway connection work and disrupted our plan to begin Mount Kumgang tourism by the land route in the middle of December. A trial tour by the land route to Mount Kumgang had also been scheduled for December 5.

The South Korean press criticized U.S. resistance as "interference in the inter-Korean relations and an infringement upon Korea's sovereignty," or as "the UNC's rigid hindrance," or "putting brakes on inter-Korean exchange and cooperation." Some press reports expressed suspicions that "the United States was helping a particular candidate of its preference as the presidential election approached."

Subsequently, our side successfully persuaded the North to accept an obvious clause in the North-South protocol ("The North-South joint management area is a part of the DMZ and the permit and the security of passages shall comply with the Armistice Agreement.") We did this to save face for the U.S. side. When the North officially agreed to this clause, the United States no longer had justification for interference. The presidential election ended with the victory of Democratic Party candidate Roh Moo-hyun. After a two-month delay, Mount Kumgang tourism via the land route started on February 14.

CHAPTER 13

THE SECOND NUCLEAR CRISIS

"Bold Approach" to Compel Subjection

Despite the progress made in inter-Korean and Japan-DPRK relations, President Bush's negative attitude did not change. In the internal division between the proponents of engagement and the hardliners who opposed negotiations, Bush sided with the hardliners.

President Bush's February 2002 public statement in Seoul, stating that all issues with North Korea would be resolved through dialogue, became no more than empty diplomatic rhetoric as it was ignored by the hardliners, who then began consistently employing delaying tactics.

I had conveyed the U.S. message to Chairman Kim Jong-il that Washington was willing to send Ambassador Pritchard to Pyongyang to explain U.S. policy towards the North, and Chairman Kim had accepted. After I returned from Pyongyang in April I met with Ambassador Pritchard, who had rushed to Seoul.

I conveyed to Pritchard that the North earnestly wished to improve relations with the United States, and that if the relations were normalized, North Korea would address all the U.S. security concerns.

I advised that the Bush administration refrain from directly vilifying Kim Jong-il and restrain from making inflammatory statements. I said, "The United States should seize the opportunity and send you to Pyongyang to confirm both sides' positions." I also advised, "If you want a quicker solution, you should talk directly to the North Korean leader, in consideration of their system. That said, I think it would be effective if Secretary Powell were to talk to him."

The State Department, which I considered an advocate of engagement, had maintained working-level administrative contacts with North Korea through the New York channel. Following Bush's Seoul statement of "no intention of attack or invasion," Pritchard and a White House representative had visited New York in March to have contact with the North for the first time there.

Pritchard shared with me, "The State Department is pleased with the good results of your visit to Pyongyang. However, there are those who do not trust the North Koreans and who favor 'regime change,' and they are not pleased with it. Therefore, the State Department was withholding open comment on it."

A few days later, I heard the news that the National Security Council Deputies Committee had accepted the hardliners' position that "the North Korean message that was conveyed by Special Envoy Lim Dong-won should not be regarded as North Korea's official intent to resume dialogue." Immediately, I sent a message to the North through the hotline, advising the North to express its intent of dialogue directly to the U.S. side through the New York channel.

A week later, on April 30, the White House announced that North Korea had invited Ambassador Pritchard to Pyongyang and that the United States had accepted the invitation. It seemed that the State Department finally managed to resume U.S.-DPRK talks.

However, for an entire month afterwards, the United States did not take any steps related to Ambassador Pritchard's visit.

In early June, Glenn Kessler of the *Washington Post* wrote that "the Bush administration was going through a hard time deciding its position on North Korea due to a confrontation within the administration between the moderates who support engagement and the hawkish hardliners who believe engagement would be a waste of time." The hardliners, who loathed North Korea as a member of the axis of evil, believed that North Korea was untrustworthy and that they should force the North to surrender or collapse instead of engaging it. In short, the hardliners were interfering with the moderate realists' diplomatic efforts to resolve the issues through dialogue.

In early June, President Kim Dae-jung planned to send Senior Secretary for National Security Yim Sung-joon to the White House to explain his position. However, the White House asked us to wait until the United States expressed its finalized position at the Trilateral Coordination and Oversight Group (TCOG) meeting that was to be held in mid-June.

The Clinton administration kept its word that "the South Korean government should lead the Korean Peninsula issue." During the Clinton administration, the United States made decisions only after having closely coordinated with our government. The Bush administration was different. While our cooperation through diplomatic channels with the State Department was relatively smooth, the State Department's position was often frustrated by the hawkish neocons. Most of the U.S. positions of which our government was informed reflected unilateral decisions made by the neoconservatives.

At the TCOG meeting held in San Francisco (June 17–18), the U.S. side stated its position: "President Bush is greatly concerned about the military threat and the human rights situation of North Korea. If North Korea showed a fundamental change by taking positive steps regarding the military threat and the human rights issue, the United States would take a 'bold approach' in response." This was a clear conditional offer. The United States also made it clear that it did not want to have unproductive prolonged talks; it desired a "bold package solution" to the pending issues at once.

In short, the Bush administration would not seek North Korean change by resolving the issues one by one through dialogue and negotiation. If North Korea demonstrated fundamental change through action, the United States would undertake to negotiate all the issues in a package deal. In other words, the United States preferred "North Korea's fundamental change first, negotiations later." The gradual step-by-step approach and road map that the State Department had said it would develop and explain to the North Koreans had disappeared and was replaced by a bold approach. However, this "bold approach" was not intended to engage the North but unrealistically force it to surrender. I did not believe this would work. I learned only later that John Bolton and other neocons had been preparing to raise the issue of the suspected highly enriched uranium program (HEUP).

Toward the end of June, Senior Secretary Yim Sung-joon went to Washington and met with National Security Advisor Rice and Deputy Secretary of State Armitage. Upon his return to Seoul, Senior Secretary Yim reported that he was convinced that President Bush had made a decision to support the hardliners' bold approach, rejecting the gradual approach roadmap supported by those who favored negotiation. Yim added that the hardliners' position had clearly been strengthened.

Yim said he was told by the United States that "the Bush administration, nevertheless, is not considering an unrealistic preemptive military attack on North Korea, but intends to bring about a bold transformation of North Korea's system and policy through non-military means." According to Yim's analysis, the State Department was likely to promote Ambassador Pritchard's visit to the North, but it was questionable whether the State Department could overcome the hardliners' opposition. Then, the second naval clash on the west coast at the end of June effectively killed the plan for a visit by Ambassador Pritchard.

Around that time, the *Washington Post* published a column entitled, "Opportunity to Change Dangerous Policy," which made the following points:

> The Bush administration is making repeated failures in its North Korea policy with an unreasonably belligerent approach. It is damaging the accomplishment of the previous administration and the U.S.-Korea alliance. The preconditions imposed by the Bush administration are out of the basic practice of diplomacy. Such an approach does not only increase tension on the Korean Peninsula but also fails to get the support of the international community. The Bush administration should engage in serious negotiations.

Secretary Powell and the negotiation supporters at the State Department continued their hard struggle against the adverse currents imposed by the hardliners. I had delivered to Chairman Kim Jong-il a verbal message that Secretary Powell wanted to meet Foreign Minister Paek Nam-sun in Brunei. At the end of July, Secretary Powell held a fifteen-minute meeting with Paek Nam-sun on the sidelines of the ASEAN Regional Forum (ARF) in Brunei. I learned that at their meeting Powell told Paek that "the United States does not have a hostile intent against North Korea and it will send a special envoy to Pyongyang." Paek welcomed this.

Despite the hardliners' opposition, Secretary Powell sent Ambassador Pritchard to attend an August 7 concrete-pouring ceremony at the light water reactor site held by KEDO in Kumho, North Korea, to show that the United States had not abandoned its commitment to the Agreed Framework.

James Kelly's Visit to Pyongyang

North-South relations, which had been moving along smoothly and energetically for a year, came to a halt. A second nuclear crisis was approaching. In early October 2002, President Bush sent James Kelly, Assistant Secretary of State for East Asia and Pacific Affairs, to Pyongyang. Kelly told the North Koreans that the United States had convincing evidence of North Korea's HEUP and demanded its elimination.

Consequently, the Bush administration took steps to abrogate the U.S.-DPRK Agreed Framework, driving the North to resume its plutonium nuclear program which had been suspended for eight years.

* * * * * * * * *

In March, the American news media published reports prepared by the U.S. DoD in its Nuclear Posture Review (NPR). The reports created a controversy within the international community. The NPR listed seven countries, including North Korea, as potential targets of a nuclear attack, discussing the sensitive development of earth-penetrating nuclear weapons able to destroy heavily-fortified underground bunkers. Since the NPR had included non-nuclear weapon states on the list of potential targets of a nuclear attack, the United States was criticized that it was bringing down the Non-Proliferation Treaty (NPT), in accordance with which the United States was committed to refrain from the threat or use of nuclear weapons against non-nuclear weapon states.

In the mid-1980s, when Gorbachev became the leader of the Soviet Union, he undertook negotiations with the United States for nuclear disarmament, aiming at building "a twenty-first century world free of nuclear weapons." Since then the United States and the Soviet Union had produced a successful agreement to dispose of all intermediate-range nuclear missiles (INF) and to eliminate one-third of their long-range strategic nuclear weapons (START I).

The two superpowers also signed a Strategic Arms Reduction Treaty II (START II), and the Comprehensive Test Ban Treaty (CTBT), which would ban all nuclear tests. However, President Bush refused to ratify these agreements, and unilaterally withdrew from the Anti-Ballistic Missile Treaty (ABM). President Bush's actions were perceived as clearly going against the current of global aspirations for the elimination of nuclear weapons.

On the night of September 25, President Bush called President Kim Dae-jung, who had just returned that morning from attending the ASEM Summit in Copenhagen. Senior Secretary for National Security Yim Sung-joon and I were with the president when he received the call in his office.

President Bush said he had decided to send Assistant Secretary Kelly to Pyongyang in early October. The United States had decided to engage North Korea to continue the progress that President Kim had made. Then he reiterated his earlier assertion: "If Kim Jong-il wants peaceful relations, he should give up his nuclear program and pull back his conventional forces to the rear." He added since the situation surrounding North Korea was different from Iraq, the way to make peace should be different. The next day Washington announced Special Envoy Kelly's visit to Pyongyang.

We were all confused by President Bush's call. We could not believe that he had suddenly changed his position. We knew he was fully preoccupied with the attack on Iraq. Nevertheless, we made the positive assessment that Bush might have at last decided to have dialogue with North Korea given the recent positive developments on the Korean Peninsula, which included dazzling progress in inter-Korean relations; North Korea's promotion of opening and economic reform; Japanese prime minister Koizumi's visit to Pyongyang and the resumption of normalization talks between Japan and North Korea; and the ASEM's "declaration of peace on the Korean Peninsula." However, it later turned out that our assessment was a miscalculation.

*　*　*　*　*　*　*　*　*

On October 2, the Kelly team came to Seoul from Tokyo before their trip to Pyongyang. At the request of the United States, Senior Secretary Yim and I received Kelly's party, accompanied by Ambassador Tom Hubbard, in a small reception room to listen to the purpose of their visit to the North.

The team was composed of Ambassador Charles Pritchard of the State Department; David Straub, Director of Korean affairs at the State Department; Michael Green, Director of Asian affairs at NSC; Air Force Major General Michael Dunn of the Joint Chiefs of Staff; Mary Tighe, Korea Desk Officer at the Defense Department; a Korean American Foreign Service Officer from the State Department's Office of Korean Affairs; and a State Department interpreter.

Unlike other times, Assistant Secretary Kelly's expression looked high-strung. He said he was going to Pyongyang to inform them that the United States had clear evidence of North Korea's uranium enrichment program. He said: "We will make it clear that the abolishment of their HEUP would be the precondition to dialogue." Kelly emphasized the purpose of his visit was to "notify" them, and not to "negotiate" with them. He said he would not expect an answer from the North Koreans, but he would listen to their position if they expressed it.

Reading from a summary of his talking points to the North Koreans, he said he would generally raise the concerns that the United States had thought were important so far, including the plutonium nuclear program, long-range missiles, and conventional forces. However, he said, the HEUP issue was most important to American interests.

Everyone on our side listening to Kelly was simply shocked. This was so different from what we had heard from President Bush. We were shocked at Kelly's words that he was going to Pyongyang "not to negotiate but to notify" them of the new development. Kelly's visit seemed to reflect the neocon hardliners' attempt to force North Korea to surrender from a high-handed posture, by unilaterally telling the North to eliminate the HEUP with a message that there would no dialogue unless the North admitted to and got rid of the program.

The American neocon hardliners alleged that the provision of heavy fuel oil and light water reactors was a "symbol of diplomatic humiliation" and the Agreed Framework was the wrong solution. We finally learned the true nature of the "bold approach." We were at a loss for words.

At the time, Korean affairs experts were commenting that the neocon hardliners had a negative perception of the trends developing to end the Cold War on the Korean Peninsula. The hardliners did not welcome improved inter-Korean relations through the North-South summit or the reconnection of the railways and roads between the North and the South. Neither did they welcome North Korea's change through economic reforms or the holding of the Japan-DPRK summit meeting.

Some neocon hardliners even frankly claimed that prolonged intensification of tension on the Korean Peninsula would be in the long-term interests of U.S. strategy in East Asia. Those who supported a hawkish policy on North Korea were led by Vice President Dick Cheney, Defense Secretary Donald Rumsfeld, Deputy Defense Secretary Paul Wolfowitz, and Undersecretary of State John Bolton. They relentlessly advocated for the collapse of the regimes in Iraq and North Korea.

In 1997, these neoconservative hardliners had established the "Project for the New American Century" (PNAC) to protect U.S. supremacy in the twenty-first century. They believed that the United States should increase its defense spending to modernize its armed forces and confront hostile countries to protect American values and interests. They further believed that the United States should establish an advantageous international order based on American values to ensure the security and prosperity of the United States.

They believed that there would not be peace until the democratization of all the countries of the world, particularly those countries in the Middle East. The Bush doctrine of the preemptive elimination of regimes that constituted the "axis of evil" stemmed from this belief.

* * * * * * * * *

On the morning of October 5, Kelly's team returned to Seoul from a two-night and three-day visit to Pyongyang. After completing his report to Washington, Kelly visited us in the afternoon at half past two to provide an hour-long debriefing on the outcome of his visit. The debriefing was held at the foreign minister's residence and was attended by all the members of Kelly's team and Ambassador Hubbard. From our side, Foreign Minister Choi Sung-hong, Deputy Foreign Minister Lee Tae-sik, Senior Secretary for National Security Yim, and I attended the meeting.

The members of Kelly's team looked tense and were acting cautiously. Assistant Secretary Kelly merely read a prepared summary report, which read as follows.

Mr. Kelly and his party arrived in Pyongyang on the morning of October 3 and checked into the Koryo Hotel. In the afternoon, Kelly had a meet-

Special Envoy James Kelly (*left*) debriefed the author upon his return from Pyongyang. The mood was gloomy as North Korea's uranium enrichment program raised concerns (October 5, 2002). Courtesy Lim Dong-won.

ing with Vice Foreign Minister Kim Gye-gwan, who denied the existence of the HEUP. The next morning on October 4, Kelly met with Kim Gye-gwan again and heard him repeat his denial. After that meeting, Kelly's team paid a courtesy visit to Kim Young-nam, President of the SPA Presidium. At four o'clock that afternoon, Kelly and his party finally met with First Vice Minister of Foreign Affairs Kang Sok-ju, who said he was updating Kelly on the all-night discussion amongst those concerned.

First Vice Foreign Minister Kang then defiantly acknowledged the existence of the uranium enrichment program that the United States had issue with. According to Kelly, Kang protested: "When the United States designates North Korea as the axis of evil and threatens to launch a preemptive attack with their enormous quantity of nuclear weapons, North Korea has no option but to develop nuclear weapons or even something more powerful for the protection of national security." Kang also rudely warned, "If the United States wants war, North Korea is ready to fight."

At the same time, Kang said that his country was willing to resolve the issue through negotiation and that it would be possible to address U.S. security concerns if the United States would cease its hostile policy. As conditions to negotiation, Kang listed U.S. respect for the sovereignty of North

Korea, conclusion of a non-aggression treaty, and the lifting of economic sanctions. In conclusion, Kang hoped for a package solution by the highest levels of the two countries.

Kelly said he was astonished by Kang's statements and attitude, adding that he could not say anything more, except that the United States would come up with some measures to cope with the North Korean response.

I was shocked that North Korea had admitted the existence of an HEUP. Yet, I said, "One needs to be prudent in accepting the North Koreans' exaggerated and emotional language." I raised a question of ambiguity regarding whether the North's expression "why should not we have our own nuclear weapons?" was an admission of the HEUP's existence or the right to have nuclear weapons. In response, Major General Dunn alleged, "Among our delegation, we had three members fluent in Korean (one interpreter, a Korean-American foreign service officer, and Straub) and they all had the same understanding. It was also repeated for confirmation."

Then I said, "Perhaps North Korea wants a rapid package solution without a delay through talks on the level of the highest authorities concerned." I had thought it was possible that North Korea had used harsh but ambiguous language to attract the attention of the United States in search of a path to a package solution.

My assessment of North Korea's strategy at that time was either the North would push the United States, which was fully focused on its attack on Iraq, to engage the North for a speedy deal, or taking advantage of the situation, the North might accelerate its nuclear development. Our request for a copy of a transcript of Kelly's meeting with Kang Sok-ju was declined by the U.S. team.

The Truth about the Highly Enriched Uranium (HEU) Program?

On October 7, 2002, forty days after Undersecretary John Bolton informed our government of the "seriousness of North Korea's HEUP," three members of the U.S. intelligence community (IC) came to Seoul to brief our side on their assessment of North Korea's HEUP. Senior Secretary Yim and I attended the briefing.

The American intelligence community's assessment, in summary, was that

> it was judged certain that North Korea was constructing an underground highly enriched uranium (HEU) facility. The location was not identified. North Korea had already obtained materials, including aluminum pipes, to make Pakistani-type centrifuges. If the program pro-

ceeded smoothly, North Korea would be able to produce enough highly enriched uranium to make two to three bombs a year by the second half of 2004.

As was later made public, the CIA submitted an intelligence assessment report to the U.S. Congress in mid-November 2002, shortly before the abolition of the U.S.-DPRK Agreed Framework. The substance of the report was almost identical to what I had heard from the U.S. IC members when they came to Seoul. In summary, the report stated that there was compelling evidence that North Korea had started building a centrifuges facility to produce HEU and it was estimated that the North could produce enough weapons-grade uranium for two or more nuclear weapons per year when fully operational, which could be as soon as mid-decade (i.e., 2005).

Having served as the director of the National Intelligence Service, I asked the IC briefers several questions, but I did not hear satisfactory answers from them. I pointed out to them that it would be risky and dangerous to present the "information" predicting a worst-case scenario without presenting any new reliable evidence as regarding the "intelligence." I also reminded them of the misjudgment about the Kumchangni underground facility, which had been cleared of the wrongful accusation by an inspection visit. I questioned the credibility of the U.S. intelligence assessment.

I was suspicious of the possible political motivations on the part of the hardliners to distort and exploit the information for their own cynical purposes. I said to them, "The ROK and U.S. intelligence agencies should cooperate with each other more closely to collect more reliable information and make a more accurate judgment."

North Korea's nuclear development had been a top concern for the intelligence communities of both the United States and the ROK, and therefore, a subject of steady exchange of information, joint analysis, and evaluation. The suspicions of North Korea's HEUP were published at length in *Jane's* and the *Washington Times* in 1997. Although the intelligence agencies of both countries had closely cooperated and exchanged information on the HEUP, no specific evidence was obtained. Until convincing evidence was discovered, I felt we needed to be cautious.

Our intelligence agency said they had also received the same information from the United States around the time I was briefed. According to our agency's intelligence report, "Since the aluminum pipes that the North had imported could be used for multiple purposes—including the production of missiles—it was necessary to find out more about their use. And there was no evidence yet showing that North Korea had secured essential equipment and materials required for the construction of an HEU plant." The report also said more pointedly that no signs of the construction of an HEU facility had ever been detected. In view of this report, I could only determine that the U.S. briefing was weak, lacking supporting information, and based on an overblown assessment of North Korea's technology.

Normally, an exchange of intelligence information between states is done through their intelligence organizations. The way in which a senior official of the Bush administration suddenly showed up in Seoul to notify us of politically-motivated information was not the standard procedure for information-sharing.

As we were pushing to get inter-Korean relations in full swing that summer, it seemed predictable that the U.S. hardliners would openly interfere with the governments of South Korea and Japan. As we saw in the case of the Kumchangni site, it was possible that some hardliners might have exaggerated and distorted the information to reflect the worst possible scenario.

The Bush administration's invasion of Iraq the following year was a telling example. While suspicions were growing about the justification for the Iraq War, the U.S. Congress undertook an investigation and the Senate Intelligence Committee subsequently released an investigation report (July 9, 2004). The report concluded, "The suspicions of the Iraqi nuclear development program or the accumulation of biological and chemical weapons were either exaggerated or fabricated without evidence, and no evidence for Iraq's sponsoring of terrorism was found." The report also charged, "President Bush started the war in Iraq based on wrong information that he pumped up and caused the loss of many precious American lives and resources, damaging American credibility in the international community." From that time, popular American support for President Bush started rapidly falling.

Based on all available information at the time, my assessment of North Korea's HEUP was that although North Korea's plutonium program was well-known, it was difficult for me to accept the assumption that the North was going to develop an HEUP, while it would struggle to keep its plutonium program. If the Agreed Framework were to be abrogated, it would be easier for the North to resume the plutonium program than to undertake a fresh HEUP.

According to experts, an HEUP would require three elements: natural uranium, enrichment technology, and necessary equipment and facilities. North Korea had a considerable deposit of natural uranium and even a refining plant, but the North was not known to have acquired the industrial technology to manufacture centrifuges. There were no signs that the North had imported centrifuges from abroad. However, I did think it was possible for the North to import equipment and parts to develop a low enrichment uranium (LEU) technology to enrich its domestically-excavated natural uranium to the level of three to four percent.

It was also possible that North Korea might have wanted to produce its own fuel for the light water reactors that would be turned over to the North in the future. This type of LEU activity was different from an HEUP to produce weapons-grade uranium of ninety percent or higher. The LEU activity would not violate the norm of international non-proliferation, if transparency were guaranteed.

To produce a uranium atomic bomb, comparable to the one that was dropped on Hiroshima, it would require 25 kilograms of highly enriched uranium. To produce that much HEU, it would take the full operation of 1,000 centrifuges for one year, letting the centrifuges run at 50,000 to 70,000 revolutions per minute—a speed that is twice as fast as a MIG jet engine.

This operation would require a high-performance motor and an electronic braking system, which, I assessed, North Korea was not able to manufacture with its own technology yet. I also judged that it was almost impossible for the North to import those types of equipment since they were prohibited for trade. It would not be easy even to smuggle in some limited quantity of centrifuges for experimental purposes. It was nearly impossible for North Korea to avoid international surveillance while building a production facility capable of making two to three bombs a year.

A few years later, a new allegation surfaced. Allegedly, North Korea's HEUP had been assisted by Pakistan. President Pervez Musharraf of Pakistan alleged in his September 2005 biography that "Dr. Abdul Qadeer Khan provided the uranium enrichment technology through centrifuges and had turned over about twenty centrifuges to North Korea since 1999." Even if this information were true, as of 2002, the U.S. intelligence assessment that North Korea was constructing a HEU facility with thousands of centrifuges to produce enough HEU to make two to three bombs a year from the second half of 2004 would have still been too far from the truth.

Trilateral Summit in Los Cabos

Special Envoy Kelly's return from Pyongyang gave a burst of encouragement to the neocon hardliners, who had demanded the abolition of the U.S.-DPRK Agreed Framework, which they had opposed from the beginning. They were boosted by North Korea's "admission of guilt" and by their allegation that the North had been violating the Agreed Framework. Now that implementing the agreement was impossible, they insisted that the United States had no choice but to abolish the Agreed Framework. If the agreement was abrogated, it was clear that North Korea would resume its plutonium nuclear program and trigger a "second nuclear crisis."

Our government had to exert its best efforts to maintain the commitment of the Agreed Framework. The NSC Standing Committee reestablished the government's position on October 10 as according to the following points:

- We would strengthen the exchange of information with friendly nations regarding North Korea's HEUP;
- Abolishment of the Agreed Framework would be dangerous, and we would use diplomacy to prevent its abrogation through various approaches;
- As agreed in the ROK-U.S. summit (February 2002), the issue of North Korea's weapons of mass destruction should be resolved peacefully, and military action should be excluded;
- We would try to arrange a visit by North Korean first vice foreign minister Kang Sok-ju to Washington in return for Special Envoy Kelly's visit to Pyongyang.
- We would develop a joint measure at the upcoming trilateral Korea-U.S.-Japan summit meeting in Los Cabos.

The Bush administration was preparing for an invasion of Iraq, and it did not want the HEU issue to be exposed until after Congress passed the authorization to use military force in Iraq. The bill to authorize the use of military force passed in Congress on October 11. The American hardliners leaked the HEU information to the press on October 12, a day after President Bush presided over an NSC meeting where their position was endorsed. It was two weeks before the next midterm elections.

As the news of North Korea's HEUP spread through headlines, an atmosphere conducive to the international bashing of North Korea was formed. In particular, the South Korean press published sizable articles on the topic, and the conservative press started publishing exaggerations and distortions.

President Kim decided to persuade President Bush first. He saw to it that Unification Minister Chung Se-hyon delivered a message to Chairman Kim Jong-il when he went to Pyongyang for the eighth round of North-South Ministerial Talks (October 19-23). He wanted him to convey that "the development or possession of weapons of mass destruction would not be tolerated," and that they should "take proactive steps to engage the United States by sending First Vice Foreign Minister Kang Sok-ju to Washington." In any situation, he wanted them to take no steps that would contribute to abolish the Agreed Framework. He also said they should be sure to announce North Korea's position before the trilateral summit in Los Cabos.

On October 25, one day before the trilateral summit at Los Cabos, Pyongyang released a foreign ministry spokesman's statement to announce its official position. It was a long statement, summarized below:

> The DPRK recently received the American special envoy in the hope that this might help fundamentally solve hostile relations with the United States and settle outstanding issues. Regretfully, however, without producing any evidence, he asserted that the DPRK has been actively engaged in an enriched uranium program in order to produce nuclear weapons, thereby violating the DPRK-U.S. Agreed Framework. He even intimidated the DPRK by saying that there would be no dialogue with the United States unless the DPRK halted its program, and that DPRK-Japan and North-South relations would be jeopardized as well.
>
> As far as the nuclear issue is concerned, the United States has massively stockpiled nuclear weapons in South Korea, thereby threatening the DPRK and pursuing a hostile policy.
>
> The United States thus first violated the Agreed Framework. Under Article 1 of the framework, the United States is obliged to provide light water reactors by 2003, but eight years after the start of construction, it has so far only dug a foundation hole. Due to this delay, we have suffered a loss of electricity.
>
> Under Article 2 of the framework, the two sides are obliged to move toward full normalization of relations. Over the last eight years, however, the United States has persistently pursued a hostile policy and maintained economic sanctions. It has said we are part of the axis of evil and it is trying to stifle us.
>
> Under Article 3 of the framework, the United States is obliged to give formal assurances to the DPRK against the threat or use of nuclear weapons. However, the United States listed us as a target of its preemptive nuclear attack. The U.S. designation of our country as an axis of evil and the inclusion of us in its list of targets for preemptive nuclear strikes is a clear declaration of war against the DPRK, as it totally nullified the DPRK-U.S. Joint Statement and Agreed Framework, and is also gross violation of the basic spirit of the NPT.
>
> Under these circumstances, the DPRK has made itself very clear to the U.S. special envoy that the DPRK was entitled to possess not only nuclear weapons but any type of weapon more powerful than that, so as to defend its sovereignty and right to existence from the ever-growing nuclear threat by the United States.
>
> We also made it clear that we were ready to seek a negotiated settlement of this issue on the following three conditions: the U.S. recognition of the DPRK's sovereignty, the assurance of non-aggression, and no hindrance of economic development.

> If the United States legally assures the DPRK of non-aggression, including the non-use of nuclear weapons, we will be ready to clear the security concerns of the United States.

President Kim attempted to persuade President Bush directly at the Asia Pacific Economic Cooperation (APEC) meeting in Mexico's famous Los Cabos resort, during which a trilateral summit was held on October 26.

From the U.S. side, Secretary Powell, National Security Adviser Rice, and White House Chief of Staff Card were attending the summit; from our side, Foreign Minister Choi Sung-hong, myself as Special Advisor for National Security and Unification, and Senior Secretary for National Security and Foreign Affairs Yim Sung-joon were at the summit. From the Japanese side, Deputy Cabinet Minister Abe Shinjo and Counselor Takano attended the meeting.

President Kim made his statement, which is summarized as follows:

> We do not condone North Korea's nuclear development. However, in view of the situation on the Korean Peninsula, we should peacefully resolve this nuclear issue. Let's mobilize all our diplomatic efforts through international cooperation. A few days ago, I sent a message to the North Korean leader through my unification minister, who was visiting Pyongyang for a meeting. The message explained our position and I asked him to present North Korea's proposal for the resolution of the issue. Yesterday, the North released a foreign ministry spokesman's statement.
>
> North Korea has proposed a package solution for the dismantlement of its nuclear program in return for a non-aggression treaty. Therefore, we can move forward to resolve this issue through diplomatic negotiations. We must be very prudent and very cautious if any of us wish to take measures to abolish the Geneva Agreed Framework in consideration of the dangerous risks involved. We should never provide North Korea with the pretext to restart its nuclear activities to make nuclear weapons.

President Bush reconfirmed that the United States had no intention of attacking or invading North Korea and that there had been no change in his will for a peaceful resolution, as he had declared in Seoul in February that year. Bush also said, "I am not like a Texas cowboy who pulls out two guns to shoot at random."

Then Bush said, "Kim Jong-il showed himself as a dangerous man through his nuclear program. But, I think he is honest, because he confessed the truth (probably in reference to North Korea's admission of the HEUP). The reason he confessed the truth is that he understood that our intent was serious, and he needs assistance from the United States." Bush also said, "I am optimistic that we can peacefully resolve the North Korean nuclear issue. But we should continue to exercise pressure on them through international cooperation."

Collapse of the Agreed Framework

As soon as the Los Cabos trilateral summit was over, the hardliners in Washington who had raised the issue of a suspected HEUP started taking steps to terminate the provision of heavy fuel oil to the North. Their logic was that since North Korea had violated the Agreed Framework first, the United States should not continue oil provision.

Although it was obvious that the termination of heavy fuel oil provision would mean the abrogation of the Agreed Framework—which would trigger the restart of North Korea's nuclear activities to produce plutonium nuclear bombs—the hardliners were determined to do so.

Around that time, the United States had mid-term elections on November 5, in which the Republican Party gained control of both the Senate and the House of Representatives. The election results were regarded as the American people's support for President Bush, who was committed to invading Iraq.

Another Trilateral Coordination and Oversight Group (TCOG) meeting to coordinate the policy on North Korea was held in Tokyo on November 8 and 9. The U.S. side claimed, "Since we anticipated no positive behavior from North Korea, it was necessary to immediately take sanction measures." The United States insisted that, to begin with, the heavy oil delivery for November should have been suspended. The United States pushed for recalling the oil tanker that had already left the port of Singapore two days earlier.

The United States insinuated that it would not make a budget request for heavy oil provision and it would soon suspend the construction of the light water reactors. In other words, the United States would soon nullify the Agreed Framework.

The United States position was that unless North Korea gave up the HEUP, there would be no talks with the North, and inevitably, economic and diplomatic sanctions would be applied. Under these circumstances, the United States opposed any new South Korean projects for the North. They wanted South Korea to be cautious regarding ongoing projects as well.

South Korean Head of Delegation and Deputy Foreign Minister Lee Tae-sik (later ambassador to Washington) proposed a cautious proposition based on government instruction:

We ought to be prudent about terminating the oil shipment because it might trigger the resumption of North Korea's nuclear activities. We should send the November shipment on schedule, while employing diplomatic efforts to persuade the North. We can send Korea Energy Development Organization (KEDO) Executive Chairman Chang Sun-sup and KEDO Secretary General Charles Kartman to Pyongyang immediately to listen to North Korea's explanation and to seek positive action by the North. If they respond negatively, we can issue a warning that the fuel oil provision could be suspended.

The Japanese side supported our position. Prior to the KEDO executive board meeting, we had worked with Japan diplomatically to prevent a recall of the oil tanker. We also sent President Kim's intentions to the White House via fax, including that "we expected a wise judgment and decision by President Bush."

Consequently, Washington informed us, "In deference to the views of Korea and Japan, the United States agrees on the November shipment of fuel oil. However, we disapprove a visit by KEDO Secretary General Kartman, who is an American, for fear that his visit might give the wrong signal, as if the United States wants to negotiate with North Korea."

The KEDO executive board meeting on November 14 announced: "The November shipment will be provided as normal. However, further shipment of fuel oil will be suspended beginning December, unless North Korea takes positive action, and KEDO activities will be reevaluated."

The following day President Bush issued a statement that welcomed KEDO's decision. Perhaps conscious of the North's demand for the conclusion of a non-aggression treaty, President Bush reiterated that the United States did not intend to invade North Korea. The United States had expressed its willingness to take a "bold approach" if North Korea had taken steps first. However, President Bush said, "Now that North Korea's covert nuclear weapons program has come to light, we are unable to pursue this approach."

It became clear that the Bush administration would not engage the North before the latter gave up its nuclear program. This position was maintained until North Korea's first nuclear test in October 2006.

In response to Bush's statement, North Korea, stressing the importance of the Agreed Framework, warned that the United States would be responsible for causing a complete breakdown of the Agreement Framework if it cancelled the heavy fuel oil shipment. At the same time, the North asked the European Union to play a constructive role to simultaneously resolve the concerns of the United States and the DPRK.

* * * * * * * * *

President Bush was accelerating preparations for an Iraqi invasion. Throughout many countries around the world—including American allies in Europe—dissatisfaction with and opposition to President Bush's arrogant attitude—one geared towards world hegemony by "force," not by "leadership," and by unilateralism not by multilateralism—and to his bellicose and arbitrary decision to attack Iraq in defiance of the international community's protests, were turning into anti-Americanism. Criticism of the Bush doctrine, which was characterized by "preemptive attack," "regime change," and "dividing countries," was spreading worldwide.

In South Korea, anti-American candlelight vigils were being held across the country. The acquittal and repatriation of two American soldiers who operated an armored vehicle that had killed two Korean schoolgirls set off anti-American resentment throughout the nation that triggered the vigils. The demonstrators demanded President Bush's immediate apology and the revision of the Status of Forces Agreement (SOFA); they were more like "anti-Bush protests" rather than anti-American demonstrations.

At that time, the *New York Times* published a column by Nicholas D. Kristof, entitled "Hold Your Nose and Negotiate" (December 20). The column said, in summary:

> Washington's failure to engage North Korea has in a few months turned a minor problem (a uranium program that would take years to produce weapons) into a major crisis (the restarting of a reactor with enough plutonium to produce five additional warheads). To avoid a catastrophic war, the administration should soon seek diplomatic solutions in cooperation with South Korea.
>
> There are three choices. First, we can negotiate with North Korea, which shows some signs of seeking the same kind of tentative opening to the West that China pursued in the late 1970's. . . . Second, we can ignore North Korea, which Washington is trying now, but it's not working. Third, we can launch a military strike on the Yongbyon nuclear facilities. But North Korea would probably respond by turning Seoul into a "sea of flames" and bring a missile attack on Japan, and there is a danger of escalation to an all-out war.
>
> The only option is negotiation. Diplomacy backed by force is fine, but force with no diplomacy will not succeed. Granted there's no good North Korea policy, but it's still worth finding a better one, like holding our nose and negotiating.

Heavy fuel oil shipments came to halt—it was announced they would be suspended beginning with the December shipment. Having quietly observed the development of the situation for about a month, North Korea finally issued a foreign ministry statement on December 12. It said, "Since the United States has actually suspended heavy fuel oil shipments, we have decided to unfreeze our nuclear program, and restart the operation and construction of the nuclear facilities, which had been put on freeze under the condition of heavy fuel oil delivery and which we now need for the production of electricity."

A week after the announcement, the North Koreans went into action. They removed all the seals and monitoring equipment from the nuclear facilities in the presence of IAEA inspectors and started taking steps to unfreeze, including preparations for loading fuel rods. On December 31, they expelled the IAEA inspectors. What everybody had been concerned about was actually happening.

At that time, the Bush administration, preoccupied with its preparation for Iraqi invasion, was not in a position to launch a preemptive strike in response to such North Korean actions. Nevertheless, the Washington hardliners were determined to ignore the North Korean response, for they preferred to maintain their hardline policy of pressure and containment, rather than negotiating with the North.

The United States would only reiterate its previous position that it would not be intimidated by North Korea's blackmail and that North Korea should first discard its nuclear program. Defense Secretary Rumsfeld warned that "the United States was capable of fighting two wars at the same time, and North Korea would learn that it had made a mistake by recklessly taking advantage of the Iraqi situation."

One thing was clear. Whereas the Clinton administration had maintained a freeze on the dangerous threat of the North Korean plutonium program by trying to obtain the transparency of the suspected uranium enrichment program through improved relations, the Bush administration had suspended the provision of heavy fuel oil based on the unclear suspicions of an HEUP, killing the Agreed Framework. The Bush administration had driven the Korean Peninsula to an extremely dangerous crisis point.

North Korea's unfreezing of its nuclear program was followed by an announcement on January 10, 2003, that it was withdrawing from the Nuclear Non-Proliferation Treaty, which made the situation even worse. The United States and North Korea were like two trains running toward a head-on collision.

* * * * * * * * *

On December 19, 2002, the South Korean people elected the Democratic Party's candidate Roh Moo-hyun as their next president. The election outcome was disappointing to the conservatives and the neoconservatives who had hoped the conservative Grand National Party's candidate, Lee Hoi-chang, would win.

Even nearing the end of its term, the Kim Dae-jung administration did its best to find a solution to the nuclear issue. We took three approaches. First, we continued to persuade the Bush administration. Second, we did everything we could do through diplomacy to gain the support of China, Japan, and the international community. Third, we continued to persuade North Korea. From the beginning of the new year, we sent our vice ministers and deputy ministers of foreign affairs to Russia, China, and Japan. Perhaps as the result of these accentuated diplomatic efforts, these three countries echoed the same voice calling for the United States to engage North Korea.

Senior Secretary for National Security Yim Sung-joon went to Washington carrying a "proposal" from President Kim Dae-jung. Yim was sent to Washington against the political backdrop of the election of the Democratic Party's presidential candidate. Even as the Bush administration sent out the rhetoric of a "diplomatic solution" while aggravating the situation by refusing to engage North Korea, President Kim thought that as the masters of the Korean Peninsula we should speak out. Our assessment was that although the American hardliners preferred long-term international pressure, we were skeptical of its efficacy. We were concerned that such an approach would only give North Korea more time to develop nuclear weapons. Our government argued in favor of an early dialogue in order to prevent deterioration of the situation. It did not take long to prove that we were right.

In Washington, Senior Secretary Yim met with several high-level officials of the Bush administration, including Secretary of State Powell, Deputy Secretary Armitage, Defense Secretary Rumsfeld, National Security Advisor Rice, and JCS Chairman General (Richard) Meyers, to explain President Kim's proposal. The gist of the proposal was:

> If North Korea explains the truth of the uranium issue and expresses its willingness to resolve the issue, the United States would guarantee on paper non-aggression and resume fuel oil shipments. North Korea would refreeze its nuclear facilities, and then the United States and the DPRK could engage in negotiations to simultaneously resolve the issues of the nuclear program and normalization of relations.

The secretary of state and the national security advisor responded positively, expecting the Seoul government to persuade Pyongyang. However,

Defense Secretary Rumsfeld did not support the proposal but simply said, "I understand President Kim's proposal." Upon his return to Seoul, Senior Secretary Yim reported on the attitudes of the American officials: "In view of the Korean people's choice in the presidential election, North Korea's strong reaction, the advice of China and Russia for dialogue, and the need to concentrate on the Iraqi war, the hawks seemed to have taken a step back in order to see how the doves deal with the situation."

After listening to Senior Secretary Yim's report, President Kim made a decision to send me again as his special envoy to Pyongyang. President Kim had only one month left in office, but he still wanted to do his best until the last day.

Winter in Pyongyang

On January 27, 2003, I visited Pyongyang again as a presidential envoy, sent to resolve the nuclear issue. Two weeks prior, I had sent a message to Secretary Kim Yong-soon of the North that "President Kim Dae-jung was going to dispatch Special Envoy Lim Dong-won to discuss with Chairman Kim Jong-il the outcome of profound consultations with the U.S. side on the nuclear issue and to come up with necessary measures." On January 22, the North notified us that it welcomed the dispatch of a special envoy.

To accompany me, I chose Yim Sung-joon, Senior Secretary for National Security at the Blue House. At President Kim's instruction, the envoy team was also to include a representative from the president-elect's side. Dr. Lee Jong-seok, a member of the transition team, was selected to join our team. He later served as deputy director of the National Security Council and afterwards as unification minister during the Roh administration.

It was snowing as my party was aboard ROK Air Force Three flying over the west coast to Pyongyang. It occurred to me that as the head of the South Korean team on nuclear negotiations, I had successfully produced the Joint Declaration for the Denuclearization of the Korean Peninsula at the end of 1991. Now I was back at the task of discussing the nuclear issue with the North Koreans. Reminding myself of arms control theory, I reflected again on the essential nature of the North Korean nuclear issue.

The nuclear issue was bound to persist until mutual confidence was built. According to arms control theory, nuclear disarmament was only possible in an environment in which nuclear weapons were not needed. Fundamentally, the North Korean nuclear issue was a product of the hostile relationship between the United States and North Korea. I determined that the resolution of the issue would require elimination of mutual threats, termination of hostile relations, and normalization of relations between the United States and North Korea.

Unlike twelve years earlier, I could not even find an opening to the solution, as the Bush administration had shown little interest in improving relations with the North. The prospects for change seemed dim. On the other hand, North Korea was unlikely to give up its nuclear card, as long as it distrusted the United States, which it accused of stifling North Korea. I felt I had to try my best to persuade the North Korean leader in order to find a clue to the solution.

When we landed at the Pyongyang Sunan Airport, the weather was penetratingly cold. Nevertheless, there was a welcome party waiting for us. The party included Lim Dong-ok, First Deputy Director of the United Front, and other principal players in South Korean affairs.

When we arrived at the Baekhwawon Guest House, Secretary Kim Yong-soon welcomed us. During our two-night and three-day stay in Pyongyang, we had three sessions of meetings with Kim Yong-soon. We also paid a courtesy visit to President of the SPA Presidium Kim Young-nam. Regrettably, I was not given an opportunity to meet with Chairman Kim Jong-il this time.

* * * * * * * * * *

The first meeting was held after a luncheon hosted by Secretary Kim Yong-soon. Through my opening statement, I explained the purpose of my visit and provided my assessment of the nuclear issue. In addition, I also presented a summary of president's letter to Chairman Kim Jong-il, handing over a copy to Secretary Kim Yong-soon as I had on previous occasions.

I also conveyed to him messages from the United States and Japan. I said I wished to meet with Chairman Kim Jong-il, and requested that Senior Secretary Yim, who had returned from Washington, meet with First Vice Foreign Minister Kang Sok-ju, who was handling the nuclear issue on behalf of North Korea.

President Kim's letter contained three parts: the North Korean nuclear issue, North-South relations, and advice for North Korea's relations with the new South Korean government.

President Kim emphasized that the current situation, related to the HEUP, should return to the previous state of October of the previous year (2002); to this end, "North Korea should make a decision to clarify the suspicions about the HEUP." President Kim's logic was that "if this is done, the United States will take steps to address your security concerns, and it will be possible to initiate North Korea–U.S. dialogue."

I first detailed the diplomatic efforts we had exerted up until that point to contribute to the resolution of the nuclear issue, as well as the international community's concerns regarding the issue. Then I recommended a proposal for the North: to revert the situation back to its previous state before October of the previous year, by resolving the suspicions regarding the HEUP as soon as possible. The proposal, a realistic approach that we had devised after consultations with the United States, suggested the following:

First, provide a clear explanation about the suspected HEUP and express an unequivocal intent against the development of nuclear weapons. Dispatch a letter in the name of the DPRK foreign minister to the U.S. secretary of state to propose bilateral talks.

On behalf of the United States, the secretary of state would provide its assurance of nonaggression and no hostile intent, thus opening the path to a dialogue. At this point, the North could seize the opportunity to promptly send another letter requesting bilateral talks. If there were a longer delay, it would be highly likely that the hardliners would move to internationalize the nuclear issue and subject the issue to time-consuming multilateral talks.

Second, express a clear intent to cancel withdrawal from the NPT as soon as possible in order to prevent a referral of the North Korean nuclear issue to the UN Security Council.

Third, given the low likelihood of the realization of the North's demand for the conclusion of a non-aggression treaty, a "three-stage approach" was advisable. In the first stage, the North should secure a letter of assurance of nonaggression from the Bush administration. In the second stage, as Russia had already proposed, they should secure a multilateral assurance against aggression among the three permanent members of the UN Security Council—the United States, Russia and China. And in the third stage, promote a legally binding treaty of nonaggression with the United States, as mutual confidence would be built along with progress in the nuclear issue. However, we drew attention to past instances in which nonaggression treaties were unilaterally discarded. In this sense, multilateral security assurance could be more secure than unilateral assurance.

With the Bush administration busily preparing the Iraqi invasion, Secretary Powell and other negotiation supporters at the State Department were back on the forefront of the nuclear issue; North Korea should use this good opportunity.

I also conveyed a U.S. message to the North: "We want North Korea to heed our public statement that we harbor no hostile intent and no intent to attack North Korea. If the North first expressed its willingness to abandon its HEUP, the United States would engage North Korea in dialogue."

I added the last part of the U.S. message that I had received shortly before my departure from Seoul. It said, "As far as the United States is concerned, it would prefer bilateral talks in the frame of multilateral talks."

The Japanese message I conveyed to the North had already been made public: "There has been no change in Japan's interest to continue normalization talks based on the Pyongyang Declaration. For this, Japan hopes to see progress in the abductees issue as well as in the security issue."

In a comprehensive response, the North said, "We have already announced our position regarding this issue yesterday through government statements." The North explained, "We have not developed nuclear weapons. We do not have the intent to develop them at present. We are willing to prove it through verification. As the nuclear issue is subject to resolution through direct talks between the United States and North Korea, we want to resolve it through fair direct talks with the United States on equal footing."

Secretary Kim Yong-soon also said, "The nuclear issue is a product of the U.S. hostile policy to stifle our country." He concluded by saying, "We hope that the South will successfully persuade the United States to come to direct talks with us without any conditions."

Our request for Secretary Yim's meeting with First Vice Foreign Minister Kang was not realized. Instead, Secretary Yim had a separate meeting with First Deputy Director Lim Dong-ok at the request of the North. Secretary Yim explained to Deputy Director Lim in detail the discussions that he had with the high-level American officials, in addition to President Kim's recommended proposal.

Next, we went to meet with President Kim Young-nam, who was formally meeting us on behalf of Chairman Kim Jong-il. He provided a positive assessment of the accomplishments from the implementation of the June 15 Joint Declaration and the development of inter-Korean relations. He then gave a logical view of the nuclear issue, although it was a familiar version:

> The nuclear issue is a product of hostile U.S. policy against our country. President Bush threatens us as the axis of evil and a target for preemptive nuclear attack, fabricating the nuclear suspicions in a big fuss, and finally unilaterally abolishing the Agreed Framework. The United States is mobilizing international pressure against us, while avoiding dialogue with us. They are trying to internationalize the nuclear issue.

When discussing the completion of North Korea's withdrawal from the NPT and the exercise of the rights to self-defense guaranteed by the UN charter, the nominal head of North Korea resolutely said, "We will reciprocate good will with good will and a hardline with a hardline." He continued,

The United States should suspend its unilateral nuclear commotion and accept bilateral talks to build mutual confidence and to resolve the issue, by respecting our sovereignty and assuring us of nonaggression. And, I cordially request that Special Envoy Lim Dong-won convey our intent to the United States.

He reiterated, "The United States should respect our sovereignty and come to bilateral talks if it wants to find a way to resolve the issue."

Multilateral Talks Substitute Bilateral Talks

Secretary Kim Yong-soon asked for my understanding, saying, "Chairman Kim Jong-il is visiting a provincial area on an important matter that requires his on-the-spot guidance, and therefore is not able to see you." He then pulled out a telephone message from Chairman Kim and read it to me:

I acknowledge the receipt of President Kim Dae-jung's letter, and I appreciate President Kim's warm advice and his dispatch of the special envoy. Concerning President Kim's advice, I will inform you of my position after a serious review of his suggestions.

The real reason why Chairman Kim suddenly changed his mind about meeting me as the special envoy was unknown. But there was a development that we should have noticed. When Senior Secretary Yim went to Washington on January 8, it was ascertained that Secretary Powell was firm in pursuing bilateral talks with North Korea, and it was agreed that South Korea would persuade the North to come to talks. Only several days after this agreement, the Bush administration's position changed.

Around the time I was preparing for my visit, President Bush again favored the position of Vice President Cheney and other hardliners who were calling for pressuring the North Koreans through internationalization of the nuclear issue. Secretary Powell seemed to have failed again in carrying out his plan to expedite bilateral talks with the North.

The hardliners in Washington started leaking an internal decision to take the nuclear issue to multilateral talks, instead of bilateral talks. Right before I left for Pyongyang, the United States suddenly asked me to tell the North the United States would favor multilateral talks.

North Korea must have interpreted this as the rejection of bilateral talks. North Korea had lost hope in the Bush administration since the abrogation of the Agreed Framework. However, when it decided to accept my visit as the special envoy, they still seemed to have some hope in the possibility of bilateral talks with the United States.

It seemed that the North Koreans had even given up their expectations for the special envoy when they discerned this sudden change in the Bush administration's position. They must have determined that there was no need for Chairman Kim to meet the special envoy.

The North Korean foreign ministry's spokesman denounced the U.S. move, saying,

> The United States is leaking information that the North Korean nuclear issue should be discussed by a multilateral meeting, including the five permanent members of the UN Security Council. This reveals the malicious U.S. intent to avoid responsibility and to internationalize the nuclear issue to pressure North Korea.

He went on:

> The nuclear issue came into being because of the United States, and it has deteriorated to an extreme limit. The United States is the only party who is threatening our sovereignty and our right to survival, and it alone has the responsibility and ability to remove the danger. We oppose the attempt to internationalize the nuclear issue, and we will not participate in any form of multilateral talks. There should be no other way than direct talks between the DPRK and the United States from an equal posture.

Now North Korea seemed to have given up direct talks with the Bush administration, for which they had hoped the past two years, and were turning toward full nuclear development.

* * * * * * * * *

On the evening of the first day of my visit, the North Korean economic observation tour group who had visited the South from October 26 to November 3 hosted a dinner banquet for my party at the Daedonggang Guest House. Director Chang Sung-taek and most of those who had been members of the tour group, as well as Secretary Kim Yong-soon, participated in the dinner.

The Wangjaesan Band played music, and singers sang songs of the North and the South. The people of the North and the South were sitting between each other, drinking wine around a big round table. We learned that the banquet was held at the special instructions of Chairman Kim Jong-il, who said, "Host a grand banquet for the South Korean delegation in return for their warm hospitality to our economic observation group when they went to the South."

The 18-member economic observation group visited 38 industrial facilities across the land of the South, including Samsung Electronics, Pohang Steel, Hyundai Heavy Industry, and Hyundai Automobiles. They also visited

R&D centers, distribution facilities, and industrial infrastructures. They all said they had "learned a lot" and expressed their "sincere thanks for the warm hospitality and love of the brethren from the South." They all concurred, in one voice, the importance of inter-Korean economic cooperation. At that time, I realized how important it was to have an exchange between high-level economic affairs experts. I knew the more exchanges of this type we had, the more likely it would contribute to change in the North.

*　*　*　*　*　*　*　*　*

On the afternoon of January 29, my party boarded Air Force Three once again, to leave the Pyongyang Sunan Airport. At under minus twenty degrees Celsius, it was still bitterly cold. While heading back to Seoul, I could see the frozen pieces of ice along the coast at Nampo Harbor. I realized that my heart was also frozen like a piece of ice, as I had not had the chance to persuade Chairman Kim Jong-il.

When I reported to President Kim the results of my visit, he did not hide his displeasure and dissatisfaction that Chairman Kim did not meet his special envoy. At the subsequent press conference, attended by more than 300 domestic and foreign reporters, I could clearly sense an atmosphere of disappointment regarding Chairman Kim Jong-il's failure to meet me.

"Although I did not personally get to meet Chairman Kim Jong-il, I was able to convey to President of the SPA Presidium Kim Young-nam and other high-ranking officials of North Korea the concerns of the international community and our recommended advice, and asked them to consider them seriously," I told the press.

The foreign correspondents issued such reports as, "although the original purpose was to meet with Kim Jong-il and persuade him to abandon his nuclear program, it did not mean a failure of the special envoy"; "North Korea displayed its hardline position to reject a multilateral meeting, insisting on direct negotiations with the United States"; and "South Korea's successful dispatch of the special envoy and North Korea's consideration deserve credit."

It was difficult for us and beyond our ability to overcome the wall of the new Cold War being set up by the neocon hardliners, or to mitigate the recalcitrant stand of the North Koreans who were reacting to the United States through nuclear development. We did not overcome the chronic pervasive mentality of the Cold War and the domestic trend of conservatism, or the legacy of flunkeyism that "we should follow the Americans without conditions." I was convinced that this was something we should overcome at some point.

Nuclear Test

The Bush administration made a serious mistake by raising an issue about the "uncertain HEUP," which led to the North restarting its "assured plutonium program." As desired by the neocon hardliners, the United States terminated the provision of heavy fuel oil and cancelled the construction of the light water reactor. It refused to accept bilateral talks with the North, while intentionally ignoring the responses by North Korea. In reaction, North Korea withdrew from the NPT in January 2003 and restarted the operation of the plutonium program that had been put on hold for eight years, in compliance with the Agreed Framework.

After the nullification of the Agreed Framework and the invasion of Iraq (March 20, 2003), the Bush administration pushed the "internationalization" of the North Korean nuclear issue. Insisting that the North Korean nuclear issue not be an issue for which the United States alone was responsible, the United States, with the assistance of China, succeeded in holding the Six-Party Talks involving the United States, China, Russia, Japan, and the two Koreas, in Beijing in August 2003. Frankly, it was a U.S. hardliner-designed scheme to form a five-state anti-North Korean front, pitting five countries against one—North Korea—to force it to surrender by pressure and isolation.

However, the initial U.S. five to one strategy, as schemed by the hardliners, failed to gain the support of the participating countries. Conversely, this strategy produced an adverse effect. The Six-Party Talks were stalemated and the North Koreans accelerated their nuclear development.

On February 10, 2005, two years after the abolishment of the Agreed Framework, North Korea at last announced that it had "manufactured nukes for self-defense," declaring itself to be a nuclear-weapons state. At the same time, North Korea announced cancellation of its moratorium on missile tests. This happened shortly after the start of the second Bush administration.

One week after the North announced itself as a nuclear-weapons state, I had a luncheon meeting with U.S. Ambassador to Korea Christopher Hill, at his invitation. The luncheon was hosted at his residence, and it was joined by Dr. Paek Jong-cheon, director of the Sejong Institute, (later Director of Policy Planning at the Blue House), and I was working as the chairman of the Sejong Foundation.

Ambassador Hill had not served long in his post, but he was appointed to succeed James Kelly as Assistant Secretary of State for East Asia and Pacific Affairs and the U.S. Head of Delegation to the Six-Party Talks. He asked me many questions about the North Korean situation and the nuclear issue.

First, I stressed to him, "You cannot bring down North Korea by pressure or sanctions." Then I expressed my views:

> It will take time but you should still induce them to change. The North Korean nuclear issue, which is a product of the hostile relations between the United States and North Korea, cannot be separated from the issue of normalization of relations. North Korea would never give up its nuclear programs before the normalization of relations. The nuclear issue has persisted more than fifteen years now, and it is not something that can be resolved by pressure and sanctions. Instead of pushing it by force, the United States should promote a peace process to end the Cold War on the Korean Peninsula.

> If the United States has the "political will" to do so, it should engage North Korea in direct talks in whatever form. Only through a gradual exchange of give and take can you reduce mutual threats and build mutual confidence.

Ambassador Hill asked me again, "What and how should we do it, in the face of the serious provocative announcement that North Korea possesses nuclear weapons?" I gave him my answer: "I believe the United States should start by contacting the North Koreans through the New York channel to express U.S. intent to talk directly with them. In my judgment, it would be desirable to start having bilateral talks under the umbrella of the Six-Party Talks."

Hill said he would report it to the higher-ups, but he did not think that Washington would accept bilateral talks. His response was negative.

* * * * * * * * *

In May 2005, North Korea announced that it had completed the extraction of spent fuel rods from the reactor. This was the third extraction following the first suspected extraction at the end of the 1980s, and the second one that had been put under IAEA surveillance until the beginning of 2003. According to U.S. intelligence assessments, the North was highly likely to soon have forty to fifty kilograms of separated plutonium, sufficient for six to eight primitive nuclear bombs.

Upon this development, the United States contacted the North Koreans thorough the New York channel. The Six-Party Talks were reconvened (July–September, 2005) and the talks adopted the September 19 Joint Statement, which reflected their agreement on the principles for the resolution of the North Korean nuclear issue. In fact, it was an agreement similar to the U.S.-DPRK Agreed Framework of 1994, upholding the principles of a comprehensive approach to denuclearization, normalization of relations, energy aid, economic cooperation, and the principle of gradual simultaneous actions. The DPRK and the United States decided to respect each other's sovereignty, exist peacefully together, and take steps to normalize their relations subject to their respective bilateral policies.

In addition, the six parties committed to joint efforts for lasting peace and stability on Northeast Asia. They also agreed that the directly-related parties would negotiate a permanent peace regime on the Korean Peninsula at an appropriate separate forum. This agreement was an important step forward for the dismantlement of the Cold War structure. The South Korean government deserved credit for its untiring efforts that contributed to the successful adoption of the agreement.

The September 19 Joint Statement represented a rejection of the early U.S. position in the Six-Party Talks that North Korea was the only party at fault, with the focus on North Korea's denuclearization, rather than what the United States and the other parties needed to do.

* * * * * * * * *

However, the Washington hardliners did not want to respect this agreement. While politicizing the human rights issue, the Bush administration enacted financial sanctions against North Korea, including a freeze on North Korean accounts with the Banco Delta Asia (BDA) in Macao. The North reacted, saying, "It was a concentrated expression of U.S. hostile policy against North Korea." This returned the Six-Party Talks back to a stalemate.

As the Iraqi war was prolonged, the hardliners realized that the possibility of launching a preemptive military attack to get rid of the North Korean regime was low. Instead, they started a new policy of "regime change through non-military means." They argued that North Korea counterfeited its currency, trafficked in narcotics and was involved in other illicit activities, threatened its neighbors with its missiles, and brutalized and starved its people. The United States said it would continue to take all necessary measures to change these North Korean policies and the political system.

While continuing to contain North Korea through economic sanctions, the Bush administration launched the Proliferation Security Initiative (PSI), Illicit Activities Initiative (IAI), and Human Rights Initiative (HRI) as specific measures to target North Korea.

As time since the abolishment of the Agreed Framework went by, the concerns about the suspected HEUP gradually diminished. The expression of "weapons-grade HEUP" was quietly replaced by a "uranium enrichment program" (UEP).

In response to the continued hostile U.S. policy, North Korea finally conducted an underground nuclear test on October 9, 2006. Although it was only a partially successful, small-scale test, it dealt a decisive blow to the Bush administration, which was forced to rethink its North Korea policy.

The Bush administration's North Korea policy, which had been led by the neocon hardliners, failed to stop North Korean nuclear development or to bring about a regime collapse. It only made the situation worse. Through repeated failures, the Bush administration found itself trapped in a situation where it could no longer continue "a policy of malign neglect."

At the same time, despite President Bush's declaration of "mission accomplished" and "a victory in the war," the Iraqi situation was worsening as internal tribal battles began to result in deaths. Bush's justification for going to war was that "Iraq was developing weapons of mass destruction and Saddam Hussein was supporting al Qaeda." However, the U.S. Senate Intelligence Committee issued an investigation report (July 2004) that refuted Bush's claim and concluded the Iraqi war was "a wrong war that started based on the wrong intelligence."

The judgment of the American people came through the November 2006 midterm elections. Bush's Republican Party suffered a devastating defeat. President Bush was shaken by the election, as the public demanded the end of U.S. involvement in Iraq, and his approval ratings plummeted. The neocons in the administration, including Defense Secretary Rumsfeld and UN ambassador Bolton, were forced to resign. The Bush administration's North Korea policy became a subject for total reevaluation.

After six years of failed diplomacy, President Bush radically changed its negotiating strategy with Pyongyang. It conducted bilateral negotiations under the umbrella of the Six-Party Talks, something that Pyongyang had desired but the Bush administration had refused to do for six years. Bush abandoned his strategy of "no dialogue with the evil regime and no rewards for bad behavior." Senior American officials met with their North Korean counterparts in Beijing, and again in Berlin in direct negotiations. In search of a breakthrough, the Bush administration promised to lift the freeze on the North Korean BDA accounts.

* * * * * * * * *

The January 2007 bilateral meeting between Christopher Hill and Kim Gye-gwan in Berlin produced an important outline of initial actions for the implementation of the September 19 Joint Statement, which led to the Six-Party Talks agreement on February 13, 2007.

According to the Joint Statement, North Korea would shut down (the first phase) and implement the disabling of the nuclear facilities at Yongbyon, destroying the 5-megawatt reactor cooling towers (June 2008). A list of the North's nuclear programs would be reported for the purpose of eventual abandonment (the second phase). During this period of initial actions, about 75 percent of one million tons of heavy fuel oil was provided to North Korea.

The United States terminated the application of the Trading with the Enemy Act (TWEA) with respect to the DPRK and removed the designation of the DPRK as a state sponsor of terrorism. The United States and DPRK started bilateral talks aimed at moving toward full diplomatic relations.

In June 2008, North Korea submitted a declaration of its nuclear program. However, the issue of verification emerged as a significant stumbling block. The position of the United States during the December 2008 Six-Party Talks was that a full verification protocol must be completed before conclusion of the disablement phase, while North Korea insisted the second phase should only include verification of the disablement measures related to the plutonium program, and that full verification should only be accomplished during the third phase of dismantlement. Unfortunately, the issue put the six-party process into stalemate again after December 2008.

However, the United States demand for a full and complete verification did not appear to be a simple issue. The second nuclear crisis was triggered by the alleged U.S. information on the HEUP, which the North adamantly denied.

The key to the resolution of the nuclear issue lay in the creation of an environment in which there would be no need for nuclear weapons and mutual confidence is constructed. Without building mutual confidence, complete, verifiable, irreversible dismantlement (CVID) would be impossible; and it would inevitably take a much longer time to resolve the nuclear issue.

Fundamentally, the North Korean nuclear issue was a product of the hostile relationship between the United States and North Korea. The resolution of the nuclear issue required elimination of mutual threats, a peace regime replacing the armistice, and normalization of relations between the United States and North Korea. It was our task to exert all diplomatic efforts to help the improvement of U.S.–North Korea relations, while moving forward to establish a lasting peace mechanism on the Korean Peninsula.

CHAPTER 14

PATH TO PEACE AND UNIFICATION

An Honorable Opportunity

The past twenty years of my life have been filled with honor, joy, and pride. Beginning in 1988, I was blessed with the opportunity to pave the path towards peace and unification. I was convinced that the Lord wanted to use me as a tool to realize His will to bring about reconciliation and cooperation between the North and the South and achieve national unification.

I worked hard, fueled by the conviction that if the seeds of unification were sown and earnestly tended, the Lord would bloom flowers of peace and produce fruits of unification. I give thanks to the Lord for giving me the opportunity to dedicate myself to peacemaking. The Lord blessed me with the ability and experience to carry out His mission. In the 1960s, the Lord allowed me to study Communism and North Korea; in the 1970s, He led me to work in the field of national security affairs; in the 1980s, the field of foreign affairs. In the 1990s, He assigned me to several important positions—including chancellor of the Institute of Foreign Affairs and National Security, and Vice Minister of Unification. After I met President Kim Dae-jung, I became Senior Secretary for National Security and Foreign Affairs, director of the National Intelligence Service, Minister of Unification, and Special Advisor to the President for National Security and Unification.

* * * * * * * *

In the wake of the end of the Cold War, two opportunities arose for peacemaking on the Korean Peninsula. The first opportunity came in the early 1990s when the North and South sought a new inter-Korean relation-

On the second anniversary of the June 15 Joint Declaration, Kim Dae-jung (*left*) presents the author with South Korea's highest award for public officials (June 15, 2002). Courtesy Lim Dong-won.

ship in the post-Cold War era. The second opportunity came when the North and the South, with the cooperation of the United States, embarked on a peace process on the Korean Peninsula. On both occasions, I did my best to fulfill my mission.

I served as a negotiator in the North-South High-level Talks, playing the role of midwife to the birth of the North-South Basic Agreement and the Joint Declaration of the Denuclearization of the Korean Peninsula. For five years during the government of President Kim Dae-jung, I worked to transform the old relationship of distrust and confrontation between the North and South into a new relationship of reconciliation and cooperation. I dedicated myself to the successful holding of the historic North-South summit at which the June 15 Joint Declaration was adopted, and to the opening of a new era of reconciliation and cooperation. Increased exchange and cooperation contributed to the building of trust and the reduction of tension between the North and the South. Threats of war diminished and expectations for peace arose. It was the beginning of the peace process on the Korean Peninsula.

In recognition of my contribution to the improvement of inter-Korea relations, the state presented me with its highest award for public officials, the Order of Public Service Merit Blue Stripes Medal, and Inje University conferred an honorary doctoral degree upon me. These honors were beyond what I deserved.

On the other hand, I confronted many challenges and ordeals at home and abroad. I was the target of harsh criticisms by the conservative press, and I was called a "pro-North Korean leftist" by the anti-Kim Dae-jung forces. I received threats of blackmail and physical harm from ultra-rightist conservatives who were hanging onto the past. As a peacemaker, I had to suffer the travail of this brutal and torturous path.

Ten Years of Work for a New National Hope (1998–2007)

Historians say that the history of national division since 1945 can be divided into two periods: one is "a period of distrust and confrontation," ending on June 15, 2000; the other is a a "period of reconciliation and cooperation" that began when the June 15 Joint Declaration was signed. This declaration was the first document to ever be signed by the highest leaders of the two governments after they met face-to-face and mutually agreed on its substance. This document did not end just as an agreement; it was the first agreement that was actually implemented between North and South.

At the time of writing this book, eight years after the signing of the June 15 Joint Declaration, that historic declaration faced many challenges and ordeals at home and abroad. These obstacles included the Bush administration's hostile North Korea policy, North Korea's subsequent nuclear development, anti-North Korean trends, and increased conservatism.

However, the ardent desire of the Korean people for the prevention of war, for reconciliation and cooperation, and peace and unification, as well as the firm political wills of the leaders of the North and the South, were the prime movers in the implementation of the June 15 Joint Declaration.

The ten-year period of governance by Presidents Kim Dae-jung and Roh Moo-hyun proved that the June 15 Joint Declaration, which called for the "consolidation of mutual trust towards gradual peacemaking and unification," was the most ideal and realistic path for the nation. Exchanges of visits between the North and South, economic cooperation, and humanitarian assistance greatly helped dissolve the hostile attitudes of both sides, contributing to confidence-building and tension reduction. During that period, there were many changes, large and small.

As the citizens on both sides—not just the two governments—began participating in the unification movement, the system of division started to crack. Unification was no longer an issue of the future, but evolved into its present progressive form.

Despite the Bush administration's hostile policy and the "second nuclear crisis," the Roh Moo-hyun administration continued President Kim Dae-jung's Sunshine policy in the name of a "peace and prosperity policy." In the process of implementation, there were some confused oscillations between linkage or parallel pursuit of the nuclear issue and inter-Korean relations. Consequently, the Roh administration's efforts experienced a frustrating pattern of stop-and-go. Nonetheless, the Roh government overcame various difficulties and observed the June 15 Joint Declaration. By steadily carrying out the projects initiated by the Kim Dae-jung administration, the Roh administration made further progress in inter-Korean relations and solidified the foundation of peaceful coexistence.

Lee Jong-seok, the director of the Blue House Office of Foreign Affairs and National Security, and the unification ministers—Chung Se-hyon, Chung Dong-young, Lee Jong-seok, and Lee Jae-jung, who commanded the policy control tower during their respective tenures—did not follow the North Korea policy of the American neoconservatives. They pursued an engagement policy of reconciliation and cooperation. In the end, the Roh administration was able to avoid confusion when President Bush completely changed his position and decided to engage North Korea, discarding the hostile North Korea policy he had insisted upon for six years.

* * * * * * * *

During the Roh administration, I served as a member of the Unification Advisory Group, occasionally helping them individually, and at other times, making speeches to gain public support for the administration's engagement policy. I felt these things to be very worthwhile. And I was very pleased to visit the sites of the Kaesong Industrial Complex and Mount Kumgang Tourism Complex, which had been part of the "five priority projects" of President Kim's administration. I also visited Pyongyang to see how the progress was being made.

Routes disconnected for a half-century were reconnected. In addition to the opening of sky and sea routes, railways and roads that were part of the nation's transporation artery were reconnected. Landmines were removed from the DMZ and two "peace corridors" were constructed in their place, enabling so many people to travel back and forth.

Although they are now used primarily for travel to Kaesong and Mount Kumgang, I am looking forward to the day when the trains can run from Busan to Shinuiju, from Mokpo to Rajin, and when the Trans-Korean Peninsula Railway is linked to the Trans-Siberian Railway. I hope that day is not too far away. As I traveled to Kaesong and Mount Kumgang, I recalled our unswerving stand against the neoconservative hardliners in Washington and our successful struggles to remove landmines and construct the peace corridors. When I look back, it is pleasing to relish the nostalgia of our struggles.

* * * * * * * *

In the first nine years of tourism to Mount Kumgang, there were 1,730,000 visitors to Korea's most scenic mountain. Undertaking of the Mount Kumgang tourism project was a green light to the reduction of tensions. With North Korea's relocation of its frontline troops and the opening of its critical navy base, tension reduction had begun. The opening of the Mount Kumgang area led to the construction of the two peace corridors and the opening of North Korea's strategic point at Kaesong.

Those who visited Mr. Kumgang all concurred that not only were they able to experience the pleasure of appreciating the beauty of the famous mountain, but the visit also made them realize the reality of the divided land, provoking a new awakening for this national issue, as well as for the importance of improved inter-Korean relations.

Mount Kumgang tourism also played a role in the improvement of inter-Korean relations. It became the venue for various North-South meetings, including government-to-government talks, reunion meetings of separated family members, and other various civilian contacts and exchanges. The mountain became a site for the sharing of sorrow for the national division; for love, trust and hope for unification through reconciliation and cooperation.

Mount Kumgang tourism, which began in November 1998, also contributed to finding a turning point in economic recovery for both the North and the South. Explicit easing of tensions on the Korean Peninsula contributed to the creation of good investments in South Korea, which had been hit hard by the foreign exchange (IMF) crisis. The tourism was invaluable in that it significantly helped to raise South Korea's "country risk" rating. For the North, facing a deteriorating economic situation, Mount Kumgang tourism served as an important revenue of foreign exchange to stave off economic crisis.

The Kaesong Industrial Complex (KIC), which began with the concept of combining the South's capital and technology with the North's labor and land, finally began operating at the end of 2004 in spite of various difficulties and delays. As of the end of 2010, 120 South Korean companies were producing goods, employing approximately 47,000 North Korean workers.

After the completion of the KIC's first phase of construction, an area of 3.3 square kilometers was cleared, and construction began on more plants. The South supplied 100,000 kilowatts of electricity to the KIC; a communications network was put in place, and freight trains started running between KIC and the South. When the KIC's first phase is fully operational, it is expected to house about 400 factories and employ more than 100,000 North Korean laborers. KIC would become a stepping stone for the building of a "North-South Economic Community." As we saw North Korean workers and South Korean engineers working together, helping and sharing with one another, we could not help but think this was indeed the process of unification in action.

The Kim Dae-jung administration was focused on the realization of reunion meetings for separated family members. For this goal, we provided fertilizer and food aid. Since the June 15 Joint Declaration, sixteen exchange meetings and video conferences between separated families have taken place and about 20,000 members of the 4,000 families were able to meet their family members on the other side of the division.

After the war, it had taken us a half-century before we started holding meetings for separated families. The North Korean side was still reluctant to implement full exchanges of meetings between separated families. This was one of the important issues we needed to keep working on.

Perhaps one of the most remarkable accomplishments during the ten-year period was the increased volume of personnel traffic between the North and the South. Between the end of the Korean War and the inauguration of President Kim Dae-jung's administration, only 3,000 people had traveled between the North and the South. During the ten-year period, however, more than 430,000 people visited between North and South. Frequently-held joint events in the areas of economic, social, and cultural affairs gave birth to a consciousness of the community of the Korean nation. More frequent contacts and exchanges would cultivate mutual understanding, confidence, and the spirit of a national community. This would be the most ideal path to peace and unification.

Since the Basic Treaty in 1972, between six and seven million West Germans visited East Germany and one to two million East Germans visited West Germany each year. In Seoul, when I met Egon Bahr, who had been the

The author converses with Dr. Egon Bahr (*left*), former West German Chancellor Willy Brandt's right-hand man, who was an architect of *Ostpolitik* (September 6, 2001). Courtesy Lim Dong-won.

architect of the *Ostpolitik* of "change through rapprochement," he shared that the exchanges of visits between the two Germanys were possible due to the practice of humanitarianism and economic inducement.

In the years from the Basic Treaty to the completion of unification, West Germany had provided about $60 billion—an annual average of $3.2 billion—to East Germany in the name of various projects. In our case, the South provided $2.4 billion, including $620 million on the civilian level, in food, fertilizer, medicine, etc., between 1998 and 2007. The South provided an annual average of $240 million, one thirteenth of West Germany's spending, which amounted to $5 per person in the South. Yet, some anti-North Korean forces and the conservative press exploited and exaggerated this subject, bashing the government as "shoveling free gifts" to the North.

* * * * * * * *

In the seven years after the June 15 Joint Declaration, more than 230 government-to-government meetings were held between the two sides, building political and military confidence and promoting economic cooperation. Broadcasts blasting mutual slander disappeared from the frontlines of the DMZ, and the two militaries cooperatively removed the landmines to build the peace corridors, which became a symbol of inter-Korean traffic.

The military hot line between the North and South troops served as a means of assisting and managing people and goods to pass through the peace corridors. On the West Sea, military confidence-building measures were put in place to prevent accidental collisions.

* * * * * * * *

In 2005, I visited Pyongyang again as an advisor to the South Korean delegation for the Grand National Festival of the Fifth Anniversary of the June 15 Joint Declaration, and there I delivered a keynote speech. Afterwards, I met with Chairman Kim Jong-il, whom I had not seen in three years. I contacted Deputy Director Lim Dong-ok of the United Front to arrange a meeting between Unification Minister Chung Dong-young and Chairman Kim Jong-il. Minister Chung conveyed to Chairman Kim the Roh administration's intention of supplying two million kilowatts of electricity to the North and secured Chairman Kim's promise to return to the Six-Party Talks and his agreement to hold an inter-Korean summit.

At the luncheon hosted by Chairman Kim, whom I was seated beside, I raised two issues. The first one was related to an early convening of the North-South Defense Ministerial Talks, to discuss military confidence-building measures and arms reduction. I said, "It will take a number of years for arms control talks to produce results. But, we should take this valuable opportunity when the United States is pursuing a new military reform to change its role, and reduce and relocate its troops in Korea."

The other issue I raised was about multilateral cooperation. I said, "Instead of continuing to insist on U.S. security assurances and a non-aggression treaty, it would be more beneficial to you if you return to the Six-Party Talks and get a negotiated security assurance involving the United States, Russia, and China, as Russia had proposed. Whereas a security assurance by a single country would be subject to unilateral abrogation, a multilateral assurance would be difficult for a single party to nullify." Chairman Kim agreed with me without hesitation, "That's right. That's the way we should go in the days ahead."

* * * * * * * *

On October 4, 2007, President Roh Moo-hyun and Chairman Kim Jong-il met in the second inter-Korean summit in Pyongyang and agreed to uphold and actively implement the June 15 Joint Declaration. They discussed concrete projects to carry out the declaration and to further expand and advance North-South relations. To expand and further develop economic cooperation, the two leaders agreed to carry out some forty specific projects, and to embark on military cooperation and build military confidence. The agreement included the establishment of a special peace and cooperation zone in the West Sea in order to change the "sea of tension" into a "sea of peace."

It was especially significant that the two sides recognized the need to end the current armistice agreement and build a permanent peace regime.

Building a Peace Regime toward Unification

Our nation's utmost task is to overcome national division and achieve unification. If the division continues, competition for monopolized legitimacy is inevitable. If so, confrontation, conflict, and tension between the North and the South will be difficult to avoid.

Moreover, in a continued state of division, it would be difficult to avoid exploitation by foreign forces and an arms race. National unification, when achieved, will bring peace, national prosperity, and advancement. To overcome the division and achieve unification, we must end the Cold War and embark on a peace process toward unification.

I argue that peace and unification will not be handed to us by others; rather, with the support of surrounding countries, we must take a joint inter-Korean initiative to realize peace and unification. However, we will not succeed with a "by-the-Korean-people-themselves" attitude. By the same token, it would be dangerous for us to subject inter-Korean relations to international relations and rely on foreign forces. If we did, national unification would be unlikely.

Rather, we ought to concentrate our efforts on the creation of an international environment in which unification is conducive to the interests of the surrounding nations, thereby gaining international support and cooperation. To this end, we must dismantle the Cold War structure, which has continued for the last half-century on the Korean Peninsula, and we must build a peace regime towards unification.

* * * * * * * *

Thus far, under the Armistice Agreement, we have strengthened our military capabilities to maintain a "negative peace." In the future, however, we must make a "positive peace" that will fundamentally remove security threats. This will pave the way to unification.

Making positive peace means dismantlement of the Cold War structure. It means that the United States and Japan, in addition to South Korea, should end hostile intentions and normalize their relations with North Korea, and all the participants in the Six-Party Talks ought to cooperate for peace and security in the region.

Making positive peace also means ending the Armistice Agreement and establishing a durable peace regime. To this end, we should realize denuclearization and arms control on the peninsula, terminate the current state of confrontation, and remove security threats.

Making positive peace also means finding a way to tear down the division toward unification. Unification is a process. Before achieving *de jure* unification, we need to realize a virtual state of unification that is *de facto* unification first for mutual exchange and cooperation. By realizing *de facto* unification, we can find the way to build a peace regime toward unification, instead of a peace regime that perpetuates the division.

The ending of the international Cold War had a positive impact on the Korean Peninsula. For the past twenty years, we have made steady efforts to end the Cold War and make peace on the peninsula.

The first attempt was carried out by the North and the South in early the 1990s when we produced the North-South Basic Agreement, in which North and South defined their relations as a "special interim relationship stemming from the process toward unification." We agreed to develop relations as partners for peace and unification. Specifically, we agreed to mutually respect each other's systems and to promote reconciliation, exchange and cooperation, nonaggression and arms control, and transformation of the present state of armistice into a solid state of peace.

The second attempt began at the end of the 1990s when the Kim Dae-jung administration embarked on a "peace process" with the cooperation and support of the Clinton administration. Subsequently, the North and the South held their historic summit meeting and adopted the June 15 Joint Declaration to open a new era of reconciliation and cooperation.

Through the process of exchange and cooperation, hostile attitudes were softened and mutual trust started growing, reducing tensions between the North and South. Improvement of relations between North Korea and the United States proceeded in parallel, through the process of denuclearization and the promotion of a U.S.–North Korea summit meeting. Also, North Korea initiated steps toward economic reform.

* * * * * * * *

Nevertheless, the peace process on the Korean Peninsula was disrupted when the Bush administration came into being in 2001. Beginning then, the Bush administration's hostile North Korea policy and the North's reactive nuclear development played undesirable disruptive roles. One lesson was learned from this experience: it would be impossible to expect peace on the peninsula unless hostile relations were eliminated between the United States and North Korea.

The Bush administration's policy started to radically change in early 2007, with the decision to pursue in parallel the resolution of the North Korean nuclear issue through the Six-Party Talks and improvement of relations with North Korea.

The September 19, 2005, Joint Statement of the Six-Party Talks reconfirmed, as did the Agreed Framework of 1994, that the nuclear issue was a product of hostile relations between the United States and North Korea and that the key to resolution was normalization of relations between them.

Dismantlement of the North Korean nuclear program and the denuclearization of the Korean Peninsula are very important and urgent issues. However, denuclearization and normalization of relations require a long, gradual, and difficult process. Denuclearization requires a thorough give-and-take approach based on the principle of action for action, while at the same time building mutual confidence through verification.

More than twenty years have elapsed since the North Korean nuclear issue arose in the early 1990s, and it is not something that can be resolved in the next few years. Throughout this long process of resolution, we must show the wisdom to pursue improved inter-Korean relations in parallel with denuclearization. We should never repeat the mistake of subjugating inter-Korean relations to the issue of North Korea's nuclear program. We should not carry out a linkage strategy between inter-Korean relations and denuclearization; rather, we should carry out a parallel strategy.

The Six-Party Talks have agreed to resolve the issues of denuclearization and normalization of relations, to discuss peace and security cooperation for East Asia and to negotiate a peace regime on the Korean Peninsula. We value and welcome the decision to comprehensively dismantle the Cold War structure that has existed for the past half-century. Now that we have the opportunity to resume the peace process on the Korean Peninsula, we should not miss this opportunity.

✳ ✳ ✳ ✳ ✳ ✳ ✳ ✳

The most urgent task facing the North and the South in establishing a peace regime towards unification is to "energize economic cooperation to construct and develop a North-South economic community," while facilitating arms control. Without the resolving the military issue, it would be difficult to expect expansion and advancement of economic cooperation. Realization of arms control and the establishment of an economic community will be mutually complementary, producing a synergistic effect.

Moreover, North Korea needs security assurances through normalization of relations with the United States and economic development through the introduction of capital and technology. The North should realize market economy reforms and transform itself through the establishment of a North-South economic community and realization of arms control.

As the European countries formed the European Economic Community and later developed the European Union towards the integration of Europe, the North and the South should form a "North South Economic Community" to increase mutual interdependence and to contribute to an integrated and balanced development of the national economy and the welfare of the entire people. The North and the South should move forward in the direction of political integration through economic integration.

As part of that process, the two sides should closely cooperate in the vitalization of joint economic projects, including the Kaesong Industrial Complex, exploration of resources, and modernization of the underdeveloped North Korean infrastructure in the areas of agriculture, energy, transportation, and communication. When economic sanctions are lifted as part of the process of denuclearizatioin, it will be possible for North Korea to have access to international financial institutions and to induce foreign investment.

We have strengthened our military defense capability to maintain a negative peace under the Armistice Agreement. In the future, we should realize arms control to fundamentally remove security threats and to establish a durable peace regime. We should implement military confidence-building measures and also realize a "reduction-oriented military balance." Through this process, we should end military distrust and confrontation, the arms race, and the excessive build-up of military arms.

The North and the South presented their respective arms reduction proposals in 1990, and through the Basic Agreement they agreed to "discuss and carry out steps to build military confidence and realize arms reduction." All that remains is for this to be implemented.

*　*　*　*　*　*　*　*

At the inter-Korean summit of 2000, the leaders of the North and South shared the view that unification is a goal as well as a process, and they agreed to achieve it by a gradual step-by-step approach on the principles of independence and peace.

Before the achievement of *de jure* unification, they agreed to realize the state of *de facto* unification for exchange and cooperation between the North and the South in various sectors. They also agreed to institutionalize a "North-South Confederation" as the joint cooperative mechanism to manage the long process of peace and unification.

I believe this peaceful unification model would meet the interests of those countries who have a stake in the security and stability of the Korean Peninsula. In my view, this ideal and realistic model can win the support and cooperation of neighboring countries, including the United States and China.

This agreement opened the way to make "peace towards unification" through energized exchange and cooperation, instead of "peace on the perpetuation of division." When we deal with the issue of building a peace regime, we should carefully prevent any elements of anti-unification and perpetuated division from interfering with it.

* * * * * * *

In establishing a peace regime on the peninsula, we must develop substantive measures to guarantee peace. Intentions for peace are important, but intentions alone will not guarantee peace. It is essential to have substantive measures for peace.

As we saw in the case of Vietnam, the conclusion of a peace treaty does not guarantee peace. We should pay attention to Europe's successful process of ending the Cold War and achieving peace. This was not done through a peace treaty but through comprehensive confidence-building measures—in political, economic, military, social and cultural spheres—and arms control.

Negotiating a peace regime on the Korean Peninsula requires the participation of four countries: the United States, China, and the two Koreas. The four parties should agree to legally and practically end the Korean War and to enforce substantive peace measures, such as the removal of hostile relations, denuclearization, and arms control. When these measures are implemented to a satisfactory extent, it will be possible to transform the Military Armistice Agreement to a durable peace regime.

A peace regime should not lead to a negative peace that will perpetuate the division and allow the arms race to continue; it should fundamentally remove security threats and guarantee positive peace toward unification. As we saw in the case of German unification, in which the two Germanys first cooperated to achieve their unification through the "2 + 4 formula," the North and South should exercise their cooperative wisdom to lead the four-party talks in the direction of the common national interests of the Korean people.

We should make sure that the establishment of a North-South Confederation will serve as the essential central authority for managing and advancing peace towards unification. Therefore, the North and the South should be direct parties in the realization of a peace regime, which the United States and China should guarantee, and the UN Security Council would later endorse. It is desirable to have this formula—"2 + 2 + UN."

* * * * * * * *

We should not forget that our immediate task is first to realize a "unification-oriented peace regime" and to bring about *de facto* unification—a virtual state of unification—before *de jure* unification. In parallel with the processes of the normalization of U.S.-North Korea relations and the denuclearization of the peninsula, we should build a North-South economic community and realize arms control to promote unification.

To repeat, unification is the goal and a process at the same time. Unification is no longer an issue of the future, but something that is taking place in the present.

APPENDIX: ESSENTIAL DOCUMENTS OF THE KOREAN PENINSULA PEACE PROCESS, 1992–2005

Agreement on Reconciliation, Nonaggression and Exchanges and Cooperation between the South and the North[1]

To enter into force as of February 19, 1992

The South and the North,

In keeping with the yearning of the entire Korean people for the peaceful unification of the divided land;

Reaffirming the three principles of unification set forth in the July 4 (1972) South-North Joint Communique;

Determined to remove the state of political and military confrontation and achieve national reconciliation;

Also determined to avoid armed aggression and hostilities, reduce tension and ensure peace;

Expressing the desire to realize multi-faceted exchanges and cooperation to advance common national interests and prosperity;

Recognizing that their relations, not being a relationship between states, constitute a special interim relationship stemming from the process towards unification;

Pledging to exert joint efforts to achieve peaceful unification;

Hereby have agreed as follows;

Chapter I   South-North Reconciliation

Article 1
The South and the North shall recognize and respect each other's system.

Article 2
The two sides shall not interfere in each other's internal affairs.

Article 3
The two sides shall not slander or vilify each other.

Article 4
The two sides shall not attempt any actions of sabotage or subversion against each other.

---

1   Also known as the North-South Basic Agreement, or simply Basic Agreement.

Article 5
The two sides shall endeavor together to transform the present state of armistice into a solid state of peace between the South and the North and shall abide by the present Military Armistice Agreement (of July 27, 1953) until such a state of peace has been realized.

Article 6
The two sides shall cease to compete or confront each other and shall cooperate and endeavor together to promote national prestige and interests in the international arena.

Article 7
To ensure close consultations and liaison between the two sides, South-North Liaison Offices shall be established at Panmunjom within three (3) months after the coming into force of this Agreement.

Article 8
A South-North Political Committee shall be established within the framework of the South-North High-Level Talks within one (1) month of the coming into force of this Agreement with a view to discussing concrete measures to ensure the implementation and observance of the accords on South-North reconciliation.

Chapter II   South-North Nonaggression

Article 9
The two sides shall not use force against each other and shall not undertake armed aggression against each other.

Article 10
Differences of views and disputes arising between the two sides shall be resolved peacefully through dialogue and negotiation.

Article 11
The South-North demarcation line and areas for non-aggression shall be identical with the Military Demarcation Line specified in the Military Armistice Agreement of July 27, 1953 and the areas that have been under the jurisdiction of each side until the present time.

Article 12
To implement and guarantee non-aggression, the two sides shall set up a South-North Joint Military Commission within three (3) months of the coming into force of this Agreement. In the said Commission, the two sides

shall discuss and carry out steps to build military confidence and realize arms reduction, including the mutual notification and control of major movements of military units and major military exercises, the peaceful utilization of the Demilitarized Zone, exchanges of military personnel and information, phased reductions in armaments including the elimination of weapons of mass destruction and offensive capabilities, and verifications thereof.

Article 13
A telephone hotline shall be installed between the military authorities of the two sides to prevent accidental armed clashes and their escalation.

Article 14
A South-North Military Committee shall be established within the framework of the South-North High-Level Talks within one (1) month of the coming into force of this agreement in order to discuss concrete measures to ensure the implementation and observance of the accords on non-aggression and to remove military confrontation.

Chapter III   South-North Exchanges and Cooperation

Article 15
To promote an integrated and balanced development of the national economy and the welfare of the entire people, the two sides shall engage in economic exchanges and cooperation, including the joint development of resources, the trade of goods as domestic commerce and joint ventures.

Article 16
The two sides shall carry out exchanges and cooperation in various fields such as science and technology, education, literature and the arts, health, sports, environment, and publishing and journalism including newspapers, radio and television broadcasts and publications.

Article 17
The two sides shall promote free intra-Korean travel and contacts for the residents of their respective areas.

Article 18
The two sides shall permit free correspondence, meetings and visits between dispersed family members and other relatives and shall promote the voluntary reunion of divided families and shall take measures to resolve other humanitarian issues.

Article 19
The two sides shall reconnect railroads and roads that have been cut off and shall open South-North sea and air transport routes.

Article 20
The two sides shall establish and link facilities needed for South North postal and telecommunications services and shall guarantee the confidentiality of intra-Korean mail and telecommunications.

Article 21
The two sides shall cooperate in the economic, cultural and various other fields in the international arena and carry out joint undertakings abroad.

Article 22
To implement accords on exchanges and cooperation in the economic, cultural and various other fields, the two sides shall establish joint commissions for specific sectors, including a Joint South-North Economic Exchanges and Cooperation Commission, within three (3) months of the coming into force of this Agreement.

Article 23
A South-North Exchanges and Cooperation Committee shall be established within the framework of the South-North High-Level Talks within one (1) month of the coming into force of this Agreement with a view to discussing concrete measures to ensure the implementation and observance of the accords on South-North exchanges and cooperation.

Chapter IV   Amendments And Effectuation

Article 24
This Agreement may be amended or supplemented by concurrence between the two sides.

Article 25
This Agreement shall enter into force as of the day the two sides exchange appropriate instruments following the completion of their respective procedures for bringing it into effect.

Chung Won-shik
Prime Minister of the Republic of Korea
Chief delegate of the South delegation to the
South-North High-Level Talks

Yon Hyong-muk
Premier of the Administration Council of the
Democratic People's Republic of Korea
Head of the North delegation to the South-
North High-Level Talks

Joint Declaration of the Denuclearization of the Korean Peninsula

To enter into force as of February 19, 1992

The South and the North,

Desiring to eliminate the danger of nuclear war through denuclearization of the Korean peninsula, and thus to create an environment and conditions favorable for peace and peaceful unification of our country and contribute to peace and security in Asia and the world.

Declare as follows;

1. The South and the North shall not test, manufacture, produce, receive, possess, store, deploy or use nuclear weapons.

2. The South and the North shall use nuclear energy solely for peaceful purposes.

3. The South and the North shall not possess nuclear reprocessing and uranium enrichment facilities.

4. The South and the North, in order to verify the denuclearization of the Korean peninsula, shall conduct inspection of the objects selected by the other side and agreed upon between the two sides, in accordance with procedures and methods to be determined by the South-North Joint Nuclear Control Commission.

5. The South and the North, in order to implement this joint declaration, shall establish and operate a South-North Joint Nuclear Control Commission within one (1) month of the effectuation of this joint declaration.

6. This Joint Declaration shall enter into force as of the day the two sides exchange appropriate instruments following the completion of their respective procedures for bringing it into effect.

January 20, 1992

Chung Won-shik
Prime Minister of the Republic of Korea
Chief delegate of the South delegation to the
South-North High-Level Talks

Yon Hyong-muk
Premier of the Administration Council of the
Democratic People's Republic of Korea
Head of the North delegation to the South-
North High-Level Talks

Agreed Framework Between the United States of America and the Democratic People's Republic of Korea

Geneva, October 21, 1994

Delegations of the governments of the United States of America (U.S.) and the Democratic People's Republic of Korea (DPRK) held talks in Geneva from September 23 to October 21, 1994, to negotiate an overall resolution of the nuclear issue on the Korean Peninsula.

Both sides reaffirmed the importance of attaining the objectives contained in the August 12, 1994 Agreed Statement between the U.S. and the DPRK and upholding the principles of the June 11, 1993 Joint Statement of the U.S. and the DPRK to achieve peace and security on a nuclear-free Korean peninsula. The U.S. and the DPRK decided to take the following actions for the resolution of the nuclear issue:

I. **Both sides will cooperate to replace the DPRK's graphite-moderated reactors and related facilities with light-water reactor (LWR) power plants.**

   1) In accordance with the October 20, 1994 letter of assurance from the U.S. President, the U.S. will undertake to make arrangements for the provision to the DPRK of a LWR project with a total generating capacity of approximately 2,000 MW(e) by a target date of 2003.

   – The U.S. will organize under its leadership an international consortium to finance and supply the LWR project to be provided to the DPRK. The U.S., representing the international consortium, will serve as the principal point of contact with the DPRK for the LWR project.

   – The U.S., representing the consortium, will make best efforts to secure the conclusion of a supply contract with the DPRK within six months of the date of this Document for the provision of the LWR project. Contract talks will begin as soon as possible after the date of this Document.

   – As necessary, the U.S. and the DPRK will conclude a bilateral agreement for cooperation in the field of peaceful uses of nuclear energy.

2) In accordance with the October 20, 1994 letter of assurance from the U.S. President, the U.S., representing the consortium, will make arrangements to offset the energy foregone due to the freeze of the DPRK's graphite-moderated reactors and related facilities, pending completion of the first LWR unit.

   – Alternative energy will be provided in the form of heavy oil for heating and electricity production.

   – Deliveries of heavy oil will begin within three months of the date of this Document and will reach a rate of 500,000 tons annually, in accordance with an agreed schedule of deliveries.

3) Upon receipt of U.S. assurances for the provision of LWR's and for arrangements for interim energy alternatives, the DPRK will freeze its graphite-moderated reactors and related facilities and will eventually dismantle these reactors and related facilities.

   – The freeze on the DPRK's graphite-moderated reactors and related facilities will be fully implemented within one month of the date of this Document. During this one-month period, and throughout the freeze, the International Atomic Energy Agency (IAEA) will be allowed to monitor this freeze, and the DPRK will provide full cooperation to the IAEA for this purpose.

   – Dismantlement of the DPRK's graphite-moderated reactors and related facilities will be completed when the LWR project is completed.

   – The U.S. and the DPRK will cooperate in finding a method to store safely the spent fuel from the 5 MW(e) experimental reactor during the construction of the LWR project, and to dispose of the fuel in a safe manner that does not involve reprocessing in the DPRK.

4) As soon as possible after the date of this document U.S. and DPRK experts will hold two sets of experts talks.

   – At one set of talks, experts will discuss issues related to alternative energy and the replacement of the graphite-moderated reactor program with the LWR project.

   – At the other set of talks, experts will discuss specific arrangements for spent fuel storage and ultimate disposition.

II. **The two sides will move toward full normalization of political and economic relations.**

1) Within three months of the date of this Document, both sides will reduce barriers to trade and investment, including restrictions on telecommunications services and financial transactions.

2) Each side will open a liaison office in the other's capital following resolution of consular and other technical issues through expert level discussions.

3) As progress is made on issues of concern to each side, the U.S. and the DPRK will upgrade bilateral relations to the Ambassadorial level.

III. **Both sides will work together for peace and security on a nuclear-free Korean peninsula.**

1) The U.S. will provide formal assurances to the DPRK, against the threat or use of nuclear weapons by the U.S.

2) The DPRK will consistently take steps to implement the North-South Joint Declaration on the Denuclearization of the Korean Peninsula.

3) The DPRK will engage in North-South dialogue, as this Agreed Framework will help create an atmosphere that promotes such dialogue.

IV. **Both sides will work together to strengthen the international nuclear non proliferation regime.**

1) The DPRK will remain a party to the Treaty on the Non-Proliferation of Nuclear Weapons (NPT) and will allow implementation of its safeguards agreement under the Treaty.

2) Upon conclusion of the supply contract for the provision of the LWR project, ad hoc and routine inspections will resume under the DPRK's safeguards agreement with the IAEA with respect to the facilities not subject to the freeze. Pending conclusion of the supply contract, inspections required by the IAEA for the continuity of safeguards will continue at the facilities not subject to the freeze.

3) When a significant portion of the LWR project is completed, but before delivery of key nuclear components, the DPRK will come into full compliance with its safeguards agreement with the IAEA (INFCIRC/403), including taking all steps that may be deemed necessary by the IAEA, following consultations with the Agency with

regard to verifying the accuracy and completeness of the DPRK's initial report on all nuclear material in the DPRK.

Robert L. Gallucci	Kang Sok Ju
Head of Delegation of the United States of America,	Head of the Delegation of the Democratic People's Republic of Korea,
Ambassador at Large of the United States of America	First Vice-Minister of Foreign Affairs of the Democratic People's Republic of Korea

South-North Joint Declaration

In accordance with the noble will of the entire people who yearn for the peaceful reunification of the nation, President Kim Dae-jung of the Republic of Korea and National Defense Commission Chairman Kim Jong-il of the Democratic People's Republic of Korea held a historic meeting and summit talks in Pyongyang from June 13 to June 15, 2000.

The leaders of the South and the North, recognizing that the first meeting and the summit talks since the division of the country were of great significance in promoting mutual understanding, developing South-North relations and realizing peaceful reunification, declared as follows:

1. The South and the North have agreed to resolve the question of reunification on their own Initiative and through the joint efforts of the Korean people, who are the masters of the country.

2. Acknowledging that there are common elements in the South's proposal for a confederation and the North's proposal for a federation of lower stage as the formula for achieving reunification, the South and the North agreed to promote reunification in that direction.

3. The South and the North have agreed to promptly resolve humanitarian issues such as exchange visits by separated family members and relatives on the occasion of the August 15 National Liberation Day and the question of former long-term prisoners who had refused to renounce Communism.

4. The South and the North have agreed to consolidate mutual trust by promoting balanced development of the national economy through economic cooperation and by stimulating cooperation and exchanges in civic, cultural, sports, public health, environmental and all other fields.

5. The South and the North have agreed to hold a dialogue between relevant authorities in the near future to implement the above agreement expeditiously.

President Kim Dae-jung cordially invited National Defense Commission Chairman Kim Jong-il to visit Seoul, and Chairman Kim Jong-il decided to visit Seoul at an appropriate time.

June 15, 2000

Kim Dae-jung
President
Republic of Korea

Kim Jong-il
Chairman, National Defense Commission
Democratic People's Republic of Korea

US-DPRK Joint Communique

U.S. Department of State, October 12, 2000

As the special envoy of Chairman Kim Jong Il of the D.P.R.K. National Defense Commission, the First Vice Chairman, Vice Marshal Jo Myong Rok, visited the United States of America from October 9–12, 2000.

During his visit, Special Envoy Jo Myong Rok delivered a letter from National Defense Commission Chairman Kim Jong Il, as well as his views on U.S.- D.P.R.K. relations, directly to U.S. President William Clinton. Special Envoy Jo Myong Rok and his party also met with senior officials of the U.S. Administration, including his host Secretary of State Madeleine Albright and Secretary of Defense William Cohen, for an extensive exchange of views on issues of common concern. They reviewed in depth the new opportunities that have opened up for improving the full range of relations between the United States of America and the Democratic People's Republic of Korea. The meetings proceeded in a serious, constructive, and businesslike atmosphere, allowing each side to gain a better understanding of the other's concerns.

Recognizing the changed circumstances on the Korean Peninsula created by the historic inter-Korean summit, the United States and the Democratic People's Republic of Korea have decided to take steps to fundamentally improve their bilateral relations in the interests of enhancing peace and security in the Asia- Pacific region. In this regard, the two sides agreed there are a variety of available means, including Four Party talks, to reduce tension on the Korean Peninsula and formally end the Korean War by replacing the 1953 Armistice Agreement with permanent peace arrangements.

Recognizing that improving ties is a natural goal in relations among states and that better relations would benefit both nations in the 21st century while helping ensure peace and security on the Korean Peninsula and in the Asia-Pacific region, the U.S. and the D.P.R.K. sides stated that they are prepared to undertake a new direction in their relations. As a crucial first step, the two sides stated that neither government would have hostile intent toward the other and confirmed the commitment of both governments to make every effort in the future to build a new relationship free from past enmity.

Building on the principles laid out in the June 11, 1993 U.S.-D.P.R.K. Joint Statement and reaffirmed in the October 21, 1994 Agreed Framework, the two sides agreed to work to remove mistrust, build mutual confidence, and maintain an atmosphere in which they can deal constructively with issues of central concern. In this regard, the two sides reaffirmed that their relations should be based on the principles of respect for each other's sovereignty and non- interference in each other's internal affairs, and noted the value of regular diplomatic contacts, bilaterally and in broader fora.

The two sides agreed to work together to develop mutually beneficial economic cooperation and exchanges. To explore the possibilities for trade and commerce that will benefit the peoples of both countries and contribute to an environment conducive to greater economic cooperation throughout Northeast Asia, the two sides discussed an exchange of visits by economic and trade experts at an early date.

The two sides agreed that resolution of the missile issue would make an essential contribution to a fundamentally improved relationship between them and to peace and security in the Asia-Pacific region. To further the efforts to build new relations, the D.P.R.K. informed the U.S. that it will not launch long-range missiles of any kind while talks on the missile issue continue.

Pledging to redouble their commitment and their efforts to fulfill their respective obligations in their entirety under the Agreed Framework, the US and the D.P.R.K. strongly affirmed its importance to achieving peace and security on a nuclear weapons free Korean Peninsula. To this end, the two sides agreed on the desirability of greater transparency in carrying out their respective obligations under the Agreed Framework. In this regard, they noted the value of the access which removed U.S. concerns about the underground site at Kumchang-ri.

The two sides noted that in recent years they have begun to work cooperatively in areas of common humanitarian concern. The D.P.R.K. side expressed appreciation for significant U.S. contributions to its humanitarian needs in areas of food and medical assistance. The U.S. side expressed appreciation for D.P.R.K. cooperation in recovering the remains of U.S. servicemen still missing from the Korean War, and both sides agreed to work for rapid progress for the fullest possible accounting. The two sides will continue to meet to discuss these and other humanitarian issues.

As set forth in their Joint Statement of October 6, 2000, the two sides agreed to support and encourage international efforts against terrorism.

Special Envoy Jo Myong Rok explained to the US side developments in the inter- Korean dialogue in recent months, including the results of the historic North- South summit. The U.S. side expressed its firm commitment to assist in all appropriate ways the continued progress and success of ongoing North-South dialogue and initiatives for reconciliation and greater cooperation, including increased security dialogue.

Special Envoy Jo Myong Rok expressed his appreciation to President Clinton and the American people for their warm hospitality during the visit.

It was agreed that Secretary of State Madeleine Albright will visit the D.P.R.K. in the near future to convey the views of U.S. President William Clinton directly to Chairman Kim Jong Il of the D.P.R.K. National Defense Commission and to prepare for a possible visit by the President of the United States.

Joint Statement of the Fourth Round of the Six-Party Talks

Beijing 19 September 2005

The Fourth Round of the Six-Party Talks was held in Beijing, China among the People's Republic of China, the Democratic People's Republic of Korea, Japan, the Republic of Korea, the Russian Federation, and the United States of America from July 26th to August 7th, and from September 13th to 19th, 2005.

Mr. Wu Dawei, Vice Minister of Foreign Affairs of the PRC, Mr. Kim Gye Gwan, Vice Minister of Foreign Affairs of the DPRK; Mr. Kenichiro Sasae, Director-General for Asian and Oceanian Affairs, Ministry of Foreign Affairs of Japan; Mr. Song Min-soon, Deputy Minister of Foreign Affairs and Trade of the ROK; Mr. Alexandr Alekseyev, Deputy Minister of Foreign Affairs of the Russian Federation; and Mr. Christopher Hill, Assistant Secretary of State for East Asian and Pacific Affairs of the United States attended the talks as heads of their respective delegations.

Vice Foreign Minister Wu Dawei chaired the talks.

For the cause of peace and stability on the Korean Peninsula and in Northeast Asia at large, the Six Parties held, in the spirit of mutual respect and equality, serious and practical talks concerning the denuclearization of the Korean Peninsula on the basis of the common understanding of the previous three rounds of talks, and agreed, in this context, to the following:

1. The Six Parties unanimously reaffirmed that the goal of the Six-Party Talks is the verifiable denuclearization of the Korean Peninsula in a peaceful manner.

    The DPRK committed to abandoning all nuclear weapons and existing nuclear programs and returning, at an early date, to the Treaty on the Non-Proliferation of Nuclear Weapons and to IAEA safeguards.

    The United States affirmed that it has no nuclear weapons on the Korean Peninsula and has no intention to attack or invade the DPRK with nuclear or conventional weapons.

    The ROK reaffirmed its commitment not to receive or deploy nuclear weapons in accordance with the 1992 Joint Declaration of the Denuclearization of the Korean Peninsula, while affirming that there exist no nuclear weapons within its territory.

The 1992 Joint Declaration of the Denuclearization of the Korean Peninsula should be observed and implemented.

The DPRK stated that it has the right to peaceful uses of nuclear energy. The other parties expressed their respect and agreed to discuss, at an appropriate time, the subject of the provision of lightwater reactor to the DPRK.

2. The Six Parties undertook, in their relations, to abide by the purposes and principles of the Charter of the United Nations and recognized norms of international relations.

The DPRK and the United States undertook to respect each other's sovereignty, exist peacefully together, and take steps to normalize their relations subject to their respective bilateral policies.

The DPRK and Japan undertook to take steps to normalize their relations in accordance with the Pyongyang Declaration, on the basis of the settlement of unfortunate past and the outstanding issues of concern.

3. The Six Parties undertook to promote economic cooperation in the fields of energy, trade and investment, bilaterally and/or multilaterally.

China, Japan, ROK, Russia and the US stated their willingness to provide energy assistance to the DPRK.

The ROK reaffirmed its proposal of July 12th 2005 concerning the provision of 2 million kilowatts of electric power to the DPRK.

4. The Six Parties committed to joint efforts for lasting peace and stability in Northeast Asia.

The directly related parties will negotiate a permanent peace regime on the Korean Peninsula at an appropriate separate forum.

The Six Parties agreed to explore ways and means for promoting security cooperation in Northeast Asia.

5. The Six Parties agreed to take coordinated steps to implement the afore-mentioned consensus in a phased manner in line with the principle of "commitment for commitment, action for action".

6. The Six Parties agreed to hold the Fifth Round of the Six-Party Talks in Beijing in early November 2005 at a date to be determined through consultations.

INDEX

RECENT PUBLICATIONS OF THE WALTER H. SHORENSTEIN ASIA-PACIFIC RESEARCH CENTER

BOOKS (DISTRIBUTED BY THE BROOKINGS INSTITUTION PRESS)

Byung Kwan Kim, Gi-Wook Shin, and David Straub, eds. *Beyond North Korea: Future Challenges to South Korea's Security*. Stanford, CA: Walter H. Shorenstein Asia-Pacific Research Center, 2011.

Jean C. Oi, ed. *Going Private in China: The Politics of Corporate Restructuring and System Reform*. Stanford, CA: Walter H. Shorenstein Asia-Pacific Research Center, 2011.

Karen Eggleston and Shripad Tuljapurkar, eds. *Aging Asia: The Economic and Social Implications of Rapid Demographic Change in China, Japan and South Korea*. Stanford, CA: Walter H. Shorenstein Asia-Pacific Research Center, 2010.

Rafiq Dossani, Daniel C. Sneider, and Vikram Sood, eds. *Does South Asia Exist? Prospects for Regional Integration*. Stanford, CA: Walter H. Shorenstein Asia-Pacific Research Center, 2010.

Jean C. Oi, Scott Rozelle, and Xueguang Zhou. *Growing Pains: Tensions and Opportunity in China's Transition*. Stanford, CA: Walter H. Shorenstein Asia-Pacific Research Center, 2010.

Karen Eggleston, ed. *Prescribing Cultures and Pharmaceutical Policy in the Asia-Pacific*. Stanford, CA: Walter H. Shorenstein Asia-Pacific Research Center, 2009.

Donald A. L. Macintyre, Daniel C. Sneider, and Gi-Wook Shin, eds. *First Drafts of Korea: The U.S. Media and Perceptions of the Last Cold War Frontier*. Stanford, CA: Walter H. Shorenstein Asia-Pacific Research Center, 2009.

Steven Reed, Kenneth Mori McElwain, and Kay Shimizu, eds. *Political Change in Japan: Electoral Behavior, Party Realignment, and the Koizumi Reforms*. Stanford, CA: Walter H. Shorenstein Asia-Pacific Research Center, 2009.

Donald K. Emmerson. *Hard Choices: Security, Democracy, and Regionalism in Southeast Asia*. Stanford, CA: Walter H. Shorenstein Asia-Pacific Research Center, 2008.

Henry S. Rowen, Marguerite Gong Hancock, and William F. Miller, eds. *Greater China's Quest for Innovation*. Stanford, CA: Walter H. Shorenstein Asia-Pacific Research Center, 2008.

Gi-Wook Shin and Daniel C. Sneider, eds. *Cross Currents: Regionalism and Nationalism in Northeast Asia*. Stanford, CA: Walter H. Shorenstein Asia-Pacific Research Center, 2007.

Stella R. Quah, ed. *Crisis Preparedness: Asia and the Global Governance of Epidemics*. Stanford, CA: Walter H. Shorenstein Asia-Pacific Research Center, 2007.

Philip W Yun and Gi-Wook Shin, eds. *North Korea: 2005 and Beyond*. Stanford, CA: Walter H. Shorenstein Asia-Pacific Research Center, 2006.

STUDIES OF THE WALTER H. SHORENSTEIN ASIA-PACIFIC RESEARCH CENTER
(PUBLISHED WITH STANFORD UNIVERSITY PRESS)

Gene Park. *Spending Without Taxation: FILP and the Politics of Public Finance in Japan*. Stanford, CA: Stanford University Press, 2011.

Erik Martinez Kuhonta. *The Institutional Imperative: The Politics of Equitable Development in Southeast Asia*. Stanford, CA: Stanford University Press, 2011.

Yongshun Cai. *Collective Resistance in China: Why Popular Protests Succeed or Fail*. Stanford, CA: Stanford University Press, 2010.

Gi-Wook Shin. *One Alliance, Two Lenses: U.S.-Korea Relations in a New Era*. Stanford, CA: Stanford University Press, 2010.

Jean Oi and Nara Dillon, eds. *At the Crossroads of Empires: Middlemen, Social Networks, and State-building in Republican Shanghai*. Stanford, CA: Stanford University Press, 2007.

Henry S. Rowen, Marguerite Gong Hancock, and William F. Miller, eds. *Making IT: The Rise of Asia in High Tech*. Stanford, CA: Stanford University Press, 2006.

Gi-Wook Shin. *Ethnic Nationalism in Korea: Genealogy, Politics, and Legacy*. Stanford, CA: Stanford University Press, 2006.

Andrew Walder, Joseph Esherick, and Paul Pickowicz, eds. *The Chinese Cultural Revolution as History*. Stanford, CA: Stanford University Press, 2006.

Rafiq Dossani and Henry S. Rowen, eds. *Prospects for Peace in South Asia*. Stanford, CA: Stanford University Press, 2005.

The authorized representative in the EU for product safety and compliance is:
Mare Nostrum Group
B.V Doelen 72
4831 GR Breda
The Netherlands

www.ingramcontent.com/pod-product-compliance
Lightning Source LLC
Chambersburg PA
CBHW020331270326
41926CB00007B/131